BATTLES OVER FREE TRADE

CONTENTS OF THE EDITION

VOLUME 1
General Introduction
By Mark Duckenfield

The Advent of Free Trade, 1776–1846
Edited by Gordon Bannerman and Cheryl Schonhardt-Bailey

VOLUME 2
The Consolidation of Free Trade, 1847–1878
Edited by Gordon Bannerman and Anthony Howe

VOLUME 3
The Challenge of Economic Nationalism, 1879–1939
Edited by Anthony Howe and Mark Duckenfield

VOLUME 4
The Emergence of Multilateral Trade, 1940–2006
Edited by Mark Duckenfield

Index

BATTLES OVER FREE TRADE

General Editor: Mark Duckenfield

Volume 2
The Consolidation of Free Trade, 1847–1878

EDITED BY
Gordon Bannerman and Anthony Howe

LONDON AND NEW YORK

First published 2008 by Pickering & Chatto (Publishers) Limited

Published 2016 by Routledge
2 Park Square, Milton Park, Abingdon, Oxfordshire OX14 4RN
711 Third Avenue, New York, NY 10017, USA

First issued in paperback 2015

Routledge is an imprint of the Taylor & Francis Group, an informa business

Copyright © Taylor & Francis 2008
Copyright © Editorial material Gordon Bannerman and Anthony Howe

All rights reserved, including those of translation into foreign languages. No part of this book may be reprinted or reproduced or utilised in any form or by any electronic, mechanical, or other means, now known or hereafter invented, including photocopying and recording, or in any information storage or retrieval system, without permission in writing from the publishers.

Notice:
Product or corporate names may be trademarks or registered trademarks, and are used only for identification and explanation without intent to infringe.

BRITISH LIBRARY CATALOGUING IN PUBLICATION DATA

Battles over free trade: Anglo-American experiences with international trade, 1776–2006
1. Free trade – History
I. Duckenfield, Mark
382.7'1'09

ISBN-13: 978-1-138-66050-2 (pbk)
ISBN-13: 978-1-1387-5033-3 (hbk)
ISBN-13: 978-1-85196-935-7 (set)

Typeset by Pickering & Chatto (Publishers) Limited

CONTENTS

Introduction ix

The Decline of Protectionism in Britain, 1846–52 1
Defeat of Protectionism in Britain
    John Lewis Ricardo, *The Anatomy of the Navigation Laws* (1847) 9
    John Charles Herries to George Frederick Young, [8?] January 1849 14
    'Protection Disinterred', *Economist* (1849) 15
    Lord Stanhope to G. F. Young, 29 May 1849 19
    Lord Stanhope to G. F. Young, 8 June 1849 21
    Minutes of a Special Meeting of the Acting Committee of the National Association for the Protection of British Industry and Capital, 15 October 1849 22
    J. C. Herries to G. F. Young, 15 November 1849 24
    Free Thoughts on Free Trade (1852) 25
    Notice of Anti-Corn Law League Meeting, *Economist* (1852) 33
    Henry Ashworth, *Recollections of Richard Cobden and the Anti Corn-Law League* (1877) 35
    Ramifications of Free Trade
Arbitration Instead of War (1848) 41
    Richard Cobden, Speech on 'Free Trade and Peace', *Manchester Times and Gazette*, 21 December 1847 44
    'Peace on Earth – Good Will Towards Men', *Manchester Times*, 8 January 1848 47
    Alexander Alison, *Universal Free Trade, by Means of a Property, Income and Wages Tax* (1852) 48
    Sir James Graham to W. E. Gladstone, 13 November 1852 53
    Sir James Graham to W. E. Gladstone, 19 November 1852 54

Diffusion of Free Trade Abroad 55
Promoters and Opponents
    Richard Cobden to Marco Minghetti, 21 May 1847 61

Richard Cobden, Speeches in Europe, in *Reminiscences of Richard Cobden*, compiled by J. Salis Schwabe (1895)	63
'Congress of Political Economists at Brussels', *Economist* (1847)	73
Free Trade Meeting at Marseilles, *Economist* (1847)	79
Richard Cobden to Michel Chevalier, 22 March 1851	82
Michel Chevalier in Dionysus Lardner, *The Great Exhibition and London in 1851* (1852)	83
Speech of M. Thiers on the Commercial Policy of France and in Opposition to the Introduction of Free Trade into France, 27 June 1851, trans. M. de Saint Felix (1852)	91
Henry Dunckley, *The Charter of the Nations: or, Free Trade and its Results* (1854)	110
The Abortive Anglo-French Commercial Treaty of 1852, 1853	117
American-Canadian Reciprocity Treaty of 1854, Despatch from Lord Lyons to Russell, 28 February 1862, *Parliamentary Papers* (1862)	126
Lord Clarendon to Lord Palmerston, 20 April 1856	129
Cardwell Memorandum on Commercial Policy towards Russia, 29 October 1854	131

Anglo-French Commercial Treaty of 1860 and the Treaty System — 137

Anglo-French Commercial Treaty

Michel Chevalier, *The History of Political Economy Taught by the History of the Freedom of Labour*, trans. W. Bellingham (1869)	143
Richard Cobden to John Bright, 16 January 1860	148
Richard Cobden to François Arlés-Dufour, 10 August 1860	153
H. Reader Lack, *The French Treaty and Tariff of 1860* (1861)	154
'Commercial Treaties and Free Trade', *Economist* (1860)	161
Robert Andrew Macfie, 'Notes on the French Treaty', *Liverpool Daily Post*, 16 February 1860	164
George Frederick Young, *The French Treaty, a Mockery, a Delusion, and a Snare* (1860)	169

Treaty System and Promotion of Free Trade

Richard Cobden to E. A. Billeroche, 12 September 1861	174
'Memorandum on the Commercial Policy of European States and British Trade' (1879)	175
Henry Charles Carey, *The French and American Tariffs Compared in a Series of Letters to Chevalier* (1864)	179
[R. Morier], *Commercial Treaties: Free Trade and Internationalism* (1870)	187
'Commercial Treaty with Austria' (1866)	196

Louis Mallet, Memorandum on Modifications of Anglo French
Treaty, 19 August 1871 207
C. M. Kennedy, 'Treaties of Commerce with, and between, European
Powers, with Especial Reference to the Trade of the United Kingdom'
(1875) 212

Free Trade Under Threat, to 1879 229
Britain, Europe, and the United States
  Manifesto of the Association of 'Revivers' of British Industry ([1869]) . . 235
  Kuklos [pseud., John Harris], *The Commercial Policy of England in
  1877* (1877) 241
  J. Slagg, 'The Commercial Treaty with France', *Fortnightly Review*
  (1877) 254
  William Bateman Hanbury, *Lord Bateman's Plea for Limited Protection, or, for Reciprocity in Free Trade* (1878) 257
  W. Farrer Ecroyd, *The Policy of Self Help: Suggestions towards the Consolidation of the Empire and the Defence of its Industries and Commerce*
  (1879) 262
  Sir Louis Mallet, *Reciprocity* (1879) 270
  Free Trade and the European Treaties of Commerce (1875) 283
The Colonial World
  Cosmopolite, *Free Trade and No Colonies* (1848) 312
  John Dunmore Lang, *Freedom and Independence for the Golden Lands
  of Australia* (1852) 323
  George Ward Cole, *Protection as a National System Suited for Victoria*
  (1860) 327
  Henry Ashworth, 'Our Colonies: Their Commerce and their Cost', in
  Henry Ashworth, *Pamphlets and Other Papers* (1872) 334
  George Reid, *Five Free Trade Essays* (1875) 338
  Letters of Henry Parkes, George H. Reid and Gower Evans, in *Free
  Trade and the European Treaties of Commerce* (1875) 348

Copyrights and Permissions 353

INTRODUCTION

The contested nature of commercial policy and limited acceptance of classical political economy was a central feature of Volume 1 of this edition. The bifurcation between liberalized tariff regimes such as that of Britain and to some degree the Zollverein was contrasted with the stubborn protectionism of much of Europe and the vibrant system of national economy prevalent in the United States. After 1846, international commercial policy assumed a slightly different aspect. For a variety of reasons most states liberalized their tariffs, though none followed Britain in dispensing with protective duties. Herein lay significantly differing national responses towards and conceptions of commercial policy. In Britain, evangelical and secular models of free trade facilitated a powerful ideological commitment, whose cross-class appeal was secured by the promise of lower food prices and an expansion of domestic manufacturing employment.[1] Conversely, a wide array of factors inhibited European support for free trade, from the political strength of protected industries and fear of British competition to the pervasive suspicion of British motives, which was in some ways strengthened by the events of 1846. Moreover, the forces of liberalism in many European nations remained weak when arraigned against absolutist, monarchist or authoritarian rulers. Despite these obstacles, a progressive European movement emerged, and within individual nations the existence of movements supportive of commercial liberalism represented a significant advance on the years before 1846.

The absence of an ideological commitment to commercial liberalism in Europe comparable to that of Britain was perhaps most starkly revealed by the mode in which free trade was extended. The 'treaty system' of the 1860s sought to extend free trade incrementally via an interlocking series of treaties which differed from the reciprocity treaties of the 1820s inasmuch as they offered no exclusive national advantages, but were extended to other nations by a most-favoured-nation clause. Ultimately, the treaty system collapsed amidst the revival of Europe-wide economic nationalism provoked by the onset of slower growth rates and falling prices of the Great Depression of 1873–96. The forces that forged a revival of economic nationalism were manifold: national rivalry, war, state indebtedness, economic depression and territorial imperialism prompted a return to high tariffs as a central component of 'national' economic policies. More widely, support for economic nationalism was fuelled by a belief in the positive attributes of state intervention against the minimal state proposed by free traders. Economic depression in the 1870s led many to question the effect of free trade on domestic employment, price levels and export values. Across Europe, and even in Britain, powerful coalitions were constructed on the basis of these grievances, and their mobilization ensured the gradual abandonment of the treaty system. On the Continent, protectionism was strengthened by the depression and emergent notions of 'national' economy, particularly in Germany, and made considerable headway against the perceived cosmopolitanism of free trade. Whilst Germany's return to protection in 1879 symbolically inaugurated a new era in international commercial relations, the return to protective measures by many states had long been implicit in their acceptance of free trade for reasons of expediency and national interest rather than ideological commitment.

Protection in Britain to 1852

If the British example of commercial liberalism was to succeed throughout the world it first had to be consolidated in Britain. Despite Sir Robert Peel's tariff reductions of 1842–6, and Corn Law repeal itself, one recent writer has drawn attention to the frequently incorrect identification of Corn Law repeal with free trade.[2] Whilst this interpretation is technically correct inasmuch as protective duties remained after 1846, the nature of British policy signalled the end of reciprocal commercial negotiations and a commitment to unilateral free trade. Yet if a reminder is needed that Corn Law repeal did not equate with free trade, one only needs to examine the period 1846–52 in Britain. For the first time, a protectionist movement, as opposed to a pro-Corn Law movement, emerged.[3] A theoretical protectionism apposite to the economic composition and development of Britain was established which emphasized balanced growth across economic sectors by moderate protective duties.[4] Predictably, the popular protectionist movement comprised economic interests threatened or damaged by foreign competition, such as silk weavers, ship owners and hatters, alongside agrarians seeking to reimpose corn duties. A commercial crisis in Britain in 1847–8, Chartist revival and the European revolutions of 1848 appeared to presage a return to protection. Yet it failed to materialize, partly from fear of revolution and, less dramatically, from the feeling that the country would not accept it. In May 1852, the Earl of Derby indicated in the Lords that, although he considered a duty on foreign imported corn desirable, the majority in the country appeared to be opposed.[5] The powerful association drawn between sectional interests and protection not only inhibited the reinstatement of protective duties, but produced a parliamentary resolution of 1852 which affirmed free trade as a 'wise and beneficial' policy.[6] The settlement of the question allowed free traders to turn their attention towards extending notions of commercial liberty outside Britain. Such a movement was attempted, somewhat indirectly, through Richard Cobden's association with the peace movement, and his campaign for arbitration between 1848 and 1853, which linked peace and reductions in military expenditure with free commerce and taxation reform.[7] Cobden's internationalism and his belief in the pacific potential of commerce were never more notably displayed. His radical 'National Budget' of 1849 proposed to reduce government expenditure to the level of 1835.[8] Whilst appearing highly optimistic, such a campaign was deemed an appropriate way to proceed, given the limited acceptance of free trade in the immediate aftermath of Corn Law repeal.

The Diffusion of Free Trade Abroad, 1847–60

The expectation that European nations would reduce their tariffs in the wake of Corn Law repeal stemmed from the belief that the Corn Laws inhibited trade with European nations and forced them to industrialize prematurely. Repeal, it was hoped, would lead to a Europe where nations would exploit their comparative advantage.[9] Such was the theory, but if Britain sought to act as a hegemonic power in guiding and informing European commercial policy, she signally failed in this endeavour. In reality, one can find little evidence of a hegemonic strategy. Britain sought rather to lead by example, by presenting her commercial policy as enlightened inasmuch as its advantages were not exclusively British. Whilst the optimism towards the progress of European free trade proved misplaced, it was not entirely without foundation. The American tariff of 1846 presented an example of the influence of British unilateralism as represented by repeal. Yet this proved to be a false dawn, as Cobden learned on his European tour of 1846–7.

Cobden found the constellation of economic interests in European nations and empires to be vastly different to that of Britain. In the 'old' states of France and Spain, industries had grown up and prospered under protection and, fully cognizant of their interests, were politically well-organized and well-connected. French industrialists and the Catalan textile industry proved far too strong for the nascent free trade movement of liberal intellectuals common to both countries. At governmental level France, before and after the 1848 revolution, remained suspicious of British motives, whilst the conservative Spanish monarchy opposed concessions to liberal progressives. Intellectually, commercial liberalism made some progress in France amongst economists, in academic circles and, pragmatically, amongst leading export trades, but political turbulence and powerful protectionist interests retarded any significant progress. In Italy, Cobden found the national question facilitated support for free trade, which was identified as a liberal, progressive policy apposite for an emerging nation. The national potential of free trade in forging links via an Italian customs union were identified, in contrast to the highly protectionist polity of the Habsburg Empire. In Italy there was little suspicion of British motives but in Austria and Germany Cobden discovered widespread support for Friedrich List's 'national system' of political economy, incorporating 'protection to native industry'. Yet even here Cobden found encouraging signs, although support appeared diffuse and fragmented. Europe then, was somewhat divided along traditional political lines on the question of free trade, with European conservative elites and entrenched protected industries opposed, whilst liberal political economy had gained some converts amongst the intelligentsia, cosmopolitan merchants and export industries.

The 1848 revolutions destroyed any hope of a rapid adoption of free trade, and indeed led to a short-lived revival of protectionism, bolstered by popular nationalism and socialism. However, in the long term, a fusion of technological and intellectual developments provided a favourable political environment for the expansion of commercial liberalism. The moral and material benefits of a policy of liberal political economy were demonstrated by the Great Exhibition of 1851, and the communications revolution promoted the concept of global markets and economic expansion, with the establishment of the International Telegraph Union in 1865 and the General Postal Union in 1874 examples of an international commercial communications network. Free trade also benefited from reconfigurations of national states and empires such as Germany, where the Zollverein was increasingly viewed by Prussia as an instrument towards German unity under Prussian and not protectionist Austrian leadership. In Italy, Piedmont continued to incorporate commercial liberty with an assertive programme of economic modernization leading to nationhood. Thus, varied influences ensured the slow diffusion of liberal political economy to the extent that by the 1860s most of Europe had to some extent embraced liberal conceptions of commerce.

The British model of free trade remained as a pre-eminent example, perhaps most notably within her own Empire. For example, the Australian Customs Act of 1850 prohibited the imposition of differential duties in the Australian colonies, whilst Canada was encouraged to develop a reciprocal trading relationship with the United States rather than the 'mother country'.[10] Nevertheless, British encouragement or coercion of other states to adopt free trade, despite a number of reciprocal treaties, was limited. Consistent with her unilateral approach, Britain relied primarily upon her own example of prosperity. More may have been done at an official level, although this would almost certainly have involved concessions on revenue duties. This was dangerous territory, with the potential to involve Britain intimately in the politics of European nations, a far cry from Cobden's 'no foreign politics', and fiscally difficult as well as politically sensitive as it would mean shifting the tax burden further towards direct taxation.[11] The British model of revenue duties only, the basic tool of free-trade advocacy, was enthusiastically taken up by commercial reformers in Europe and the United States. As a route towards cheaper government, reductions in the tax burden and in encouraging peace betweens nations, this model was capable of universal application, and was accurately if idealistically described as the Charter of the Nations.[12] By the third quarter of the nineteenth century, such a view had advocates across Europe, and its wide diffusion is a testimony to the influence of commercial liberalism.

Anglo-French Commercial Treaty and the Treaty System

Despite the increasing incidence and prominence of theories of commercial liberalism throughout Europe, by the late 1850s it seemed clear that little actual progress had been made. The Crimean War obviously represented a setback to normal commercial intercourse, but even in its aftermath there were few signs that European nations would follow the unilateralist model of free trade adopted by Britain. It was political instability and the threat of war in 1859 that provided the impetus for progress.[13] An Anglo-French treaty had long been aired as a device for reforming the French tariff, and providing a model for other nations.[14] The political aspects of the treaty were important, and it can be viewed as an old-fashioned agreement in which geopolitical disputes and problems were resolved by the device of a commercial pact.[15] Napoleon III viewed the treaty as a means to allay British opposition to his designs on Nice and Savoy, and his contesting Austrian domination of northern Italy. For Britain, the prospect of reforming the French tariff, and the avoidance of war, were cited as the main advantages.[16] The treaty was generally recognized as favourable to France, at least in the short term, but it was hoped it would stimulate further support for commercial liberalism. This was a reasonable assumption, for the terms of the treaty lowered British duties on French silks, wines and spirits, and renounced any restrictions on the export of coal, whilst France abolished prohibitory duties and admitted British goods at a maximum of 25 per cent within five years with immediate reductions on coal, iron and machine tools.[17]

The method of agreement was as, if not more controversial than the terms. There was predictable opposition from silk manufacturers, wine merchants and victuallers, as well as from the shipping interest. Political opposition came from doctrinaire free traders who opposed treaty-making as it represented a return to bargaining and negotiation, and as such violated the unilateral principle. Yet, what made the treaty different from the previous model of reciprocity treaties was the clause stipulating most-favoured-nation status. This provision made the treaty the 'cornerstone of a new international trading system' and the first in a series of international commercial agreements.[18] In Europe, the treaty system, combining specific tariff reductions and the advantages of most-favoured-nation status, reduced tariffs and inaugurated an era of unprecedented commercial liberalism on the Continent. Even hitherto highly protectionist states such as Austria moved slowly away from prohibition and high protection.[19]

As a policy instrument, treaties could extend commercial liberalization, but this required the will of statesmen who in many cases retained traditional prejudices against an open commercial system. Many were guided towards free trade by other considerations rather than a principled belief in commercial liberalism. Otto von Bismarck, for example, used free trade as a means towards Prussian hegemony in the Zollverein and towards combating Austria within the German Confederation. Similarly, Russia's lowering of import duties in 1857 and 1868 was made in order to aid Russian industrial development, and did not represent any departure from protectionism as state policy.[20] Despite the progress of Continental liberalism, it was perhaps industrial expansion and development that was more important in determining European policy options of the 1860s. For a brief moment there appeared the prospect that the treaty system could advance commercial freedom to the point of establishing a free European market.[21] However, political and economic pressures eventually brought an end to the system, and calls for a return to national commercial freedom presaged a powerful wave of economic nationalism in the 1870s.

Free Trade under Threat?

The liberal vision of European progress based on free trade, peace and democracy, values enshrined in the treaty system and strongly pursued between 1846 and 1865, were undermined by the changing political complexion of Europe from the mid-1860s. As Cobden indicated in his earlier campaign, there was a close relationship between peace and free trade. The Austro-Prussian War of 1866 and the Franco-Prussian War of 1870 represented the first challenges to maintaining policies of commercial liberalism. Economic depression from 1873 aggravated the fiscal crisis, and prompted a decisive shift back towards protection across Europe. Britain's ability to influence the European economic order was damaged, but perhaps more serious in the long term was the renewed popularity of theories of economic nationalism which gained strength from national rivalry and economic depression. If the interlocking nature of the treaty system was its strength, its weakness lay in its vulnerability to any one participating nation breaking ranks. This was likely to have a cumulative impact as other countries sought to retaliate. Another inherent weakness lay in the time period for which treaties were in force, thus subjecting them to the political vicissitudes of European nations. In the aftermath of the Prussian victory in the war of 1870, France was compelled to grant Germany permanent most-favoured-nation status, somewhat transforming an instrument of voluntary association and friendship into an instrument imposed by military defeat. Simultaneously, domestic support for a liberal commercial policy ebbed, with free trade associated with the failures of the Napoleonic regime. Protectionist pressure groups were formed, comprising industrialists, which were coherent, informal blocs in the Chamber. By 1878, the protectionists had succeeded, in the face of falling prices and wages, contracted profits and British dumping, in forcing the French government to postpone the negotiation of new trade treaties.[22]

The movement of opinion in France was not unique. Across Europe there was a reaction against the perceived cosmopolitanism of free trade which constituted a powerful challenge to ideas of a Europe characterized by commercial freedom. Whilst there were purely protectionist organizations motivated primarily by support for higher tariffs, a wider critical movement emerged, with divergent motives and objectives. Economic nationalism, although more fully developed in the 1880s, began an assault on free trade in the 1870s, with German historical economists in the vanguard of intellectual opposition. The advocacy of economic nationalism was more than a protectionist movement but one that encompassed and redefined the role of the state. Many attacked the tenets of classical political economy for failing to address the wider interests of the nation, aside from wealth and individual self-interest. For others, reacting to, and reflecting the increasing militarism of Europe, the military ramparts of the state were better served by a protective policy which harnessed national resources and protected a broad economic base. The essential element in all these policy prognostications was a higher degree of state intervention, and whilst the intellectual stimulus for such theories emanated from Germany, their impact was felt across Europe. Only in Britain was there no significant intellectual challenge to the primacy of free trade and the centrality of consumer interests.

The intellectual challenge to free trade would have been much more difficult to sustain without the Great Depression of 1873–96. Characterized by falling prices, declining exports, overproduction and unemployment, the depression affected the entire European economy. In searching for causes, free trade was an obvious target, with cheap foreign imports damaging domestic industries, and, an old concern, even threatening national survival through dependence on food imports.[23] Broad coalitions of those who had suffered under free trade were now mobilized with far greater effect. The most important example of this process was in Germany, where the alliance between agrarians and industrialists, with differing grievances but a shared interest in protective tariffs, was exploited by Bismarck.[24] The protectionist movement in Germany had also witnessed theoretical refurbishment. As Friedrich List was no longer applicable to a mature industrial economy, the emphasis now shifted towards the argument of securing the home market for industry, and rejecting the concept of free trade as an international community of interests. Such views owed something to List, but more to Henry Carey and his emphasis on domestic economic interdependence. In the context of a Europe-wide depression this type of emphasis on nationality was common. Even in Britain, movements emerged calling for an end to 'one-sided Free Trade'. Lacking the support of a political party, such movements struggled, but, elsewhere in Europe, constructing alliances on the basis of economic grievances was far more successfully achieved.[25]

Against this formidable movement of opinion, it was the task of European statesmen to attempt to renegotiate the commercial treaties. Not for the first time, Britain's wish to continue to advance a liberal commercial policy appeared to face insurmountable obstacles, in the form of strong support for protection in the councils of Europe. In Britain, there was a growing dissatisfaction with treaty-making, from doctrinaire unilateralists such as Robert Lowe, and from those advocating reciprocity. A return to unilateralism or the 'restoration of commercial freedom' was widely touted as the most apposite policy for Britain. This proved premature, for in 1873, the French treaty was renewed until 1877. In the interim, anti-free trade elements gained strength across Europe. The dogged pursuit of renewing commercial treaties was undermined by protectionist organization, whose aims were now shared, for fiscal reasons, by many governments. British and French attempts at Europe-wide cooperation to implement a European tariff, an interesting early example of the idea of a common market, came to nothing and bilateral agreements were again sought. As France's commercial treaties expired in 1877, her policy inclinations were recognized as having a profound effect on the future commercial trajectory of Europe. The political instability of the Republic scotched any prospect of further tariff reductions. In any case, Britain was in a weak position, for, as critics of the 1860 treaty had pointed out, Britain had divested herself of bargaining counters.[26] Wine duties, one of the few remaining negotiable duties and essential to British revenue, could not be reduced further.[27] By the end of 1878, a return to protection across Europe appeared imminent, and on 31 December 1878 France renounced the 1873 treaty with Britain, once again raising the question, in acute form, of the role of commercial treaties in the pursuit of commercial liberalism.[28]

In the colonial world, free trade was also in retreat. The anti-imperialism of free trade had a long intellectual tradition, including Adam Smith, Josiah Tucker and Jeremy Bentham. For the 'Manchester School', colonial free trade was equated with colonial self-defence, with the colonies bearing the burden of expenditure for their defence.[29] This was all the more necessary given the protectionist inclinations within the Empire. In Australia, the Australian Colonies Government Act allowed the separate legislatures the freedom to determine their own commercial policies.[30] The popular rhetorical trappings of protectionism in Australia were not dissimilar to those of the United States earlier in the century.[31] There was a similar emphasis on harnessing national resources and providing employment, and an aggressive colonial nationalism which promoted national economic policy as an integral component in freedom from imperial control. In Canada, the National Policy of 1879 entrenched protection as state policy, thus imitating their southern neighbour, for in the United States, the strength of protectionism remained unabated.

Sources

The source material used for this volume comprises official documentation, private correspondence, newspaper articles and printed material from pamphlets and rare books. The latter sources are perhaps more prominent in this volume of *Battles over Free Trade* than in Volume 1, reflecting the wide diffusion of printed material relating to commercial policy, and the readiness of politicians and the mercantile community to publish their thoughts and ideas. As with Volume 1, the material seeks to be broad-ranging and representative of different bodies of opinion, whilst reflecting the main trends of thought over particular issues. Consistent with its themes, the present volume is perhaps less Anglo-centric than Volume 1, although the centrality of Britain towards global commercial policy debates cannot be denied. Once again, the material seeks to illustrate the contested nature of commercial policy, which formed an important component in a vital period of state formation and reconfiguration of 'Great Power' rivalry.

Notes
1. Whilst food was cheaper under free trade, manufacturing employment was much more variable, although foreign competition was merely one factor in serious unemployment and underemployment. Despite this, a Spitalfields silk weaver asked: 'When is the people of England to see that there big loaf they was promised – that's it – the people wants to know when they're to have it', E. P. Thompson and E. Yeo (eds), *The Unknown Mayhew: Selections from the Morning Chronicle 1849–1850* (London: Penguin reprint, 1984), p. 134.
2. J. V. C. Nye, *War, Wine, and Taxes: The Political Economy of Anglo-French Trade, 1689–1900* (Princeton, NJ, and Oxford: Princeton University Press, 2007), p. 94.
3. See John Charles Herries to George Frederick Young, [8?] January 1849; Lord Stanhope to Young, 29 May 1849; Stanhope to Young, 8 June 1849; Minutes of a Special Meeting of the Acting Committee of the National Association for the Protection of British Industry and Capital, 15 October 1849; and Herries to Young, 15 November 1849, all below, pp. 14, 19–20, 21, 22–3, 24.
4. For protection balancing interests, see Derby's speech, 25 May 1846: 'It is a system under which, and in accordance with which, each surrenders some advantage to himself, for the purpose of partaking in the general advantage of all', *Hansard* (1846), lxxxvi, c. 1166.
5. Speech in the Lords, 24 May, *The Times*, 25 May 1852, p. 2a; describing his reception at Leeds, Cobden informed Charles Pelham Villiers: 'The feeling amongst the mass of the people is most intense ... It is very different to what it was when I went to carry on a *middle class* agitation for the repeal', 5 March 1852, Cobden Papers, BL, Add. MS 43662, fols 106–7.

6. See Sir James Graham to W. E. Gladstone, 13 November 1852; and Graham to Gladstone, 13 November 1852, 19 November 1852, both below, pp. 53, 54.
7. R. F. Spall, 'Free Trade, Foreign Relations, and the Anti-Corn Law League', *International History Review*, 10 (1988), pp. 405–32.
8. W. N. Calkins, 'A Victorian Free Trade Lobby', *Economic History Review*, 213 (1960–1), pp. 90–104, on p. 100.
9. For the view that many British manufacturers, and possibly Cobden, sought an agricultural Continent and an industrial Britain, see M. Taylor (ed.), *The European Diaries of Richard Cobden, 1846–1849* (Aldershot: Scolar Press, 1994).
10. A. Howe, *Free Trade and Liberal England, 1846–1946* (Oxford: Clarendon Press, 1997), p. 62.
11. See H. Reader Lack (ed.), *The French Treaty and Tariff of 1860* (1861); and 'Commercial Treaties and Free Trade', *Economist* (1860), both below, pp. 154–60, 161–3.
12. See H. Dunckley, *The Charter of the Nations: or, Free Trade and its Results* (1854), below, pp. 110–16.
13. Howe, *Free Trade and Liberal England*, pp. 94–5.
14. See The Abortive Anglo-French Commercial Treaty of 1852, below, pp. 117–25.
15. P. K. O'Brien and G. A. Pigman, 'Free Trade, British Hegemony, and the International Economic Order in the Nineteenth Century', *Review of International Studies*, 18 (1992), pp. 89–113, on p. 99.
16. For the 'invasionism' gripping Britain, see A. L. Dunham, *The Anglo-French Treaty of Commerce and the Progress of the Industrial Revolution in France* (Ann Arbor, MI: University of Michigan Press, 1930), p. 118.
17. For the debate on the extent of protection in both countries, see J. V. Nye, 'The Myth of Free-Trade Britain and Fortress France: Tariffs and Trade in the Nineteenth Century', *Journal of Economic History*, 51:1 (1991), pp. 23–46; cf. D. A. Irwin, 'Free Trade and Protection in Nineteenth-Century Britain and France Revisited: A Comment on Nye', *Journal of Economic History*, 53:1 (1993), pp. 146–52.
18. O'Brien and Pigman, 'Free Trade', p. 100.
19. Howe, *Free Trade and Liberal England*, p. 103.
20. O'Brien and Pigman, 'Free Trade', p. 102.
21. See the comments of T. Michell, Attaché to St Petersburg, on the commercial coalition of European states, except for Russia, in his 'Memo on Trade between Great Britain and Russia', 4 December 1865, in D. Lieven, K. Bourne, and D. C. Watt (eds), *British Documents on Foreign Affairs: Reports and Papers from the Foreign Office Confidential Print, Series A: Russia, 1859–1914*, vol. 1, Russia, 1859–1880 ([Frederick, MD]: University Publications of America, 1983), p. 93.
22. See M. S. Smith, *Tariff Reform in France, 1860–1900: The Politics of Economic Interest* (Ithaca, NY: Cornell University Press, 1980).
23. See Volume 1 of this edition.
24. For the coalition, see C. Schonhardt-Bailey, 'Parties and Interests in the "Marriage of Iron and Rye"', *British Journal of Political Science*, 28 (1998), pp. 291–330, on pp. 293–6.
25. B. H. Brown, *The Tariff Reform Movement in Great Britain, 1881–1895* (New York: Columbia University Press, 1943), p. 15.
26. See 'Commercial Treaties and Free Trade', *Economist* (1860); and Robert Andrew Macfie, 'Notes on the French Treaty', *Liverpool Daily Post*, 16 February 1860, both below, pp. 161–3, 164–8.

27. See Lack (ed.), *The French Treaty and Tariff of 1860*, below, pp. 154–60; the Tory Chancellor Sir Stafford Northcote refused the request of Sir Louis Mallet of the Board of Trade to reduce the wine duties, Dunham, *The Anglo-French Treaty of Commerce*, p. 338.
28. Ibid., p. 343.
29. See John Dunmore Lang, *Freedom and Independence for the Golden Lands of Australia* (1852), below, pp. 323–6; R. L. Schuyler, *The Fall of the Old Colonial System: A Study in British Free Trade, 1770–1870* (New York: Oxford University Press, 1945), p. 211.
30. C. D. W. Goodwin, *Economic Enquiry in Australia* (Durham, NC: Duke University Press, 1966).
31. Most apparent in David Syme's *Outlines of an Industrial Science* (1876); Syme was known as the father of protection in Australia.

THE DECLINE OF PROTECTIONISM IN BRITAIN, 1846–52

The period 1846–52 witnessed the effective disintegration of protectionism as a political force in Britain. In retrospect, the rapidity of its decline appears surprising, and as the next section demonstrates, Britain was unique in this respect. One can view the decline of protectionism as emanating from the dissolution of a winning coalition of economic interest groups or, in ideological terms, as a result of many strands of support for free trade, encompassing evangelical, economic and moral issues, emerging with full force in the late 1840s. Either way, the ability of free trade to obtain cross-class support was strikingly demonstrated between 1846 and 1852, and stands in stark contrast with the pleading of vested interests associated with protectionism. Despite this success, attempts to extend internationalist and pacific conceptions of free trade met with less success.

Corn Law repeal removed one of the main pillars of the protective system, but the Navigation Laws, the long-standing body of laws protecting British shipping, remained. For protectionists, defending the Navigation Laws assumed great significance, not only as the last bastion of the protective system, but also by attributing to them Britain's rise to greatness. Thus, abolition would result in the decline of the British shipping industry and naval power, which in turn would threaten Britain's global position.[1] Indeed, protectionist defence of the Navigation Laws was not primarily based on questions of free trade or protection per se, but on Adam Smith's dictum that defence was more important than opulence.[2] Whilst the shipping interest was broadly opposed to repeal, the economic case for maintaining the Navigation Laws was seriously undermined by Corn Law repeal.[3] For a free trade in wheat to be effective, it was necessary to free shipping from restrictive regulations. It was impossible to restrict the shipping of colonial goods, especially since the effective abandonment of colonial preference. If Canadians, for example, as well as losing preference were restricted to the higher freight charges of British ships, they would be disadvantaged. Thus, the protectionist case of 'justice for the colonies' was appropriated by free traders. Alongside such considerations were more fundamental aims of freedom of commerce, with John

Lewis Ricardo, the ardent free trader and nephew of David Ricardo, calling for repeal on the basis of restoring the natural order in commerce.[4]

Despite the events of 1846, the Corn Law question was far from resolved. With the Conservative Party split between Peelites and protectionists, it was expected that re-imposing the Corn Laws would be the fundamental priority of any protectionist government, particularly in light of the agricultural and industrial depression after 1846. Political and economic conditions appeared conducive towards restoring protection, yet the period ended with the triumph of free trade, alongside broad recognition that the question was now resolved for a number of years. Why protection was not restored remains one of the most vexed questions in British history in the aftermath of Corn Law repeal.[5] The inability of protectionists to obtain popular and political support emanated from the powerful association drawn between protection and higher food prices. It was significant that Corn Law repeal generated far greater public controversy than repeal of the Navigation Laws, although the latter remained a divisive political issue, and the parliamentary battle over repeal was keenly contested. The ideological force of the anti-Corn Law agitation may not have solely converted Sir Robert Peel, but its impact was felt long after 1846.

The protectionist movement of 1846–52 was a fascinatingly diverse coalition. No single issue, other than dissatisfaction with free trade, united the disparate groups. Although primarily agrarian, the movement incorporated shipping, colonial and industrial interests.[6] Whilst protection had parliamentary advocates such as Conservative politician John Charles Herries, after the resignation of Lord George Bentinck as leader in February 1848, many leading figures sought to distance themselves from protection.[7] The main impetus for protectionist agitation was extra-parliamentary, provided by the National Association for the Protection of British Industry and Capital, formed in 1849.[8] The founder, George Frederick Young, saw protection as a policy which reflected and encouraged 'a lofty and ennobling patriotism' compared to the 'vague and impracticable cosmopolitanism' of free trade.[9] Another leading figure was Charles Stanhope, who sought to build on Bentinck's ideal of urban support to accompany the movement's rural base.[10] Whilst the popular movement was composed of economic interest groups, a coherent protectionist philosophy and critique of free trade existed amongst the intelligentsia of the movement, which assessed commercial policy in broad constitutional, economic and imperial terms.[11] There was little moral or religious basis for the movement, but economic interests were conflated with themes of self-sufficiency, national independence and balancing of fiscal burdens and class interests within the British polity.[12] The fundamental premise of protectionist political economy was a denial of Ricardo's theory of international comparative advantage. A differentiation between 'old' and 'young' states was drawn, operated on by a 'fundamental law of nature' between the different effects of progress on agriculture and manufacturing. The old state could undersell the young in manufacturing, but the young could undersell the old in agriculture. This was an ingenious argument that could justify agricultural protection in Britain, and industrial protection in nations where manufacturing was at an early stage of development.[13]

Why then, was protection not restored in Britain in the period 1846–52? Part of the problem was the difficulty of squaring the expediencies of party politics with the commercial policy revolution of 1846. It seems clear that many 'protectionists' who opposed Peel in 1846 would not continue to advocate protection. Benjamin Disraeli, for example, saw no possibility of restoring the Corn Laws, but sought to placate protectionist demands by advocating fiscal readjustments. In 1849, a year of severe agricultural depression and low prices, he proposed revision of local taxes and poor rates as measures of agricultural relief.[14] Under pressure from a revival of popular protectionism in agricultural constituencies, he eventually succumbed to advocating an increase of import duties on foreign products which would facilitate a surplus in the Sinking Fund.[15] Whilst this programme bore similarities to Bentinck's earlier plans, it met with a hostile reception from within the party.[16] Disraeli's proposals have been viewed as a coherent response to the loss of protection, whilst retaining its theoretical trappings by balancing fiscal burdens between the propertied interests of the State.[17] Yet he could not convince the protectionist movement, which demanded nothing less than protection, and facing renewed protectionist agitation, Disraeli decided to drop the idea of a Sinking Fund.[18]

Young's National Association, although originally formed to oppose the Navigation Laws, aimed at constructing a broad popular protectionist alliance in the constituencies.[19] The Association agitated in agricultural constituencies, and successfully harnessed the anger of farmers at the loss of protection and falling prices. Many were alarmed at the farmers' independence, and viewed their aggressive language and activity as a sign of the erosion of the traditional deference of county society. Fear of revolution and the establishment of a Republic were heard throughout 1850.[20] Young sought to enlist working-class support, some sections of which were clearly sympathetic to protection, if not protectionist. For many, it was a short step from 'protection of labour' to protection of native industry. The formation of the National Association of Organized Trades for the Industrial, Social and Political Emancipation of Labour (NAOT) in March 1848, an alliance of Chartists and trades unionists, was 'an important attempt to concentrate working class energies against the ideology of laissez-faire political economy'. The movement emerged from concerns over unemployment amongst London trades, and was influenced by Louis Blanc's organization of labour in National Workshops in France.[21] In looking to government to protect labour, the movement was at odds with classical political economy, signified by Richard Cobden's colourful description of government intervention in employment conditions as 'communism'. The prospect of an anti-free trade alliance of protectionists and Chartists disappeared when the NAOT leadership declared support for protection of labour, not protectionism as it existed before 1846.[22] The failure to construct a popular movement, separate from what were perceived to be vested interests, was a fatal blow to the hopes of restoring protection.

With the defeat of the Whig government in February 1852, a minority protectionist government came to power. The Anti-Corn Law League made preparations to renew its agitation, with Cobden stating 'when we find a body of men taking possession of the reins of power, we expect that they will drive in the direction in which they have always professed to be heading'.[23] Meetings were held to orchestrate parliamentary action, and force an admission from government that protection would not be restored, which was confirmed in May by the Earl of Derby's speech in the Lords.[24] Parliamentary sanction was given to this admission later in 1852 with Palmerston's motion attributing British prosperity to the reform in commercial policy.[25] With free trade unilaterally established, protection widely regarded as an electoral liability, and with the disbandment of the National Association in 1853, protectionism disappeared from British politics for a generation.[26]

In the immediate post-1846 period, free traders were also occupied in attempts to extend free trade. The internationalism of free trade was nowhere better displayed than in the International Peace Congresses held annually between 1848 and 1853, a testimony to the optimism of the age. The utopianism of the Cobdenite analysis of foreign policy converged with the pacifism of Quakers and Benthamites, underscored by concerns with financial retrenchment. Curbing military expenditure and extending peaceful conceptions of commerce were viewed as part of the same struggle.[27] Cobden played an important role in providing a secular critique of excessive military expenditure. His political agenda of the late 1840s was shaped by the experience of his European tour. Considering tariffs inextricably linked with militarism, Cobden argued that by controlling military expenditure and curbing warlike propensities, peaceful conceptions of freedom of exchange and international commerce would flourish.[28] For Cobden, escalating military expenditure was, in fiscal terms, the 'taproot of protection'. He hoped to make converts to free trade through peace, and to broaden the European base of the movement by linking it with the Mazzinian Republican movement.[29] As he told George Wilson, 'I consider this struggle against armaments to be the real free-trade battle'.[30]

Cobden's campaign to commit European governments to international arbitration was another facet of his belief in the connection between peace and commerce.[31] Linking foreign policy considerations, notably renunciation of balance of power international politics, with peaceful conceptions of free commerce was perhaps Cobden's most fundamental principle. Arbitration was an instrument that would promote international cooperation and progress rather than international rivalry and balance of power conceptions of international relations. Whilst critics pointed to the idealistic and visionary aspects of this type of analysis, Cobden's arbitration motions created some agitation, which perhaps owed as much to concerns over financial retrenchment as to support of arbitration per se.[32] Motions for international arbitration of 1849 and 1851 were defeated, amidst considerable debate over its merits.[33] Yet no government was willing to sacrifice vital interests to the vagaries of arbitration, and the failure of the peace movement to curb military expenditure and to promote disarmament and arbitration was signalled by the Turkish declaration of war on Russia in 1853.

Notes
1. G. F. Young's evidence to Select Committee on the Navigation Laws, Fourth Report, *Parliamentary Papers* (1847), 556, x.[371], questions 5234, 5300–2, 6125, pp. 69, 76–7, 152.
2. D. Walker-Smith, *The Protectionist Case in the 1840s* (1933; New York: Augustus M. Kelley, 1970), p. 77; *Parliamentary Papers* (1847), 556, x.[371], questions 6121–5, pp. 151–2.
3. A. Howe, *Free Trade and Liberal England, 1846–1946* (Oxford: Clarendon Press, 1997), p. 116; A. Howe, 'Free Trade and the City of London, c. 1820–1870', *History*, 77 (1992), pp. 391–410, on p. 404.
4. See John Lewis Ricardo, *The Anatomy of the Navigation Laws* (1847), below, pp. 9–13.
5. J. Vincent (ed.), *Disraeli, Derby, and the Conservative Party: Journals and Memoirs of Edward Henry, Lord Stanley, 1849–1869* (Hassocks: Harvester Press, 1978), pp. xiii–xiv.
6. 'A Protectionist League: The Navigation Laws', *Economist*, 7:289 (10 March 1849), pp. 255–7.
7. Vincent (ed.), *Journals of Lord Stanley*, 29 March, 19 and 20 May 1849, pp. 3, 8, 9.
8. *The Times*, 27 June 1849, p. 5c.
9. A. Macintyre, 'Lord George Bentinck and the Protectionists: A Lost Cause?', *Transactions of the Royal Historical Society*, 5th series, 39 (1989), pp. 141–165, on p. 160.
10. S. Palmer, *Politics, Shipping and the Repeal of the Navigation Laws* (Manchester: Manchester University Press, 1990), p. 173; Macintyre, 'Lord George Bentinck', p. 163.
11. A. Gambles, 'Rethinking the Politics of Protection: Conservatism and the Corn Laws, 1830–52', *English Historical Review*, 113:453 (1998), pp. 928–52, on pp. 932, 950.
12. See *Free Thoughts on Free Trade* (1852), below, pp. 25–32; Gambles, 'Rethinking the Politics of Protection', p. 951.

13. Macintyre, 'Lord George Bentinck', pp. 156–7; cf. W. Cunningham, *The Growth of English Industry and Commerce in Modern Times: Laissez Faire*, 6th edn (Cambridge: Cambridge University Press, 1925), p. 869.
14. See 'Protection Disinterred', *Economist* (1849), below, pp. 15–18.
15. T. L. Crosby, *English Farmers and the Politics of Protection, 1815–1852* (Hassocks: Harvester Press, 1977), pp. 158–9; 'Mr. Disraeli's New Plan', *Economist*, 7:320 (13 October 1849), p. 1133.
16. See Minutes of a Special Meeting of the Acting Committee of the National Association for the Protection of British Industry and Capital, 15 October 1849; and Herries to Young, 15 November 1849, both below, pp. 22–3, 24.
17. Gambles, 'Rethinking the Politics of Protection', p. 951; P. R. Ghosh, 'Disraelian Conservatism: A Financial Approach', *English Historical Review*, 99:391 (1984), pp. 268–96, on pp. 269–70.
18. See Minutes of a Special Meeting of the Acting Committee of the National Association for the Protection of British Industry and Capital, below, pp. 22–3; R. Blake, *Disraeli* (London: Eyre & Spottiswoode, 1966), p. 191.
19. Crosby, *English Farmers and the Politics of Protection*, p. 160.
20. See Stanhope to Young, 29 May 1849; and Stanhope to Young, 8 June 1849, both below, pp. 19–20, 21.
21. M. Finn, *After Chartism: Class and Nation in English Radical Politics, 1848–1874* (Cambridge: Cambridge University Press, 1993), p. 89; J. Belchem, 'Chartism and the Trades, 1848–1850', *English Historical Review*, 98 (1983), pp. 559; Finn, *After Chartism*, p. 69.
22. Ibid., p. 191; Belchem, 'Chartism and the Trades', pp. 577–81.
23. Cobden's speech at Leeds, *Manchester Examiner and Times*, 6 March 1852; see Notice and Details of Anti Corn Law League Meeting, *Economist* (1852); and H. Ashworth, *Recollections of Richard Cobden and the Anti-Corn-Law League* (1877), both below pp. 33–4, 35–40.
24. Cobden to George Wilson, 10 March 1852, Wilson Papers, Manchester Central Library, vol. 18, M20/10/3/1852; *The Times*, 25 May 1852, p. 2a.
25. See Sir James Graham to W. E. Gladstone, 13 November 1852; and Graham to Gladstone, 13 November 1852, 19 November 1852, both below, pp. 53, 54; *The Times*, 26 November 1852, p. 5a.
26. 'Protection Decently Interred', *The Times*, 9 February 1853, p. 4f.
27. 'They are one & the same cause', Cobden to Henry Ashworth, 12 April 1842, in A. Howe (ed.), *The Letters of Richard Cobden, Volume 1, 1815–1847* (Oxford: Oxford University Press, 2007), pp. 266–7; D. Nicholls, 'Richard Cobden and the International Peace Movement, 1848–1853', *Journal of British Studies*, 30:4 (1991), pp. 351–76, on p. 354.
28. Cobden shared with Richard Whateley and Nassau Senior the 'optimist' view that foreign commerce would promote international peace and create sufficient wealth to solve all problems of distributive justice, B. Hilton, *The Age of Atonement: The Influence of Evangelicalism on Social and Economic Thought, 1795–1865* (Oxford: Clarendon Press, 1988), p. 54.
29. Howe, *Free Trade and Liberal England*, pp. 84–5; Nicholls, 'Richard Cobden and the International Peace Movement', p. 364.

30. 17 January 1848, Wilson Papers, Manchester Central Library, vol. 14: M20/17/11/1848; M. Taylor (ed.), *The European Diaries of Richard Cobden, 1846–1849* (Aldershot: Scolar Press, 1994), pp. 29–32.
31. M. M. Robson, 'Liberals and "Vital Interests": The Debate on International Arbitration, 1815–72', *Bulletin of the Institute of Historical Research*, 32 (1959), pp. 38–55, on pp. 44–6.
32. See *Arbitration Instead of War* (1848), below, pp. 41–3, for a skilful analysis with an emphasis on financial retrenchment.
33. *Hansard* (1849), cvi, cc. 53–121; *Hansard* (1851), cxvii, cc. 916–49.

CONSOLIDATION OF FREE TRADE IN BRITAIN

Defeat of Protectionism in Britain

John Lewis Ricardo, *The Anatomy of the Navigation Laws* (London: C. Gilpin, 1847), pp. 213–17, 220–2.

THE VALUE OF THE COMPETITION CRY.

We have now done with the facts and the figures of competition.[1] The result of them are –

That England has advantages, superior to every other country, for the build of first class ships.

That those first-class ships are the best and cheapest.

That they stand the wear and tear of sea more than three times as long as cheap foreign ships, and do not in the first instance cost any thing like three times as much.

That our own colonies build, of the cheap class, the cheapest ships, and of the dear class the most long-lived ships in the world.

That British ships do not carry, tonnage for tonnage, a greater number of seamen than foreign ships.

That foreign ships carry a greater number than ours.

That our ships are not better victualled than foreign vessels.

That the sailors on board most foreign ships are better cared for and better found than in our ships.

That foreign ships are not navigated more cheaply than ours.

That, on board American ships, the captains, petty officers, and men are much better paid than they are in English ships.

That British vessels lay in their stores as cheaply as any ships in the world.

---

1 [Ed.: The previous section demonstrated the increasing tonnage (1,256,909 tons) of British ships in the period 1821–46, and a comparative analysis of British, colonial and foreign shipping.]

That of all tonnage, that of England has increased the most continuously and rapidly.

That the increase is greatest in the face of foreign competition.

That of all the tonnage entering British ports, not one-third is foreign; and the proportion of British increases.

That in all other ports the foreign tonnage either exceeds their own, or is increasing in proportion to their own.

That British ships have nearly the whole carrying trade of Russia, as well with other ports of Europe as with foreign ports.

That the ports of Russia are open to all ships on equal terms.

That every month, from January to December, British ships enter the Austrian port of Trieste with cargoes from European ports and foreign countries, alike open to all the shipping of the world.

That the port of Trieste is open to all shipping on equal terms.

That at Hamburgh the number of British ships is greater than their own, and is nearly half the whole number of ships entering the port.

That the port of Hamburgh is open to all on equal terms.

That of all the foreign tonnage entering the ports of the United States, more than two-thirds is British.

That the ports of America are more free to other ships than to ours.

That America has adopted our own Navigation Law against ourselves.

That to all other countries she gives such liberty as they give her.

That efforts are being made to form a Zollverein Union Flag by way of Prussian and German retaliation for our Navigation Law.

We have proved that British shipping can compete with all the shipping of the world.

That it does compete and has long competed successfully.

That the Navigation Laws are not a help, but a hindrance to our shipping, by giving rise to foreign retaliation hostile to trade. In addition to our natural advantages, shipping has been enriched of late years by the increase of many large branches of trade, to some particulars of which we claim the attention of shipowners.

BENEFIT TO SHIPPING FROM TRADES OPENED AND DUTIES REPEALED.

Of late years, the East India trade has been opened to all our ships, and the employment for them has increased more than five-fold. The China trade has been opened, and is year by year increasing.

The duties on timber have been equalised or repealed, and more than 500,000 tons additional of timber have been shipped from Canada alone in a single year.

The duties on sugar have been lowered and equalised, and the trade opened to our ships throughout the world; and this year there has been an increased import of 100,000 tons.

The Corn Laws have been abolished, and all the ships of the world have not been enough to carry corn.

Cattle, sheep, pigs, &c., have been admitted, and quarter by quarter the numbers brought increase.

The wool, cotton, and silk duties have been abolished, and there are more of each to be carried to and fro, raw and manufactured.

The provision trade has been opened, and the imports are already great, and show a steady and rapid increase.

In fact, the staples of India, China, the Foreign West Indies, Brazils, the Havannah, and the whole Continent of South America, of Russia, the Baltic, Spain, all corn-growing Europe and America, have been admitted to our ports, either duty free, or at only revenue duties; and from and to all these places, trade has increased, and is growing.

We hear nothing from the Central Committee of British Shipowners as to the rich harvest that must have fallen to them, from the employment of hundreds of thousands of tons of shipping in all these trades, made for them by the abolition of monopolies like their own, regardless of the outcries of the several vested interests.

But when their turn has come, and it is demanded of them that they (as all the others have been made to do) shall cease to put difficulties in the way of trade, and to impose taxes upon the consumer, for their individual benefit, we are met over again by the old policy of mystification and patriotic pretences; and are told particularly to believe, that the safety of the state is in danger, from the fir wood of Finland and the cheap sailors of Dantzic.

In every case, the dread of foreign competition was unfounded; but in some there might be the excuse for it, that the foreign resources were not known; but in this of shipping they are known, and ours outweigh them all.

Curious enough, when we come to look closely at it, is this dread that our shipowners have of foreigners. They seem to have become possessed by an idea that, shut up in some deep hidden bay or other, there floats ready for sea some million tons of shipping, waiting merely the signal of the repeal of our Navigation Laws to heave anchor, spread every sail, stand out to sea, and carry everywhere, everything, from every place. It seems never to occur to these shipowners, that there are no ships idle now; that one way or another they all get freights; that the abolition of the Navigation Laws might cause here and there a different distribution of trade; but that there would be none the fewer goods to carry, and no less distance altogether to carry them; for by some ships or other they must be all brought from their several places of production to the manufacturer and the consumer. The repeal of the Navigation Law would neither dry up the sea, nor bring Europe, India, America, or Africa, one whit nearer to us; nor could it make England, or the Continent of Europe, grow the productions of the tropics, nor transport our factories to India; nor can it change our commercial spirit and aptitude for maritime enterprise.

All it can do is, to put an end to the memorials of shipowners' societies, and to the absurd notion that shipping is an interest distinct from trade, leaving all ships free to find how they may best contrive never to be idle nor empty. [...]

CONCLUSION.

In the year 1660 a compact was entered into between Parliament and the shipowners, which compact has been modified and confirmed by one hundred and forty-four other Acts, all of which are now represented by the 8th and 9th Victoria, cap. 88, and the auxiliary Act, 8 and 9 Victoria, cap. 89.

Parliament, on the one hand, undertakes to give encouragement to the shipowners, by means of a monopoly of the carriage by sea, so far as other nations will permit. The shipowners, on the other hand, undertake to find men for the manning of the Royal Navy, and to that end to register their seamen – to carry useless apprentices – and to submit to have their crews abstracted from them by desertion or impressment, when and where to the Admiralty it shall seem fit.

However sincerely either party may have intended to carry out the contract, it is quite evident that both have most signally failed.

The Act of Parliament does not encourage and increase the mercantile marine.

The sacrifices of the shipowners do not find a 'large, constant, and ready supply of seamen for the Royal Navy.'

The Act of Parliament fails –

Inasmuch as the mercantile marine has flourished least where it is most protected;

Inasmuch as monopoly has produced inferiority;

Inasmuch as restriction has produced retaliation; –

Because, by restriction on the one part, and retaliation on the other, the field of enterprise is narrowed, the cost of transport is enhanced, and so fewer ships are required altogether.

The shipowners fail –

Inasmuch as by carrying apprentices they displace able seamen, and so drive them to seek employment in foreign service;

Inasmuch as by registering the sailors, they advertise to them their purpose; and these objecting altogether to fight for lower wages than they could earn by trading, when they are most wanted are least likely to be found; and

Because the seamen of merchant ships are not adapted for the Royal Navy, and are not such as modern naval warfare requires;

And so the preamble of the Navigation Law is not proved, and the preamble of the Registration Act is not proved.

But there are other classes of the community, of whose interests the statutes take no note, to whom the arrangement is a source of unmitigated and admitted injury, who demand the demonstration of the necessity of the sacrifice they are called upon to make.

The colonists must know why it is indispensable that they should be crippled in the competition which has been forced upon them.

The merchants require to have satisfactory justification for the contraction of their commerce, and the vexations and impediments to their trade.

The manufacturers require proof of the urgency of a law which limits their markets, curtails the supply of their raw materials, and forces the capital of their customers from barter into competition with them.

The working classes must be told what real ground there is for denying to them the freest possible import of the articles upon which their labour is expended.

The merchant seaman asks of right what paramount need there is that he alone, of all skilled workmen, should be held to be at the disposal of the State, and to have no full property in his own skill.

Finally, the whole community must be persuaded of the soundness of the policy which enhances to them the cost of every article for consumption or manufacture which is brought from beyond the sea.

And as a distinct advantage has not been shown, the colonist, the merchant, the manufacturer, the workman, the merchant seaman, and every class of consumer, have a just claim upon Parliament for the repeal of the laws through whose agency the injury is inflicted.

John Charles Herries to George Frederick Young, [8?] January 1849, Herries Papers, BL, Add. MS 57423, fols 104–6.

S:t Julians
[8?] Jan.y 1849
(Copy to G.F. Young)

My d:r Sir

The time is at hand when we must again give battle for the Navigation laws.

We have now the Gov:t Bill before us. Have you looked at it? – To me it appears to agree in all Material points with their programme.

The first question for our Consideration in the present advanced stage of the discussion is as to the best mode of meeting the reintroduction of this most dangerous measure.

The alternatives which obviously suggest themselves are – 1:st A Single, persevering determined resistance to the propositions of the Gov:t –

2. To Oppose to their sweeping abolition of the Navigation laws a modification of them so framed as to uphold the principle of preference & protection to our own Shipping – especially in our Colonial & extra European trade – but at the same time to introduce some relaxation partly for the relief of our own Commerce & partly also for the advantage of other Countries which may be able and willing to concede corresponding benefits to us:– And thereupon to take the sense of Parliament & the Country on the respective plans.

I confess that I incline to the latter Course.

But if it be adopted we must lose no time in settling the Main point of our antagonist Measure.

You & I had some talk upon the view of the subject while our fight in the H:o C:o was in progress. And you partly opined to me the view of what the Shipping interest might be disposed to accept with satisfaction.

If you Continue to hold the opinion which you then expressed I should be very glad to receive them more in detail before I consult our friends here in both Houses on this most important subject.

For my own part I am so thoroughly convinced of the enormous detriment & danger to the Country with which the Gov:t measure is pregnant, that I am prepared to oppose it in one shape or other to the last extremity. If the result be unfavorable to us those who concur with me in this resolution, will, at least, have their Consciences clear of all responsibility for the evils which will inevitably follow.

Believe me
JCH

'Protection Disinterred', *Economist*, 7:289 (10 March 1849), pp. 254–5.

The bad wheat crop of last year has proved a sort of political godsend to the protectionists. That party was rapidly wearing away; and now, with the questionable advantage of a deficient harvest – which, if they had had their own way, might have produced a famine – it is doubtful whether Mr Disraeli and his friends will betray their weakness by dividing the House of Commons. But, whatever may be the protectionists' tactics in the house, there is that in their out-door and preliminary movement which calls for a passing notice.

Up to the month of February 1848, when commenced that constant succession of wet weather which will render the last year one of the worst seasons of the present century, it was wonderful with what equanimity the farmers, whose ruin from free-trade had been so passionately predicted, regarded the coming event. In fact, they had experienced an anticipatory interval of free trade, and, upon the whole, they rather liked it. Had the wheat crop of last year been one of average productiveness, we have no doubt that the opening of the corn trade would have passed by, so far as the farmers were concerned, with little remark. It is admitted that farmers of average capital and skill did well during the two previous years; and had last year's crop been only moderately abundant, the most we should have heard about agricultural duties would have been an occasional fling at the perfidy of Peel, or the atrocity of Cobden, in putting an end to the contingent possibility of a monopoly price for wheat. But the wet weather of last year has occasioned to the growers of wheat – in the counties south of Trent, at all events – a misfortune analogous to that which the potato failure inflicted upon Ireland. The peculiarity of the season has caused a serious deficiency in that portion of his produce on which the farmer relies – perhaps relies too exclusively – as a money-bringing crop; and we do not deny, for we know, nay feel, that much inconvenience and distress among English farmers have been the result. From no fault of their own, but from the incessant rains, all the farmers' calculations have been upset; the chief source of their money income has in a great measure failed them, and amongst the weaker members of the body it is, we fear, but too probable that there are many whom nothing but the assistance of friends, or the forbearance of those to whom they are under engagements, can save from ruin. We have always frankly expressed our opinion as to the deficient capitals with which so many English farmers carry on their business, and have often pointed out the hazard they run by so doing. Now, one of the great risks in husbandry is that of a bad season. A farmer with a weak capital may contrive to keep his ground in productive years, but in adverse seasons he must go down. And even farmers possessing considerable means cannot undergo such a year as that of

1848 without vexation, anxiety, and loss. We can readily believe that many farmers must this year pay rent out of their capital; or from extraneous resources; but with that free trade in grain has the remotest possible connection. The only way in which free trade can be said to have injured the English farmer is by preventing – as it probably has prevented – corn reaching a famine price. Will any discreet and rational politician venture to object to free trade on that ground?

We have, however, in the protectionists, a political party neither discreet nor rational; and accordingly we find the natural discontent of the farmers attempted to be used for party purposes. Of this the meeting at Willis's Rooms is an illustration. To those who can go through the dreary waste of words on the speeches (as reported in the *Morning Herald*), at the meeting of the 'Central Protection Society,' on Tuesday last, the disinterment of fallacies and fictions long since exposed and disposed of, the inconsequential reasoning, the silly and coarse abuse of all public men, who, in office or out, have shown any capacity for statesmanship, the ill-concealed servility, and the simulated violence, present a combination which is as ludicrous as it is tiresome. The speakers were exclusively of that small section of agriculturists well known as political hangers-on of the Duke of Richmond; men who are altogether without influence over the farmers as a body. Many of them are land agents, and were used to get up that abortive imitation of the League, the Protection Society. The protectionist members of Parliament who attended said not a syllable, with the exception of the Duke of Richmond, the chairman, who thanked the meeting for having re-echoed his own expressed opinion – for making which he admitted he was 'nearly laughed at' – 'that protection would again become the law of this country,' and recommended them to rally round their 'leaders:' *i.e.*, the Duke himself, Lord Stanley, and Mr Disraeli, and not to follow any other politicians. The resolutions passed were a paraphrase of that proposed to the House of Commons by Mr Disraeli, a little altered to suit the taste of the farmers.

Apart from the suggestion of repeal of the malt tax, upon which we have before fully stated our views, the only topic in either set of resolutions which is worthy of the slightest notice is the reference to local taxation both contain. As we have said, the phraseology is raised to suit the audience, but the idea is the same. At Willis's Rooms they ask, 'in order to mitigate as far as possible' the loss of protection, 'the immediate revision of all general and local taxation which presses with unequal severity upon the cultivators of the soil;' while Mr Disraeli proposed to the House of Commons to affirm 'that the whole of the local taxation of the country for national purposes falls mainly, if not exclusively, on all real property,' and sought a committee of the whole house 'to take into consideration the removal of the grievances of which the owners and occupiers of real property thus complain, and to establish a more equitable apportionment of the public burdens.' A resolution more obviously framed as something on which to hang a speech and nothing else, than Mr Disraeli's proposition, cannot be conceived; nor are the Central Society's resolves much more definite. But there is this point of the incidence of local taxation raised, though somewhat vaguely and obscurely. Let us see what it really means; and first, let us dismiss the farmers from this discussion; for except accidentally or temporarily they have nothing to do with it. On taking his farm, the farmer ascertains first what are the local rates and taxes – the poor, highway, church, and county rates, the tithe rent charge, and so forth – and then he calculates what rent he can afford to pay. If these local charges be high, the rent will be reduced in proportion; if low, more rent will be given to the owner of the farm. To the farmer, therefore, in a pecuniary point of view, it is a matter of indifference whether he pays a larger or a smaller proportion of the aggregate amount, compounded of rent and local charges, as rent to his landlord or as local taxation. Both items must be paid before he has either gross or net profit for himself, and both form the first and most important considerations on hiring a farm. Unless, therefore, local taxation increase during the currency of his lease, if he has one, or during his yearly tenancy – the probability of which is one of the contingencies a farmer must take into his calculation – local taxation is exclusively a landlord's question. The effect of removing the local rates and taxes from real property; and the conversion of those charges into a tax upon all kinds of property, would be simply a transfer of the obligations of landed property from the shoulders of landowners to those of other people.

But there is another class of local burdens on the occupiers of land, which the speakers at Willis's did not mention, from which they suffer far more than from local taxation, and for relief from which they require no legislative assistance: we allude to the burdens caused by obsolete customs, covenants, and restrictions, game preservation, precarious tenures, and the like, the whole of which may be removed by more rational and business-like contracts between landlords and tenants than at present prevail. As an instance, let us mention a statement made by Mr Worsley at the East Grinstead meeting, when he said that if his landlord would give him the land he occupies, rent free, he would not hold it upon condition of cultivating it according to the customs of the country. Let the farmers turn their attention to these things wherein they must succeed, instead of wasting their time and losing their temper in beating the air at the bidding of the political protectionists who use them and dispose them.

Mr Disraeli's argument is, that local charges are for matters of national utility, that poor rates prevent mendacity and crime, by which the owners of other than real property receive a benefit; and that in some instances, as in the case of county rates applied to criminal prosecutions, matters only occasionally local occasion great local expense. This is shallow and fallacious. The burden of poor rate is in all cases made more or less by the circumstances of the locality in which it is charged, and may commonly be in a great degree controlled by local good management. In rural parishes, where poor rates are heavy, the causes will almost invariably be found to be dependent on mismanagement of the land, which owners and occupiers have it in their power to correct. And the same thing applies to some extent to the other local charges. But the short answer to Mr Disraeli's fallacies is, that though by the progress of modern society the purposes to which local rates are applied have a wider utility than in former times, yet that progress had conferred upon the owner of landed property benefits far more than equivalent to the increased local charges to which they are subject.

If the country gentleman of the midland counties, whom Mr Disraeli impersonates, complains that the industrious capitalists engaged in trade and commerce do receive occasional, or even constant, benefit from his local expenditure, and asks that the rest of the community should ease him of one-half of that expenditure, let him know how much his rental has been increased – without any effort on his part, nay, in despite of obstacles he has persisted in maintaining – by the wealth and industry of the rest of the community. If this country gentleman desires to go back to the local burdens of past ages, let him be content also with the rents of the same period.

The truth is, that instead of landed property in this country being unduly burdened, it is rather the reverse. At all events, the industrious part of the landed classes, the occupying tenants, have no permanent interest in Mr Disraeli's motion, and he has altogether thrown overboard their panacea, repeal of the malt tax.

Lord Stanhope to G. F. Young, 29 May 1849, Young Papers, BL, Add. MS 46712, fols 97–8.

> Chevening, near Sevenoaks,
> May 29th, 1849
>
> Dear Sir
> I am favored to day with your Letter, & shall feel much obliged if you will have the goodness to inform me what has been the result of the enquiries which you directed to be made.
>
> It gives me very great concern to find that your opinions differ so widely from my own in respect to the course which ought in this crisis to be pursued, & which may decide the fate of this country. The Masses are not, I think, in favor of Free Trade, & I should feel no apprehension as to their decision at any Public Meeting when the question is argued with reference, not to the interests of any particular class, but of every class which is engaged in Native Industry. The immediate object of the Meetings which ought every where to be held in all the Sea Ports, & on the most extensive scale at Blackheath, would not be the restoration of Protection, but a Dissolution of Parliament which could not be opposed by Free Traders without tacitly confessing that the majority of the Electors is opposed to their views.
>
> There can be no doubt that a strong Reaction will at last arrive, but before it takes place I see every reason to expect that the lamentable destitution to which the Labouring Classes will very soon be reduced, in the Agricultural Districts as well as in the Sea Ports, will produce Anarchy & Revolution. Those who now decline to guide the Masses may then find that they will become the dupes of designing demagogues & be led either by Chartists or by Communists.
>
> It is in my opinion quite obvious that Parliament will not be induced to retrace its steps unless it is compelled to do so by a Popular Movement, or what was called 'a pressure from without.' Unless the Society which was formed in the Meeting at the Hall of Commerce intends to organize such a movement & to act with the energy & union which are now more than ever indispensably requisite I can take no interest in its proceedings which would be utterly useless, & even worse than useless as they might excite hopes & expectations which could not possibly be realized.
>
> A continuance of inactivity, if indeed the country had the patience to allow it, would, I am confident, encourage Ministers to propose the repeal of the Navigation Law & as far as regards even the Coasting Trade, to which they admitted in the late Debates the same principles of Free Trade are applicable, although they asserted, what is contrary to fact, that it could not be pursued profitably by foreigners. We have seen for many years the disastrous & deplorable results which have arisen from the apathy & inactivity of those who ought to have defended

zealously their rights, & which if continued cannot fail to terminate in a Social Revolution the most awful & desolating that the world has yet witnessed.

very sincerely your's [*sic*]
Stanhope

Lord Stanhope to G. F. Young, 8 June 1849, Young Papers, BL, Add. MS 46712, fols 99–100.

no. 29 Albemarle Street,
June 8th, 1849

Dear Sir

I feel much obliged by your Letter which reached me this morning & by the explanations with which you have favored me. I have long perceived & with very deep regret the apathy & delusion which prevail, & which seem indeed to indicate a 'judicial blindness' that is, I fear, the precursor of destruction. We ought however to derive some encouragement from the examples of so many County Meetings in which the Protectionists have been every where successful, & also from the reaction which now takes place in public opinion.

Although our exertions should prove to be ineffectual, & although I cannot flatter myself with the expectation that a Revolution will be averted, it might be very dangerous to delay them, for the extreme destitution to which the Labouring Classes will soon be reduced may be such as would ~~soon~~ lead to Anarchy with all its awful results. The scenes of November 1830 may be renewed throughout the country, but in a much more formidable manner, for the Artizans of Towns would probably unite with the Agricultural Labourers.

It gives me great satisfaction to learn that a Public Meeting is to be held on the 25th Inst. & I shall be very happy to attend it if the County Meeting in Kent should not be fixed for the same day, which I will endeavour to prevent. The Meeting in London ought, I think, to be held in the open air, as no room is sufficiently capacious to contain all those who might wish to be present, & I cannot too strongly recommend to you to send to it many Spitalfield Weavers & other Artizans who have been the victims of Free Trade. Amongst them there are several excellent speakers whose observations might have very great weight, & would very clearly prove a community of interests. It appears also very important that our Friends & Adherents should go to the Meeting so early as to occupy the greatest portion of the Room, or of the space, in which it is held before the arrival of any Free Traders.[1]

I need not assure you that it will always give me very great pleasure to be favored with communications from you when you think that I can be of any service in a cause which I have very much at heart.

very sincerely your's [sic]
Stanhope

1 [Ed.: For a critical account of this meeting, see *Economist*, 7:289 (30 June 1849), pp. 711–13.]

Minutes of a Special Meeting of the Acting Committee of the National Association for the Protection of British Industry and Capital, 15 October 1849, at the London Tavern, Chaired by G. F. Young, Herries Papers, BL, Add. MS 57423, fols 143–4, enclosed in G. F. Young to Benjamin Disraeli (copy), 17 October 1849, fols 145–6.

National Association for the Protection of British Industry and Capital

At a Special Meeting of the Acting committee held at the London Tavern on Monday the 15th day of October 1849, for the purpose of taking into consideration the policy of making arrangements without delay for convening Public Meetings throughout the Country for carrying out the objects of the Association.

George Fred^k Young Esq: in the Chair.

Resolved,

That in the judgment of this Committee, considering that great variety of opinion prevails on the subject of specific measures of relief to British Interests, while all concur cordially in desiring a return to Protection, it is indispensable to the success of the efforts of this Association, that it should by every means in its power, discourage the advocacy of any particular measure of relief, and urge on its friends throughout the Country to restrict their exertions to energetic endeavors to reestablish the principle of Protection as the ground work and guide of legislative policy.

That this object can obviously only be attained by a dissolution of Parliament and the appointment of a Protectionist Ministry, to whose unfettered discretion should be confided the consideration of the particular measures best adapted for carrying out the principle.

That it is through the pressure of a strong expression of public opinion alone that a dissolution of Parliament can be obtained, and that appeals to elicit that opinion ought therefore forthwith to be made.

That, from the information now before this Committee, it appears that District and Town meetings throughout the Kingdom, carefully arranged and conducted, would produce indisputable proof of reaction in the Public mind on the subject of Free Trade; and that, restricted to the endeavor to procure a dissolution of Parliament by addressing the Crown, they would concentrate the energies of the friends of Protection, and most effectually conduce to the attainment of the objects desired.

That it be referred to the Committee for Publication to adopt without delay such steps as may appear advisable for giving effect to the objects of the Foregoing Resolutions.

That from the high respect entertained by this Committee for the talents and conduct of M#r# Disraeli, it anxiously desires that the Resolutions it has this day sanctioned, should not, from want of accordance with any course of action publicly recommended by him, diminish that cordiality towards the Association on the continuance of which its Members greatly rely for success in the struggle in which they are engaged.

That the Chairman, with M#r# Freshfield, M#r# Ball and M#r# Foskett, be requested to wait on M#r# Disraeli to explain the views of the Committee.

Extracted from the Minutes
Charles Stokes Sec#y#

J. C. Herries to G. F. Young, 15 November 1849, Herries Papers, BL, Add. MS 57423, fols 147–8.

St. Julians
15 Nov: 1849
(Copy to G.F. Young)

Copy
Private

My dear Sir

I have to thank you for the 'Morning Herald' of the 14th Inst: which I had not previously seen.

There must I think be some mistake (so far as I am concerned in it) in the Report of that part of the speech of Sir John Tyrrell in which he is made to say that the measures propounded by D'Israeli in Bucks and in Essex 'had the confidence of Lord Stanley Mr Herries & Lord Granby.'

I have had no communication whatever from D'Israeli on the subject, and I have had no opportunity of expressing my opinion to him upon the merits or practicability of his views and suggestion.

I should not envy the position of a Chancellor of the Exchequer upon whom might devolve the task of proposing to Parliament practical measures for raising by general taxation the whole amount now provided by local rates, and at the same time for creating an effective Sinking fund. I should be glad enough to see such measures adopted and enacted by Parliament. But however desireable [*sic*] they both of them may be, we know by experience that they are not indispensable to the well doing of the country, under a wiser system of Commercial and maritime policy than that of the late and present governments.

The reversal of that policy is the point to which all my wishes and my hopes are directed. I use the word hope advisedly, inspired as that sentiment is in me by the contemplation of the manifestly growing change in the public mind upon the subject.

Believe me & c.
(Signed) JC Herries

Free Thoughts on Free Trade (London: John Ollivier, 1852), pp. 18–27.

THE RATIONALE OF COMMERCIAL RESTRICTION.

PROTECTION, it must be owned, is a restrictive, artificial contrivance; Free-trade is, undoubtedly, the simpler and more natural system. This, however, suggests no argument in its favour, but altogether the contrary; for civilisation itself, viewed as a whole, has become so complex and conventional, that we have no right to look for simplicity in the institutions and arrangements which form its component parts.

Restriction, indeed, appears to be one of the most universal laws of society, and its chief element of order – a fundamental condition of our imperfect nature, directly consequent upon that imperfection. Pure, unrestricted freedom exists nowhere in creation. The Creator alone possesses it: His creatures are his slaves – happy only in submission and obedience. Even the winds and waters, with their living denizens, those freest things in nature, are fettered by His laws; but man is the greatest slave of all, because he struggles against those beneficent laws; and by thus violating the conditions of his being, becomes the slave of his own passions also. To counteract the evil consequences of such a state, he is necessitated to impose upon himself innumerable artificial checks and restraints in his various social relations. The radicals and socialists of all countries are striving to emancipate themselves from this necessity – this general law of restriction. Their efforts to establish the lie that all men are equal; to confound merit with worthlessness, sense with folly, in one impossible and insulting bond of fraternity, and to perpetuate the licence which they mean by the word liberty, are now arriving at their natural, and we may add, proper result, the 'solidarity' – not of the peoples – but of military despotism; and furnish a spectacle that ought to be a lesson to the human race.

The English public, meanwhile – that is to say, its responsible classes – although too experienced a political community to embrace the wild theories of ultra-democracy, have caught the sympathetic furor so far, as to apply the very same principle to their idol, commerce, which the continental revolutionists would adapt to political institutions. Warned by the examples of the present and the past, we have not yet ventured to carry out to their fullest extent the principles of popular government, and, by means of universal suffrage, to sink the fair fabric of society in the dull, dead, stagnant level of political equality. We, therefore, still limit the elective franchise, respect the ancient privileges of classes, and endeavour to maintain something like a balance of power between town and country – between rustic inertness and urban cunning. But though thus prudent in matters purely political, the operations of commerce, we have solemnly decided, may be safely freed from all restraint and state supervision.

Is there, then, anything so innately pure, scrupulous, and disinterested in the spirit of trade – anything so simple and unentangled in its various relations, as to entitle it alone to exemption from this general law of restriction? Is there any greater sacredness in the natural commercial rights of man than in his natural political rights? Property itself, in its modern acceptation, is an artificial thing, created by laws and regulated by restrictions; why then may not the distribution and exchange of property be subject to analogous control? Honourable as industry and production are, trade or barter in the articles produced must, from its innate tendency, be viewed as a selfish and encroaching thing. Trick, adulteration, and overreaching – the unequal balance and the unjust weight – have been its common attributes and accompaniments in all ages. To aggressive wars and dishonourable peaces it has been alike guilty of instigating. The inconceivable atrocities of the slave trade, the gold trade, the opium trade, the spirit trade among doomed aboriginal races, with those of the truck and the infant slavery system at home, are all of its producing. The habitual vitiating of food, for the sake of an extra profit; the detestable impostures of the puffing system; the reckless competition which deprives the fair trader of his legitimate profit, and is alike the offspring and the parent of insolvency; the wholesale gambling carried on in the manufacture and transfer of joint stock shares of various kinds, to the demoralisation and ruin of thousands annually – these are but some of the evils generated by its spirit. The falsity of the dealer furnished a simile to the all-observing Shakspere; the patriotism of the merchant was a theme for the satire of the gifted Burke, and for the warning cautions of the sagacious Franklin. The 'clamour and sophistry of merchants and manufacturers' is animadverted on even by Adam Smith.

We speak on this subject thus boldly, believing commerce, at least commercial success, to be unduly venerated in this country. We have the less scruple in so speaking, because the class of traders, properly so called, are remarkable for the severity with which they question the integrity of motive and conduct evinced in other pursuits. The farmer is a trader when he brings his products to market, and, as a trader, is also open to similar temptations and accusations. We may, however, venture to affirm that, whether from the greater simplicity of country life, or from the more ennobling character of his labours, bringing him into closer contact with nature, and directer dependence upon God, there is less of falsehood and fraud in his dealings – more of the principle of 'live and let live,' than in any other sort of traffic. The lawyer, medical practitioner, soldier, sailor, clergyman, and artist, all bring their talents and acquirements to market, and not a little uncharitable are the regular trading classes in the judgment commonly passed upon their professional conduct. Unquestionably, all varieties of trade, all actual money getting, is, viewed morally, a dangerous occupation, and requires both self-control and public interference, because it offers direct incitement and opportunity to the inherent selfishness of man. But it may, at least, be urged that this incitement must be stronger in him who, unlike the professional man, is a trader only, and has not necessarily any loftier collateral pursuit to refine and elevate him.

There can be nothing personally offensive in these free remarks, which relate to the spirit of trade, not to the individual trader. We believe in the existence of a noble army of upright, honourable dealers, in every grade of society, and we believe of such, that, as a body, none are nobler and worthier; but this nobleness and worth is in spite of their avocations – not owing to any elevating influences which they impart; on the contrary, it is because those influences are not elevating, and because the temptations are strong, that such peculiar merit attaches to unsullied integrity in commercial pursuits. The trader's occupation is his probation. The glory lies, not in it, but in resisting its temptations. [*sic*] Honour, though happily it may accompany, springs not from it; industry and usefulness form its only intrinsic recommendations; but strong as these are, and necessary as it is that trade should flourish, can it be possible (and here lies the relevancy of our observations) that a pursuit, in its natural tendency and unquestionable history, thus mercenary and acquisitive, should have a title to act in the social system without any of that legal check and control common to other human institutions? And if this be answered in the negative – is there any weight in the favourite final appeal of the adroit, scheming free-trade manufacturer, or the shallow unreflecting free-trade consumer, who, when desirous of shifting from themselves responsibility for the distress their selfish measures may have brought on other classes, resort to the argument, that they have nothing to do with the result, as it affects any class, nor, as in the case now chiefly in question, with the assumed fact that the British corn grower cannot compete with the foreign; all they contend for is the simple, the inalienable right, to buy where they can buy cheapest, whatever may be the effect on any particular interests?

Viewed purely on commercial grounds – namely, with reference to the immediate result of any transaction, as it affects their own pockets, there is indeed weight as well as plainness in this argument. But the question – the great question on which the whole subject mainly hangs, is this – are there no considerations superior to those of a commercial character, which should influence the policy of a community? above all, are there not NATIONAL CONSIDERATIONS? – under which, the simple claim to buy in the cheapest market, would have to be referred to a select committee, whose business would be to enquire how far this abstract claim of the individual buyer might be found practically compatible with that most involved and complicated arrangement, whose result is the general welfare of the community.

Salus populi suprema lex, is a political axiom which economists and commercial speculators have, before now, been pronounced guilty of disregarding; in recent proof of which, witness the checks that it has been found necessary to impose upon Free trade as carried on under the nefarious truck system, and the still more glorious triumphs of philanthropy in rescuing infant life from wholesale destruction under the long-hour system of labour, upon which Herodian policy, our manufacturing prosperity was said to be dependent. Here, political and philanthropical considerations have been esteemed more imperative than those of political economy: let us see if the same considerations, the same principle of restriction, may not be justly extended to the regulation of our foreign supplies.

FREE-TRADE INCOMPATIBLE WITH NATIONAL INDEPENDENCE.

PROTECTION is an artificial thing – so is that division of nations, of which Protection is, in fact, the result. It is, indeed, the division of the world into separate political communities, with the varied complications to which it gives birth, that our Free traders appear so singularly to overlook, or at least to make so light of; although it is it alone which renders their theories impracticable.

As long as it subsists, political interests must always rank paramount among the different societies into which the world is divided. So far as the sustentation of the population is concerned, industrial interests, it is true, are of primary importance, but this is still on political, not commercial grounds. Production, equal in quantity to the demand of the people, in which case the price will never be above their means, is a great national consideration; but the traffic in productions is chiefly a question of commercial interest, and commercial and political interests often jar; the true commercial aim being the individual accumulation of capital – the first political or national consideration being, not so much that one class should amass great wealth, as that wealth should be so diffused as to ensure at least moderate prosperity to every class, and above all, that the community, whether wealthy or poor, should remain independent, that is, preserve its nationality.

The barest conception of the word *nation* instantly suggests ideas of opposing foreign interests, and possibility of war. National barriers, like legal restrictions, are ordained and wisely regulated consequences of the unjust and selfish nature of man. The same may be said even of the wars to which nationality gives rise, consequences, and, at the same time, useful though severe correctives of human error and violence. To seek a substitute in cosmopolitan institutions, without in the first place ameliorating human nature, is a conception worthy of our contentious modern peace-mongers and slave-produce consuming abolitionists – a pleasing dream of wealth-amassing millocrats, from which they may be awakened when it is too late. These men, absorbed in the pursuit of gain, do not understand their true position as citizens. They have been so long accustomed to peace and its uninterrupted commercial facilities, that they cannot realise the possibility of any of those disturbing causes which the more expansive mind of the statesman is bound to take into account.

Even religion, which detests war, admits its necessity, and legalises the profession of arms. The spread of religion may, however, be looked to as an influence that will, sooner or later, bring about a millennial state of peace and universal brotherhood. But we know that it has not yet effected this; and meanwhile, many will agree with us in thinking it almost impious to expect that aught so mercenary in its aspirations as commerce, will be the glorious means of working so benign an amelioration. The spirit of trade is as likely, under many possible circumstances, to excite the warlike principle as to control it; valuing peace not for its own moral excellency so much, as on account of its general tendency to promote commercial security.

As this tendency has varied, so has it varied also[1], and provoked perhaps as many unjust and bloody wars, as the prouder thirst for military glory, or the wild fanaticism of religious zeal. On the possibility of war, then, we have no right to cease to calculate, however long periods of peace may happily last. They who would have us act as if it were otherwise, are grossly deluding us: deceived themselves, perhaps, by mistaking material progress for civilisation. Indeed, we all now see the probability of war as more than ever imminent. On the continent, whether the madness of democracy, or its natural consequence, the present military despotism predominate, war is equally probable. Across the Atlantic, the restless disposition and the anomalous institutions of the United States people forbid us to conclude that the world has really grown so much wiser and better, as to justify us in beating our swords into plough-shares, our spears into pruning-hooks. It is, therefore, as imperative as ever that nations, to be in a position to repel injustice or encroachment, should continue carefully to foster and maintain all their attributes of nationality. The first of these, far beyond the keeping up of vast armaments, is the being self-subsistent – the producing within themselves the necessaries of life, without dependence on foreigners, who may at any time become enemies. However large a people's foreign trade, in the exchange of their own superfluities for foreign luxuries, or even for semi-necessaries, yet if they look to the foreigner for that which they cannot do without, they are, in spite of every dogma in political economy, unworthy of the title of a nation: at all events, they cannot continue in the position of a first-rate power; but must sink into that of a mere city or free port, and, whether nominally or not, will be virtually the dependency of the power that feeds them. That power, it is true, need not in all cases go to war to assert its supremacy. When the foreigner becomes the farmer of a neighbouring state, he, generally speaking, will have but to close his ports to reduce that state to terms, or at least, greatly to influence its policy. Supplies might indeed come in from different quarters, so as to divide the dependence;

---

1   Take, for a recent example, the conduct of the Cape gunpowder traders.

but numerous possible and easily imagined contingencies, such as the partial or comparative decline of naval force, concurrent with extensive political confederations in one quarter, and unpropitious seasons in another, would be liable and likely to teach, sooner or later, the lesson we are endeavouring to inculcate – and for the mere liability we are content to contend. Show but the *possibility* of such concurrence, or partial concurrence of circumstances, and enough has been done for the establishment of our principle that the production of the necessaries of life within itself, is the indispensable element of a nation's independence.

The instinctive consciousness of this possible concurrence would, in fact, influence the policy and free action of a state that had sunk into the unworthy position of foreign dependence we have been contemplating. And yet, a people which has, like ourselves, gradually imbibed the passion and the habit of looking to the accumulation of wealth as its chief good, may at length become disposed to undervalue and to barter this birth-right of nations, this inestimable privilege of independence, for the bribe of an increased lucrative foreign trade. The landed interest is not thus tempted. It produces immensely, and lives by its production, but it is, as regards necessaries, self-subsistent, and it rarely accumulates. With the manufacturing and commercial community it is very different; and we presume it was the prospect of this ever increasing foreign trade, which, like golden shackles, glittered in the imagination of one of the great leaders of the League, when he intimated amidst loud applause, that foreign coercion might, after all, be no such evil thing for the people!! Well might Benjamin Franklin warn the political power to be watchful of the tendencies of the commercial – well might Adam Smith talk of 'the clamour and sophistry of merchants and manufacturers'! And, undoubtedly, it is one of the chief duties of a government, – especially of a body of high minded, unpaid legislators, of independent position and proud historic name – such as still partially survives in our own land – to oppose these grovelling tendencies of the commercial mind, and to preserve us, not merely as a community of traders, but as a great, free, and powerful nation, intact – and this, even though the country remain less wealthy than it might otherwise have become.

Such doctrine is, we admit, very questionable political economy, according to the present guides in the misty regions of that dubious science. They would, in fact, persuade us that legislators have never any business to interfere in the sacred mysteries of commerce: but though bad political economy, it may, nevertheless, be sound doctrine in the higher range of politics. In political economy, the teachings of a Johnson and a Goldsmith would be derided as poetical rhapsody. In politics, it is still as practically true as it is finely expressed, that

> ' – States of native strength possest,
> Though very poor may yet be very blest.
> That trade's proud empire hastes to swift decay,
> As ocean sweeps the labour'd mole away;

While SELF-DEPENDENT POWER can time defy,
As rocks resist the billows and the sky.'

If this be too good poetry to be trusted as philosophy, let us substitute the prose of Lord John Russell, written when the powers of that noble lord's mind were in their early vigour, and when his moral courage was still unquestioned: – 'Were there no such thing as war – no such thing as commercial disputes – no such thing as a national debt – it might be easy for the ministers of different communities to come to an understanding to regulate the world according to the rules of commercial liberty; but the existing fact is – that every nation is obliged to guard its independence with the utmost jealousy; to avoid, with the greatest care, putting itself under the control of any other power; and to check its industry by taxes which are absolutely necessary for the preservation of its separate existence.' – *On the British Constitution.*

On the principle, then, that to be truly and permanently independent, a nation must be self-subsistent, in other words, must mainly produce its own food, we found the fact, so galling to our aspiring millocracy, that agriculture is necessarily the first and most important industrial interest in the state; first, in its indispensableness to political position, as it is first, *de facto*, in the annual value of its products: that a nation, although it may, under many circumstances, safely allow another to become its manufacturer and its purveyor of comparative luxuries, cannot, consistently with sound policy, allow the foreigner to become its farmer; and that, therefore, the farming interest has, on high national grounds, quite irrespective of commercial results, especial claim to the fostering care of the state; requiring to be maintained and promoted if even at a certain national cost. Just as we would willingly vote a sum of money or an additional tax for a necessary armament, so should we be ready even to tax ourselves for the maintenance of this great arm of national defence, if it can be shewn that such taxation is, by circumstances, rendered necessary.

That such circumstances may occur, can be shown on various grounds. The first and most obvious case is that of natural disadvantages of soil and climate, operating, not to such extent as absolutely to discourage cultivation, but so as to render it more difficult and less remunerative than the average of occupations. Another case would be that in which the general taxation of the community fell, whether owing to unequal assessment, or to less means for bearing the same burden, in undue proportion on the landed interest, giving at once a claim to some special protection, or, which is the same thing, to some direct, countervailing exemption; not in order to enrich that interest at the expense of other classes, but simply to place it on equal terms with them, so as to encourage it to persevere in raising a production required to be raised at home upon political grounds. But this inequality of taxation, with the many other causes hereafter to be noticed, which may be supposed to render agriculture a less remunerative branch of industry in one country than in another, would right itself very easily without any legislative assistance, were it not for international influences. The interest placed, by whatever cause, at a disadvantage, would raise the price of its product in proportion to the extent of its burden – competition among its own members preventing it from carrying this further than was necessary – so long, at least, as the home supply was equal to the demand. While that was the case, home competition would always bring the commodity to its proper home price – the price that ought to be given for it. If the supply was not equal to the demand, the case would be altered, and foreign resources would become necessary – but still on restrictive principles, that is, within defined limits. If these limits be observed, the case, however, is not altered. But when full competition between different nations, founded on free unrestricted imports, is permitted, this corrective self-adjusting principle, applicable to home competition only, is destroyed; the home production thus undersold, will gradually decline, the nation must look more and more to the foreigner for supplies, and thus will free commerce be found incompatible with political independence.

Notice of Anti-Corn Law League Meeting, *Economist*, 10:445 (6 March 1852), p. 276.

NATIONAL ANTI-CORN LAW LEAGUE

At a Meeting of the Council and Friends of the late League, held this day, March 2, 1852, in the Large Room, Newall's Buildings, Manchester: GEORGE WILSON, Esq., in the chair;

It was moved by Richard Cobden, Esq., M.P.; seconded by Robert Ashton, Esq., of Hyde; and carried unanimously:–

That an administration having been formed committed by every pledge that can bind the honour of public men to attempt to reimpose a duty on corn, it is resolved that the Anti-Corn Law League be re-constituted, under the rules and regulations by which that body was formerly organised.

It was moved by the Right Hon. T. Milner Gibson, M.P.; seconded by James Heywood., M.P.; and carried unanimously:–

That the council of the League be requested to put themselves into communication with their friends in all parts of the Kingdom, urging them to immediate action to prevent the return to Parliament of candidates in favour of the re-enactment under whatever pretence or form, of any duty upon the importation of foreign corn.

It was moved by John Bright, Esq., M.P.; seconded by T. Bazley, Esq.; and carried unanimously:–

That, considering how essential it is to the welfare of the agricultural, manufacturing, colonial, and shipping interests, as well as to the peace and prosperity of the great body of the people, that the free-trade question should be permanently settled by an appeal to the country, – resolved, that a memorial to the Queen praying for an immediate dissolution of Parliament, be signed by the chairman, on behalf of this meeting, and transmitted for presentation to Her Majesty.

TO THE QUEEN'S MOST EXCELLENT MAJESTY

May it please your Majesty, – We, your Majesty's loyal and devoted subjects, conscious of the earnest solicitude which your Majesty feels for the welfare and happiness of your people, and impressed with a deep sense of the danger which now threatens the security of those great measures of commercial policy which, during the last four years, have conduced so greatly to the prosperity and social contentment of all classes of your Majesty's subjects, have seen with distrust and apprehension the occasion to power of a Government pledged by the obligations of personal honour and public duty to attempt the restoration of odious restrictions on the trade and industry of this country.

That your memorialists, whilst recording their solemn and emphatic protest against any and every attempt to reimpose, in whatsoever shape, taxes on the food of the people, are firmly persuaded that an overwhelming majority of the British people are, by every constitutional means, prepared to resist and defeat such a policy, as an unjust and dangerous aggression on the rights of industry, the freedom of trade and commerce, and the social welfare and domestic happiness of the great mass of your Majesty's subjects.

That your memorialists believe that doubt and uncertainty on this subject are calculated to disturb and jeopardise all trading and industrial operations; to keep alive a spirit of agitation and restlessness throughout your Majesty's dominions; to foment false hopes, and foster injurious apprehensions; and that every sound maxim of state policy demands an immediate and decisive settlement of a question fraught with such manifold elements of disunion and disquietude to all the great interests of the nation.

Your memorialists, therefore, would loyally and respectfully beseech your Majesty not to suffer the interests of your subjects to be postponed to the exigencies of a temporising administration, or any party difficulties that may conflict with sound maxims of commercial policy; but that your Majesty, in the just exercise of your royal prerogative, would cause the great issue now pending between the responsible advisors of the Crown and the people at large, to be forthwith and finally determined by a speedy dissolution of Parliament.

GEORGE WILSON, Chairman.

Henry Ashworth, *Recollections of Richard Cobden and the Anti-Corn-Law League* (London: Cassell, Petter and Galpin, 1877), pp. 347–57.

'Gentlemen, when we in 1846, resolved to lay down our arms, and to commit suicide as an Anti-Corn League, it was said, even by our enemies, that the fairest and best part of all our conduct was the close of our existence. Everybody admitted that the Anti-Corn-Law League had kept faith with the world at large – that we did not seek to divert the influence and power which we had obtained by the successful advocacy of our one question, to be the means of aggrandising any individual, or any bodies of men, in any other direction. I can say for myself, and I am sure too, I can say for all those around me, that so far as concerns any influence we acquired, by having been mainly instrumental in placing a new government in power, we have never sought at the hands of any government any recompense or reward, official or otherwise; we have never sought to obtain influence over any administration, nor in any way to use the power which we obtained through your confidence and kindness, to promote any personal objects. (Cheers.) I say this now, because in appearing before you and proposing to take part, if you think proper, in renewed efforts for maintaining the ground we have already won on this question, I intend to pursue entirely the same course as in former times. I have no other object in view, and no wish to serve any party of politicians. If we renew our effort, it shall be under the same rules and regulations which led us triumphantly to victory on the last occasion. We will strictly confine ourselves to the object for which we have met together. I solemnly declare for myself, that in the most exaggerated flights of fancy, I never expected so great a result from the labours of the League, as has been witnessed during the last four years. (Cheers.) Take for instance a single fact, which comprises almost our main case. Since the day when we laid down our arms, there has been imported into this country in grain, and flour of all kinds, an amount of human subsistence equal to upwards of fifty millions of quarters of grain – a larger quantity than had been imported from foreign countries during the 31 years preceding 1846, that is, from the peace of 1815 down to the time at which we brought our labours to a close. Now, gentlemen, in that one fact is comprised our case. You have had at the lowest computation, five millions of your countrymen, or countrywomen, or children, subsisting on the corn that has been brought from foreign countries. And what does that say? What does it say of the comfort you have brought to the homes of those families? What does it say of the peace and prosperity, and serenity of domestic life in those houses, where fifty millions of quarters of grain extra have been introduced, and where, but for your exertions, the inmates might have been left either in hopeless penury, or subsisting on potatoes? But I need not go into statistics to show what the beneficial consequences have been, you may see for yourselves your triumph in the nation's eyes, you may read it in the countenances of the people of all classes, you may trace it in their improved clothing, and in their improved habits – you may see it in the diminished pauperism and crime throughout the whole country. You may see it in every aspect in which you can test, as touching the pulse of society, the condition of the great mass of the people. Well, gentlemen, if we have done so much, what have we averted? How much of pain and anguish lies behind the privations which the mass of the people must have suffered, if it had not been for your triumph? How much of vice and crime, and consequent misery, must have pervaded the great mass of the people, if they had been kept in the state of destitution and privation, which they must have been, but for the introduction of this great amount of human subsistence? These, then, are our reasons, and they are surely a sufficient justification for renewing the effort to maintain the ground which we have achieved, assuming that we confine ourselves to the one question we have in hand, as we did before. It cannot be concealed that there are many gentlemen who say – 'Why don't you go for a large measure of parliamentary reform, which will not only enable you to carry Free-Trade in corn, but to do a great many other things also?' Now, the fallacy that underlies this argument, or entreaty, is this. It is assumed that because we are going to make an effort to put an end for ever to this controversy of Free-Trade, that therefore we intend to exclude other people from entering on the consideration of other questions. We do not say, that because gentlemen join in this new movement of the Anti-Corn Law League, they are to abandon those other principles, and neglect those other movements in which they are now or may be hereafter engaged; but having shown you the vast social benefits that have arisen from the emancipation of the people in the article of food, and from the establishment of Free-Trade in this commodity, we say that while we feel morally certain that in a few months we can put this question for ever out of the category of controversial questions, we do not feel justified in placing ourselves at a disadvantage, by taking up other questions, on which the public are not so well informed, or so well united. We, the men who have had a responsible position, and who have taken an active part in this agitation before, do not think it justifiable that we should change our position in the House of Commons from a majority to a minority, or retard the definite settlement of this question, from three or four months, to as many years. (Cheers.)

Now, gentlemen, with regard to the course which has been recommended in the resolution you have just heard, it is proposed that you should reorganise the League – that you should send our circulars to your old friends and colleagues throughout the country, to arouse them into action, in order to prevent the return to Parliament of anyone who is not pledged to Free-Trade in corn. But it is proposed further, that you should memorialise the Queen, and that you should call upon your friends in all parts of the country to organise societies, and arrange public meetings, in order to memorialise Her Majesty to the same purport, viz. – to dissolve the Parliament, and to give to the country an opportunity of recording a final judgment on this question. In the terms of the resolution, you are to memorialise the Queen to dissolve Parliament at once – immediately. Now it will very likely be said, why should you dissolve Parliament and seek an immediate issue on this question? Gentlemen, I have the strongest belief that we are safe from every thing but delay, and the tricks of politicians which will be practised during that delay. (Great cheering.) I want to bring this question to a definite issue, without its being mixed up with any other questions. We have not only friends amongst us who wish to blend other questions with ours, by which as I think we might materially damage our cause, and probably altogether sacrifice it; but our enemies will play the same game, for it is their only chance. Leave this question in suspense during the whole session of Parliament, and what will be the result? In the first place, we all know from experience that it is not very easy to keep popular enthusiasm for any extended period in that high and fervid state to which you can probably bring it in the course of a few weeks; you cannot possibly keep it up for a number of months. But whilst your enthusiasm may be cooling, your enemies will be practising their arts of deception and misrepresentation; and one of those arts will be, to try and mix up other questions with this, and, if possible, to thrust some other question before it. Already I see the enemy hoisting the flag, and trying to raise up the banner of intolerance in religion, so that you may have the questions of Protestantism and Popery thrust before the bread tax. It is the old thing over again; your enemies will try to be religious; *they* will pretend to be the only religious part of the community; *they* who tax the people's bread will profess to be the great champions of religion. (Cheers and laughter.) You know, in olden time, they that devoured widows' houses made long prayers for a pretence. And you will have infidelity, popery, and all sorts of charges held out against you, if by that means our opponents can change the issue from Free-Trade to some other question. I should not wonder if they even tried to raise the issue of the monarchy itself! You in Lancashire will be denounced by these bread-taxers, with being enemies of the monarchy, and promoters of revolution. I should not be surprised at any charge that may be brought against you, with a view to direct attention from this question, if you will only give your enemies time. Now, I say, give them no time; let this question of the Corn Law occupy the front rank; let this be the only question for those who think that it can be settled by one effort more, in the course of the next three months; let this question take precedence of all that the enemy can bring to baffle and confuse you; and then you will soon bring it to a successful issue. (Cheers.)

But I am told that we must allow the protectionists to remain in office for twelve months, because that will give them the opportunity of abandoning all their professions and principles, and of cheating their friends. Now, I tell you candidly, I do not believe Lord Derby and his colleagues are one half so base as these advisers take them to be. What! the men who hunted that illustrious statesman (Sir R. Peel) almost to his grave, for having abolished the Corn Law – whose sole political capital, from that time to this, has been the sarcasms and obloquy with which they have covered his name and fame, and the abuse and denunciations with which they have loaded the gentlemen of the Manchester school – are these men going to do, not what Sir Robert Peel did, but ten times worse! Are we now to believe that Lord Derby and his colleagues are coming into office simply and solely that they may immediately get rid of the principles which they have hitherto advocated, and which they have denounced their former leader for having abandoned? I say I do not believe it. I believe that such a thing would show that we have fallen into a lower status of political morality than it is alleged they now have in France. I, on the contrary, believe the ministry to be sincere in their professions. I believe they came into office with a view to carrying out those professions. But are you going to allow them to remain in office, to be sharpening their weapons in order that they may stab you when they find you off your guard? (Cheers.) Then if I correctly interpret the feeling of this meeting, the course we have to pursue is clear. We must raise this question at once, and keep it as *the* question before the House of Commons and the country, until it be finally disposed of. You know Mr. Villiers, our old and trusty representative in the House, has given notice – (great cheering) – of a motion to bring the House to the test in this question. Now, as it has been said that Mr. Villiers is the brother of Lord Clarendon, and that he may have a Whig object in bringing forward this motion, I may as well state at once that it was at our instance, at the instance of those with whom you are associated, that Mr. Villiers gave notice of that motion – and that he foresaw – (I speak it from my own knowledge), he foresaw what would be said as to his wishing to reinstate the fallen ministry, and he proposed to leave out the part which refers to the administration; because he did not wish to give it the semblance of a party attack on the government. But I do say that if there be any difficulty in bringing this question to an issue by the terms of the motion of which Mr. Villiers has given notice, I am sure that Mr. Villiers will be ready to yield to your wishes on the subject; and if it be necessary to bring forward a vote of want of confidence in the ministry, I hope he will do it, rather than let this question remain undecided before the country. (Cheers.) You are told that it is a very wrong time for dissolving Parliament. Now I tell you candidly – and it is perhaps a secret, as coming from a member of Parliament – that I never yet knew a proper time, in the eyes of members of Parliament, for a dissolution. (Laughter.) And, if by possibility, two or three months might be gained, why such is the dread of a large portion of the representatives of the people, to be sent back to their constituents, that they are willing to make any possible compliance and sacrifice in order to put off the evil day. But if you memorialise the Queen, and communicate to members of Parliament that you think it desirable that in April or May this question should be settled, – if the House of Commons are made to understand that that is the determination of the country – well, then, when a motion is brought forward to suspend the voting of supplies, by merely voting a sum on account instead of the whole estimates, or when a direct vote of want of confidence in ministers is proposed, – if you are thus vigilant, the House of Commons will then pluck up courage and face the dissolution, rather than incur the liability of your displeasure in another way.

'Now, I think the greatest of all evils which the country can suffer is, to have all the great trading interests kept in suspense on this vital question. (Cheers.) I see every newspaper now contains columns of electioneering proceedings; every member of Parliament is beginning to look after his seat, or is beginning to show great attention and civility to his constituents. But besides these gentlemen, you, manufacturers and merchants, and our shipowners and colonists, all require to know how and when this thing is to be finally settled; for you and they want to enter into transactions extending over a year or two years; in fact all the wages and profits of this empire are bound up in this one question. (Cheers.) When this question is settled the protectionist party will disappear. You will have one dissolution on this question, and then you will never find a politician tying to his tail the tin-kettle of protection afterwards. (Cheers.) They are all anxious to get rid of it, no doubt; and when you have abolished the protectionist party, it will not be so difficult to manage the business of the House of Commons. The whole of the difficulties have arisen from the fact that you have had 200 or 230 gentlemen bound together apparently with the most intense self-interest, and with the determination to upset any government that did not consult their interests. This party, led on by a gentlemen [sic] (Mr. Disraeli), who, I think, has at all times shown himself to be a tactician, who is willing to take all advantages, you have seen constantly upsetting the Whig government; and why? Because they have believed that upsetting the Whigs was the necessary preliminary to the accession of the protectionist party to power. And the great difficulty in carrying on the government has been from the existence of this, the most compact body in the House of Commons, led on by the gentleman who is now their Chancellor of the Exchequer. But I say, if a dissolution abolishes that protectionist party, you will no longer be in the same difficulty, you will no longer have these attempts to trip up the government. Only put these protectionists out of the way, and after a dissolution shall have settled this question, you will never again have a party in Parliament founded on the principle of protection; you will no longer have some people claiming merit for being Free-Traders, for all will be Free-Traders; and the politicians who have hitherto, perhaps, getting a little popularity by declaiming against Free-Trade, will have to take in a reef of their sail, or to go on a new tack altogether; and I have some confidence that the protectionist leaders, when they find they have no longer protection to talk about, will find something else, something intelligible, useful, and patriotic to talk about instead, and which we may be quite as much interested in carrying as they are. (Cheers.) I have thus got rid of the objection as to the difficulty of carrying on the government. But ours is not a question of tactics; I say, in conclusion, we are not here to discuss the pretensions of Whigs or Tories, or what can be done in Parliament by this party, or by that party. We have a plain, straightforward course to pursue. I am not surprised that, on a great question, which involved the interests of the whole community, and which divided parties on their most sensitive point, their material interests, we have had the effect of breaking up governments. I have said, years ago, we shall destroy two or three governments before this question is settled; and now I say, not dreading the consequences, not caring for the consequences – let us all unite in this country, the humblest as well as the richest, who all live by bread – let us put this government to one of three courses; – either they must fully recant this principle of protection, or they must resign their places in the government, or they must dissolve Parliament; and one of these three causes we will compel them to take. (Cheers.)

When you have accomplished either of these objects, then you will have effected all that you have in view. Don't doubt but the government of this country will be carried on; I do not see that there is any necessity for our despairing of finding other men, as good in every other respect, if not as good protectionists, as the present government; but let everybody join in forcing the government to one of these three causes; and having done so, let us not be alarmed at any bugbears, but pursue our straight course as we did before; and you will, in less than four months from the present time, be relieved from all the labours on which you are now embarking.' (Great cheering.)

Ramifications of Free Trade

Arbitration Instead of War (London: Peace Society, 1848).

ARBITRATION INSTEAD OF WAR.

MR. COBDEN has engaged to bring before the House of Commons at an early period of the next Session of Parliament, a motion in favour of Arbitration Treaties between England and Foreign countries, binding them in case of future misunderstanding, to refer the subject-matter of dispute to the decision of Arbitrators. But as the subject is somewhat new as a matter of popular discussion, it may be necessary, in a few plain sentences, to explain the nature, object, and manifold advantages of this proposed method of Arbitration. By Arbitration then, it is intended to apply to nations the same rational principles for the settlement of differences, as have been long ago adopted between individuals in all civilized communities.

There was a time when in this and other countries, not only were criminal cases decided by wager of battle, that is, by the accused asserting his innocence by fighting with his accuser, but even civil cases, such as related to disputed property, &c., were adjudicated by a similar appeal to brute force. This preposterous method of seeking justice has long ago been exploded, as between man and man, and any person who would propose it now, would be laughed out of society for his absurdity. But what is War but the perpetuation of this folly in regard to nations, an attempt to decide questions of right by violence and blood, which nothing but the inveterate power of habit could have so long saved from the reprobation and contempt of mankind.

If it be said that this project of settling international disputes by Arbitration is impracticable, we can confidently appeal to history and fact, in proof of the contrary. It has been tried in a large number of instances, and it is evident from these, that whenever fairly applied, it is equal to any emergency that national affairs can present. Iceland and Norway have preserved peace, between their respective countries, for 600 years, by Arbitration alone; and by the same just and rational method, the Helvetic Union preserved peace among its different members for more than 500 years. A disputed question between Great Britain and America was decided by the Arbitration of the Emperor of Russia; and another between the same nations was submitted to the Arbitration of the King of the Netherlands, and finally settled without War. A difficulty that arose between Britain and France, was satisfactorily terminated by the Arbitration of the King of Prussia. The dispute on the 'Sulphur question,' between Great Britain and Sicily, was also adjusted by the Arbitration of Louis Phillipe, then King of France. To these many others might be added, but the instances adduced are sufficient to prove that Arbitration *can* decide great national disputes without War; and all that is now required is, to adopt this *as a fixed and regular law of nations, instead of leaving it to be uncertain and occasional.*

The advantages of this method over War are so obvious, that they must strike the common sense of every man that has the courage, for a moment, to think for himself.

It is more rational: – War is the proper resource of brutes, not of beings endowed with reason. It reduces men to the level of tigers, it tramples right under the foot of might, and yields the victory to the strongest alone. History abounds with examples, where the superiority of mere brute force has triumphed over justice, humanity, patriotism, and liberty. But Arbitration, calmly weighing contending claims in the scales of equity, and by the light of reason, will decide the question in harmony with their dictates.

It is more humane. – The horrors and cruelties which War perpetrates are unutterable. Destroying the fruits of the earth, laying waste cities, towns and villages, burning the hearths and homesteads of the poor, and without pity or ruth, involving in one indiscriminate massacre all ages, sexes and conditions, helpless childhood and venerable age, creating widows and orphans by thousands and tens of thousands, deluging the earth with blood, and filling the air with wailing voices of agony and terror. Arbitration will avoid all these atrocities, and leave the people in peaceful possession of the fruits of their industry, and the quiet happiness of their homes, while the quarrels of their rulers are settled by an appeal to reason and justice.

It is incomparably cheaper than War: – The enormous taxation which War entails is absolutely crushing down the industrial energies and resources of the people, hindering the development of commerce, and exhausting the earnings of labour, and not unfrequently endangering government itself, by making it the instrument of its own rapacious demands. In Great Britain it takes away 17s. 6d. out of every 20s. paid in taxation, and this year (1848) it will absorb the almost incredible sum of forty-seven millions sterling of the people's money, in paying the interest of its past and the cost of its present exorbitancy. Arbitration, by a far more economical mode of adjusting disputes, will effect an all but incalculable saving, and thereby diminish in every way the burdens of the country.

It is more consistent with the spirit of Christianity. – War involves an inversion of all the principles of morality, a perpetual outrage and affront to the genius of the gospel, an insolent and contemptuous disregard of the temper inculcated, by precept and example, by Him who came not to destroy men's lives but to save them. Arbitration, on the other hand, by appealing to Truth, Justice and Mercy, is in strict accordancy with that benignant system which pronounces its choicest blessings on the meek, the merciful, and the peace-maker.

Such then, as compared with the custom of War, is the method of settling the disputes of nations to which Mr. Cobden is about to direct the attention of the British Legislature. But Mr. Cobden can do nothing effectually without the support of the public. The *people* must determine whether the absurd, wicked, sanguinary, and costly system of War is to last for ever; or whether Arbitration shall take the place of the sword. To them, therefore, do the friends of Peace appeal and say, Unite without delay earnestly to petition Parliament to substitute Arbitration for War. Let your petitions for this purpose be signed universally, and send them to your *own Members* for presentation, accompanied by a respectful, but decided request to support their prayer, as well as the motion, whenever it shall be brought before Parliament. The *Electors*, especially, should remember that they have in their hands the destinies of their country, and to a great extent those of the whole world. Let them see to it, that by a faithful discharge of the trust reposed in their keeping by possessing the franchise, none may have occasion to charge them with supineness, indifference, or neglect on this great occasion.

Christians of Great Britain! You surely have at heart the cause of peace and humanity; let not the present opportunity of forwarding that cause pass away unimproved. Let a petition be prepared in every Christian congregation throughout the land, and signed universally by those who bewail the portentous insult and wrong which the continuance of the war system inflicts on Christianity, and who desire to advance the kingdom of Peace upon earth.

The British Public at large! You have now a solemn duty to discharge, and a proper opportunity for discharging it. You groan under heavier burdens than any other people on earth; and unless by timely, earnest, and united exertion, you use the means to effect a change, your children will have to groan and suffer too.

As you would relieve your country from a weight of taxation, which is hurrying us to the verge of national bankruptcy – as you would advance the interests of truth, justice, and humanity – as you would discharge your own consciences from blood-guiltiness, by participation in the iniquitous system of War, rally around Mr. Cobden, and let the House of Commons be deluged with *Petitions for Arbitration.*

Richard Cobden, Speech on 'Free Trade and Peace' at Newton, Proposing Henry for South Lancashire, *Manchester Times and Gazette*, 21 December 1847.

RICHARD COBDEN, Esq. M. P. then arose, and was greeted with several rounds of most enthusiastic applause, from every part of the room...

But, gentlemen, there is another view of the question of free trade, which, I venture to say, our friend Mr. Henry is disposed to take. I want not only free trade in corn, and free trade in sugar, and free trade in ships; I do not want merely to have more bread and sugar to put in our mouths; I want the spirit of free trade to enter into the hearts of this community. (Cheers.) I want the legislature to be really alive to the really great moral revolution which free trade necessarily implies, if understood. (Applause.) Why, what is it we propose? We propose to abolish, or, at all events, greatly to modify our navigation laws, to give access to our ports to ships coming from all parts of the world, and bringing all kinds of produce. We wish to throw open our ports to all the commodities of the world, without regard to differential duties or the protection of native industry. (Hear, hear, and cheers.)

What does all that imply? It implies a growing demand and sympathy between the people of this country and the people of all the civilised world. (Hear, hear.) Well, to what must that conduct us? Must it not conduct us, if we are right in our principles, to a spirit of friendship – (Hear, hear.) – to a spirit of amity and peace throughout the world? (Cheers.) Well, then, gentlemen, if that be the moral tendency of our principles, – and I never should myself have given twelve months' labour to the cause if I had not believed that that was the tendency of our principles – what is the use of talking about increasing our armaments? (Loud cheers.) I ventured, in Stockport, the other day, to allude to this subject, and I see it has been stated that I would save the country the whole £17,000,000 annually expended on our army, navy, and ordnance. Gentlemen, I did not promise you anything so good as that; but what I did say was this, that if we are right in our free trade principles, we must be very wrong here, after having adopted them, to begin putting up fortifications all along our coast. (Cheers.) And I said, moreover, that the great item of our expenditure in this country – that upon which you can make a diminution of your expenses, is that horrible item of £17,000,000 sterling, this year, for the army, navy, and ordnance. (Applause.) And I said then, as I say now, that if you cannot make a reduction in that item, I do not believe that you can make any reduction of taxes which will ever be sensibly felt in the pockets of the people. (Hear, hear.) And I said that that reduction could only be made by effecting a change in the opinion of this country – by your having free-trade, not only in your ledgers and counting-houses, but by having it in your hearts and principles. Now, gentlemen, since I have been in this room a gentleman has put into my hand a paper upon the subject of the tea duties. I have not read it yet, but I can guess what it means. They want to have a reduction of the duty on tea – 1s. instead of 2s. Well, and that is a very necessary and proper change. Then comes the question, how can the revenue be dispensed with – how will you make up the revenue? I perfectly concur with the gentleman that it would be to the advantage of the people of this country, in every way, to make that reduction; nay more, I say that if you could make a reduction of 1s. per lb. on tea, it would do you far more good, in extending your trade with China, than it does in sending out two or three extra line of battle ships thither, or taking possession of some fresh territory in the Indian archipelago, to serve as a midway station to China. Reduce the duty on tea, and you would augment the trade to China, without sending out another line of battle ship or another regiment. (Cheers.) But, gentlemen, you want money – you want the means to enable you to reduce this duty, and I see no one coming before the country with any proposition for reducing our expenditure. Different plans for charging and shifting taxation have been propounded; but, shift the burden as you will, put it on as you may, you will find that the load will still gall your shoulders. (Cheers.) I am one who believes that this country has nothing to fear from any foreign country, so long as you advance in your present principles of free commercial intercourse with all the world.

The great jealousy, and rivalry, and hatred of this country has arisen from our monopolising spirit, and from that grasping ambition which has led us everywhere to seize on territory, that we might have the exclusive trade with that territory; but, the moment that you proclaim to the civilised world that your ports are open, and that your colonies are open – because the colonies claim that right now – the moment that you say you will abandon the whole privileges of your navigation laws, you change the whole face of the civilised world towards you; they will be as ready to enter into that peaceful career, to entertain amicable relations with this country, as they have on former occasions been excited to a spirit of antagonism and hatred by your monopoly, and by the spirit of war and aggression which this country has manifested during the last century. (Cheers.) I therefore do not speak here as an Utopian. People will try to identify me with Utopian views. The views which I am now expressing are those which first made me acquainted, out of my own business, with the people of Lancashire – I mean as the author of certain pamphlets which I published twelve years ago. (Hear, hear.) Free trade has been only a labour of love with me, in order that I might carry out those views; – (Applause.) – and I believe that we are fast tending towards the time when the whole community will be brought to the conviction, that it is not by warfare and armaments, and brute force that the interests of this country can be advanced. (Loud cheers.) I want us to hold out, not the nettle with which diplomatists have been constantly stinging foreign powers, but the olive branch; and if we do so, you may depend upon it that the moral influence will be such that the rest of the world will be glad to follow our example. (Cheers.) It is not only in Great Britain, but in the whole of Europe, that the people are groaning under the weight of their taxation for warlike armaments. Take France. She has an enormous army of 300,000 or 400,000 men, with bayonets in their hands; but France, in proportion to her frontier, has not a larger army than Russia, Prussia, and Austria. They are all armed, and because they have the same spirit of jealousy towards each other; but they are equally burdened with us, and the burden is not popular in any country. (Hear, hear.) France has suffered as much as we have. Their military expenditure increases their duties and taxation as much as it does in England. In Russia, Prussia, and in Austria, it is the same.

I have a high mission for English statesmen. I want England to take the lead in disarmamenting [*sic*] the great European powers. (Cheers.) Instead of sending diplomatists over to the continent to quarrel about the marriages of boys and girls – (hear, hear, and loud applause) – or to squabble over invitations to dinner, I want England to send her diplomatists to those countries, and to say, 'We have been pursuing wrong and foolish courses; we have been building more ships of war than are necessary; you have been doing the same thing in France; France has been increasing her army; Russia, Prussia, and Austria have been doing the same; so that we should all of us have been on the same level, if none of us had taken any step in this false direction. Now, instead of increasing our armies and navies let us agree like rational beings, to a pro rata reduction of our armaments; we shall then be all on the same footing, and shall save to the people heavy expenses which they are now incurring; and if, hereafter, we should be so unfortunate as to be engaged in war, we shall then be better prepared for it than under the present oppressive system.' (Cheers.) Do you think that there is anything Utopian in this? (No, no.) It is common sense, and I have faith in common sense. If governments and statesmen were actuated by such a spirit as I have thus indicated, and if they understood the noble mission which now awaits them, I am sure – and I speak from personal observation, and from intercourse with eminent men of all countries I have named – I am sure, I say, that it would be practicable for the government of this country to lead the nations of Europe back into that course from which they only departed to the injury of their people, and to the scandal of Christianity. (Enthusiastic applause.)

'Peace on Earth – Good Will Towards Men', *Manchester Times*, 8 January 1848.

'Peace on earth – good will towards men.'

We direct attention to two letters of correspondents. The subjects will, we hope, be promptly considered. If the north of England and other manufacturing districts do not wait for their tone from the mercantile community of Manchester, they will at least be stimulated by the example of those who have carried the cause of free trade. While the leading journalists, in their sympathy, or from misapprehension, pander to the policy and selfish interests of a still dominant aristocracy, it is needful that the merchant princes of Britain look well to the interests of trade and the claims of commerce. Let this nation become a garrisoned and military cantonment, to please or subserve the schemes of martial dukes and place-hunting nobles, and trade will soon sink to secondary consideration. It is the duty of the principal merchants, whose trade is with every nation, and whose success depends on the maintenance of peace with all lands, to look well to this clap-trap *ruse* about national defences. RICHARD COBDEN should not stand alone. Let his wonted colleagues rouse themselves. We shall be glad to see our correspondents' suggestion adopted, and such a meeting convened in the Free Trade Hall as will leave no doubt as to the abhorrence in which this hated war cry is held by the myriads of England. Let the Peace Society co-operate. It is their duty, surely. The second topic, alluded to by our correspondents, is the bill of Lord JOHN RUSSELL for removing the Parliamentary Disabilities of the Jews. Lord ASHLEY has brought his plausible influences to support Sir R. H. INGLIS. The antagonists of equal liberty, and those who abhor, most of all, liberty of conscience, are moving all their forces to oppose the bill. Petitions will be poured into Parliament to prevent the bill becoming law. The advocates of civil and religious liberty are quiescent and torpid, not because they are indifferent to the principles involved, but from a confidence that the measure must be carried, – that the opposition of bigotry and fanaticism is ridiculous and futile. This confidence is presumptuous, and may be fatal. We should rejoice to see a Town's meeting as well as a Corporation petition in favour of the removal of Jewish disabilities and all other badges of prescriptive inequality by which any people dwelling in our land are degraded. There are also modes in which the community may signify their liberality, as by congregational petitions, &c. What other means will so convince the Jews that Christianity is a generous and beneficent religion. The Christians who seek to convert the Jew may thus practically prove the influence and superiority of their principles.

Alexander Alison, *Universal Free Trade, by Means of a Property, Income and Wages Tax* (London: James Ridgway, 1852), pp. 54–64.

CHAPTER III.

We now come to the question how Universal Free Trade and Direct Taxation may be carried.

Prior to 1842, the ancient rights and privileges of the higher classes were religiously maintained, and when these privileges were assailed by the Reforms of Sir Robert Peel in 1842 and 1846, an opposition which cost that greatest of statesmen the estrangement of many of his best friends and supporters was evolved. In retiring from office in 1846, Sir R. Peel said: –

'My name may perhaps be execrated by monopolists who clamour for Protection, because they seek some benefit for themselves, but I am not without hopes that I shall leave a name perhaps remembered with kindly feelings in the abode of those whose lot is to labour, and who earn their daily bread by the sweat of their brow, and who will eat henceforth a more abundant meal of untaxed food, sweeter because it is not leavened by Injustice.'

When good is to come from Legislation, it must be by withholding unjust privileges from the privileged classes, and bestowing the benefits of such reforms on the unprivileged classes. By completing the Income Tax, and by abolishing all protective taxes many privileges which Sir Robert Peel did not touch will be withdrawn. This at first sight indicates an amount of opposition painful to contemplate; but a little consideration will shew that the case is now strangely altered since 1842 and 1846.

The privileged classes – never partial to discourses on principles – have now Statistics to look to. In 1842 and 1846, they had nothing but promises of future good in return for present sacrifices. The Country party know what the Income Tax has done, and what it is capable of doing when complete, and they are now willing to sacrifice their prejudices to their interests. If we may judge from the election speeches of Ministers on taking office, the Conservatives, instead of being the determined opponents of Free Trade, only quarrel with it because it does not go far enough. A great revolution in public opinion is in progress. Those who were once Protectionists are becoming Free Traders, and interested individuals, formerly Free Traders, may possibly become Protectionists!

We are not surprised that they, who in 1846 were the opponents of Free Trade, should now become the supporters of impartial Free Trade. Public opinion has foreclosed the possibility of a return to Protection, and in the position of suffering from the present partial state of Free Trade, the Country party have no alternative but to demand universal Free Trade. If Ministers decide upon bringing forward an impartial scheme of Taxation – which is now more than probable – they must expect opposition. In pressing the privileged classes with the universal extension of Free Trade, they will come in contact with the prejudices of interested parties. But the cause of justice and humanity will prevail, especially when the question at issue is one which no liberal can consistently oppose. No Minister can carry a comprehensive Reform of Taxation, without the cordial co-operation of the people, and as Ministers are about to appeal to the Nation on the subject of Taxation, the future policy of the Government will probably be determined by the result. Much will depend on the forthcoming expression of public opinion.

But there is another reason why the people must take up the subject of Taxation. Their great champion is no more. It is true that Sir Robert Peel left many noble-minded men behind him, on whom his mantle has fallen, but the inert state of recent Parliaments shews that there is no man to fill the place of the departed statesman. If progress is to mark the future history of this nation, the people must look to their own interests, and not rely on the unaided efforts of any member or party within the House. They must inform Parliament of their wishes on the great question of Trade and Taxation. *Is it the will of the nation that all be taxed according to their means, and that Free Trade be extended to every branch of Industry?* That is the question submitted to the nation.

Even Sir R. Peel, with all his influence and power, could not have carried the Corn Bill without agitation out of doors. And in admiring the patriotism of Mr. Cobden and his party, and in reaping the fruits of their unwearied exertions, we say to the supporters of Direct Taxation, go and do likewise, – a golden harvest is before you.

Protectionists, whether Conservative or Whig, will expatiate on the amount of the proposed Tax. They will maintain that it is better to pay more in an indirect and unknown way, than in an open and honest manner! To intelligent men, this language is childish, and a libel on the understanding of Englishmen. No tax is agreeable. But that tax which amounts to the least at the end of the year is the best. We have not so low an opinion of the People's intelligence as to suppose them incapable of calculating whether they shall pay more by the purchase of the necessaries of life loaded with taxes, or by a direct tax on their Income, with food, clothing, and house-rent free of tax. We hope the information conveyed by the present work will enable every man to make the comparison for himself. The question only requires to be freely canvassed in order to convince every man that he will gain by the change. That which benefits the country at large must benefit individuals; for what is a nation but the aggregate of its members.

It is alleged that Indirect Taxation is to some extent voluntary, *i.e.* if you choose to deny yourself the use of taxed articles you may escape Taxation. To comply with this condition we may as well go out of the world at once. Whether the articles used are called necessaries or luxuries, habit has made them necessaries; and if we mean to live, there is no choice but to suffer ourselves to be taxed. By direct Taxation he that has nothing to pay will not be taxed – he that has little will have little to pay – and he that has much will pay much. Here there can be no hardship and no injustice, and as indirect Taxes can offer no such advantages, we shall not institute any further comparisons.

In proposing a comprehensive reform of Taxation, we shall be asked why we are not content to reform by degrees. This language would have been proper in 1842 and 1846, but after having watched the operation of the Income Tax for ten years, and after having – both from experience and principle, – been convinced that the operation of that description of tax is beneficial, we know no reason why any more experiments should be tried.

Did Sir Robert Peel reform bit by bit when in 1842 he altered or repealed the duties on twelve hundred articles of import, and thus disturbed the entire trade of the kingdom? Did Sir R. Peel, assisted by Mr. Cobden and his party, reform by degrees when they abolished the Corn and Provision Taxes in 1846? Wherever great results have been realized, they have come, not from small and partial reforms – but from large and comprehensive changes. These great reforms are as extensive as the Reform now proposed, and if the argument of precipitancy can be used in either case, that can only apply to past reforms. In 1842 and 1846 Reformers had no data to guide them as to the effect of their measures, hence, these reforms were much bolder measures than that which we propose, for abundant proof is before us to indicate the result of Universal Free Trade.

It must not be forgotten that every branch of Industry and Trade has suffered in its turn from the constant changes of Taxes, and it is high time that this cause of distress and bankruptcy should cease. Until all indirect Taxes are abolished, the Government will be beset by vain expectants, and the attention of producers will often be more turned to watching the Government than attending to their own affairs. By a comprehensive change, once for all, all branches of Industry and Trade will be settled on an immoveable basis. To all there will be a fair field and no favour. And then none will fear that some day they may find their honest gains swept away by some sudden and arbitrary change. The loss to particular trades, owing to the constant meddling with Taxes, has been too much overlooked, and as our Scheme is a complete remedy for this evil, we get a strong argument in favour of a complete demolition of arbitrary Taxation. Ever patching and changing, and never perfecting anything, is not the way to produce general good, and it is because the Reforms of 1842 and 1846 were large and comprehensive, that they have been so successful.

Were life longer than it is, we could afford to talk about bit and bit Reforms as preferable to complete Reforms; but it is poor consolation for people toiling all day long, and getting little for their work, to be told that some twenty years hence the Free Trade policy will be complete, and then they shall enjoy the fruits of general prosperity. Unless good reasons for a succession of partial reforms can be stated, the nation is entitled to demand the immediate and entire abolition of all restrictions on Industry; and as the admirer of the close system can no longer say that such a demand is impracticable, it will be the People's own fault if their immediate emancipation be not secured. Let the united demand of the nation be for justice, and let them be satisfied with nothing less than justice, and all difficulties will vanish, and peace and plenty will reward the industry of all.

It is a comprehensive, and not a partial change of laws, which can produce any appreciable change in the general welfare. Partial changes only produce results on the trade particularly affected, and the general good remains untouched. Extensive changes are disliked, and as a general rule we sympathise with this feeling; but of this we are certain, that until we see our way to venture on a comprehensive reform, we must fail to carry the benefits of Free Trade into every family of the land in any degree corresponding with our wishes, or with what Universal Free Trade would give. Prosperity must not be confined to the Exchequer, or particular branches of Industry – that is not the general prosperity we speak of – we desire to see a marked improvement in the circumstances of every family, and in estimating the prospects of Universal Free Trade, we do not hold out this hope without at the same time shewing how it may be realized.

That particular Reforms may effect the general good, other laws must be adjusted to the change. In this manner a simple reform becomes a comprehensive reform; and with respect to the Scheme of Reform now proposed, it will be observed, that none of the changes indicated are unconnected with the great object in view – General Prosperity, nor with the means by which that object is to be accomplished – Universal Free Trade.

No financial reform, which falls short of removing all restrictions from Industry and Trade, can be either just or complete. We cannot redress class suffering, or remove the strife of classes, but by an impartial adjustment of our laws affecting Trade and Industry. We cannot neutralize opposition without offering the benefits of impartial Free Trade to parties who are called to make present sacrifices. We cannot be delivered from the endless exactions and annoyances of Customs and Excise officers, – we cannot dismiss the Coast Guard, nor receive the benefits on the saving of collecting the Revenue, by any half measure of Reform. These facts shew that a large and comprehensive scheme is not only the best for all parties, but a Reform easier to be carried than any partial measure.

The Legislative Enactments necessary to complete the Reforms suggested are four in number; viz.:

I. An Act to extend the present Income Tax from 3 to 8 per cent, and to apply to all Incomes without exception. This Act will repeal all other Taxes, both direct and indirect.

II. An Act to relieve the Bank of England from the obligation to purchase Gold at a fixed price, and empowering the Commissioners of the Mint to vary the weight of the several Coins of the Realm according to every important change in the value of Gold.
III. An Act repealing existing Entails, and making it illegal for any Proprietor to destine his property beyond one heir or heirs in succession.
IV. An Act to repeal the Law of Settlement and make it illegal to give relief to persons able to work.

Not only is this scheme of reform necessary to eradicate those evils which ever mar the efforts of the Legislature to advance the welfare of the Nation, but it would not be difficult to prove, that it is the only adequate remedy. Without more harmony of interests there can be no progress, and nothing but an equitable adjustment of our laws can produce peace and union. Legislation has hitherto consisted chiefly of compromises between opposing interests. By the abolition of unjust privileges, principle takes the place of compromise; and injustice and strife, and all the ills arising from disunion are removed. It is one of the properties of Justice to dissipate strife, and we know of no other remedy for that greatest of evils.

Divide a gift or burden unequally, and you produce strife; divide it equally, and there is peace. So is it with Trade and Taxation. Divide the gift of freedom partially, and the burden of the Revenue unequally, and you have discontent and disaffection; but let even handed justice be dealt out to all, and the result must be peace and contentment.

Until the Reforms of 1842 and 1846 are either repealed or completed, there will be no peace. Protection is possible, and Free Trade is possible, but a mixture of these opposite principles cannot be long endured. Every deficient harvest and every period of low prices, will revive the demand for Protection, and in every case they must be met by the revival of an Anti-Corn Law League. Thus until Free Trade is complete the entire nation will be periodically divided against itself. Those whose interests are damaged by partial Free Trade will never be satisfied until Free Trade is either pushed to its utmost limit or repealed. In these circumstances it must be the desire of every friend of his country to complete the Free Trade policy forthwith, for until Free Trade is Universal the Free Trade and Protection controversy must continue.

No one who gives the subject the slightest consideration will doubt the truth of this statement, and it is one which calls for serious thought, with a view to putting an end to strife, least '*a kingdom divided against itself be brought to desolation.*'

Sir James Graham to W. E. Gladstone, 13 November 1852, Gladstone Papers, BL, Add. MS 44740, fols 167–70.

'Nov. 13
 Resolutions as drafted by Sir J. Graham & Lord J. Russell & agreed to by us.'

Humbly to assure Her Majesty that in the ~~conviction~~ <opinion> of this House principles which have been applied <by recent Parliaments, and > the laws relating to commercial legislation <and in conformity with the fiscal emancipation of the people> especially <many important measures adopted> within the last ten years have eminently contributed <both> to that <present> prosperity of the country and to the stability of ~~you its~~ your Majesty's Throne & of the institutions with which it is surrounded:

 That ~~in~~ <in the opinion of> this House ~~decrees it to be~~ <~~and humbly desires~~> ~~its bounden duty thus emphatically to express it is for the interest of Her country~~ <deems it of the utmost moment that no doubt should exist in the public mind <either> as to the permanency of those laws ~~& of the system of legislation to which they belong~~ <or as to the view taken> by Her Legislature of the common sense principles on which they are based.

 Humbly ~~to pray Her Majest~~ That this H. fulfils a bounden duty in expressing to Your M. its conviction that ~~all future measure~~ it is essential to the welfare of Her community that the measures of commercial & financial policy which may be submitted to Parliament by ~~H~~ Your M.s. advisers should be framed in conformity <fidence?> with the principles ~~which have~~ during the last ten years generally formed legislation with reference to those subjects.

Sir James Graham to W. E. Gladstone, 19 November 1852, Gladstone Papers, BL, Add. MS 44163, fols 64–5.

Private
Grosvenor Place
19. November
1852

My dear Gladstone

I send you the [...][1] copy of the Resolutions, which I submitted to you for approval on Saturday Evening. I struck out 'mainly' and inserted 'in great measure', because you preferred the latter term; and I sent the words, so altered, to L$^d.$ John Russell in a letter, which I subsequently send to you.

In gist the alterations, which have since been made and which do not appear to me to be Improvements. It is not, however, not possible for us to refuse assent to the opinion, that the Repeal of the Corn Laws was 'a just and beneficent' measure. It might have been generous to spare our Adversaries and not to insist on passing them under the Yoke; you know, that I was willing and even anxious so to do; but the great majority of the Free Traders are resolved to record their Triumph; and I must own, that Peel's implacable Enemies, whom Time and Death have not softened, can urge no claim but that of compassion on our forbearance.

You may take a copy of the words, which I enclose; but I will thank you to return to me the Original.

I am
Y^{rs} very sincerely
Jas. Graham

[Enclosure]

Nov. 19. 52
Sir James Graham

It is the opinion of this House that the improved condition of the country & especially of the industrious classes is in great measure the result of recent legislation, wh[ich] has established unrestricted competition, wh[ich] has abolished Taxes imposed for the purpose of protection, & wh[ich] has thereby diminished the cost of the principal articles of food.

It is the opinion of this House that this policy, firmly maintained & prudently extended, will without inflicting injury on any important interest, best enable the industry of the country to bear its burdens & will thereby most surely promote the welfare & contentment of the people.

That this House will be ready to take into cons$^{n.}$ any measures consistent with these principles, wh[ich] in pursuance of H.M.s gracious speech & recommendation may be laid before it.

1 [Ed.: Illegible word.]

THE DIFFUSION OF FREE TRADE ABROAD, 1847–60

The repeal of the Corn Laws in Britain in June 1846 was viewed by many of its supporters as only the start of a European- or even world-wide process, whereby tariffs would be lowered and free trade re-established between nations. As Richard Cobden predicted 'if you abolish the Corn-law honestly, and adopt Free Trade in its simplicity, there will not be a tariff in Europe that will not be changed in less than five years to follow your example'.[1] But in retrospect, despite claims that Britain exerted its hegemonic power to remould the world in its own free-trade image, it is the limitations to free trade that remained most obvious in the aftermath of repeal.

Even so, free traders drew immediate comfort in 1846 from the adjustment of the American tariff, which they interpreted as an encouraging response to the British unilateral model of free trade.[2] Mutual tariff liberalization was seen as demonstrably in the interests of both countries. Much more difficult was the attempt to diffuse commercial liberalism to the empires and nation states of Europe, although in 1846–7 Cobden, the leader of the Anti-Corn Law League, undertook a long Continental tour in order to propagate the benefits of free trade.[3] He was, however, soon convinced of the unlikelihood of the rapid conversion of the Continent. In France, for example, Cobden found a small enthusiastic band of French liberals who had responded to the moral appeal and emancipatory rhetoric of the Anti-Corn Law League in England, forming their own Association. But most of those in government circles who favoured a simplification of the tariff did so for pragmatic rather than doctrinal reasons. The cause of free trade also suffered from the political inexperience of the French liberals, unused in the constrained politics of the restored monarchy to organizational and pressure group activity.[4] Not only this but the free traders soon found themselves exposed to the counter-politics of the protectionists, able effectively to mobilize economic interests under threat, including industrialists in textiles and iron, and, according to Cobden, the King himself, a timber monopolist. Not only did these groups successfully mobilize support from workers threatened with unemployment, but work/industry was reconstructed as a distinct 'national'/French interest now threatened by free trade, the latest disguise by which 'perfidious Albion' sought to undo the prosperity of her neighbour. The popular resort to the appeal of economic nationalism easily overpowered the intellectual currency which free trade retained in French academic life and among the economists whose *Journal* remained the main bastion of the French free trade movement.

In Spain, free trade also made a strong appeal to liberal intellectuals, and Cobden found himself fêted by the members of Spain's numerous economic societies, professors of political economy and progressive merchants; but again such elements for the most part lacked weight in the rigid politics of the early liberal monarchy. Cobden put his faith in the fiscal potential of moderate duties, which by removing incentives for smuggling would, he argued, help restore the fiscal capacity of the Spanish state. Whilst this argument was attractive to reformist ministers, it cut little ice against the powerful Catalan textile industry, a monarchy distrustful of the liberal press, and progressive urban elites whose members included many scions of long-standing Anglo-Spanish mercantile families.[5]

If Iberia proved a predictable disappointment to Cobden, this was to some extent compensated for by the enthusiasm for free trade he found in Italy, where those he met from the Pope downwards, including the Chief of Police in Naples, claimed to be favourable to the cause. The powerful 'Cobdenian moment' in the Italian Risorgimento was the product of a conjuncture in which states sought to exploit the economic potential opened up by repeal, while free trade was readily identifiable with progress, prosperity and nationhood. In particular, free trade within an Italian customs union offered not only a stage towards economic modernization but a stage towards nationhood, readily embraced by moderate liberals, for whom Cobden acted as a surrogate 'national hero'. In addition, free trade helped to distinguish an emerging Italy from the interests of the Habsburg Empire which still controlled large parts of the Italian peninsula, while adhering strongly to a protectionist tariff, deemed necessary to protect Austrian industry and to raise revenue.[6]

But the Habsburg Empire and the German states more widely were no strangers to the ideological battle between free trade and protection. Cobden himself reported the strong appeal of the Listian doctrines of protection to native industry, and intellectually and politically free trade seems to have had less purchase in the Empire than almost anywhere in Europe (save Russia). The rejection of English-style free trade had of course long been advocated by Friedrich List, who had argued that it merely served to maintain the economic subjection of 'young' states, to offer them simply the status of agricultural appendages to an industrialized Britain.[7] Nevertheless, Cobden's visit to Germany provided evidence of considerable division in German opinion; Germany's intellectual traditions had shown the strong impact of Smithian political economy and free trade enjoyed the support of disparate groups of merchants, landowners and journalists.

Overall, therefore, Europe in 1846–7 was widely polarized between protection and free trade; on the one hand, protection was identified with the status quo, with monarchy, well-established mercantile elites and established industrial interests, who feared the power of British economic competition, and who could draw on engrained traditions of popular economic nationalism. Against them were the far weaker forces of liberal economic opinion, internationally-oriented merchants, technologically-modernized industrialists and export-oriented landowners, together with those especially in Italy who saw in free trade a tool to help fashion a new nation-state. Both the strength and the weakness of the latter were well revealed at the first World Congress of Economists, held at Brussels in 1847. The most numerous group attending was Belgian, but the participants included many representatives of Europe's progressive liberal intelligentsia, social reformers, and peace activists, who met with suspicion from both the right and the growing left. Finally, what Cobden had hoped would be a rising tide of free trade in Continental Europe was shortly to be submerged in the revolutionary tide of 1848. This had paradoxical results; it briefly encouraged a rhetoric which linked free trade, peace, fraternity and federalism in a 'United States of Europe'. More lastingly in France free traders, such as Frédéric Bastiat, believing in a minimal state, found themselves confronted by republican and socialist forms of interventionism; while more widely the failure of revolution helped re-entrench the very forces that had long opposed freer trade, for example economic petitions to the Frankfurt Parliament sought protection, not free trade.[8]

The revolutions of 1848 dashed the Cobdenite hopes of 1846; yet by the 1860s Europe was to be refashioned on free-trade lines. This outcome was the result of a slow but cumulatively powerful realignment of domestic and international forces. For example, the intellectual and moral ascendancy of liberal political economy was bolstered by the Great Exhibition of 1851, a triumphant demonstration of the material, economic and moral benefits of free exchange. The technological progress celebrated by the Exhibition was also now extended into a global communications revolution – with railways, steamships, canals and the electric telegraph all reducing space and distance in the world economy in a way unparalleled until the late twentieth century. In this context, especially in France, economic modernization was now seen as the way to avoid revolution in the future; technological modernizers, including the Saint-Simonian socialists, now joined hands with the imperial state in order to promote free trade and prosperity, admittedly with due deference to protectionist interests. In Germany too, free trade was no longer seen as a threat to the state (for example by threatening the livelihood of its handicraftsmen) but as a means towards successful nation-building, by promoting the consolidation of the Zollverein through a series of commercial treaties. Above all, Otto von Bismarck saw free trade as the best means by which to counter Habsburg schemes for an Austrian-dominated German confederation, or a protectionist-inspired Mitteleuropa.[9] In Italy too the leading state of Piedmont continued to vaunt its loyalty to British-style policies of free trade as part of its own search for nationhood and modernization.[10]

The British model of free trade also remained as a pre-eminent example for policymakers abroad. As the above section on 'The Decline of Protectionism in Britain' has shown, protectionism had lost political and economic plausibility in the world's most advanced nation; free trade had been extended from agriculture to shipping and the British Empire, and was now promoted as the means towards a golden age in the metropole and its colonies; trade, not military conquest, was averred as the means towards national greatness, however much this might conflict with British policy in the East or the Crimea. For example Canada was now encouraged to develop reciprocal ties of trade with the United States rather than to depend upon the 'mother country'.[11] Nevertheless, Britain's ability to encourage or coerce other states was limited; she did agree a series of reciprocal treaties with a host of states, from Morocco to Russia, designed to lower tariffs, while the so-called unequal treaties opened up new markets in Asia. But Britain primarily relied upon her own example of prosperity to argue the case for free trade. Thus, periodically the Board of Trade compiled statistics of British prosperity since 1846 which were sent on to the French government. Arguably Britain might have done more to encourage French liberalization, as some argued, by abolishing sooner her wine duties, but governments were still reluctant to rely excessively on direct taxation. Nevertheless, the British model of revenue duties only remained the basic tool of free-trade advocacy, taken up by a variety of customs reform associations, which sought to cheapen government, reduce the tax burden on the people, encourage consumer welfare and increase peace betweens peoples. As Henry Dunckley had argued, free trade was the Charter of the Nations, not just that of the British nation.[12] Significantly, by the third quarter of the nineteenth century this was a case which was extensively argued throughout the parliamentary assemblies of Western Europe at a time when economists played a uniquely prominent part in political life.[13] But the case also retained powerful advocates in the New World, with the United States responding to the depression of 1857 by its historically greatest downward revision of customs duties (to levels of around 20 per cent), hoping to encourage cheap foreign imports and to expand its exports of agricultural produce. In many respects this was the culmination of the age of Ricardian comparative advantage.[14]

Notes

1. Speech at Manchester, 15 January 1846, in J. Bright and J. E. T. Rogers (eds), *Speeches on Questions of Public Policy by Richard Cobden*, 1 vol. edn (London: MacMillan, 1878), p. 185.

2. S. C. James and D. A. Lake, 'The Second Face of Hegemony: Britain's Repeal of the Corn Laws and the American Walker Tariff of 1846', *International Organisation*, 43 (1989), pp. 1–30.
3. M. Taylor (ed.), *The European Diaries of Richard Cobden, 1846–49* (Aldershot: Scolar Press, 1994); A. Howe (ed.), *The Letters of Richard Cobden, Volume 1, 1815–1847* (Oxford: Oxford University Press, 2007).
4. A. Tyrrell, '"La Ligue Française": The Anti-Corn Law League and the Campaign for Economic Liberalism in France during the Last Days of the July Monarchy', in A. Howe and S. Morgan (eds), *Rethinking Nineteenth-Century Liberalism: Richard Cobden Bicentenary Essays* (Aldershot: Ashgate, 2006), pp. 99–116.
5. E. Lluch, 'EL "gira triomfal" de Cobden per Espanya (1846)', *Recerques*, 21 (1988), pp. 71–90; S. Almenar and R. Velasco, 'Una Etapa en la Considacion del Librecambio en España; el Viaje de Richard Cobden por Andalucia' (1846), in G. Ruiz (ed.), *Andalucia en el Pensamiento Economico* (Malaga: Arguval, 1988), pp. 105–18.
6. See especially R. Romani, 'The Cobdenian Moment in the Italian Risorgimento', in Howe and Morgan, *Rethinking Nineteenth-Century Liberalism*, pp. 117–40.
7. F. List, *The National System of Political Economy*, trans. S. S. Lloyd, ed. J. S. Nicholson (London: Longmans, 1904); for a contemporary critique, see J. Austin, 'List on the Principles of the German Customs Union; Dangers of British Industry and Commerce', *Edinburgh Review*, 1807 (July 1842), pp. 515–56.
8. The proceedings of the Congress were published in French, *Congrès des économistes réuni à Bruxelles par les soins de L'Association belge pour la liberté commerciale* (Bruxelles: Deltombe, 1847); for the broad context, see A. Howe, *Free Trade and Liberal England, 1846–1946* (Oxford: Clarendon Press, 1997), pp. 73–86.
9. See esp. H. Böhme (ed.), *The Foundation of the German Empire: Select Documents*, trans. A. Ramm (London: Oxford University Press, 1971).
10. G. Are, 'Economic Liberalism in Italy, 1860–1915', *Journal of Italian History*, 1 (1978), pp. 409–31.
11. D. C. Masters, *The Reciprocity Treaty of 1854* (1937; Toronto: McClelland and Stewart, 1963); R. E. Ankli, 'The Reciprocity Treaty of 1854', *Canadian Journal of Economics*, 4 (1971), pp. 1–20.
12. Henry Dunckley, *The Charter of the Nations: or, Free Trade and its Results* (1854), below, pp. 110–16.
13. M. M. Augello and M. E. Guidi, *Economists in Parliament in the Liberal Age (1848–1920)* (Aldershot: Ashgate, 2005).
14. A. Howe, 'Free Trade and Global Order', in D. A. Bell (ed.), *Victorian Empire and International Relations in Nineteenth-Century Political Thought* (Cambridge: Cambridge University Press, 2007), pp. 26–46.

DIFFUSION OF FREE TRADE ABROAD

Promoters and Opponents

Richard Cobden to Marco Minghetti, 21 May 1847, Minghetti Papers, Bibliotecha comunale dell' Archiginnasio, Bologna.

Turin 21 May 1847

My dear Sir

On applying at the post office at Genoa & here I do not find any copies of the Felsineo – Perhaps you have been good enough to send them & they may have miscarried In any case I should feel much obliged by your forwarding me two or three copies by the first courier addressed to the care of the Count Petitti – I shall remain here a week & if I should have left before they arrive, the amiable Count Petitti will be good enough to forward them after me – As I only arrived here last evening I have not seen many of the good people yet – We are however to have a banquet on monday where I expect to make the acquaintance of many intelligent men. After leaving this place I shall enter the Austrian states, where I shall I suppose confine myself to private intercourse with the natives for there will not be any public demonstrations allowed in Lombardy – – Shall I tell you as the result of my experience in Italy what I should do were I an Italian? Here is my practical course – In the first place I should of course do all in my power to urge forward reforms in the particular state or sovereignty to which I belonged – Next I should endeavor to promote union amongst the Italian people, & this I should do by means of a Customs house union – This is in my opinion the only practical mode of effecting the object so near the heart of you all – I have not heard of any other plan worth a moments thought As for the union of princes, whether by marriage or treaty, we know how unstable are such alliances, & how little guarantee they afford to the people – As to the idea of Italy becoming one empire under one sovereign, I regard it as a childs dream – I should advocate the union of the Italian states within one line of Customs, like that of the Zollverein, upon the ground that the *railways* now projected & in progress render such an union absolutely indispensable – I should show that railroads with the present division of territory into separate *fiscal* sovereignties are quite impracticable – I would deprecate all interference with existing governments excepting for the purpose of a Ligue Douanière - This is the work I would engage in if I were an Italian – The work is difficult but not impracticable – All other attempts at Union are a pure waste of time because they are aiming at an impossibility – There! you have the progression of my faith, who am almost entitled, after so many acts of cordial fraternisation on the part of your Countrymen, to consider myself an Italian –

Hoping you & my good acquaintances at Bologna are all well
I remain
My dear sir faithfully Yours

Rich[d] Cobden

I need not add that I should make the basis of my customs union the principle of Free trade – that is, I would repudiate all protective duties – The Tuscan rates of duties should be the model for the whole, with such modifications as are necessary

Richard Cobden, Speeches in Europe, in *Reminiscences of Richard Cobden*, compiled Julie Salis Schwabe (London: T. Fisher Unwin, 1895), pp. 13–16, 30–4, 44–5, 48–53, 62–5.

Mr Cobden's Speech at the Free Trade Banquet at Madrid. 14th October 1846.

Gentlemen, – I accept with the deepest gratitude this demonstration. I accept it as a proof of your approbation of the principles of Free Trade, and of the means by which the Free-traders of England obtained their victory. We advocated commercial liberty, not in the spirit of a political party, nor for the benefit of a particular class, but for the interests of the whole community, and we effected our object solely by such moral means, as all good men in every country will, I hope, be able to approve. From the commencement to the close of our struggle, we renounced all resort to physical force, and trusted solely to the power of reason and argument. The sharpest weapon we wielded was the pen, and our loudest artillery was the voice of the orator. We never sought to *slay* an opponent, but only to *convert* him. It is true we made many prisoners, but they were the willing captives of conviction. For seven years a civil contest was waged in the midst of twenty-seven millions of people without shedding a drop of blood. The battle was long and arduous; but a victory achieved by discussion is in no danger from a re-action. Once gained, it is gained for ever.

You are probably all aware of the precise object of our Free Trade struggle in England. A great principle was at stake. We claimed for every Englishman the right of freely exchanging the produce of his industry for the productions of every quarter of the globe. We demanded the removal of all protective custom duties. We said to our Government: 'Make your Custom-House officers the collectors of revenue for the public Treasury, and nothing more; do not make them protectors of this or that industry, at the expense of the rest of the community, and, above all, do not make them subservient to the smuggler.' We applied this principle with even-handed justice to all classes. We claimed for the British manufacturers the right of buying the corn, the cattle and the wool of Spain, on the same terms as the like productions of our own soil. We proposed to levy equal duties upon the sugars of Cuba and Jamaica. We demanded also for the agriculturists the right of buying every article of manufacture from foreigners on the same terms as from the British manufacturers. This is now the triumphant policy of the English people. Gentlemen, Free Trade is not the cause of one country alone, it is the cause of every people which is alive to the interests of civilisation and humanity; and where ought I to expect to find a sympathy for our principles, if not in this enlightened centre of the Peninsula? To no country does Free

Trade offer greater advantages than to this, for nowhere has Nature been more bountiful in bestowing a super-abundance of those productions which other nations desire to obtain in return for the produce of their skill and industry. But, I need not tell you, that commerce is nothing but an exchange of equivalents, and that a nation must consent to import, or it cannot export. I know that there are individuals to be found in every country, who say, 'We will produce everything we require within our own boundaries; we will be independent of foreigners.' If Nature had intended that there should be such a natural isolation, she would have formed the earth upon a very different plan, and given to each country every advantage of soil and climate. My country, for example, would have possessed the wines, oils, fruits and silks, which have been denied to it, and other countries would have been endowed with the abundance of coal and iron with which we are compensated for the want of a warmer soil. No, Providence has wisely given to each latitude its peculiar productions, in order that different nations may supply each other with the conveniences and comforts of life, and that thus they may be united together in the bonds of peace and brotherhood. Gentlemen, I doubt not that ere long the public opinion of this great nation will emancipate its commerce from those restrictions which recently fettered the industry of my country. I remember that more than three centuries ago a great man sailed from your shores to discover a new hemisphere. Let me not be accused of undervaluing the glory of that great achievement if I say, that the statesman who gives to Spain the blessings of commercial freedom will, in my opinion, confer greater and more durable advantages upon his country than it derived from the discovery of America. The genius of Columbus gave to your ancestors an uncultivated continent, thinly peopled by a barbarous race, but Free Trade will throw open a civilised world to your enterprises, and every nation will hasten to bring you the varied products of their ingenuity and industry to be offered in exchange for the superabundant produce of your favoured and beautiful country. In conclusion (said Mr Cobden in Spanish), I drink to the univeral [*sic*] success of Free Trade, the surest guarantee of the peace of nations. [...]

FREE TRADE BANQUET at Cadiz, with Mr COBDEN'S SPEECH.

(Translated from the *Comercio* of Cadiz.)

9th Nov. 1846.

The banquet was prepared in one of the beautiful saloons of the Casino, given up for the purpose by the society of the establishment. The table was adorned with fine flowers, and covered with rich dishes and a profusion of fruits and sweetmeats.

At half-past five p.m., Mr Cobden arrived, accompanied by his friend and fellow-traveller, Mr Salis Schwabe, of Manchester, and by Don Jorge Urtetegui, a respectable merchant, and a friend of the great English League leader. The latter, we learn, was the first to conceive the idea of giving to Mr Cobden, in this *fête*, a proof of the lively sympathies entertained for his doctrines in Spain.

At six o'clock the festival commenced. Don Jorge Urtetegui presided, supported by Mr Cobden on his right, and Don Jose Maria Elizalde on his left. There were altogether forty-four persons present, all gentlemen of high standing in society, and, for the most part, interested in commerce.

The President rose and said: – Gentleman, – I am about to propose a toast, which I am sure you will all drink with much pleasure; it is the health of the illustrious guest who this day honours this table by his presence – 'Mr Richard Cobden. May Heaven prolong his life, so as to enable him to behold the complete triumph of his sound doctrines throughout Europe, as he has already done in England!'

Mr Cobden then rose and replied as follows: –

Gentlemen, – I regret that I cannot express my gratitude for this kind reception in a language which is intelligible to all present. It gives me no surprise, however, to find that the commercial principles which I have advocated in England should find admirers in Cadiz; it is to those *principles*, and not to their unworthy *advocates*, that we have now met to do honour. Gentlemen, the English Free-traders have had but one object in view, and it may be expressed in one word – *Liberty*. We found our commerce subject to a thousand restraints. The Legislature was everywhere thwarting the operations of individuals – our merchants and manufacturers carried their enterprise into every corner of the globe, but, on their return home with the productions of foreign countries, they were repulsed from their native shores by absurd and illiberal tariffs. It was to put an end to this interference with the right of individuals that the English League was formed. We resolved to restrain the functions of our Legislature within their proper limits, by withdrawing from it altogether the power of regulating or protecting commerce, and leaving every individual free to exercise his industry in whatever way he pleased. This was the object of the League, which it accomplished after a struggle of seven years. Henceforth no merchant in England can be thwarted in his undertakings by the Government, under the pretence of protecting the interests of some other man at home or in the Colonies. Every individual is placed upon the equal ground of freedom, but no one has any privilege over his fellow-citizen. I need not say a word to convince you how favourable *liberty* is to commerce. All history proves it – compare the different nations of the world at the present time with each other, and you will find that everywhere commerce flourishes or fades in proportion to the liberty or the restraint which it encounters – compare even a seaport which is free with another that is not, and see the great difference. You all remember that for a year Cadiz enjoyed an extraordinary prosperity. You remember the fleet of vessels which crowded your bay, the vast traffic which filled your streets, and your warehouses charged with the productions of every clime? What was it that occasioned such a magical change in Cadiz? The climate, its harbour, its productions, everything was the same as they had been before – there was but one alteration which accounted for all the prosperity – *for one year Cadiz was a* FREE *port*. In every country there is some particular interest which is afraid of freedom. In England, our agriculturists were frightened out of their senses at the prospect of Free Trade in corn. But they now laugh at their former terrors. In Spain, you have the Catalonians, who are terrified at the mere name of Free Trade. They will live to laugh at their present fear like my own opponents the farmers of England. I never knew an industry suffer from freedom. I have known many trades perish under the enervating shade of protection, but never one which failed to gain strength in the invigorating breeze of liberty. Gentlemen, if you think that Spain would be benefited by adopting the policy which now prevails in England, you must follow similar means to those which were pursued for advancing Free Trade opinions. You must promote the discussion of the subject in every possible way. Each man who is convinced of the truth of our principles must make it his duty to convert his neighbours. It is only by individual efforts and sacrifices that great truths, whether in religion, philosophy or politics, can be propagated. It is useless to expect Free Trade measures from your Government until the people have been convinced of its advantages. In my opinion, almost all the Governments in Europe are in advance of their people in intelligence upon economical questions, and they are only waiting for the removal of public ignorance and prejudice to advance in the path of commercial freedom. I see many gentlemen round this table who, I am sure, will devote themselves to the patriotic task of propagating sound economical doctrines, and I assure them that, however far I may be removed from them, I shall always take a lively interest in their labours. In conclusion, I drink prosperity to the ancient city of Cadiz. [...]

Mr Cobden's Speech at Genoa.

Gentlemen, – Let me beg you to accept my warmest thanks for this kind and hospitable reception, and, still more, let me thank you for the sympathy you have expressed for the principle with which my name has been associated. The Free-traders in England have only had one object in view, the removal of those restrictions which impede the progress of commercial intercourse between the different nations of the earth. We never entered upon the field of party politics; we abstained from all interference with the forms of government; we confined ourselves strictly to a question of economical science, which effects equally the prosperity and happiness of every nation, whatever be its forms of government – for where is there a government which is not interested in ruling over a rich, flourishing and contented people? We look for the progress of Free Trade in all countries, because it will promote alike the interests of the governors and governed. There is a great lesson to be learned by governments – a lesson as yet learned by but two nations – which will teach them how to increase their revenues by reducing their customs duty, – a process which augments the population, commerce and wealth of a nation, and thus increases its ability to contribute to the revenue of the State. I will give you a fact or two in illustration of what I mean. The United States of America enjoy probably the most moderate tariff in the world. In that country nine-tenths of all the revenue is derived from the customs. In England, where for the last quarter of a century we have been marching in the path of Free Trade, one-third of our enormous income is yielded by the customs. In France, which has yet to take the first step in the reform of its tariff, one-tenth only of the taxes is raised from the customs; and in Spain, where the restrictive system reigns supreme, so small a fraction as one-thirteenth of the revenue is all that is raised at the custom house. If I were to take other countries, I could show that, in proportion as they depart from the principles of Free Trade, they diminish the resources of the Treasury. Seeing, then, that the interests of the Government and the people are identical in this matter, I feel confident in the extension of sound commercial principles everywhere.

I need not remind you, gentlemen, that the removal of commercial restrictions must promote the interests of Genoa. Nature has given you a deep and capacious port in a sea that is not famous for good harbours; your merchants possess capital and enterprise; your sailors have always been renowned for their courage, sobriety and perseverance. I do not forget that from amongst them sprung that great and daring genius who sailed upon the discovery of a new world. You have here the elements of commercial greatness, and require only free scope for your energies to achieve the highest prosperity for your beautiful city – a prosperity which will be desirable, because it is based upon principles of justice and humanity.' [...]

ACCOUNT *of a* DINNER *to Mr* COBDEN *at Rome.*

(From the *Roman Advertiser*, February 13, 1847.)

On the 10th instant a dinner was given by many of the nobility and the most influential citizens of Rome to Mr Cobden. Amongst those present were Prince Corsini, Prince de Canino, the Marquis Dragonetti, the Duke of Bracciano, and the members of the Chamber of Commerce; the only English guests were Count Henry Arundel, Mr Sharpe, and Mr Freeborn, the British consular agent. The dinner was given in the large saloon of the Chamber of Commerce. The Marquis Patinziani was in the chair, and spoke as follows: –

'May God, Who by a manifest wonder has accorded to the Church and the State Pius IX., preserve him for long years to come! Long live the magnanimous Pius IX.! Long live Her Majesty the Queen of England! Long live Sir Robert Peel! Long live Richard Cobden, and long live the liberty of commerce!

'The great Christian family, impressed with admiration for the sublime and beneficent virtues which adorn the Sovereign Pontiff, beholds in him the Universal Pastor destined by Providence to bind a general and indissoluble knot of fraternal charity. Under his empire the virtues that gladden and honour our epoch will triumph over the vices that afflict and disgrace it; the people amongst whom the faith of the gospel has not yet penetrated will behold in the Chair of St Peter the source of all truth, the seat of all justice, the centre of civilisation; in fine, the pontifical subjects will behold realised all their desires and all their hopes. God, who has given to this best of princes a mission so sublime, will inspire him to dictate laws adapted to the age in which we live, and to maintain with firmness their exact observance. Thus we shall enjoy the benefits of order, law, peace and prosperity, and shall have cause to bless him daily as the author of our happiness.

'And you, sir, as an illustrious Englishman, who has the glory of identifying your name with the grand principles of free commerce, accept from me, as a veteran in the profession of the same doctrines and as spokesman of those now present, our most sincere homage, united with thanks for the visit made to our country, and the honour done to this hospitable banquet. We, with all our fellow-citizens who love the just and useful, shall never be able to praise as we should desire your ardent endeavours to unite all the nations of the earth in the indissoluble bonds of true and reciprocal interests, and thus to destroy that national egotism which, flourishing under the protection of Monopoly, has produced so many prejudices, rivalries and sanguinary discords among nations. This will be the commencement of a new era, when nations, by means of the well-established principle of free traffic, shall acquire and maintain mutual independence and peace, internal prosperity, order and tranquillity. The prodigious activity of the present generation shall have a proportionate field for development, and the young man of to-day shall have a way opened to useful occupations, failing which, rather than be condemned to intolerable inaction, he would abandon himself to the pursuit of chimeras, which ever prove the constant source of error, misfortune and loss. Free Trade, which has nothing in common with the intricacies of politics, is pre-eminently the true element of order in every government. It ameliorates the condition of the people, it produces a lasting and stable prosperity, which stimulates the moral progress of society, and triumphs over all obstacles.

'We honour in you, Mr Cobden, the principles you represent, and the generosity which has done so much to revolutionise the old uncivilised commercial system – principles which, in the Middle Ages, gave wealth and grandeur to Italy, and which you have revived in England, which holds so high a place in modern civilisation.'

The health of Sir Robert Peel, proposed by the President, was then drunk with loud applause. The Marquis Dragonetti then spoke as follows: –

'Let us all join in wishing long life and prosperity to our illustrious guest. He is an admirable example of that tenacity of purpose and firmness of will which triumphs over all obstacles.

'Mr Cobden had against him a powerful aristocracy of almost fabulous wealth, whose prestige was firmly established by a long record of great deeds. They bitterly opposed the bold but liberal project of removing a burdensome tax on the people's bread. Even those Liberal ministers, who a few years before had themselves promoted a memorable reform, looked upon this idea as extravagant folly, and shuddered at the thought of undermining those legal privileges, the basis of all the national greatness.

'We honour, sir, your unrivalled perseverance, and we rejoice to entertain you in the city of eternal triumphs, and near the rock where stood the Capitol of ancient Rome. The conquerors of old drove to the citadel in golden chariots, because they had made the entire world a province of Rome, and subjected all nations to her empire. You, with your peaceful and legal victory, have given the strongest impulse to the universal association of nations, and the glory of sanguinary conquest pales before the splendour of yours, sanctified by that love which sanctifies all things – the love of virtuous liberty.

'We specially revere in you the virtue of perseverance, which we, the sons of Italy, most need to regenerate our country, and we therefore desire from henceforth to enshrine it in the very spot, where of old stood the Temple of Capitoline Jove.'

Mr Cobden spoke as follows: –

'Gentlemen, I am not surprised, however delighted, to find in this august capital, the mistress of the arts and patroness of learning, many enlightened men who take an interest in a question of commercial policy. It is a question which is historically connected with this country, for modern Europe is not more indebted to Italy for its arts and letters than for the revival of its commerce and manufactures; England preserves to this day many proofs of this origin of its commerce. The very account books of her merchants are kept upon the Italian model, and the street in London, where our bankers are congregated, still bears its Italian name (Lombard Street). I am bound to say, however, that a fatal error pervaded generally the policy of the commercial states of the Middle Ages – an error which has been more or less imitated by all modern nations. The warlike spirit of a barbarous age was too generally introduced into the pursuits of commerce. Each country regarded its neighbour with the jealousy of a rival and the hatred of an enemy. People did not understand that trade, freely carried on between two countries, could promote the prosperity of both. They thought that commerce necessarily involved the sacrifice of one for the aggrandisement of the other. Hence arose those mercantile wars between neighbouring commercial states, each aiming at that impossibility, an exclusive trade, which led to the constant destruction of human life, and the waste of all those elements of wealth which are the great resource and support of commerce. Modern political economy, a science to which Italy has largely contributed, has shed a new light upon the true principles of trade, and has raised its character to the level of a more civilised age. It teaches us that commerce, if free, is a mutual interchange of benefits – that where two countries voluntarily trade together, it cannot permanently serve the interests of one without conferring equal benefits on the other, and that, therefore, under a general system of Free Trade, every commercial community has an interest in the prosperity and wealth of all other states. It destroys the motive which formerly tempted mercantile nations to enter upon wars to conquer customers, by proving that they can obtain the various productions of the earth's surface on more advantageous terms by Free Trade than by the exclusive conquest of territory. I do not mean to say that this principle is as yet generally understood in the world; but it has been long demonstrated in theory by learned and philosophical writers. England has already led the way in the practical adoption of Free Trade, and other governments are preparing to follow her example. Everywhere it has become the theme of discussion, and I am glad to find that it is a favourite topic in Italy, for I calculate much upon the co-operation of your countrymen, whose acute, logical and practical genius never fails to shed a light upon whatever sciences it may undertake to elucidate. It would be to me an easy task to show how greatly the States of the Church might be benefited by the application of the principles of Free Trade. But I abstain; for I think it would be unbecoming in me to comment upon the public affairs of countries where I am hospitably received as a foreigner. But I see around me several gentlemen far more competent than myself to make the application of my views to their native country; and I conclude, thanking you for this kind reception, and with the expression of the confident hopes that the illustrious man who now fills the pontifical throne, and who has filled the world with the fame of his public virtues, will signalise his reign by carrying out in his dominions the peaceful and philanthropic principles of Free Trade.' [...]

PUBLIC BANQUET to Mr COBDEN at Florence.

(From *Morning Chronicle* of 14th May 1847.)

A banquet was given on the 29th April to our distinguished countryman in the magnificent gallery of the Borghesi Palace in Florence. Signor Vincenzi Perruzzi, the Gonfaloniere of the city, presided. Upon Mr Cobden's health having been drunk with enthusiasm, he rose and spoke as follows: –

'Gentlemen, – I should feel much embarrassed if I believed this splendid demonstration was intended as a personal compliment to myself; for, whatever may be thought of my merits in other countries, I can have no title to pre-eminence as a Free-trader in an assembly of Tuscans. But no; we meet here as brethren in a common faith, myself a younger brother, to unite our vows in favour of that commercial liberty, which Tuscany, of all the nations of the earth, was the first to put in practice upon sound economical principles. Other people, as for instance the Dutch and Swiss, owing to the accidents of their geographical position, may have always enjoyed peculiar exemptions from commercial restrictions, but to Tuscany is undoubtedly due the glory of having preceded by half a century the rest of the world in the application of the theories of economical science to its legislation. Here political economy was first erected into a commercial code. Let us render a solemn homage to the memories of those men who gave to the world so great a lesson in statesmanship. Honour to Baudini, who, a century ago, discovered the truth, of which more than half the civilised world is still ignorant, that liberty of commerce is the only safeguard of nations against the evils of scarcity, and their surest guide to agricultural and commercial prosperity. Honour – immortal honour – to Leopold, who, taking the torch of science from the hand of Baudini, entered upon the then dark and untrodden path of Free Trade, and, guided only by its pure light, proceeded onwards with an unfaltering step, undeterred by the obstacles which ignorance, prejudice and self-interest threw in his way. Honour to Neri, John Fabbroni, Fossombroni and the rest, who preserved from the attacks of sophistry his great work to our day. These are the real benefactors of mankind, to whom we ought to decree honours and monuments, whose peaceful triumphs will shed blessings upon myriads yet unborn, long after the causes and consequences of blood-stained victories are lost in oblivion and nothingness.

'Gentlemen, I am not in the habit of addressing my hearers in terms of flattery, and I should like it to be understood that the few words I have to add are intended for those who may chance to read my remarks in other countries rather than as complimentary phrases offered to a Tuscan audience. Upon this, my first visit to Italy, I have felt naturally curious to witness the effects of Free Trade, particularly in corn, upon the moral and material condition of a people. I must confess that I entered Tuscany with feelings of enthusiasm such as a devotee experiences in visiting the shrine of his faith. But I have endeavoured to cast an impartial eye upon all that I have seen, and if what I state as the result of my observation be erroneous, it will be open to correction by others. During the last eight months I have been travelling in nearly all the countries of Southern Europe, and I am bound to state, without wishing to disparage other nations, that

I find the condition of the population of Tuscany superior to that of any people I have visited. The surface of the country resembles that of a well-cultivated garden; the people are everywhere well dressed; I have seen no beggars, except a few lame or blind; and in this season of general scarcity there is less of suffering from want of food here, with a perfect freedom of export and import of corn than in probably any other country in Europe. I find such industries as are natural to Tuscany carried on with success; and that, in particular, of its indigenous straw manufacture, has attained a development which has surprised me. But I do not confine my observations to the material condition of the people. Where a country had enjoyed for fifty years the advantages of commercial liberty, I expected to find the spirit of Free Trade entering into the character of its people, abating their natural prejudices, destroying the spirit of egotism, and imparting to them a sentiment of brotherhood towards other nations. And in this respect I have not been disappointed in the inhabitants of Tuscany. I am only repeating the opinion of every traveller when I say that they are eminently courteous and mild towards strangers. Foreigners make this country their favourite abode, not merely because here there is no impediment to a cheap and abundant supply of luxuries and comforts from every part of the globe, but because they find a charm in the amiable cordiality of the Tuscan people. Such is a description of the only country in Southern Europe which enjoys the advantages of Free Trade, and I will not add a word of comment, but leave the facts I have stated for the instruction of other nations.

'Gentlemen, I thank you heartily for this cordial reception of a fellow-labourer in our good cause. The remembrance of this happy evening will always be a source of the highest gratification to me. I conclude by drinking to the rapid extension of Free Trade principles all over the world.'

'Congress of Political Economists at Brussels', *Economist*, 5:211 (11 September 1847), pp. 1048–9.

CONGRESS OF POLITICAL ECONOMISTS AT BRUSSELS.

By a circular, of which the following is an extract, the Belgian Association for promoting free trade has invited political economists to meet at Brussels on the 16th instant:–

The usefulness of a meeting of the friends of *economical science*, of all countries and all descriptions of opinion, is impossible to be disputed, marked advances having been made in various branches of social knowledge through the instrumentality of congresses like the one now determined on.

By assembling at Brussels the individuals who, from their exertions and position, are at the head of the politico-economical movements of the world, the Belgian Association for the Liberty of Commerce apprehended it should take the shortest road for reducing the difficulties, and destroying the prejudices, which continue to be opposed to the extension of the commercial relations between different countries.

It seems needless to insist on the importance of the questions to which this politico-economical congress will be called to apply itself. For centuries they have been the objects of continual study to the most eminent men that have appeared.

It is hoped, Sir, you will consent to contribute to these serious objects, by giving the meeting the advantage of your information, and of the character you possess for acquaintance with the science which it has long been our common object to promote.

Advantage has been taken of a meeting at Brussels for the extension of reformative punishments (*congress penetentiare*), and of the fortunate coincidence of an exhibition of the products of Belgian industry, to call together the present congress of the friends of political economy and statistics. Its meetings will take place four days before those of the meeting on reformative punishments – that is to say, on the 16th of September.

The civic authorities of Brussels have placed the great hall of the Hotel de Ville at the disposal of the committee.

A numerous meeting, embracing the most distinguished professors of the science in France, Germany, and England, will, we believe, assemble and be instrumental in attaining the objects proposed. It will help to reconcile conflicting opinions, and destroy the prejudices which are still opposed to the extension of commercial relations between the subjects of different Governments. There is a kind of moral fitness in Belgium originating such a congress. Prospering at an early date from the growth of trade, before politicians meddled much with it, and subsequently going to decay from the loss of freedom under the successive Governments of Spain and Austria, Belgium supplies ample means of illustrating the vicissitudes in national prosperity caused by erroneous and restrictive legislation. She has heretofore supplied a battle field for the warriors of Europe; now, aspiring to a more noble renown, she offers herself as the site of a congress to promote intercommunication and general peace. The victories now to be obtained will be bloodless, but important. Prejudices, numerous, and strongly fixed in many minds, are to be conquered. The very class who brought the armies together to fight must now be subdued by opinion. The principles of political economy derived from nature, concern equally the whole family of mankind, and apply to all times and places; the local, fiscal, and commercial regulations of each government are always at variance with these principles, and the bulk of politicians continually try to evade, thwart, or resist them. Their prejudices must now be conquered, and it seems appropriate that the attempt should be made where, in support of their systems, they have caused so much blood to be shed.

Amongst the prejudices in the minds of our continental neighbours hostile to the admission of truth, there are none more inveterate than those derived from the superficial acquaintance with the politico-economical history of England, which is common abroad. Her great progress in wealth, mainly owing to inventions and arts, which restriction had not reached, having taken place in conjunction with several unsocial and restrictive laws, the belief has become firmly fixed in many minds that they caused her prosperity. England has made, they think, the most she can by those laws, and now finds it her interest to have free trade for herself. She is anxious, they say, to prevent other nations from following in her career, and obtaining a like prosperity by a like series of navigation and corn laws and colonial restrictions. In accordance with the general and false conclusion, that the effects of laws are always identical with the intentions of law-makers, they believe that our wealth was created by laws passed with an intention to make us rich, and imagine our present advocacy of free trade is intended to make them forego advantages which our laws have secured to us. Our new policy is not recommended by our past prosperity, and it would have been more acceptable were England not the most wealthy of nations. Envy bars out truth: in recommending free trade England is suspected to have a sinister object in view; and good principles are looked on with jealousy or rejected, because they have her advocacy.

But we, in England, have had experience of partial free trade. We relaxed our navigation laws in 1824, and the rate of increase in our shipping in the last six years was nearly four times as great and rapid as in the six years immediately preceding 1824. In ten years on an average before 1824, our trade, as indicated by shipping entered inwards and outwards, increased at the rate of 34.83 per cent, while in ten years subsequent to 1824, it increased at the rate of 67 per cent. If foreign vessels have at the same time increased to a small extent in our trade, it is also a fact that English vessels, engaged in the trade with the United States and France, have increased in a much greater proportion than the vessels of the French and the Americans engaged in their own trade. It is a fact, too, that while our shipping has increased since 1824 only at the rate of 94.37 per cent in our colonial or protected trade, it has increased at the rate of 182.98 per cent in the unprotected trade. Since 1842 there has been a tolerably free trade in cattle, and never did the graziers of England, after recovering from the effects of their own unfounded panic, thrive more. Foreign silks have been admitted into our own market, and the silk manufacture of England has thriven more than before it was exposed to competition. Our flock masters predicted ruin from allowing foreign wool to come in; it was allowed, and they have almost ever since ceased to complain. So in every branch of trade to which freedom has been given, and which has been exposed to competition, a great increase has taken place, and the progress of our country in material prosperity has been much more rapid since we began the relaxation in our system, than when restrictions existed in full rigour. Even those who were most opposed to the relaxations when they were first mentioned, have long since ceased their hostility. They have witnessed the effects; and have tacitly become converts to the propriety of abolishing restrictions. Nearly the whole of the community, certainly the bulk of the most advanced and intelligent portion, including the Government, which has had for several years to rejoice over a tranquil people and continually increasing revenue and power, is convinced, from experience, of the immense advantages which free trade has conferred on England.

With this knowledge of its effects, were Englishmen hostile to the prosperity of the continent, as continental politicians frequently assert, instead of urging free trade on its acceptance, we should keep it carefully to ourselves. We should guard it as the secret of our future greatness. We should prevent our neighbours, if we could, from sharing its manifold advantages. Supposing us actuated by envy and malignity towards other nations, we should recommend them, the French for example, to maintain all their restrictions on the importation of cattle, and iron, and cotton-twist which we and the men of Marseilles know to be injurious alike to the wealth of individuals in France, and the power of the Government; we should say our prosperity has been caused by our restrictive laws; and though we now find it necessary to abolish them, you should maintain them as long as possible; we should exceed any of the Paris journals in praising M. Guizot and the system of protection, and extol his firmness in not giving way to the clamour of speculating merchants and indiscreet manufacturers; we should praise the patriotism of the ironmasters and owners of forests, and never hint that they might possibly be biased by expecting, though erroneously, to get larger rents and higher profits by advocating what they call the good of the country. Englishmen being now generally convinced that free trade is the only policy, that can give the utmost scope – the natural scope – to individual industry, is the surest way to enrich the nation, not only demand free trade for themselves on all points, even requiring the abrogation of the navigation laws, the last important remnant of the worn out restrictive system, and the one most cherished as the source of their maritime superiority, but they also, from a thorough conviction that free trade will be beneficial to other countries, and promote the best interests of humanity, urge them to follow the modern example of England.

We do not seek to disguise the fact, indeed we boast of it as the Christian or Divine attribute of free trade, that the abolition of restrictions in one nation benefits other nations; that the restrictions on the importation of iron and cotton twist into France are disadvantageous to England: but those restrictions are far more injurious to the nation which enacts them, and to some portion of which they chiefly apply, than to other nations. In opening our ports to French commodities, lowering our duties on French wines, or abolishing them altogether, we shall undoubtedly help forward the prosperity of France, but we should much more promote the prosperity of England. Whether France allowed a free importation or not, of English goods into France, every Englishman who was engaged in bringing in French goods, or used them, would be benefited by allowing a free importation into England. What benefited them could not injure the community, which is composed of the individuals benefited. By continuing to exclude our cotton twist and iron, France would only keep up the price of her own cloth and cutlery, and exclude herself from entering into competition with us in foreign markets. She would insure us the complete possession of those markets. By not taking twist and iron from us, the French contribute to keep down the price of those articles here, and facilitate their exportation to other countries that do take them.

Every species of importation – abundance of any and every kind – tends to keep down prices generally, and promotes exchange. A part of the price of wheat is made up of the price of the instruments the farmer uses, and of what he eats, drinks, and wears while he is cultivating the ground. If wine or beer be a part of his consumption, his corn will be grown cheaper by the free importation of wine. The same is true of all manufactures. If the cost of the customary maintenance of the labourer be diminished by the importation of foreign wine or foreign corn, cotton cloth may be sold cheaper, and we shall have greater advantages in the markets of Brazil and China. Thus, while we admit that it is for the mutual interest of both countries to abolish all restrictions, all exorbitant duties on the produce of each other, it is the interest of either to admit the produce of the other freely, whether that other reciprocate or not. Nay, we affirm that it is the duty of the Government, which is bound to protect, not to injure, its subjects who would profit by foreign trade. If we wished to injure France or any other foreign country, therefore, we should content ourselves with reducing our own duties, abolishing our own restrictions, and should encourage other nations to preserve restrictions and high duties, which destroy trade, lessen revenue, impede national prosperity, promote dissatisfaction and discontent, and impair political power. The very reverse of this Englishmen do. Convinced of the equal utility to all of free trade, we adopt it ourselves, we urge the Government to extend it as far and as fast as possible, and zealously recommend it to other nations.

The Governments which oppose it act inconsistently. There is not one of them but wishes to promote the prosperity of the people, and to increase their wealth. But every individual, almost, in the present condition of society produces something or other for sale. There are few persons in any part of Europe who live, each one, exclusively on his own produce. Even the serfs of Hungary, clad in the untanned skins of their masters' flocks, buy their knives. It is nearly the universal condition of mankind, that they labour to sell the produce of their labour. They perform services for one another. M. Bastiat properly says, that all trade is barter; that services are exchanged for services; and governments which wish their people to be industrious and rich, encouraging them to labour and trade, and at the same time shut out importations, only deprive their own people of the services of other people which are their proper reward. They at once encourage labour and deprive it of its pay. They excite their own people to diligence, and try to prevent the diligence of another people, by which alone the diligence of their own people can be rewarded. They stimulate as far as they can the industry of the farmers (say of Normandy), and they will not allow the merchants of Havre and Marseilles to import the real price of their produce. Almost all labour, we repeat, is now performed in order to sell its produce; and the government which restricts or prevents importation, which hinders trade, deprives that labour of its proper market. It makes the diligence of its subjects comparatively profitless, lessens the motives for exertion, and diminishes the national wealth.

Immense prejudices, however, chiefly nourished by politicians, are yet to be surmounted. They are not entertained by the people. At least those portions of different nations who come into contact with each other, who are willing to trade with each other, know them not. Politicians, with their well meant regulations for each particular people, necessarily interfere with these general laws, which are called political economy, and they are hard to be convinced that their own little contrivances are not superior to the contrivances of nature. It is a part of their creed, and a part of the creed of all who believe in them, that nature regulates nothing in society, and that they are appointed to fulfil the duty which she is supposed to have neglected. This is a great prejudice which, amongst others, the congress will have to combat; and the order which has not ceased to reign in all the transactions of men, since free trade was extended, which seems, indeed, to have become more firm as free trade has extended, will serve to dissipate the prejudice of politicians. They are anxious to promote the order of society and the happiness of mankind; but it is now distinctly ascertained, that no means of accomplishing these ends are equal to free intercourse and free trade between all individuals and nations. From them a mutual dependence both of individuals and of nations arises, which is the soul of social order as well as of peace. To promote such lofty ends, to contribute not merely to the material prosperity of mankind, without which, however, there can be no contentment, but to the promotion of good will amongst all the nations of the earth, the preservation of peace, and the extension of that social order which is the offspring of nature rather than of political contrivances, the congress of Brussels is to meet, and has our hearty wishes for its success.

Free Trade Meeting at Marseilles, *Economist*, 5:211 (11 September 1847), pp. 1050–1.

We cannot allow the meeting of the Marseilles Free Trade Society (*Association Marseillaise du Libre Echange*) on the 24th ult., to pass without some further mention of it than a couple of lines amongst our foreign intelligence. 'More than a thousand persons,' says the *Courrier de Marseilles*, 'crowded the large room, too small for the multitude assembled, to hear the two deputies of Marseilles, MM. Clapier and Reybaud, M. Fred. Bastiat, the zealous apostle in France of Free Trade, and with the hope of applauding one of the most eloquent orators of the age, M. de Lamartine, who had promised to honour the meeting by his presence.' They were not disappointed. The great poet was there; the two deputies were there; and there was assembled an audience of merchants, and others, of Marseilles – almost comparable, in numbers, to those which crowded Covent Garden to hear the orators of the League. A great number of ladies were present, as at Covent Garden, to listen to the dry discussions of political economy. Such an event, to be followed by the approaching meeting of a Congress of Political Economists at Brussels, on the 16th instant, is one of the significant signs of the progress of that 'new faith' on the continent, which has wrought such great changes in England, and which, according to the President, M. L. Luce, 'is consistent with the designs,' (if we may not say it is based on the acts,) 'of Providence, sharing unequally its divine gifts amongst the numerous families of mankind. Practically adopted in England, and theoretically favoured by the leading minds of Europe, it must, ere long, become the creed not of one nation or of one sect, but the universal creed of mankind.'

The business of the meeting was opened by M. L. LUCE, who gave a neat account of the proceedings of the Society, and informs us that the principles of free trade were adopted almost unanimously by the merchants of Marseilles. In Marseilles, as here, the shipowners, not yet taught by experience, but blindly believing still that what the law promises it performs, trusting to a Navigation Law instead of to their own exertions, were amongst the opponents of free trade, but were successfully combated by the Society. In Marseilles, as in London, it was demonstrated that protecting laws, such as those passed between 1819 and 1825, in France, and confirmed by the law of 1832, had caused the dearth of 1846 to assume the intensity of famine. In Marseilles, we learn from M. L. Luce, the proposed tariff had been the subject of discussion, and it was considered, as only intended, like too many ministerial schemes, to mark time in the march of protection, without granting anything to commercial freedom. M. L. Luce was followed by M. CLAPIER, deputy of Marseilles, who expatiated, in a luminous and animated speech, on the great progress free trade principles had made since they had issued from the Study of the philosopher and become the means of influencing the opinions of the masses. M. Clapier expressed an opinion that the French Ministry was favourable to free trade, but disposed to wait till public opinion was ready to second it in carrying out the principle. M. L. Reybaud, the other deputy of Marseilles, explained clearly the disadvantages which the South of France suffered from the protecting laws, as distinguished from the North of France; but the results being influenced by enterprise, turned out by comparison to the advantage of the South. He said, –

> The north of France produces cereals, cattle, beet-root, oleaginous grains–all of them protected articles. The south produces madder, silks, brandies, and wines – all of them articles which protection has left exposed to general competition. And yet, such is the elasticity which liberty imparts, such the state of languor inspired by monopoly, that we have no rivals in the world for those commodities which our fiscal legislation neglects or oppresses, – our silks, madders, and wines,– whilst those which the laws protect – corn, cattle, oleaginous seeds – at the best barely supply our markets, acknowledge superiors in every region, and seem doomed to an irremediable inferiority. So true is it that protection resembles the 'deadly tree' under the shadow of which the vital faculties grow dull and are extinguished.

After the Secretary, M. Estrangin had made an appeal to the ladies, by showing them how free trade would enrich their households and allow them to expand their benevolence, M. F. Bastiat delivered a speech to establish the 'political economical axiom, that products are exchanged for products, or, still better, that services are exchanged for services.' – a mode of expression which might be adopted here, to show the complete reciprocity – the mutual benefit – of freely exchanging service for service. He also showed that a financial reform would be the inevitable consequence of adopting free trade doctrines, by which the industrious classes would be relieved from taxation, at the same time that the revenue would be increased ... M. Bastiat concluded by a very well timed compliment to M. de Lamartine, quoting his fine phrase, 'La liberte fera aux homes une justice, que l'arbitraire ne sau rait lui faire;' 'and M. de Lamartine crowned the exertions of the day' – we quote from a contemporary – 'with one of those masterly orations in which the matured ideas of an observant life are given forth with all the fervour of early youth, tempered by the judgment gained from experience in the contests of the senate.' His discourse, we are assured, was repeatedly interrupted by the most animated applause. So elevated and so elevating – so assuring for the rapid progress and not long postponed triumph of free trade in France, was the proceeding of the 'Association Marseillaise du libre Echange,' on the 24th of August, 1847.

We will take the opportunity to remark, with a view to forestall a possible objection to our doctrines, that the present unfortunate condition of France, financial and political, is not owing to free trade. France has not had free trade, and her condition is worse than that of England. By-and-bye it will be generally found out, even in England, that there is something more to be dreaded in society than a fall of rent, or a decay of agriculture, supposing either were to be the inevitable consequence of free trade, or *laissez faire* – something worse than a bad smell, and even a blast of miasma, supposing that they were sure to be continued, because the Government did not interfere with the proper business of the inhabitants of every town, and clean it for them. There is to be generally dreaded that want of self-reliance and prostration of mind in an over-governed people, which, whenever the too much ruling government falls into disfavour, as fall it must, exposes society to all the great evils of a great and sudden revolution. In France, where everything has been regulated by the Government, a dissolution of society is anticipated from events, that in England, where we have not yet gone the length of French statesmen, would scarcely cause a change of ministry. We may add, as the condition of France is mainly caused by the over-regulating system, so the present uncomfortable condition of society in England, – the commercial embarrassment and stagnation of trade – are not the consequences of the removal of the laws which oppressed trade, but of those laws. Though contemporaneous with the success of free trade principles in legislation, or rather, in the squabbling of parties, they are not the consequence of that success, which has been too short a time in operation to produce such a result. They are the lingering consequences of the system which has been superseded. The present embarrassment and stagnation of trade would have been much greater and more disastrous had protection been allowed to remain in full force, than they have been under the mitigated system. Every day makes us more thankful that Sir Robert Peel saw in time the terrible consequences which might ensue from a great dearth, and saved the nation from having to meet a famine with laws which excluded foreign nations from growing food for our use. Our greatest auxiliary has been the Indian corn of the United States, and, fortunately for us, the total abolition of the duty on that grain in 1846, enabled and encouraged the inhabitants of the United States to grow it for our present use, and saved many, if not all, the Irish from actual starvation.

Richard Cobden to Michel Chevalier, 22 March 1851 (copy), Cobden Papers, West Sussex Record Office, CP 290, fols 271–3.

103 Westbourne Terrace London
22 March 1851

My dear Sir

    I received your favor yesterday, and was very sorry to hear that so much dissatisfaction existed in Paris, amongst the French Exhibitors at our forthcoming 'Worlds Exposition'. – I immediately consulted Lord Granville, the Chairman of the Executive Committee, and from the explanation I received from him I have reason to hope that everything will be adjusted to the satisfaction of our French friends. We are aware how much the success of the Exhibition & the consequent pleasure of the visitors from all quarters of the globe, will depend upon the beautiful contributions of yr countrymen; & therefore be assured that in the midst of the great Enterprise itself, every possible effort will be made to afford you as large and prominent a space in the building as is compatible with a sense of fairness to the other Exhibitors. If you will take the trouble to ascertain how large a portion of the space applicable to the whole world is devoted to the products of France, I think you will admit that we have not underrated your rank in the scale of civilized nations.– Lord Granville tells me that M. Salandrouse[1] left London for Paris yesterday, and that he will carry full & satisfactory explanations to your committee – I duly received your pamphlets & have sent a copy as you desired to Col. Thompson. It delights me to see you still persevering in the advocacy of Free trade principles, for since the ever lamented death of our dear friend Bastiat it is to you mainly that we look as the champion of commercial Freedom. Do not be alarmed at anything you may hear about reaction in England. We shall not go back one penny of duty upon corn, & you know English society well enough to be assured that whilst we can prevent the landed aristocracy from robbing us under the name of 'protection' we can easily keep the fingers of the smaller 'interests' out of the people's pockets. I shall trouble you with another letter in a day or two upon another subject meantime

Believe me faithfully Yours
R. Cobden

---

1   Salandrouse de Lamornaix

Michel Chevalier in Dionysus Lardner, *The Great Exhibition and London in 1851* (London: Longmans, Brown, Green, and Longmans, 1852), pp. 560–72.

No, this age is not servilely devoted to the worship of matter. The civilization of Europe has been accused of having fallen into the slough of materialism, and of sinking every day still deeper in it. This is an extreme injustice. Certainly there are, in our day, corrupted and avaricious individuals. Alas! all vices are common in all ages. It has come within the designs of Providence, as everything teaches us, that men should be incessantly warned of the fragility of their nature, by examples always afflicting, and sometimes hideous. If, at certain moments, materialism has appeared to spread itself over the social body like a furious leprosy, these moments have been short, and they also offered the striking spectacle of devotedness and virtue. If there was licentiousness in France under the Directory, is it to be thence inferred that there was no disinterestedness and heroism in our armies, that our magistracy was not pure, and that the people despaired of liberty? Because the Jewish people worshipped the golden calf during the few days that Moses passed on Mount Sinai, has it been ever said that idolatry was their worship after they quitted Egypt?

No, the age is not marked by materialism as by the seal of the beast. Taken in its *ensemble*, and observed in its most general and most salient characteristics, it is more spiritualist than any of the ages which have preceded it. I find the proof of this written in indelible characters on the greater number of the pages of contemporaneous history. And what then are the advantages in the pursuit of which civilisation has hurried on for the last sixty years? What is the device that it has inscribed on its standard? What are the words which have had the power of electrifying men's souls? Is it the paradise of Mahomet, the voluptuousness of Sybaris, or the luxury of Heliogabalus, that the generous minds in whose steps the human race has followed, have promised to men? Can it, in good faith, be maintained, that it is to satisfy coarse appetites, that France has, since 1789, shed her blood in torrents, and lavished her treasures, and that everywhere throughout Europe the people for the last sixty years have addressed to heaven their ardent prayers, and multiplied their efforts with untiring perseverance? I have listened in vain to the imposing clamour which proceeds from the bosom of nations; constantly the words which dominate over all the rest, and to which myriads on myriads of voices serve as the echo, are appeals to liberty, and claims for justice, under the name of equality; and what imports it, that, in the midst of this majestic choir, some individuals should murmur forth some sensual hopes? It is for justice and liberty that Europe agitates herself, and that the world is in labour. That the labour may be painful I dispute not; for pain is its necessary attendant. But justice and liberty, those sovereign benefits which more than ever excite the transports of men, these springs of joy and grandeur, at which civilisation wishes to quench its thirst at the price of a thousand evils and the hardest sacrifices, and which she is at length on the point of attaining – is all this, I ask, material substance? I beg to be told the specific weight, the colour, and the taste of it; and I call on the ultra-Christians, who erect themselves into a tribunal from which there is no appeal, and pronounce against the age these uncharitable judgments, to inform us whether it is not, on the contrary, the groundwork of Christianity, and the commencement and the end of that august religion.

No, the age is not materialist, although some of its children may be so. I see a striking demonstration of this in the very fact of this Universal Exhibition; which is, nevertheless, devoted to the glory of the arts, by which man acts on matter and appropriates it to his wants. The Universal Exhibition is nothing less than the bringing together of all the nations of the earth on one ground, where national hatreds may be effaced, without the genius peculiar to each being enervated.

The sentiment which was nobly expressed in the speech of Prince Albert, has been repeated in twenty other speeches to which the Universal Exhibition has given rise. It was more particularly found in that delivered by Lord Ashburton on the 20th May, 1851, when he presided at the banquet given to the Foreign Commissioners of the Exhibition at Richmond. This sentiment is thus constantly on the lips of English orators, because it is in the heart of the English nation, and because it is also felt by us and by all Europe. It is not, therefore, an ephemeral fruit, nor a phraseology invented for the occasion. It is an idea the germ of which is old, like the Christian religion; for that has always taught us that all men are brothers, being all children of the same God. But this germ has become a magnificent tree, the fruit of which has, in our day, arrived at maturity. The sentiment of the unity of the human race, on which Prince Albert and Lord Ashburton insisted, is the same which has been so often cried up under the name of the fraternity of nations. It is this which Beranger has sung under the name of the *Holy Alliance of Nations*. As we are now sufficiently removed from the events, so disastrous for us, of 1815, to render it possible for a Frenchman to be just towards all those who took part in them, without exciting a painful feeling of surprise around him, I may add that it is the same as the Emperor Alexander, under a form peculiar to his mind and position, pursued when he organised with ardour a Holy Alliance of Governments. Some years further back in our history, this same sentiment gave birth to the scene where Anarcharsis Clootz, *the orator of the human race*, pompously harangued the Convention at the head of a group of personages of every country. But the London Exhibition is advantageously distinguished from all the manifestations which have hitherto been made of this great and fruitful idea. The ceremony in which Clootz celebrated, in a declamatory tone, the fraternity of nations, looked like an insult to good sense, because we were then at war with the whole of Europe. After 1815, the Holy Alliance of Governments became almost immediately a league against all liberal ideas; and the Holy Alliance of Nations, extolled by the Tyrteus who consoled France for her reverses, tended to organise a campaign of people against sovereigns. The Exhibition came at its point and at its hour. Everything was at length ripe for the accord of all the civilised men in the world to reveal itself with *éclat*. Thirty-five years of prosperous and fruitful peace had effaced all distressing reminiscences, and there was at length discovered a neutral ground where the old quarrels which divided nations could not find a place – that of labour, where the domination over nature by the human mind, for the common welfare, common independence, and common dignity of mankind, was displayed.

I must here be allowed to make an observation on the character of our general policy. We are proud of being Frenchmen, and the world, in its days of equity, feels for our country an admiration blended with gratitude, because France had contracted the habit of taking fact and cause as the great principles of civilisation. She has considered and treated the affairs of the human race as her own. She has been the heart of the world, and her beatings made themselves felt from pole to pole; the events of 1848 loudly attest this fact. She has lavished the life and patrimony of her children to support the honour of her ideas. She has sometimes violated equity or abandoned herself to the inspirations of an arrogant policy; and it has even happened that she has outraged good faith. What would we not now give to be able to tear from our annals the overbearing conduct of Louis XIV. towards Holland, or the scenes at Bayonne between Napoleon and the Spanish princes? But, even in her outbursts and her errors, the foreign policy of France has almost constantly testified a great respect for humanity; and this policy has always distinguished itself by being sympathetic. It has been sometimes railed at, and styled sentimental and humanitarian. But I do not think that any policy can be great, if it is not in accordance with the general instincts of humanity; and I do not know of any nations or individuals who have ever effected anything great or durable, unless they had been animated and supported by a good and elevated sentiment. It happens that England has, for some time past, taken a very ample part in that noble initiative which appeared to belong to us, and which the assent of the human race recognises among our attributes.

The element which an egotistical and weak philosophy has called by a name, but which, however, I accept, – that of *humanitarian*, – has made for itself in British policy a place which one had not been accustomed to see there. Formerly England, as if to justify the expression of the classic poet, kept herself in her plans apart from the human race. She had an insular policy. For some time past this has been changed. Look at what she has done during the last twenty years. She wished to enfranchise the slaves, and she has accomplished it with that calm resolution which is the glory of the English character, and which gives to English policy so much consistency. The slave-holders were largely indemnified at the cost of twenty millions, and the emancipation was effected in her colonies; and it is a cause which has now gained ground in the world. Afterwards, taking in hand the cause of humanity in favour of the African negroes, she recognised and accepted the right of search, against which a spurious patriotism raised such an outcry with us; a right which was in no way humiliating for either of the two nations, since it was perfectly reciprocal. At a later period, when England concluded a treaty of peace with China, she therein stipulated that the Celestial Empire should renounce the state of isolation in which she had before placed herself; and she stipulated this, not for herself alone, but for every nation without distinction. If, at the same period, the French Government, placed under similar circumstances, had acted in the same manner, and had abstained from reserving to herself particular advantages for her national commerce, violent complaints would have been raised against her. She would have been attacked in the press, and it would have been repeated in the national tribune that she had sacrificed the interest of the country to foreigners; and, wretched as the charge would have been, the pretended patriotic accusation would have obtained credit with a great majority of the public.

The Universal Exhibition of London, or, to speak more correctly, the commercial system connected with it, has the same tendencies, but more strongly brought forward. Contrary to the spirit of Christian civilisation, the old commercial system amongst the English, as well as in the rest of Europe, was founded on the system of hostility of one nation to another. It was admitted in principle, that in commercial matters, the profit of the one constituted the loss of the other, as was said by Montaigne: a notion, however, which is materially false; for when two parties, freely contracting, exchange their merchandize, it is fair to suppose that each finds his advantage in so doing, and that, in fact, each finds in it the means of best satisfying his wants. When two nations freely exchange their productions, they enrich each other, for he is enriched which acquires the means of satisfying his wants. And by what combination of circumstance can a transaction favourable to both parties when it takes place within one state, and between two individuals belonging to that state, cease to have that character when it takes place between different nations? The old commercial system which England abjured in 1846, suggests to each nation this singular pretension, that she has sufficient for all her wants, but that she could furnish much merchandize to foreign countries; as if these terms were not contradictory. In fact it is nonsense, an impossibility, and an hallucination; for if the system is in vigour in France, if we proclaim it excellent, is it not recommending our neighbour to apply it also? When I exclude the merchandize of another nation, in boasting of thus having found the means of enriching myself, do I not induce him to exclude mine? Moreover, I cannot sell him mine without purchasing his. The rule is absolute.

Gold and silver themselves, when they enter *de facto*, and not merely nominally into transactions, make no infraction of it; for these two metals, whether coined or in ingots, are merchandize, like lead, or copper, or iron, or like any other productions of industry, and each nation only requires them in a certain proportion as compared with other merchandize.

Negotiators, however, endeavoured, by every means in their power, in the bargains which they made, to sell without purchasing. They were necessarily defeated by the force of circumstances, and it was very fortunate; for in order to succeed in this strange programme, it would have been necessary that those to whom the sales were made, should become bankrupts. I defy any one to point out any other means of arriving at the plan of selling without purchasing. And, nevertheless, I could quote administrative or parliamentary documents of the most recent date, in which some parties in France pride themselves on having solved this fine problem, of selling abroad and skilfully avoiding purchasing; and this absurdity finds admirers.

In 1846, the English Government, through the organ of Sir Robert Peel, repudiated this isolation, which was pretended to be crafty, but was in reality silly. He admitted that the purchaser is not the victim, or, as he is called in protectionist language, the *tributary* of him who sells, any more when the transaction takes place between an Englishman and a Frenchman, than when the two parties are of the same nation. He understood and proclaimed, that the interest of all nations, as well as of all individuals, was to come to an understanding and concert together for the purpose of satisfying their common wants, each furnishing that which he most excelled in, and stimulating each other by mutual competition; an idea eminently favourable to the majority for several reasons. It supposes the peace of the world, and it is the masses on whom falls the heavy load of war. From the very fact of its supposing peace, it prepares and will determine the suppression of the exclusive privileges with which certain classes have been formerly invested, in view of the necessities of war. War was formerly the ruling hypothesis in the policy of all governments. The new rights which have been called into being by the progress of civilisation, require peace. England, by the commercial policy which she has started, has replaced the hypothesis of war by that of peace. A nation who, not content with adopting for the first of its manufactures cotton – of which the raw material is derived from regions far beyond the seas – counts upon foreign corn for its sustenance, erects itself by that very fact into a defender of peace; it obliges her to wish for the concert of nations. It becomes a necessary partisan of fraternity of races, and of nations. It closely unites its cause to the maintenance of Christian principles. Is this, I ask, materialism? Does an age or a nation which gives such an example, and to which all other nations, whether willingly or unwillingly, prepare to conform their laws, live in the lowest depths of a sordid materialism?

In the internal policy of states, the idea, the development of which led to the Universal Exhibition, has introduced a progress not less beneficent, and the morality of which is not less striking. Under the feudal *régime*, nations were divided into small groups, who fortified themselves one against the other. The lords guarded themselves in their vultures' nests, with their men-at-arms. The commoners, the cradle of the *tiers état*, surrounded themselves with walls and towers. The corporations of arts and trades had around them, as a protecting barrier, the monopoly which was recognised by the law, and they maintained the prerogative of it at great expense before the parliaments. Times sadly whimsical; a tissue of contradictions which would be inexplicable, if we did not see in it a necessary transition between the *régime* founded on the absolute subjection of the great number, and the era of liberty.

Finding the world around it divided into small brutal sovereignties, into a thousand exclusive privileges, and into jealous jurisdictions, the genius of liberty was then compelled to place herself under the auspices of privilege and of monopoly, and the *tiers état* organized itself in consequence. Hence a multitude of abuses and of inequalities which in our time could not be justified, and the greater part of which the current of civilisation has already swept away, and shaken the rest. All that was condemned and virtually abolished on the day when the eminently salutary principle of common right – a principle of the highest morality, for it was equity itself – was inaugurated. The idea of common right has become the foundation of the public law of civilised states at home. No one can withdraw himself from it. All that is opposed to it is destined shortly to perish, and it is for that reason that the protectionist *régime* cannot much longer exist with civilised nations. It is in vain that it assumes a threatening attitude, its airs are more worthy of pity than of anger.

Common right cannot, in fact, accommodate itself to the privileges which display themselves under the standard of protection. When once the principle of common right had entered into our habits, it was inevitable that we should ask ourselves whether it were lawful for the State to interfere between certain classes of producers and the public consumer, in order to compel the latter to pay to the former, for their merchandize, more than it was worth in the general market? The question, in fact, was raised from the moment when the principle of common right, or, what amounts to the same thing, equality before the law, was proclaimed. The men of 1789 were strongly opposed to the protective *régime*, and in favour of free trade. What fine remarks were those written by Turgot, who was their friend and master, in order to advocate the cause of commercial freedom against those private interests which pretended that they were the personification of national labour! The proceedings of the interested parties, and the national prejudices, raised to the highest pitch by the inveterate wars of the French revolution, had, for a time, made the balance lean on the side of the protectionists; but, in 1838, the discussion was resumed with vigour in England, and it was done in a manner which well justified the proverb – 'A question well put, is more than half solved.' Is it just, exclaimed some generous-minded men, that the public should pay dues to others besides the State, to others who, in the eyes of the law, were nothing, and did nothing, more than the rest of their fellow citizens? A momentary assistance to necessitous men, a temporary subsidy to men who tried their strength, was a social expediency; but a permanent tax, and an indefinite tribute to men who pretended that they dispensed without paying a tribute to the foreigner, is incompatible with modern civilisation. It is necessary that this should disappear, and take its place in the dust of the tombs with the other institutions of the past, which might formerly have been indispensable, but which, in our days, are repugnant to equity and good sense.

No sophistry or paradox can overthrow this argument. It is a glory for England, it is a proof of the reason of that nation, and of the strength which the sentiment of equity has there acquired, that she was the first in which, before that claim (which was, it must be allowed, supported with much vigour and considerable talent), all opposition, all the coalitions of private interests, and all the intrigues of parties were compelled to give way. The interest of the aristocracy itself, all powerful as it was, was obliged to bend and submit itself. This triumph of the principle of common right realised itself with a mass of attendant circumstances, which showed what progress public opinion had made, and how much it had released itself from the hateful prejudices with which patriotism had formerly nourished itself. The word foreigner was synonymous with that of enemy. The neighbouring nations were hated, not only in their armies and in their persons, but even in their manufacturing products. In the heat of their real or pretended passions, political men, who hunted after popularity, included in their maledictions all that the foreigner might manufacture or derive from his soil. The idea of a foreigner reaping any profit by his relations with one of their countrymen, made them start with horror. It was of little consequence to them that their countrymen also had their share of profit; the foreigner derived an advantage, and that, in their eyes, was enough to make them condemn it. The English; when they returned to free trade, have placed themselves above this disastrous error. Their statesmen have not sought to measure what the foreign nation would gain by England purchasing its productions, they did not wish to look at that; they saw that the consumers, that is to say, the mass of the people, would derive an advantage, and from that moment their decision was taken. They proclaimed the principle of free trade, and they have applied it without demanding reciprocity from any one. Before 1846, when the protective system was accredited in the councils of their government, they had opened negotiations in which they offered to lighten the conditions of admission for some foreign productions, provided an equivalent advantage were granted to English articles. On this occasion nothing of the kind has taken place; no negotiations have been entered into on the subject. The foreigner was left to his free will. If, they said to themselves, he will not enjoy the benefits of liberty, let him commit the fault; let him continue to exclude the merchandize of other countries; let him in this manner impoverish his people, and lessen their welfare, if such be his good pleasure. Let us respect his liberty, even in his aberrations; but we will not make our intelligence subservient to that of our neighbour.

England has reaped the harvest which she sowed. She has passed through the last period of revolutions without receiving any shock. The Continent has been shaken to its very foundations, England has been exempt from the slightest shock. She offers to other nations a model worthy of imitation, and, confident in their good sense, they do not deign to perceive that rhetoricians, like the serpent in the fable, which exhausted itself by biting at a file, use their eloquence in vain efforts to turn that majestic reform into ridicule in the eyes of their fellow citizens.

From the character and the direction which she has given to her foreign and domestic policy for a certain number of years past, England has taken a high rank in the mind of the friends of humanity, and of the partisans of exalted principles. She does not draw up preambles of constitutions, in which she boasts of serving as an example to all other nations, she does better; she takes the part of *coryphée*, which she finds vacant, and leaves us in the rear with our boastings. It gives me a bitter pang to see my country thus thrown into the second rank; but I hope that, once more restored to good sense, she will not delay to dismiss the flatterers who abuse her, and will bring herself rapidly to a level with her old competitor. In ideas and general sentiments, France is well advanced; it will not be difficult for her, if she wishes, to overtake any nation whatever; for it is the advancement of sentiments and of ideas, that it is to say, moral progress, which determines progress of every kind, and in the practice of industrial arts she has proved, at the Universal Exhibition, that she fears no comparison with any one.

Speech of M. Thiers on the Commercial Policy of France and in Opposition to the Introduction of Free Trade into France, 27 June 1851, trans. M. de Saint Felix (London: Ollivier, 1852), pp. 3–14, 15–19, 47–59, 67–8.

Gentlemen,

Although I by no means agree with the opinion which M. Sainte-Beuve has just expressed at this tribune, I wish, in the outset, to thank him for having raised so important and extensive a question – a question which, I do not hesitate to say is agitating the whole world, and one which ought to have as much interest for France as any that can be discussed in the present day.

I, for one, have heard the honourable M. Sainte-Beuve with the greatest attention. I beg that the kind patience of the assembly may also be accorded to me; for the investigation of this question must be useless unless complete; to be distinctly understood, it must be thoroughly fathomed; if such be not our course, it would be better to leave the subject entirely untouched.

I hope, Gentlemen, that you will favour me with the attention necessary for going into those details without which the question would remain vague and obscure to your minds. I will endeavour to be brief; but it is impossible that a question which affects the interests of the whole country, and, after the examples which have been adduced as authorities, I fear not to say, the interests of the whole civilized world, it is impossible that a question of such magnitude should not require much time for bringing it to a serious decision.

For my part, (and I have for thirty years, been engaged in the public business of my country) I have never varied on this question. Experience, practice in business, the most scrupulous observation of facts, have convinced me that the prosperity of France is bound up with the industrial and commercial system which she has constantly followed.

M. Sainte-Beuve, whose studious mind and independent character I honour, has, if he will allow me to say so, very roughly handled the opinion opposed to his own. Towards him individually, I shall show all that respect which he deserves, but shall, in my turn, roughly handle the opinion which he upholds. (a laugh.) He has said that our opinion checks the prosperity of the country; but I will soon prove to you that his would shiver that prosperity, like a glass. Three years ago, you saw a government fall in a few hours; if any of the new doctrines should ever attain the ascendancy, you will see the fortune of the country fall in an instant. (marks of approbation.) Of this fact I have a profound conviction which nothing has been able to alter, and which the great spectacle I have recently witnessed in London, has only strengthened and deepened.

I shall begin with a statistical fact, one only, to set against that with which M. Sainte-Beuve concluded. He has told you, and I am sure you ought to have been moved by the statement, for I should myself have been moved had I not been prepared with the answer, – he has said 'You are languishing, whilst in England, from 1830 to 1850, the exports have increased from £38,000,000, to £70,000,000, that is have nearly doubled. You have no doubt been struck with the graveness of this result, and justly so: but take care you do not attribute to other than the true causes, this remarkable developement [*sic*]evidently owing to the peace, the tranquillity, and the calm, which England has enjoyed. France also, from 1830, to 1848, enjoyed a profound repose, and I will show you the effect. I accept the proposal of passing judgement on the two systems according to the amount of the increases which have attended them. England, you say, has advanced from £38,000,000, to £70,000,000; then it has not doubled. And what has France done? In 1830, the exports were 452 Million fr., in 1849 they were One Milliard, 32 Million fr. France then has more than doubled. These figures are taken from the official returns. Whilst England, in the same period of 18 years, has not doubled, we have more than doubled. Our system is not then so very bad. If the systems are to be judged by this standard, you are condemned.

Let us now go into the question in detail: and, in the first place we will look at this great experiment, in speaking of which, permit me to say, too much stress is constantly laid on the statements collected by writers, who may be endowed with some degree of talent, but whose authority I dispute as correct observers of facts.

You advise us to imitate England's great experiment. I will soon prove to you that such an experiment could not be made in France; not from any inferiority on our part, but by reason of a situation which cannot be appreciated without a close acquaintance. And even were the circumstances the same, it would be better to wait, till time shall have decided the question in regard to England, before urging us to follow her example.

I do not hesitate to say that, in certain points, in which her superiority was indisputable, England has not altogether adopted Free Trade, and wherever she was not superior, the experiment has been ruinous. The enlightened men of the age, question not the genius of Sir Robert Peel, nor the great services which this illustrious man has rendered to England, but the prudence with which he has acted. I should be very ungrateful were I to speak of Sir R. Peel with any want of respect; for, in the senate of England he referred to me in terms of which I will only say that I wish I had deserved them. (A murmur of applause.) I shall not then speak of Sir R. Peel without the profoundest respect, but I have not met with an intelligent and enlightened man in England, who has not acknowledged, that, great as Sir R. Peel was, he was rather too fast, and exposed his country to a rough trial, by the boldness with which he altered her commercial system.

Permit me, without immediately entering into a minute examination of the experiment that is being made in England, and of which so much is said amongst us, to point out in a few words those parts of her policy, which can be imitated (disastrously in my opinion) but still which *can* be imitated, because circumstances permit, and those parts which cannot be even tried in France, because circumstances absolutely preclude the idea.

In one word, this is the experiment which England has made. There are in England very few direct taxes, and a large number of taxes on consumption, as well of those collected by the Custom House on the imports, as of those collected on home produce by the Excise. I will show you, by statistics, the difference in the importance of the two budgets.

In England, the Customs, as M. Sainte-Beuve has told you, bring in 550 million francs (I use french money to make myself better understood.) The Excise, brings in 350, making a total of 900 million francs raised from articles of consumption. So much for indirect taxation. The amount raised by direct taxes is only 100 million francs.

M. Sainte-Beuve. – And the local taxes?

M. Thiers. – What are called the assessed taxes, (answering to our direct taxes) including taxes on land, windows, and some articles of luxury, realize about a hundred millions. As I have just said, the taxes which fall upon articles of consumption amount to 900 millions. – 100 millions to 900 millions! The stamp duty, the post office, and other sources of revenue raise the amount to 1200 or 1300 millions.

In France, on the other hand the direct taxes show 450 millions; the indirect taxes, *i.e.* the customs and excise, give not quite 450 millions. Stamps, forests, and the post office, raise the French revenue to 1200 or 1300 millions, like the English.

This shows in the most striking light, the difference between the two countries, and between their systems of taxation. In England, 100 millions of direct taxes, against 900 millions of customs and excise; in France, 450 millions against 450. In England, nearly all the taxes fall on articles of consumption, either foreign or domestic.

In time of war, what did they do? They were obliged to press heavily on articles of consumption. When peace returned, what taxes did they find it necessary to remit? Those on articles of consumption. And do you know what they taxed in England? Not only such kinds of foreign raw produce as England produced, which ought to have been taxed for the purpose of protection, but also such kinds of raw produce as England did not produce; timber for example, for England has no wood, or none of any account. They even taxed raw silk, an article not produced in England at all. They have taxed gypsum; and in the interior, English coal, carried from port to port coastwise, or shipped to Ireland. They taxed bricks, glass, leather for shoes, candles, calico manufactured in England, and used by the people for clothing. They taxed paper: – and when peace permitted the system to be modified, what did they do? What France did, under different circumstances, when she suppressed the lottery, and lightened the land-tax and wine duty.

This was the first part of the experiment originated by Mr. Huskisson, and continued by Lord Grey and Sir R. Peel himself.

In suppressing these duties, one after another, they brought upon themselves a considerable deficit. They were right in not allowing themselves to be stopped by an inconvenience of this kind; for the abolition of these taxes which they had begun to repeal was desirable. They substituted a direct tax – the *income tax*. But is it for us to imitate England in this respect? On the contrary, it is she who has here imitated us, and is still far behind us. In France both in all the assemblies since 1789, and in the council of state whose duty it is to watch over the system of taxation, we have never permitted any article of consumption, except those which have been long regarded in every country as proper objects of taxation, such as wine, tobacco, salt; we have never permitted clothing, building materials, glass, calico, leather, articles which serve to cloth and nourish man, to be subjected to any tax. The council of state has taken care, ever since 1789, that no such taxes should be established in the country; and the assemblies have never admitted them, except on the ground of taxing foreign for the benefit of native produce, as in the case of iron and coal. But never since 1789, has that system of taxation been adopted, which imposes burdens, not on such foreign articles as we produce at home, but on national articles of the first importance. And do you know what has for a long time been the policy of England? what we did abruptly, – violently, – in one day, by the revolution of 1789, England, thanks to her magnificent system of liberty, is doing gradually – successively – peacefully, as all progress ought to be made. She is replacing most of the taxes on articles of consumption, by direct taxation; and by what tax? The *income-tax* universally repudiated on the other side of the channel, because, instead of being like our income-tax, which comprises land-tax, furniture-tax, window-tax, and licences for trade, but without partiality in the distribution, the English income-tax is the representative of all these imposts, coupled with an odious partiality which renders it insupportable in England.

(Many voices. Very good, very good!)

M. Thiers (continuing) – England having supplied the place of all these imposts, whose successive abolition had caused a deficit of 50 or 60 million francs at the accession of Sir R. Peel, (which was afterwards increased by the new reductions which he made) taking into the account the 140 millions of income-tax, has to show 240 millions of direct taxes against 900 millions, whilst we have 450 against 450.

This first part then of the experiment which is proposed as our model, the part most indisputably good, and not called in question by any one in England, consisting in the substitution of direct taxation for taxes on articles of consumption, is, I repeat, already carried out in France. As to the second part – free-trade, that indeed is not an imitation of France, and I hope that France will never seek to imitate it. We are not in the way to free-trade; and I hope, I say it again – that France will never adopt it.

I shall not enter upon our industry as a whole, though that might be very instructive; I shall take some of its principal branches, examine them, and show you their condition. We shall then be in a situation to determine whether an experiment could be made upon them with any prudence and good sense. This order is the reverse of that of M. Sainte-Beuve. He has begun with theory, and finished with facts; I shall begin with facts, and finish with theory.

Let us then begin with facts.

Every thing is protected in France, even M. Sainte-Beuve admits that, but he says all is not equally protected. M. Sainte-Beuve, though still very young, has diligently applied himself to the study of political economy. Unfortunately for me, I have devoted myself to it much longer. If he had as often sought the means of ascertaining *les prix de revient*, that is to say, *clear profits* as I have, he would have found out that it is the most difficult thing in the world, and he would also have learnt that it is extremely difficult to determine whether one branch of industry is more protected than another. So far however as it is possible to form an exact estimate on these matters, I shall prove to you, gentlemen, that agriculture is one of those branches which have the most liberal protection, and, moreover, that it is the branch which most needs it.

In France we protect corn, cattle, pasture, wood, oleaginous plants, and all kinds of industrial cultivation, as well as all branches of manufacturing industry, coal, iron, cotton, woollen cloths, and even silk.

A voice from the left. – And wine!

M. Thiers. – Wine itself. (Whispering on the left and laughter.) I know that the wines are very independent, and disdain protection. I allow that those of Bordeaux do not need it; but, though I am a great admirer of the grandeur and superiority of my country, I should not wish to bring our wines of the South into competition with those of Italy and Spain.

Now let us take each branch of industry in turn.

CORN.

M. Sainte-Beuve says, 'Corn is not protected in comparison with other national products, there is a sliding scale for corn, whilst there is none for iron.'

I do not wish, gentlemen, to weary you with details, (cries of 'go on') but I must explain to you the action of the sliding scale. The object of its establishment was, to secure to every producing country a price, which, judging from previous experience, would be remunerative. Thus, in the South of France, it was thought that, to secure remuneration, a price of 24 francs per *hectolitre* of wheat, was necessary; and yet all existing leases in that part of the country were based on an average price of 20 francs; whilst in the North 18 francs per hectolitre was sufficient. Well the new tariff for wheat was made on the supposition that a price of 24 francs was necessary. When the price drops one franc, the duty rises two francs, &c. To illustrate this mode of calculation; – In the district to which Marseilles belongs, the price of wheat has fallen to 14 fr. 88 cent. or 15 fr. The fall has been from 24 to 15 fr. that is to say, has been 9 fr.; the duty, being double the depreciation, is 18 fr. per hectolitre. I have here some tables, taken from the books of the houses which trade in wheat, showing that the best Odessa wheat can be imported to Marseilles at 13 fr. Here then is a branch of industry which has a protective duty of 18 fr. on the value of 13 fr., that is, nearly 150 per cent. I am speaking from the tariffs themselves.

M. Sainte-Beuve tells me, 'iron has no sliding scale, and profits when they become high, are not stopped. With corn, on the contrary, if the price rises, the profits that would result are prevented, by the sliding scale dropping, and admitting foreign *corn*. You are shocked at this; but we must remember that the sustenance of the people is concerned, and, however much we may wish to protect grain, we nevertheless do not wish to enable the producers, after two, three, or four bad harvests, to maintain a famine price.

'But' you may say 'you allow iron to bear a famine price.' I will answer you. When you have a bad harvest, then a second, and a third, can you, in an instant, double or treble the produce of wheat, to make up for the quantity that is deficient? No; the cultivation of wheat extends very slowly. With iron, the case is far different. When railways sprang up, so suddenly and extensively, an increase of supply took place, which astonished the world, and, which could not, at first, be believed. There were 38 large furnaces in 1844; – I was a member of the commission of customs in 1847, and, as the result of six months care and close attention, we found that whilst there were thirty-eight large furnaces in 1844, sixty-one more were made in two years, and the supply had increased to such a degree, that, from home competition alone, the price became nearly as low as in England.

This, then, is the principle on which your tariffs are framed. In the case of manufactured articles, if there is a year of dearness, home competition brings the corrective in the following year. But with cereal crops it is not so: when there have been two, three, or four bad years in succession, (and ancient experience testifies that such years generally come together,) you have famine prices. This I repeat is the reason why a sliding scale has been preferred to a fixed duty, in all countries where it has been found necessary to protect agriculture.

Thus, in fact, corn is protected in France by a duty which, at the present time amounts to about 150 per cent.

M. Sainte-Beuve, who is very original in his ideas, adds, 'wheat has no protection, and wants none. If you abolish your tariffs, you will introduce foreign corn into France – the Odessa wheat; and that will make no difference.' I first ask him, how people could obtain bread so cheap by the introduction of Odessa wheat, if this introduction did not lower the price of wheat. What! when you want to have the measure adopted, you speak of the interest of the people; when you afterwards want to reassure the producers, as to the effect of the measure, you say, 'it will make no difference.' But let us know what you mean, either it will *make no* difference, or it *will make a* difference. I shall show you that it will make a great difference.

You are not the only person who has made this statement; you did not invent the argument; the English reformers also said that it would make no difference.

M. Sainte-Beuve. – I did not say so.

M. Thiers. – Indeed you did say so; and you reasoned in this way, – that in England, though the price of wheat was higher than in France, the Odessa wheat was not imported; and you concluded that it would not be imported into France. You then maintained, – I appeal to the memory of all present (yes yes) that the measure would produce no sensible result.

I have not here the documents necessary for making quotations – I should besides be afraid of protracting the discussion too far, – but I will prove to you that the same thing was said by the Free-trade party in England. When they wanted to draw to themselves the landlords – the farmers – all the prudent men, who were apprehensive as to consequences, they said, 'it will make no difference.'

You have spoken of the price of wheat. A week ago I was in London, and, after a rather difficult enquiry, in the course of which I was brought into contact with official and highly enlightened persons, I am able to state correctly the price of corn in England. As in France, it was said 18 fr. in the North, and 20 fr. in the South, were necessary to yield a sufficient remuneration to the producer, always with the condition that wheat will often be higher. This is the calculation on which the leases were based, and it is not disputed by any one, either Free-trader or Protectionist. A month or two ago, the price was 38, 39, and 40 shillings. Every one acknowledges that agriculture has lost more than 30 per cent. Thus if we think that the introduction of foreign corn will make no difference, we deceive ourselves; here is the first proof to the contrary. At the present time, Odessa wheats are selling in England, at 34 or 36 shillings, but the average of wheat a few weeks ago was 38, 39, and 40 shillings. Just now in consequence of a reaction which is taking place in grain throughout Europe it bids fair to increase. All leases were based on a price of 56 shillings! You say that the abolition of a protective duty would make no difference. I repeat it here is one proof which confounds you; since, in England, a third part of the value of grain has already disappeared. M. Sainte-Beuve has often spoken of unanswerable arguments. There are no such things as incontrovertible reasonings, but there are incontrovertible facts; and I affirm that this is one, for it is disputed by no one. Fifty-six shillings was the price acknowledged as necessary in England, corresponding to 24 fr. per hectolitre, and the price has fallen to 38 or 40 shillings, *i. e.* to 16 or 17 fr. per hectolitre.

In England, Gentlemen, the question in which we are engaged has taken a form which has greatly facilitated the solution; it is the aristocratic party against the democratic. In England, the land is exclusively the property of great landowners, and is entirely cultivated by the farmers, an opulent class of persons, who join in field-sports with their landlords, keep horses, and constitute a veritable middle class. In England, the question has taken the form of aristocracy on *the* one side, and democracy on the other; for on the one side were all the popular classes, and on the other the landowners and farmers. But you know the state of things in France. If you ruin the cultivators, is it the rich whom you ruin? I have here a list of direct taxes; and I will read you the number of quota of each value, premising that the same individual often has several quota. There are 5,441,000 quota of the value of 5 fr.; 1,818,000 from 5 to 10 fr.; 1,614,000 from 10 to 20 fr.; 791,000 from 20 to 30 fr.

You see then, (and you knew it before, from the simple observation of facts) that the peasant is a landowner in France – the people are landowners; and this is one of the best features of our civilization. (Very good, very good.) You see it is not as an aristocrat that I am speaking. The land is not the property of a particular class, but of all classes; and when you ruin the land, you ruin all classes. [...]

Oh! they say, we must go to the cheapest market! This is the great argument of the economists, these literary gentlemen of a new kind, inventors (begging their pardon) of the least amusing of all literature. They will have the opportunity of taking their revenge to morrow, and they will not fail of taking it; but let them permit me to say, they have created, not a science, but a literature, and a very dry literature. (General and sustained laughter.) Not that cotton, corn, sugar, iron, coal, are dry subjects; they are the elements of the greatness of nations. But it is only when spoken of from exact observation of facts, that these subjects become interesting. When, on the contrary, they are only made matter of speechifying and pamphleteering, they become the subjects of the vainest, the most puerile, and sometimes the most disastrous of literatures. (Loud applause from many benches.)

M. Sainte-Beuve. – I demand audience.

M. Thiers. – For goodness sake, we old prejudiced protectionists, who are always treated as narrow and weak-minded, speak but very seldom; those gentlemen are incessantly writing: we shall surely be allowed to say, for once, what we think of so many discoveries of genius, destined to produce so much prosperity. If they complain, they will at least allow that our reprisals have been very tardy.

These gentlemen, then, pretend that wheat must be bought in the cheapest market. It must be bought then at Odessa, Naples, and Seville, and I have told you in what a situation the wheats of our country would in this case be found.

The sensible men who honour Sir Robert Peel, honour him as the chief of a great aristocracy, who has said to that aristocracy, and to royalty, 'we must make some sacrifices;' and, in England, the aristocracy sustains itself only by means of the concessions to which it, with great tact, consents. Yes, it is necessary to know when to yield; and I honour in the persons of Mr. Huskisson, Sir R. Peel, and the Duke of Wellington, an aristocracy which has shown that it knows how to make sacrifices. But is it so in France? Have we an aristocracy from whom we could demand sacrifices? But this is plainly not the question under debate. I do not hesitate, notwithstanding the glorious and just fame of Sir Robert Peel, to say that there was in the measure to which he has attached his name, a temerity which in some respect must be considered as an imprudence.

England at this time is obliged to take from abroad one-third part of her consumption of wheat, viz. – 30 millions of hectolitres. These supplies being conveyed by vessels of 200 to 300 tons, require from 8 to 10,000 vessels. It is true that the same vessels make the voyage several times, which reduces the number to 2 or 3,000 vessels plying constantly on the seas. England has said, 'I am the mistress of the seas.' It is true that if we look into the history of the present century we find that whilst victory, for a time at least, accompanied us constantly on the continent, at sea on the contrary, in spite of the heroism of our men, every thing was misfortune. I know that in her last struggle with us England conquered; but it is also known of what formidable navigators Napoleon foresaw the future destiny when abandoning Louisiana to the United States, he said to M. Marbois: 'I may perhaps be conquered, but I prepare my revenge.' (Very good, very good.)

Those formidable navigators whose maritime genius I will show you, and of whom the English talk more than M. Sainte-Beuve appears to think, (without speaking of us, who after all have remained something in the maritime world,) can change the face of things. Then let me ask what will become of that country which will be obliged to have 2 or 3,000 vessels always under sail to bring to her, her food.

I know well what will happen; at the present time in England they are turning much land into pasture, they will hasten to grow corn again on this land, but at what price! they provide bread for the English people at present at a very low price, I do not deny it; but suppose a war: although England should remain mistress of the field of battle, the charge for insurance alone will raise the price of bread in time of war, just as it raises the price of sugar. Then that nation will see in a few days bread doubled and perhaps trebled in price; whatever they may say, this is a future which no prudent nation ought to defy. (New marks of assent.) Now, whilst England remains the mistress of the seas as she likes to style herself, that noble and generous nation which does not blame us for speaking of Austerlitz and of Iena, speaks also of Trafalgar, nothing is more natural; it is a noble feeling for a nation to glorify herself; although vanity in an individual is ridiculous, vanity in a nation is a noble sentiment which produces noble deeds. (Very good, very good.)

Let England call herself the mistress of the seas, she is at liberty to do so, she is right, for she is the mistress of the seas as we were for a brief period of the continent. What if calling herself the mistress of the seas she says to the world with overweening confidence, I do not fear you, I throw open my ports, I am making this great experiment of consenting to feed myself with wheat coming from the banks of the Volga and the Mississippi; let her act and speak thus, it is an act of noble pride which may perhaps be punished by the result as daring projects sometimes are.

But we who have been for a moment the masters of the continent, but unfortunately not of the seas, if under the pretext of yielding to certain self-styled liberal ideas we were to expose ourselves to see the third part of our consumption depend upon the sea, we should be but children or fools. (Very good, very good.) So much for corn.

If my strength and the patience of the Assembly permitted I would treat our other branches of industry with equal detail. (Go on, go on.) But I am obliged to hasten a little for there could be a book made on this subject, and one cannot make a book at the tribune.

I will proceed then to examine the different products of agriculture, cattle for example; which is protected in France by direct and if I may be allowed to say so, by an indirect taxation. It is protected by a direct duty charged on its entrance upon each head of cattle: it is 50 fr. for bullocks, and 5 fr. for sheep, it is also protected by a duty on foreign wool.

You know that wool is one of the principal products of cattle. It is true that statistics are still uncertain things, but however they have made in France, very great and honourable progress. People agree generally to estimate French agricultural and manufacturing products at 12 milliards, it is the amount I affixed myself in the discussion on paper money; however I have an intimate conviction that it is more than 12 milliards, that it is probably 13 or 14 milliards.

But what remains true of statistics is the relative value of the productions among themselves. If cereal crops in a production of 12 milliards, representing nearly 3 milliards, 3 or 400 millions, cattle represent either by the product of slaughtered meat and milk, or by that of hides and of wool, about 1 milliard, 400 millions; pasture 600 millions. Thus cattle includes a production of nearly 2 milliards which is protected by the duty of 50, and 5 fr. on cattle, and by the duty of 22 per cent upon wool.

M. Sainte-Beuve has told us, Free-trade in England has been extended to cattle without any injury to the country. It is true, but what is the reason? It is that the cattle of England is of a quality superior to the cattle of the whole of Europe, and because England is an island and that the countries which could bring cattle in good condition into England are separated from her by the whole breadth of France. Those countries are Wurtemberg, Switzerland, and Piedmont. To transport live beasts by sea is extremely difficult, and they have not yet succeeded in overcoming the difficulty of making these transports with advantage.

The experiment of England then proves nothing. [...]

Let us speak then of that English experiment which they say has succeeded so well and done such great wonders. Well, this is what the English have done. They were the strongest in certain industries, and for those industries they defied foreign competition, and here you will see the great difference between English and French industry, a kind of comparison very useful and very instructive which can be made, especially so in the Crystal Palace, where are exhibited the works of all nations.

We were the first inventors of exhibitions. The English, who often profit largely by our inventions, as it is permitted to profit by the inventions of others, for there is nothing more beautiful than the struggle between these two great nations, now that it is peaceful and loyal and accompanied by mutual good feelings; the English I say, have profitted [sic] by that idea and have largely developed it, making an appeal to all nations to send them their productions.

Well, let us see what people are learning in the Crystal Palace, from those two great countries, I will even say from those four great countries which are engaged in an industrial struggle, for the Russians and the Americans each already a Hercules in infancy, who have taken their first steps with giant strides, deserve to enter into that comparison. Let us see the characteristics of industry of these different people and their peculiar ways.

Do you know what is the real distinctive character of English industry? It lies particularly in this, that it manufactures certain products with an indisputable superiority and with a cheapness that no one can equal: they extract coal, manufacture iron, cotton, and even woollen cloth so well and so cheap that they fear nobody; they manufacture so cheap because they do it in large quantities; but the consequence of such a state of things was that their national market, although very large, was not sufficient for the sale of their products.

Then they said: what can we do better? it is to try to solicit other nations by our example, to receive those special productions which we manufacture so well, so largely and so cheap. For that we must make some sacrifices; our neighbours are very clever in industries of luxury; let us give up to them some of these industries, and then the English gave up to us silk goods, printed calicoes and gloves. After having done this the manufacturers of printed calicoes, especially Mr. Cobden, a very distinguished man certainly, a great man, that will come. (They laugh.) Mr. Cobden a man of indisputable merit, said: but in order to procure a sale for those special productions which you manufacture so well and so extensively, you must sacrifice the manufacturers of products of luxury, of whom I am one, (for he was a manufacturer of printed calicoes;) you will have to sacrifice the printed calicoes, the articles of silk and many other products, well; but then liberty for every one! and from that instant, owing to a natural sense of justice, they who held the reins of government, the nobility of the country, have been obliged to proclaim free-trade in corn. They were obliged to *finish* by that. However after that great effort, Sir Robert Peel was removed from office and was replaced by the Whigs. It has been asked how the Navigation Act came to be abolished? I assure you there was much astonishment felt at seeing come out of the portfolio of free-trade the abolition of the Navigation Act. The Whigs who succeeded to Sir Robert Peel and who wanted to prove that they were desirous of continuing the system of free-trade, sought for something to reform in their turn. They found the famous Navigation Act of Cromwell, which was still in existence, they destroyed it, and before long you will see the consequences.

Here then you see the succession of ideas and facts in England! they say: there are products which we manufacture admirably and for which we have nothing to fear; these are iron, coal, and cotton. Well, we are about to deliver up some of our manufactured products as silk and printed calicoes to induce other nations to accept our best products; and that being done they were led by a concatenation of events to grant free-trade for agriculture, and then even the abolition of the Navigation Act, in order that all interests might pay their tribute to the same system. What has been the result? It has been judged very differently and even at the present time it is not known what will be the final decision to the British nation.

Well, I do not come here to foretell the future, which in our age arrives so quick, I will not say before-hand that such a thing will happen and such another will not; I should expose myself to a false reckoning; I will not compromise myself by prophecies or show in this tribune an unbecoming temerity; I have never committed any, either in the tribune or elsewhere that I am aware of. But in short, what has been the result? upon iron, cotton and coal it has been nothing. How could it be otherwise? Nobody can manufacture iron, cotton, and extract coal at such a cheap price as the English. This is not an argument which proves much for Free-trade. As to silk articles, printed calicoes and gloves, there has been a sensible result. Thus for silk articles there has been a great suffering. But in this industry as in those exposed to a foreign competition, the inferior product was guaranteed either by cheapness or by tariffs! and this is the secret of the English experiment. They have preserved the duty sufficiently protective of 15 per cent. on inferior articles of silk: they have preserved one of 10 per cent. upon some works in cotton; and as to the former duty they added to it a power for the Custom House officers to adopt a peculiar mode of weighing, which sometimes raises the duty to more than 20 per cent. It is thus that even with Free-trade the English have protected with a duty being sometimes up to 20 per cent. the inferior products which are the most considerable.

Thanks to that combination, the inferior products which are always the most important owing to their quantity have been saved, and there has been suffering only for the products of luxury; but these even with a duty of 30 per cent. would not on that account have run less risk. Here is the reason: the English are too rich to be stopped by an increase of duty, and as our silk articles are the finest, they would have been bought even with a duty of 30 per cent.

After all, the experiment for articles of silk being confined within these limits could not give a great result; but there is something else now preparing. The English are very uneasy at the present moment about the plain silks which are manufactured at Elberfeld and Zurich, and it may happen (I do not affirm that it will,) that they may be obliged one day to raise the tariff on plain silks.

For printed calicoes which for the most part are very cheap, what has happened? There again the inferior productions are still sufficiently protected by a duty of 10 per cent.[1] The superior products alone are unprotected. We manufacture at Mulhousen, owing to that French taste of which I shall speak presently, admirable products which would be bought at any price, unless there should be an absolute prohibition; then under any circumstances the fine products would have suffered, but very little as shown by the experiment.

Thus for instance, England which consumes from one milliard to one milliard 200 millions of cotton, receives scarcely 20 millions of our calicoes printed in Mulhousen, but they are the finest, and the most beautiful and the most esteemed by people of fashion. Then she has only exposed the head whilst the rest of the body has remained protected; but with us it would not have been so if we had tried the same experiment.

Here then the reform was but of little importance, and the English purchased at a trifling sacrifice the chance of seeing other nations imitate them for coal, iron and cotton. This is all the secret of the experiment, (Very good, very good.)

A Voice. – Perfidious Albion!

[1] I have committed here an error of not much importance I believe, in my argument, but of which advantage has been taken against me. The English tariff mentions a duty of 10 per cent. upon some works of cotton. This tariff is not applicable to printed calico, I am aware; but my argument is not on that account less conclusive and just.

Those products of considerable importance in which the English exposed themselves to competition, were either covered by the cheap price or by a tariff which protected the bulk of their production. They were protected by cheapness for the tissues of cotton and by a tariff of 15 per cent. at least for the articles of silk. The printed calicoes of Mulhousen, owing to the taste which distinguished them, the figured manufactured silks of Lyons, owing to their rare beauty, would have been imported into England, whatever might have been the tariff. As I have said before, they exposed only the head of each industry, the rest being protected; they got in exchange of a light sacrifice, the chance of holding in the world a prevailing commercial liberty which might insure the sale of the overplus of their immense products.

M. Thiers. – Give me leave to say the English were not guilty of any perfidy, it would be ridiculous to call it perfidy. No, they well calculated their tariffs and they saw how far they could accept Free-trade. But they had not so much prudence on the subject of corn. This was a political question, a party question, and it is from political reasons that they have been obliged to yield to the coalition they had provoked.

In the present day you hear of many things about the condition of property in England. The free-traders of that country make up their minds about it; they say, the farmers are rich enough and the great land-owners too rich; both the one and the other are suffering, so much the worse. They will find at last some compensation, and after all if they do not find any, they will not be quite so rich, the misfortune will not be very great. I confess I cannot reason altogether in this manner. England which at the present time enjoys an admirable tranquility, I do not wish, God forbid that I should wish misfortune to that great nation which is really our friend, which notwithstanding the difference in the form of government, is a nation truly liberal, which in the great events which may happen one day in the world, will, if we do not commit any fault, be our ally, who has at this time, only feelings of a loyal and generous rivalry towards us, as it is proved by the two tribunes; a nation which conjointly with us would hold up the torch of civilization for the happiness and tranquility of the world. (Bravo, bravo.)

I am far, I repeat it, from wishing misfortune to that great nation; it would be impious and barbarous; but do you believe that Sir Robert Peel did a thing indifferent and of little consequence in bringing forward this corn question, which widely separated those two classes, and tended to lessen for a long time the good feelings which had hitherto existed between them. The land-owners are the wisest, they are resigned although they suffer cruelly. And do not imagine they suffer only a loss of 10 or 15 per cent. The large properties in England bear numerous charges of every description: there are younger sons, cadets, something must be done for them; there is a kind of family common debt which is transmitted from generation to generation and for which they must provide; and indeed among those great houses which have formed the glory and grandeur of England, there are some of which the property was lately seized and brought to the hammer to pay hereditary debts, which were not always incurred for unworthy purposes, being often caused by an excessive taste for the fine arts, magnificent edifices and philanthropical purposes.

Well, those families have not perhaps even one half of their apparent income and are in most difficult circumstances. Those great families however are the safe-guard of English liberty, for if the English aristocracy no longer existed, the ballast of that great vessel would be lost, and the vessel most probably wrecked. (Murmurs on the left. – Applause on the right.)

I do not speak, Gentlemen, as an aristocrat, but as an observer of facts. (Cheers and murmurs.)

It is to your honour, Gentlemen, that you hear from my lips, without being too much irritated, these words about the English aristocracy; you do yourselves an honour in listening to them, and I do myself an honour in pronouncing them. (Very good!)

Yes, truly the English aristocracy are the authors of English liberty, and I should see them perish or impoverished with a deep regret, and the English people think as I do; when they see in the streets of London, those fine equipages and beautiful horses, they do not cry out against them, they think they have a share in those riches as they contribute to better their condition. (New applause on the right. – Noise on the left.)

Well, let us leave the aristocracy. But the farmers, that agricultural body who cultivate the land, who are attached to it and cannot separate themselves from it, what have we to say about their situation? Sometimes it is said to make the evil appear less, 'the farmers do not quit their farms and the landowners do not turn them out;' 'then things are not so bad as they are represented to be.' But one judges incorrectly from appearances. The farmers do not quit their farms, and the land-owners do not turn them out, because they are bound together in a common misery.

They suffer in common, looking for some unknown end to their sufferings. But there are now opposed to each other, on one side the class of farmers and land-owners who cannot exist with the present price of corn, and on the other side a class quite as numerous of working men who are not willing to relinquish the low price of bread which has been so hastily procured for them. Do you think this an indifferent thing? Is it not on the contrary the cause of a great and just anxiety? I hope the difficulties will be removed, I wish it for that great nation in which the whole civilized world is interested; but there still remains this indisputable temerity, the having exposed England to the necessity of importing from abroad one-third part of her consumption.

For my part I am not aware of any satisfactory explanation or means of lessening the importance of such result. I agree that boldness will succeed, that perhaps the Americans will be beaten if they should one day engage in a struggle; but should they be beaten which is very doubtful, there will be a terrible day of reckoning for the English; It will be with bread in England as it has been with sugar among all nations; on the simple declaration of war, by the change in the charge for insurance they will see the price of bread once more rise to a price much superior to that they would not submit to before, and which was really but the medium between peace prices and war prices. But after all, whatever may be the result, the experiment was possible for England, for she is a nation peculiarly situated, manufacturing certain products largely, being able to send them to others, instead of procuring them from abroad; and in order to obtain the sale of those products which she manufactures so well, she could consent to the sacrifice of some industries of luxury; and once drawn in, she has made an experiment on corn of which no one can foresee the result, but which is very daring, and the merits of which time only can determine. Thus suppose a nation in the same condition as England is, and able to try the same thing without more peril, you would say to her, before trying the same experiment, wait until time has given its decision. But for a nation placed in quite a different situation, it would be a double folly not to wait until time had decided.

Now I am naturally led to say a few words upon French industry. You will see directly by the simple quotation of its distinctive character that we cannot do what England has done. The characteristics of our industry are universality, perfection, and some relative dearness.

Permit me to describe them fully.

Universality, yes we manufacture every thing and very well. England extracts coal, manufactures iron and cotton to a great extent and with a wonderful cheapness; but she manufactures silk indifferently; as to woollen cloth she is very far behind us. Last of all she has no wine. It is not her fault. (Laughter.) She grows fine grapes under glass, but she cannot make wine. Now compare yourself with Germany. Germany properly speaking has no fine articles of silk, only common ones; she manufactures remarkable woollen cloth in Saxony, but she does not make machinery as you and the English do; in this respect she is yet in her infancy; she has not your wines; she has a small quantity on the Rhine, but it is not to be compared with yours for quality and quantity.

Italy has silk fabrics, but much inferior to yours; she manufactures but indifferently woollen cloth. It is the same with Spain, for Italy and Spain are nearly in the same condition; but these countries have not what you possess, they do not manufacture as you do very fine articles of cotton and much iron and coal.

Thus if you compare yourselves with other nations, you will see you are in full possession of all things. A nation is always as it were all of a piece, and in every thing like itself. The celebrated Cuvier used to say, in his course of comparative anatomy, 'Give me a single bone of any animal whatever and I will re-form the whole animal.' One might say of a nation, 'Give me one of its pictures, one of its books, one article of its manufacture, and I will tell you the whole character of that nation.' Indeed this distinctive character of universality which is shown in our literature, in our arts, we carry into industry, we make every thing with almost an equal superiority. If our superiority wounds sometimes, every body becomes satisfied by saying, 'France possesses wit and taste.'

Gentlemen, France has more than this; taste is certainly a great thing, it is the genius of the arts; but France possesses a high degree of intelligence. It was necessary, for instance, in the construction of machinery to economise the combustible: well, France has made fixed steam engines which consume only

2 *killogrammes* of coal per hour for each horse power, whilst the English fixed steam engines consume 4 *killogrammes*.

It was necessary to apply the Helix, a kind of winged screw, to men of war, and place it beneath the line of flotation. France made the principal discovery; but the English who possess more money have better applied it and on a larger scale.

France has then a great degree of intelligence. This is what delighted me so much in the Exhibition of London, for I experienced at that sight, the greatest patriotic joy I had ever felt in my life. Forty years ago our armies covered us with glory, and that consoled us for our political sorrows.

In the present day it is our industry which does us honour; this it is which heightens our glory in the eyes of Europe and which makes them say, that in spite of all our troubles we remain the most civilized of nations. (Numerous marks of approbation and applause.)

Yes, we make every thing; our workmen so quick of temper, so hot, so ungovernable, set them to work file in hand, and they will execute with an admirable perfection and precision. And as a proof of it, the instruments of precision, the great clock work, the instruments of astronomy and those of navigation are taken only from our hands with a feeling of perfect security. Our workmen who possess an admirable intellect, have besides, when they are at work, a patience and care which render them an object of universal admiration.

Certainly we possess that great quality of universality; we manufacture every thing, silk admirably, our woollen cloth is acknowledged to be the most beautiful in Europe; but in Germany and Switzerland, they manufacture inferior articles of silk which owing to their low price would be dangerous for us. In Saxony, they have began to manufacture woollen cloth which although inferior to ours, is already fine, and owing to their wool has an advantage in regard to price which would render their competition dangerous.

We manufacture cotton admirably, especially for the application of dye; we produce those printed calicoes of Mulhousen of which M. Dollfus wishes to manufacture a greater quantity at the risk of seeing our white spun and woven articles diminish. These fabrics are the finest and are superior to any other. But when one comes to the price, one can see they are dearer on account of the perfection itself. Here again and in this respect we have reason to fear our neighbours the English.

We grow corn and we grow it as well as England; we produce flour better than England, as a proof, she buys a large quantity of our flour; and yet if our corn is cheaper than that of England, we have down yonder in Russia, an opponent who might put even that in danger.

You see then we produce every thing with a rare perfection, but it is this which causes us to have rivals every where; it is the reason we have in all parts and for every thing an opponent against whom we must defend ourselves. We have universality, but on account of that very universality we are obliged to defend ourselves every where against rivals who could put us in peril. Those are the Russians for wheat, Swiss and Germans for manufactured silk; the Saxons for woollen cloth; English for cotton, iron and coal.

This indicates the wide difference between the English and the French nations. Yes, the special nation which makes certain things in abundance and with great superiority, and which wants to find an outlet for them, can afford to sacrifice some articles of luxury in order to obtain in exchange the means of disposing of those surplus products. But that nation which makes every kind of article and makes it well has peculiar need to avert competition, she ought to keep her own market to herself, she has kept it to herself, and it is so good and so extensive that she has had no reason to regret it.

Yet does it follow from such a situation, which involves a certain relative dearness (for it is necessary to consider the connexion of things under the penalty of not comprehending them; that universality involves protection, and protection involves dearness;) does it follow from such a state of things that we cannot have exportation? By no means. Next to the English we have the finest exportation, and that in consequence of the perfection of our products. Yes we sell dear, but we are like those merchants who selling dear, yet sell much more than their neighbours who sell cheap, because they offer to their customers better articles. The English export to the extent of 1 milliard 500 millions to 1 milliard 600 millions. This is far beyond our exportation. But when our maritime existence is considered, and that we have not India as they have, that we have scarcely any colonies, (for our colonies are quite trifling compared with those of England,) when it is considered that we have only 3 millions of tons of shipping whilst the English have 12 millions, we ought to look upon it as remarkable that we have reached an exportation of 1 milliard 100 millions, that is to say that we press so close upon the heels of the English. In short we export 200 millions of silk goods, 60 millions of cotton goods, 50 millions of cloth, 120 millions of woollen tissues, and some hundreds of millions in furniture, jewelry, dressed skins, choice wines, fine flour, &c.

I cannot give a complete account of all our exports, but all those products of luxury which are the delight and admiration of the world, it is we who furnish them.

Such is our industry.

For the bulk of things, we reserve for ourselves our own market; and it is so good that one could not say he is unfortunate in being shut up in it. We find moreover in the perfection of our products, the means of exporting a quantity of goods, approaching pretty nearly that of the English exports, which are the greatest in the world. [...]

Do you know what is intended to be expressed by the difference of tariffs? Not that foolish pretension of wishing in all times and in all countries, to produce, under impossible circumstances what the climate and the soil refuse to produce; but it expresses that patience of genius, that resignation which consists in doing laboriously, slowly, and dearly at first, that which afterwards can be done better, and at last with perfection. This is the condition that God has imposed upon all men in placing them here below, to produce every thing with effort.

I would say in concluding, that the contrary would be impious. Come, cast your eyes on the temperate zones and see the small space that we occupy on the surface of the globe: there are from 15 to 16 degrees of latitude and 45 of longitude. Take a map in your hands, the whole of Europe is nothing as compared to the rest of the world. Well! what has nature given to it? Oaks, Fir trees, pastures, scarcely any corn, cattle large in size, middling in beauty; and on the other hand, she gave to China, silk; to India, cotton; to Thibet, the most beautiful breed of sheep; to Arabia, the horse; to America, precious metals and the most beautiful kinds of wood. In a word, she lavished every thing upon these other parts of the world. But in Europe what was there that possessed any superiority? One single thing, Man! Man! (Warm applause, prolonged sensation.) Every thing was inferior in Europe, except man, because the temperate countries are the best fitted for the development of the human organization. In cold countries man is benumbed; in hot countries he is idle and sensual. There only man could be great, proud and ambitious. Yet he went to take every thing from those countries so well gifted by nature; he took from China, silk; from India, cotton; from Thibet, sheep; from Arabia, the horse; from America, metals and wood; with all those things he has adorned Europe, his beloved country: he made it the theatre of civilization; and then he had recourse to powerful machines to conquer and civilize those remote countries where he was not born, and from which he had taken every thing which they possessed.

It is then the design of the Almighty you insult when you say 'do nothing,' and 'leave every thing to chance.'

I protest then against that doctrine, and I counsel my country to persevere in her noble and faithful traditions.

Henry Dunckley, *The Charter of the Nations: or, Free Trade and its Results* (London: W. & F. G. Cash, 1854), pp. 160–2, 412–21.

We have now taken a brief but comprehensive survey of our commerce, as it is placed before us in official records; we have seen it rise from its previously depressed state, and advance in a few years as much as fifty per cent.; we have seen it multiplying our relations with states which have been our customers from time immemorial, and at the same instant opening new channels in parts of the world which have hitherto scarcely echoed the British name, and bringing vast districts, which have lain for ages beneath the night of despotism, for the first time in modern history within the magic spell of civilisation. We have beheld the gladdening sight of plenty scattering the countless treasures of her golden horn around the thresholds and hearths of the labouring poor, and industry, sustained by comfort, lured back again to the silent loom, and sending her cheapened products to clothe millions in distant lands. It would require no ordinary measure of hardihood to withhold from Free Trade the credit of these facts. The connexion between the two is natural, obvious, and indisputable. If we plant a tree we forthwith expect to see it grow, and, at the proper season, bear fruit; and if this result follow we should as soon think of asserting, against the evidence of our senses, the nonexistence of the tree, as of ascribing the result to any other cause than that of suitable culture. If a person chose to deny this, and to ascribe its fruitfulness to the colour of the garden wall, or the form of the garden-gate, or the appearance of some new star in the heavens, it would be difficult perhaps to prove him mistaken; – we could carry him no higher than the demonstration of his senses. It is precisely so with our commerce. It was once fettered, it is now free. Ever since its fetters were knocked off it has progressed with unexampled rapidity, and there are some who venture to believe that it progresses the faster because it is free. If any one chooses to say that it moves faster than when its limbs were bound, not because they are unbound, but because an earthquake happened five months since, it is hopeless to attempt a mathematical demonstration to the contrary, but we can point to the facts as amply sufficient to obtain the verdict of all unprejudiced men. The repeal of the corn laws, and the abolition of the imposts previously laid on many hundred articles, occasioned an influx of those commodities which former regulations had kept out. But imports and exports are reciprocal. Protection to native industry says – 'You shall not receive,' and the corollary to this is 'You shall not give.' Once obtain permission to *import*, and the nation will forthwith begin to *export*. The cheapness which Free Trade produces expands all our markets. One of the heaviest burdens formerly sustained by our manufacturer was the necessity of competing with the lightly-taxed foreigner. The reduction which Free Trade has effected in the price of food and the raw material places him nearer to a position of equality, and helps to decide the battle of cheapness in his favour. But cheapness is the magic power of trade; at its approach the market gives way on all sides, nation after nation crowds into it, and protective measures, adopted by enlightened communities in self-defence, are thrown up as gross anachronisms. Free Trade is, as we shall see, the means of introducing greater economy into our manufactures, and stimulating all engaged therein to the attainment of greater excellence. Protected interests invariably languish; those who engage in them resemble a number of well-salaried officials who are guaranteed the enjoyment of a fixed income whether they work or not, and who content themselves, in consequence, with the minimum of ingenuity and exertion. Once deprive them of this support, once leave them to take care of themselves, and their conduct will undergo an instant change. Like the man who is reported to have run away with great agility when a set of thieves plundered him of his crutches, they will be compelled to do their best, and will soon equal, if not beat, their rivals. These are all the inevitable results of Free Trade, and the one expression for the whole is just – increased exportation. The condition of our commerce is scarcely more flourishing than it was expected to be. All was foreseen. It blossomed in theory before it blossomed in fact. The Free-trader always said – 'Only open your ports to the produce of other nations, and your factories will soon be in motion, and the sea will be covered with your shipping, conveying your merchandise to every clime.' This was the prophecy again and again uttered; in the prosperous times which are passing over us we witness its fulfilment. [...]

PROBABLE INFLUENCE OF FREE TRADE ON THE MORAL RENOVATION OF THE WORLD.

From this point we may look abroad, and contemplate for a moment the effects of Free Trade, thus socially, religiously, commercially, and politically developed among ourselves, upon the rest of the world. For this purpose it will be requisite to form a definite idea of the changes which may be expected in the future history of our race. The orator and the poet tell us of a 'good time coming,' a time which they depict in the warmest colouring of fancy. The inherent conviction and aspirations of the noblest minds point them onwards to a distant goal, at which humanity is to rest after the toils of centuries. What estimate may we calmly form of these hopes? How do we expect to see them fulfilled? By what particular tendencies will Free Trade hasten their fulfilment?

I. We own, at once, that, in assuming the certainty of a future political and moral 'millennium,' we take for granted what some deny. Many are thorough 'infidels' with regard to man's destiny on earth. They have no confidence in his real progressiveness, or in the permanence of any moral results. The future presents to their mind's eye a scene of gloomy disorder; a dim vista of social and political earthquakes. It is to them a looking through the twilight of some inorganic world. They think that time will continue to re-enact his old horrors, play off his old impostures, and exercise, in new shapes, the tyrannies of king and priest: – that civil blood will still be shed; armies, scaffolds, and dungeons still raise their brute barriers against the holy march of peace, till, at length, the power which shall have borne with us too long will totally destroy a race which is proved at last to be unworthy of His protection. Such a faith as this is not enthusiasm, it is fanaticism in its most malignant form; it is itself the grim and faithless thing that throws so dark a shadow on the future. If such is life, of what use is it living? If history has no better escutcheon to hold up to the universe than one which is crowded with follies and crimes, to what end have good men suffered, why have patriots and martyrs bled? Grant the views we oppose, and where is the moral of man's existence? The nobler spirits of the race, Plato, Dante, Luther, Shakspeare, Milton, Bacon, Descartes, Pascal, Howard, Washington, – have they lived in vain? Did HE, who came to 'save that which was lost,' depart unsolaced by any hope that His bitter travail would some day be rewarded by the spread of love and justice throughout the world? If the history of man shows us nothing better than the utter failure of moral principle when brought into collision with injustice, it is a picture of hopelessness in reference to the moral destinies of the universe which we can but sorrowfully wish it had been consistent with sovereign wisdom to withhold.

II. There is a disposition in some men, when two alternatives, equally probable, are offered, to prefer the more terrific. The fascination sometimes felt in circumstances of great danger, which almost tempts us to rush headlong into it, gives us a clue to the nature of such a disposition. They love to think that the present age is the prelude to a tragedy, and the spice of misanthropy which mingles with the feeling only makes it the more palatable. There are, however, two opinions which influence the growth of this feeling: one of these we have just mentioned. It is that man is not really progressive; that revolutions bring on reactions; and that a season of freedom, by leading to wild democracy, brings back despotism – that man, instead of following an ever onward course, walks perpetually, like the mill-horse, round the same circle. An inference of this kind may be drawn from a contracted and partial study of history, but it disappears before reflection. Viewed aright, history rather represents an unfinished drama, with many acts and interludes, but all centering in one plot, and all contributing towards the same *dénouement*. In social and political changes action and reaction are not equal; what is true in mechanics is in this respect false in humanity. So far as human revolutions are mechanical, the maxim holds good; but, though they always spring, in part, from mechanical causes, they spring from a cause far deeper – from life; and the law of life is, not reaction, but progress. Experience proves this. Who will say that the prospects of mankind are no better now than they were when Xerxes filled the Persian throne, and kidnapped strangers were exposed for sale in the market of Athens? – or when the Roman Empire was sinking in collapse, and countless hordes of barbarians poured over the Danube into Italy and Gaul; – or when English troops were using their long knives at Cressy, when Europe was without any international law, and its populations, as well as its rulers, seemed animated with a common desire to rob and murder each other? Or, coming down to more recent times, is British liberty no more secure than it was under the Stuarts? Are the prospects of France less hopeful than they were under Louis XIV.? Has Germany made no advance in political knowledge, and aptitude for enjoying political freedom, since the close of the seven years' war? With states of Anglo-Saxon origin fringing the eastern coast of the Pacific; with British settlements at Borneo, Hong Kong, New Zealand, Natal, and the Cape of Good Hope; with India under British rule; new communities rising in Australia; with Chinamen emigrating to California; a marvellous revolution rending in twain the Celestial Empire; a line of steamers from San Francisco to the Sandwich Isles; Turkey adopting the principles of Christian civilisation; canals and railroads connecting the Atlantic and Pacific; and the electric telegraph enabling us to converse over an extent of a thousand miles, who will say that the prospects of civilisation are no better than they were some centuries ago?

In estimating the probable influence of any moral agency, a very important element is time. There is an impression somewhat prevalent that the world is hastening to some crisis, and that the period allotted for its moral development will soon expire. Neither experience nor reason, nor, we may add, religion, gives ground for any such sentiment. Granting its truth, then, our faith in moral agencies, and especially in the effects of Free Trade, as a means of humanising the world, is shaken. Our own social development, the wealth, the knowledge, the fitness for political action, which we enjoy, is the growth of 1,500 or 2,000 years. It may be expected that, with better means of progress, other states will grow faster, but when we reflect on the condition of two-thirds of the population of the globe; when we think of their present ignorance, barbarism, superstition, and political incapacity, we cannot, consistently with known laws, expect that their elevation will be achieved in the course of one or two centuries. Analogy supports this view. The works of Providence are slow; the universe is never in a hurry. If, as geologists tell us, the world occupied some millions of years in being fitted for man's abode, surely a few more thousands of years may have to pass before his destiny here is over.

II. Recognising, therefore, the reasonableness of the hope which all feel, that a future period of political and moral perfection is in reserve for the world, how will Free Trade influence its approach? We answer, in a threefold way: –

Free Trade will elevate the physical and social condition of the world. The groundwork of civilisation is labour; a sense of its value, and an economising of its results. The effect of Free Trade on civilised communities with respect to the value of labour, is very plain, – it creates a demand for it, and gives the labourer a proportionably greater share in the enjoyments of life. But it will produce the same results, in some measure, upon barbarous communities too. It will induce the peasant to till more ground, to sow more wheat than he can consume himself and exchange with his neighbours, and, in return, it will bestow upon him comforts of which he before knew nothing. This reward will expand his views, and stimulate his exertions; gradually he will learn to invest capital, his wealth increasing, step by step, till at length he becomes an owner of estates and ships, and an extensive civiliser in his turn. One such individual cannot rise alone; others will be stimulated by his success, and, in time, national opulence will be the result. By stimulating a demand for labour, and conferring its rewards, commerce will build up mankind in that social well-being which affords the most favourable opportunity for the due development of every political and moral virtue.

Free Trade will tend to spread the knowledge and the practice of purer political sentiments. On this subject there prevails much ill-judged enthusiasm. Justly grateful for the freedom which we enjoy, assured that freedom is necessary to attain man's highest well-being, and, also, that it is his inalienable right, we are apt to forget the only condition on which it can be possessed. We are ready to imagine that all which is necessary for the happiness of a people, is a constitution like ours; constitutional government is with us a recipe for every disease. If the question at issue were merely one of political systems, our views would probably be correct; but the question is too often a social one. Physical force is, in many cases, resorted to, as a means of obtaining political rights, and too often only to occasion a closer rivetting of the chain. The sure mode of enfranchising mankind, is to raise them in social comfort and moral excellence. Without these attainments, liberty could not be kept if it were won, but with these attainments liberty will come of its own accord. Hence commerce is the emancipator of mankind – it creates wealth, it inspires with energy and self-respect, it fosters habits of justice and moderation, it strengthens the love of property, and thus opens so many sources of political power. A commercial people almost necessarily become in time a free people. We have been pointed, again and again, to the serfs of Russia, – with thousands Russia is a hateful name, the symbol of oppression and wrong. How then might we best aid the slave population of Russia in the work of emancipation? By sending our men of war into the Baltic and Black Seas, and scattering eloquent manifestoes on liberty? – Nay, trade with them, and in time they must be free. Commerce brings nations together, unites communities by the ties of reciprocal benefit, till at length, the people loving each other, the wrath of princes falls as harmless as a spark on granite rocks.

Free Trade will aid in spreading beliefs which exalt and stimulate the faculties of those who receive them, and thus lay the foundation of all political and moral greatness. We need not say that the special beliefs to which we refer are those of

Christianity. We waive here the higher aspects of Christianity, and claim for it nothing but what the mere historical student admits, on the ground of experience and fact. It will not be denied that religion is the most influential element in moulding individual and national character, and that on purely political grounds merely, the choice of beliefs is no matter of indifference. We find in Hindostan, for example, a religion which developes [sic] the passive qualities; which favours contemplation, endurance, mysticism, rather than vigorous exertion: – Hindostan has never been free from a foreign yoke. We find in Turkey a faith which inspires every man with the conviction that all things are under a law of inevitable necessity; that it is an act of impiety to attempt to arrest the progress of a fire, or to escape from death, and which, at the same time, calls the voluptuous passions into play by visions of celestial houris: – Turkey is at this moment at the mercy of Christian powers, and silence on the part of France and England would seal its doom. In Britain and the United States we see a faith which tells us that man's destiny is practically in his own hands; which stimulates inquiry and independent thought, asserts the equality of all men in the sight of God, and bases all virtue on an intelligent appreciation of his will: – These two nations are now exerting a moral and political power, which we shall hardly exaggerate in pronouncing equal to that of all the world beside. This comparison might be carried into the minutest details, and exemplified in the largest variety of instances, and it would be found fully proved, as a matter of fact, that where the elements of Christian civilisation have been most vigorous, there the greatest triumphs of industry and political greatness have been achieved.

But what is Free Trade? – It is itself a Christian idea. It is the embodiment of the Christian thought that men are brothers. It takes the olive branch which Heaven in mercy sends to earth, and bears it to every land. Free Trade tells us that war is wicked; that the millions of armed men that cover Europe should beat their swords into ploughshares, and their spears into pruninghooks. In proportion as mankind accept the principles of Free Trade, they will admit the morals of Christianity, and may be the more easily led to adopt the doctrines from which they spring. But it exerts a still more direct tendency in the same direction. As our commercial connexions extend, so also will our moral power; with the prosperity occasioned by Free Trade, our population will increase, to be drafted off by thousands to our colonies in distant parts of the globe. Nothing will tend so much to people Australia, Southern Africa, and New Zealand, as the effects of Free Trade. By the life it will infuse into commerce, and the political freedom which it will give to our dependencies, it will tend to spread throughout the world, at a rate of which we have no conception, the language, manners, literature, and faith of Britain. But the colonisation of the Pacific will be its Christianisation too. Bring the shasters and the gospels together, as they are seen in the languor and servility, or the energetic independence of their professors, and the result will not be long doubtful.

Free Trade says: – 'Let men come together.' We hail the bidding; such contact is vital for truth. The figments of superstition will then vanish, priestly sanctities and impostures will be scorned away, and man everywhere stand up erect, wearing the image, and blest with the liberty of God.

The Abortive Anglo-French Commercial Treaty of 1852, 19 February 1853, PRO, FO 881/551, fols 81, 85.

No. 29

Lord John Russell to Count Walewski.

M. l'Ambassadeur, *Foreign Office, February* 19, 1853.

HER Majesty's Government have taken into their serious consideration the note which your Excellency addressed to my predecessor on the 25th of September last, relative to the conclusion of a new Treaty of Commerce between Great Britain and France; and whatever delay has arisen in replying to that communication, must be attributed solely to the minute and careful investigation which was rendered necessary by the contents of your Excellency's note, which differed widely from the communication which Her Majesty's Government had been led by the Government of France to expect from your Excellency on the subject of the proposed Treaty.

When, in September last, M. Drouyn de Lhuys expressed to Lord Cowley his anxiety that the scale of duties should be modified on goods imported respectively from France into England, and from England into France; and that a Convention should be concluded on the subject, Lord Cowley was instructed to remind M. Drouyn de Lhuys, that Her Majesty's Government had long ago evinced the utmost readiness to enter into negotiations for this purpose; and that those negotiations were only stopped by the unwillingness of the French Government to admit the statements of the British Government upon the subject of local exemptions in certain British ports.

M. Drouyn de Lhuys stated in reply, that instructions would be given to your Excellency to enable you to resume the negotiations for a new Treaty. But your Excellency's communication of the 25th of September, instead of proposing the resumption of the negotiations, was almost entirely restricted to the above-mentioned point of local exemptions, which matter Her Majesty's Government had considered as already exhausted and set at rest: and your Excellency concluded your note by stating that this matter must be definitively set right before any negotiations could be resumed. You accordingly proposed one of two alternatives; either that a mixed commission should be appointed to inquire minutely into the local exemptions in question; or else that all port-charges should at once be abolished on French and British vessels in both countries.

This unexpected proposal naturally rendered necessary a further reference to the Board of Trade, and a reconsideration of the whole question on their part; and the result of that reference and reconsideration is that Her Majesty's Government find it impossible to agree either to the proposal for the mutual abolition of all port-charges; or to that for a fresh inquiry into the matter of local exemptions, a subject which has already undergone repeated investigation of the most searching kind, to which investigation the French Consul-General was a party.

Her Majesty's Government deeply regret, therefore, the obstruction which seems to oppose itself to the resumption of negotiations which appeared to have been so much desired on both sides. But so long as the two above-mentioned alternatives are insisted on by the French Government, it is not easy to see how the negotiations are to be resumed.

I am anxious, however, in making this communication to your Excellency, to enable you to point out accurately to your Government the real position of the subject, and I accordingly inclose herewith a memorandum which has been drawn up at the Board of Trade, pointing out the errors into which the French Government has fallen in commenting upon the details with which they have been furnished by their own agents as well as by Her Majesty's Government.

I think it may be desirable at the same time to recall briefly to your Excellency's attention the origin and general course of the negotiation which is now pending between the two Governments.

When, in 1849, the British Navigation Laws were amended, and greater facilities and advantages were given to French and to other foreign vessels in their commercial intercourse with the British dominions, Her Majesty's Government invited the French Government to reciprocate the liberal policy of Great Britain; and the French Government, in reply to that invitation, proposed in the following year to Her Majesty's Government a draft of a new Convention, accompanied by explanations of the principles upon which it was founded.

That draft of the Convention certainly embraced the question of the extension and improvement of the commercial relations of the two countries; but the French Government at the same time introduced the subject of local exemptions as a grievance alleged to be contrary to treaty; and that subject has unfortunately been allowed to supersede, as it were, the main question of the mercantile relations between the two countries, and has ever since been made the chief matter of discussion by the French Government.

Now, Her Majesty's Government have always regarded this point as one of an entirely subordinate, and indeed extraneous, character; but they, nevertheless, consented to investigate the subject of local exemptions, in order to prove to the French Government that the effect produced upon French shipping by these local exemptions was scarcely appreciable; and Her Majesty's Government conceive that they have clearly demonstrated this to be the case. But, in undertaking this investigation, Her Majesty's Government never for a moment intended to admit, nor can they ever admit, the interpretation which the French Government desire to put upon the Treaty of 1826; since that interpretation, if adopted, would have the effect of placing French vessels in British ports upon a footing not merely of equality with British ships, as provided by the treaty, but of superiority over British ships, a position which it is manifest that no treaty of reciprocity could contemplate. The views of the British Government in this respect are clearly set forth in the well known communication made by Viscount Palmerson to M. de Bacourt in the year 1833, when a complaint was preferred on the part of the French Government of certain exemptions in the Channel Islands. To those views Her Majesty's Government still strictly adhere.

The French Government, indeed, itself, in 1851, evinced a manifest disposition to coincide with the views of Her Majesty's Government in this matter; for M. de Marescalchi, in his note of the 20th of June in that year, stated that if it were found that the grievances complained of were trifling, no further point would be made of them by the French Government. Now, it has been clearly shown, by repeated investigation, that the said grievances, if grievances they can be called, are scarcely appreciable; and it is therefore with much surprise and concern that Her Majesty's Government see them still put forward in the foreground of the discussions by the French Government. Nevertheless, out of courtesy to the French Government, Her Majesty's Government, although they cannot consent to renewed official investigation, and feel bound to close all further discussion upon the point, are still willing to allow the French Consul-General to enter into friendly communication with the Board of Trade, in order that he may satisfy himself of the completeness and accuracy of the information upon which the statements of Her Majesty's Government respecting local exemptions are founded.

Notwithstanding the present unpromising aspect of the discussion between the two Governments, I am still willing to hope that your Excellency may be enabled to inform me that the negotiations for placing the commercial relations of the two countries on a footing satisfactory to both may be proceeded with; and I cannot conclude without reminding your Excellency that the trade of the United Kingdom is at this moment subjected in the ports of France to disqualifications which apply to no other country; that those disqualifications were originally imposed by France in retaliation for the British Navigation Laws; that the British Navigation Laws have been amended in favour of France, but that the disqualifications abovementioned have not as yet been removed; and that, in consequence of the hope held out by the French Government that steps would be immediately taken to remedy this evil, Her Majesty's Government have not, up to the present moment, adopted, by way of retaliation towards French shipping, any of the measures which are authorized by the British Navigation Act of 1849.

If, setting aside, as inconsiderable and almost inappreciable, the question of local exemptions, the French Government is disposed to enter into negotiations upon a Treaty of Commerce and Navigation between the two countries founded upon liberal principles, mutually advantageous to both, Her Majesty's Government will be ready to enter into such negotiation.

I am, &c.
(Signed)   J. RUSSELL.

[...]

No. 31.

Mr Booth to Mr. Addington. – (Received

Office of the Committee of Privy Council for Trade,

Sir,   *August* 3, 1853.

WITH reference to the negotiations between Her Majesty's Governments and the Government of France on the subject of the conclusion of an amended Treaty of Commerce and Navigation between this country and France in substitution for the existing one of 1826, I am directed by the Lords of the Committee of Privy Council for Trade to request that you will inform the Earl of Clarendon that a Royal Commission, copies of which are herewith inclosed, was issued on the 19th of March last, for the purpose of inquiring into local charges upon shipping in the ports of the United Kingdom.

It will be in the recollection of Lord Clarendon that their Lordships, in their letter of the 29th January last, stated their opinion that it would be unadvisable in the highest degree to subject the question of the temporary continuance of local exemptions in British ports to the interference, as proposed by France, of a Mixed Commission emanating from the demand of a Foreign Power, the subject being one appertaining to the internal administration of this kingdom alone. My Lords see no reason to alter, on the present occasion, the views then expressed by them; but they would suggest that Her Majesty's Ambassador at Paris should be made acquainted with the fact of the issue of the Royal Commission for the purpose of examining into all cases of local exemption so far as relates to the several harbours of this Kingdom.

It will be for Lord Clarendon to consider how far it may be expedient to draw the attention of the French Government in any way to that controverted subject. Meanwhile, it appears to their Lordships desirable to take this opportunity of calling Lord Clarendon's attention to the general subject of the existing commercial relations between this country and France, and to that end they have caused the inclosed memorandum to be prepared, recapitulating the negotiations which took place from 1839 to 1843 for the establishment of improved relations between the two countries, and exhibiting, from the statistics of their trade during the last twenty years, the state of their commercial progress as influenced by the policy, whether of free trade or of protection, pursued in each country respectively.

It will be seen on reference to the memorandum that while England has, with a view to her own interests, been constantly occupied with the task of modifying her commercial policy in a liberal sense, and with happy results to herself in every point of view, the few changes that have been made in France have been in a contrary direction. Consequently, the conditions which formed the basis of the Treaty the negotiations for which came to an unsuccessful close in 1843, are no longer applicable to the altered position of the commercial relations of the two countries; and, without now expressing any opinion on the general subject of the expediency, under our present commercial system, of regulating the tariff of the United Kingdom in connection with Treaty arrangements with Foreign Powers, my Lords consider that nothing less than an entire revolution in the whole policy of France in matters of commerce could suffice to ensure to this country a real reciprocity of treatment, and that the conclusion of any Treaty providing for a mere readjustment of existing duties on either side to compensate for equivalent alterations to be made on the other, would altogether fail to place British imports into France on a footing in any way corresponding to the very favourable footing on which French imports into this country are at this moment placed.

The eminent success which has attended the practical application in Great Britain of the principles of commercial freedom cannot, in the opinion of my Lords, but have its weight in tending to convince the Government and people of France of the advantages to be reaped by that country by adopting a corresponding policy; and the contrast to be observed between the progress of the trade between England and France on the one hand, and that between England and the United States on the other, is so remarkable that it may well induce on the part of France an anxious examination into its cause.

In each case this country, which is now enjoying an unprecedented amount of commercial prosperity, is exhibited trading with one of the two most powerful nations in the world, – nations possessing, moreover, in their own hands the means of extending their commerce almost indefinitely. In each case this country has taken care to secure from the other a supply of whatever that other produces which it stands in need of itself. Whether in the case of France or in that of the United States, England has equally succeeded in profiting by the permission which she gives to both alike to find an unrestricted market within her territory. But while the latter of the two countries has been moving in the same direction, and relaxing the restrictions which were in full force there a few years ago, the former has pursued an opposite policy; and the result in each instance is to be seen in the statistics contained in the memorandum relating to each of them respectively, of which the one relating to France accompanies this letter, and the corresponding one relating to the United States was inclosed in their Lordships' letter of the 20th April last.

At the time when England stood alone in her commercial policy, she felt its beneficial effects; when joined by the United States, those benefits became still further developed, and were fully shared in by that country; and, both from analogy and from every other consideration, the same happy results to her own commercial industry may be looked forward to by France so soon as she shall have resolved to adopt the same course.

In addition to the information contained in the inclosed memorandum, the Parliamentary Paper (No. 318, of this session) of which I am directed to inclose copies, will be found to contain detailed statistics of the trade and public income and expenditure of this country, showing the many ways in which she has benefited by the policy she has now been steadily pursuing for so many years, in her increased trade both in imports and exports, in the augmented employment of her shipping, in her diminished taxation, in her flourishing revenue, and in all the items that serve to indicate the material prosperity of a nation. Testimony to the same effect is borne by the decrease of pauperism, the abundance of employment for the working classes, the high rate of wages, and the reduced cost of provisions and the necessaries of life in this country.

The memorandum also contains striking evidence of the effects produced upon France by an equally steady adherence to an opposite policy. It exhibits an actually declining revenue of Customs, notwithstanding the increase of population and the absence of any reduction of duty. There an amount has been lost to the revenue which has not been saved to the public; in this country a great advantage has been conferred upon the consumer, with little or no loss to the revenue.

The memorandum shows, further, the annual drain upon the French Exchequer entailed by the system of bounties, whereby commerce is diverted from its natural channels, and the public in France is taxed in order to enable the merchant to supply his foreign customer with the goods which he exports at less than their actual cost, or, at all events, at a less price than he can afford to dispose of them to his own fellow-countrymen.

The result which might be expected from a policy which consists in fostering the export trade of a country by means of bounties, and, at the same time restricting its import trade by means of prohibitory duties, will be seen detailed in that part of the memorandum which shows the extraordinary excess of French exports to this country over British exports to France, even when the trade in the specie which might have been supposed to form the means of payment of that excess is taken into account.

There can be little doubt that the great discrepancy between these two trades, exhibited by the statistical returns, is to be explained in a two-fold manner: by the extensive smuggling that takes place into France, and by the circuitous manner in which England is compelled by French legislation, to pay for the excess of her imports from France, by which the price of the English commodities so imported into France is enhanced to the French consumer of them; whilst by the smuggling, the revenue of France is exposed to serious loss.

The importance to an agricultural country like France of being able to procure at the least possible cost those articles of manufacture of which a large labouring population such as hers stands in need, is as evident as is the corresponding advantage of securing a more extended market in foreign countries for the agricultural produce with which she is so well able to supply them. Nor is it less important to her manufacturing population to be furnished with the cheapest and most abundant supply that can be obtained, of those raw materials of industry which form the basis of their employment, but the cost of which it has hitherto been the policy of France to enhance by means of import duties.

With regard to the shipping interests of France, a reference to the memorandum will serve to show what has been the practical effect of the restrictive policy pursued in that country. Lord Clarendon will be aware that by the French Tariff, almost every single article imported there experiences a specially favoured treatment when imported in national vessels. The object of this has, of course, been to throw the whole commerce of France as much as possible into the hands of French shipping, a result which the returns of the employment of French and foreign shipping respectively in the Foreign trade of France, might therefore have been expected to show. But it will be seen by these statistics, that only 40 per cent. of the total tonnage so employed is French, the remaining 60 per cent. belonging to foreign nations. In this country, on the other hand, where employment is found for more than three times the amount of shipping that is required to carry on the commerce of France, the relative positions are exactly reversed; the proportion of British tonnage considerably exceeding 60 per cent. of the whole, and the tonnage of foreign nations only amounting to between 30 and 40 per cent.

It is also to be observed that the constant tendency in France is towards a decrease in the size of the vessels employed, the tables showing the average tonnage of each French vessel employed in 1847 to have been 120 tons; while in 1852 it has fallen to 115 tons. In this country, on the contrary, the stimulus given to trade by the competition induced by the repeal of the Navigation Laws, has led to the employment of a better class of vessels than heretofore, the average tonnage of the British shipping employed in our foreign trade in 1847, having been 223 tons, while in 1852 it had increased to 240 tons.

But no more decisive evidence of the unsatisfactory state of the French commercial marine under her existing restrictive policy, is to be found, than that contained in the despatch of the French Minister for Foreign Affairs, of the 30th

January, 1850, submitting the draft of the proposed Navigation Convention. In that despatch, General de la Hitte employs the following expression;

'En présence de l'infériorité actuelle trop bien établie de la Navigation Française dans l'intercourse direct avec la Grande Bretagne, nous sommes malheureusement obligés de reconnaître que notre marine marchande n'est en position de retirer de fait que peu ou point de profit réel de ces nouvelles facilités. Pour l'intercourse direct, en effet, par suite des restrictions applicables jusqu'ici dans les deux pays aux pavillons tiers, la Navigation Française n'a eu à lutter jusqu'à présent qu'avec un seul concurrent, le pavillon Britannique. Votre Excellence connait déjà les résultats fâcheux de ce concours inégal.'

Upon the change which took place in the British and American Navigation Laws in 1850, a new trade arose, by which goods to the amount of 2,000,000*l*. annually are sent to this country from France for export to America. It is unnecessary to say one word upon the commentary which this simple fact must afford of the gain England has derived from freedom of navigation as contrasted with the failure of a restrictive policy in France.

The above observations upon the results to be gathered from a review of the facts contained in the memorandum, and which are of more value than any arguments drawn from theory, have not been made by my Lords from any wish to recommend that the views they have expressed should be unseasonably urged upon the attention of the French Government, especially as they feel that any change in the commercial policy of France, is to be looked for only in a conviction on the part of that Government and nation, of the essential importance to the future well-being of the empire, of the adoption of a different policy.

But to this end, their Lordships conceive that it will be very desirable that Her Majesty's Ambassador at Paris should be made fully acquainted with the feelings entertained by Her Majesty's Government in reference to this important subject; and that he should be instructed to take every fitting opportunity of pointing out to the French Government the very great benefits which have ensued from the adoption of a policy of free trade to this and to the other countries that have entered upon the same path. It is a happy characteristic of that policy that its beneficial effects are participated in by all alike – by the country that adopts it as the principle of its commercial intercourse with other States, no less than by the country whose commerce it may appear, or may be designed, more especially to favour; and that under it, self-interest is not only compatible with the bestowal of the greatest amount of advantage upon others, but in direct proportion to its extent. My Lords cherish the hope that the time is not far distant when from the adoption on both sides of enlightened principles of commercial policy, the trade between England and France will expand to those proportions which it is only natural to look for in the case of two countries so eminently calculated to minister to each other's wants and requirements, and to find in the bonds of commercial intercourse, the sure pledge of friendly union and cooperation.

I have the honour to be,
Sir,
Yours very obedient servant,
(Signed)   JAMES BOOTH.

H.U.Addington, Esq.
    &c.   &c.

American-Canadian Reciprocity Treaty of 1854, Despatch from Lord Lyons to Russell, 28 February 1862, *Parliamentary Papers* (1862), [2993], lxii.839, pp. 841–2, 844, 862.

Concurrent Resolutions of the Legislature of the State of New York in relation to the Treaty between the United States and Great Britain, commonly known as the Reciprocity Treaty

'Whereas, under the Treaty made by the United States with Great Britain, on behalf of the North American Colonies, for the purpose of extending reciprocal commerce, nearly all the articles which Canada has to sell are admitted into the United States free of duty, while heavy duties are now imposed upon many of those articles which the United States have to sell, with the intention of excluding the United States from the Canadian markets, as avowed by the Minister of Finance and other gentlemen holding high official positions in Canada; and similar legislation, with the same official avowal, has been adopted by the imposition of discriminating tolls and duties in favour of an isolating and exclusive policy against our merchants and forwarders, meant and intending to destroy the natural effects of the Treaty, and contrary to its spirit; and whereas we believe that free commercial intercourse between the United States and the British North American Provinces and Possessions, developing the natural, geographical, and other advantages of each, for the good of all, is conducive to the present interest of each, and is the only proper basis of our intercourse for all time to come; and whereas the President of the United States, in the first session of the thirty-sixth Congress, caused to be submitted to the House of Representatives an official Report, setting forth the gross inequality and injustice existing in our present intercourse with Canada, subversive of the true intent of the Treaty, owing to the subsequent legislation of Canada; and whereas the first effects of a system of retaliation or reprisal would injure that portion of Canada known as the Upper Province, whose people have never failed in their efforts to secure a permanent and just policy for their own country and ourselves, in accordance with the desire officially expressed by Lord Napier when British Minister at Washington, for the 'confirmation and expansion of free commercial relations between the United States and British Provinces:' Therefore –

'*Resolved*. That the Senators and Representatives in Congress for the State of New York are requested to take such steps, either by the appointment of Commissioners to confer with persons properly appointed on behalf of Canada, or by such other means as may seem most expedient, to protect the interests of the United States from the said unequal and unjust system of commerce now existing, and to regulate the commerce and navigation between 'Her Majesty's Possessions in North America and the United States in such manner as to render the same reciprocally beneficial and satisfactory,' as was intended and expressed by the Treaty. And

'*Resolved*. That the foregoing preamble and Resolutions be transmitted to our Senators and Representatives in Congress, with a request that they be presented to both Houses thereof.'

The chief points for consideration are the extent, population, position, and resources of the British North American Provinces and Possessions; the present so-called 'Reciprocity Treaty;' the existing condition of our commercial and fiscal relations with Canada, and the line of policy most conducive to the interest and welfare of both countries; the tendencies of modern inventions and civilization on the intercourse of nations, including the leading principles of the German Commercial Union or *Zollverein*, and their applicability to the United States and the co-terminous or adjacent British Provinces and Possessions; the mutual relations of Great Britain and Canada, and the Colonies, so far as they affect the United States; and a method of negotiation for the removal of existing difficulties.' [...]

Date of the Treaty, and Policy advised by Agents of the United States' Treasury

With the intention of establishing a system thus mutually advantageous, a Treaty was made in 1854 by the United States with Great Britain on behalf of the Provinces of Canada, New Brunswick, Nova Scotia, Prince Edward's Island, and Newfoundland.

Various representations having been made as to the unfriendly, adverse, or restrictive legislation of Canada, the Hon. I. T. Hatch, of the State of New York, and James W. Taylor, of Minnesota, were appointed as Agents of the Treasury Department of the United States, to inquire into the operations of the Reciprocity Treaty. They reported the results of their investigations in 1860. Minor differences of opinion exist between the two Commissioners, but they fully agree as to the ultimate object of our national policy towards the Provinces, that of unrestricted commercial intercourse. [...]

Method of Negotiation

The Committee on Commerce believe, with the Legislature of the State of New York, that 'free commercial intercourse between the United States and the British North American Provinces and Possessions, developing the natural, geographical, and other advantages of each for the good of all, is conducive to the present interests of each, and is the proper basis of our intercourse for all time to come;' and that such measures should be adopted as will fully carry into effect the principles announced by the British Minister at Washington, in 1859, 'for the confirmation and expansion of free commercial relations between the United States and the British Provinces,' and to 'regulate the commerce and navigation between Her Majesty's Possessions in North America and the United States in such manner as to render the same reciprocally beneficial and satisfactory,' as was intended and expressed by the Treaty made between the United States and Great Britain, and commonly known as the 'Reciprocity Treaty.'

The Committee on Commerce would, therefore, recommend that three Commissioners be appointed by the President of the United States to confer with persons duly authorized by Great Britain in that behalf, with a view to enlarging the basis of the former Treaty, and for the removal of existing difficulties.

Lord Clarendon to Lord Palmerston, 20 April 1856, PRO, FO 27/1169.

I called yesterday to take leave of Count Orloff and to speak to him upon various matters respecting which I had received application from British Subjects. These were discussed in the most friendly manner by His Excellency who assured me that on his return to St Petersburg he would do his best to meet my wishes.

Afterwards in the course of conversation Count Orloff said that the present Emperor of Russia had always been opposed to the policy of his late Father, who, His Majesty thought, had sacrificed the true interest of Russia to vast military armaments, which were more than was required for the defence of the Country, and which he did not intend to use offensively.

His Majesty considered the real way of making Russia a great and thoroughly European Power was to develop her vast internal resources which were as yet almost unexplored. In financial, commercial and agricultural matters, Russia had as yet everything to learn, and as his Majesty was determined that she should be thoroughly instructed in them, he intended by all the means at his command to turn the Peace to good account.

And now that we have made peace, 'added Count Orloff', Heaven forbid that it should again be disturbed. I remarked that the prospect of maintaining peace would much depend upon Europe having reason to believe that the present Emperor did not intend to pursue the aggressive policy for which [his] Father had made such vast preparations.

Count Orloff answered I solemnly declare that the Emperor Nicholas never intended to take possession of a single inch of Turkish territory. I am now speaking of a dead man from whom I have nothing to hope or to fear, but whose inner thoughts I knew as well as his failings and have no object in misrepresenting them. From the moment he ascended the throne he entertained the conviction that the Ottoman Empire must fall to pieces, and that it was his duty to concert therefore with other powers and more especially with England as to the provisions to be made for that event in order that war might be prevented.

It was an 'idée fixe' with him, and he made no secret of it but when he informed me of the language he had held to the Duke of Wellington and Lord Aberdeen I told him he had been making proposals which responsible English Ministers would not listen to, I combated his wild scheme for making Constantinople a free port like Hamburg to be garrisoned by the troops of the five great Powers, but it was of no use. I declare however that he never entertained the notion of obtaining for Russia any portion of Turkey and that he never intended to go to war in 1853 and did not believe that war was even possible until owing to mismanagement and imprudence it had become inevitable.

Count Orloff further stated as his own opinion that the prohibition for Russia to have a fleet in the Black Sea would ultimately prove of great advantage to her, for that Russia though powerful was not sufficiently to have a large Fleet both in the Black Sea and in the Baltic, and that this prohibition would remove the apprehensions of Turkey and other Powers and would give free scope to commercial enterprise. With regard to the Emperor Louis Napoleon, Count Orloff said that he was much pleased with the frankness and calm judgement of His Majesty and his manifest desire not to create erroneous impressions – as an instance of the latter Count Orloff said that when he had appealed to His Majesty's generosity in order to make the terms of peace less onerous to Russia, the Emperor had been cautious and reserved, and had not given him the least expectation that he could would do anything singlehanded. With regard to France, Count Orloff believes that red republicans and other elements of disorder still exist and are only kept in subjection by a strong arm and by the Police, the activity and organization of which he described as wonderful and that if the present Emperor were by any accident to be removed that France would give as much trouble to Europe as ever. His Excellency implied though he did not actually say so, that no government could rely exclusively upon a French Alliance.

Count Orloff spoke with contempt of the Emperor of Austria and did not disguise his ill will towards Austria, not alone with reference to her late conduct towards Russia, but for the perfidious manner in which she always carried out her selfish and shortsighted policy, and he added that Hungary and any other province of Austria were eager to throw off her yoke.

He said with great satisfaction that Count Buol had left Paris disconcerted and depressed and when he took leave of the Emperor he had said to His Majesty that Austria was on the worst terms with Russia, that her relations with Prussia were not friendly, that she was treated with coldness by England, and that if he could not rely upon an intimate alliance with France his position would be one of dangerous isolation. Count Orloff promised me that no harm should befall the Tartars in the Crimea, who had taken part with the Allies and particularly those who had been engaged in the British Service.

His Excellency mentioned that when the Emperor was recently in the Crimea He had received numerous deputations from the Tartars professing loyalty and devotion to His Majesty.

Count Orloff said that as soon as diplomatic relations were established between Russia and the different Powers it was the intention of Count Nesselrode to retire from the direction of Foreign Affairs, but that he would still retain the office [of?] Chancellor of that Empire.

Cardwell Memorandum on Commercial Policy towards Russia, 29 October 1854, PRO, 30/29/23/4, fols 181–8.

Printed for the use of the Foreign Office.   October 31, 1854.

CONFIDENTIAL.

Remarks by Mr. Cardwell on the Commercial Policy of this Country towards Russia.

SO soon as it was determined, on the part of Great Britain, to waive those doctrines of the last war which aimed at destroying the trade of the enemy with neutrals, it was obvious that we must practically permit the Queen's subjects to trade with the enemy. The consequence of adopting any other course would have been to drive away trade from ourselves to neutrals; in other words, Russia would not have suffered. Her trade would have continued, though diverted into other channels. Our trade would have been destroyed. At the same time a premium upon neutrality would have been created; another result most prejudicial to the allies.

These considerations induced the allied Governments to relax the strictness of the Law of Nations, by Orders in Council, &c.

It is now observed, that British capital is still embarked in trade with Russia, and that the blockade of the Russian ports has driven the trade to the ports of Prussia nearest to Russia. It is therefore proposed to adopt new measures, namely, to prohibit British subjects from trading with Russia, and, by means of a system of certificates of origin, to prohibit the importation of Russian produce, whether through Prussia or through any other channel.

The Orders in Council are framed, as has been said, upon the supposition that the trade of Russia could not be wholly checked; and that it was not expedient to drive away from ourselves, in favour of neutrals, that portion of it which must inevitably continue to exist. Again, when the Russian ports were blockaded, it was known that so much of the Russian trade as could bear the cost of transport, would evade the pressure of the blockade, by passing through the ports of Prussia. Both consequences, therefore, were foreseen, and their actual occurrence only shows that the Orders in Council have answered the intention of their framers, and that the blockade has been effectual.

Have, then, any new considerations arisen, inviting the British Government to adopt new views?

Are we prepared to revert to our ancient doctrines, and, for the purpose of crushing the trade with Russia, to incur the hostility of all neutral Powers, and to sever our maritime policy from that of France?

Are we so dissatisfied with Prussia as a neutral that we are prepared to make her an enemy? or are we dissatisfied upon the whole with the effect of a blockade which has transferred to the ports of a neutral so much of the enemy's trade as it has not been able to destroy?

I understand that the proposal now under consideration simply is, that we shall prohibit any trade between Russia and ourselves, in the belief that by so doing we shall inflict a greater injury upon Russia than we shall sustain ourselves.

Before this conclusion is adopted, I think the following considerations should be weighed, viz.:

1. In point of fact, the trade and manufactures of Russia have, by means of the blockade, been seriously injured. It is a mistake to suppose that our measures have failed to inflict commercial pressure upon Russia.
2. The measure now proposed would have little or no effect upon Russia, while it would in no inconsiderable degree injure ourselves. It would also benefit neutrals: and this result, which we deprecate now when the benefit to Prussia is temporary, and obtained at the expense of Russia, would under the new plan be permanent, and would be obtained at our own expense, and not at the expense of our enemy.

1. In illustration of the first point, viz., that Russia is actually suffering a great pressure, I would observe upon –
   a. The annihilation of the Russian merchant navy.
   b. The diminution of the trade and manufactures of Russia.
   c. The diminished price of Russian produce at St. Petersburgh, owing to the cost of conveyance through Prussia.

Of these heads, the first needs no illustration; the second is fully set forth in two letters hereto appended: viz., one from the Foreign Office to the Board of Trade, inclosing a dispatch from Berlin to the effect that for some months past (i.e., ever since the blockade was established) the transport of raw material was too expensive to be borne, and the manufactories in Russia had been closed; the other a letter from the Board of Trade to the Foreign Office, showing the great diminution in the exports and imports of Russia; also the great diminution in the exports and imports of Russia and Prussia together, and the tendency of that diminution to induce a supply to the British market from other parts of the world; in other words, that England is obtaining what she wants, but ceasing to obtain it so much from Russia.

IMPORTS into this Country, January to September 1853–54.

From Russia and Prussia together.

	Tallow	Flax	Hemp
1853	288,455	978,447	468,940
1854	113,760	708,443	176,225
Decrease	174,695	270,004	292,715

From other Countries

	Tallow	Flax	Hemp
1853	249,727	266,937	319,972
1854	334,904	390,170	567,220
Increase	85,177	123,233	247,248

The third head requires some elucidation, and is of great importance. The system of carrying on trade with Russia has been that the English merchant is a year in advance of money to the Russian producer. It consequently follows, that in the first year of hostilities, the contracts being already made, the purchaser must bear the loss occasioned by any unforeseen expenses incurred in bringing the produce from Russia. But so soon as the time for new contracts comes, the English merchant will only give such a price as, after allowing for the additional cost of transit, he can pay. In other words, the pressure will, in the first year, fall upon England, and will in all future years fall principally upon Russia. This is apparent from reflection; but it is illustrated by the following figures, taken from a paper which has been furnished to me by the Governor of the Bank:

		October 1853	1854
Hemp.	St. Petersburgh	26 ½	21 ½
	London	36	60
Tallow.	St. Petersburgh	44	29 ½
	London	58/9	66

These figures show that while the general course of trade in the world has established a great rise both in tallow and in hemp, Russia is so far from participating, that she sells a much smaller quantity at a much lower price. Before I leave this subject I would observe, that the blockade has scarcely been operative at all in the White Sea, and that the apparent pressure upon Russia in another year will be so much greater.

It is then manifest, that already a very serious blow has been inflicted upon the trade of Russia.

2. Let us inquire what would be the probable effect of attempting to exclude all articles of Russian origin from the English market. First. Is it possible? Did Napoleon succeed in the like attempt? Are not the frontiers of France crowded with smugglers at this time? If it be answered that we have means of exclusion

which continental countries have not, I ask in reply, – If that be conceded, would it be wise to establish a stringent law operative in England and inoperative in France? Would it benefit England? Would it be effective against Russia? Would it tend to cement the good understanding between the allies?

But again; let our coast-guard be ever so effective, is not the scheme impracticable? What consular officer can ascertain the origin of tallow? or even of hemp? The provinces of Prussia, adjacent to Russia, produce both. Who can say from which country a given consignment springs?

Further; suppose it were possible. Is it wise to create a premium on the partial manufacture abroad of those articles which now come here as raw materials? If the fat of a Russian beast may not come to England in its first state of preparation, who can prevent its being boiled up with its Prussian neighbours, and imported as stearine with a valid certificate of origin? Is it desirable to transfer to Prussia either the whole, or any part, of the manufacture of soap, or of candles? Is it for us, who complain of the advantages which Prussia has already derived from the war, thus indefinitely and permanently to increase them?

Once more; suppose all that has above been referred to as impracticable could be effectually accomplished. Why has Russia been, hitherto, the chief producer of hemp and of tallow? Because she produces them best and cheapest. It has been shown that our measures have directly tended to impair her powers of production; and this is a serious injury to her, while we only share it as consumers, *i.e.*, as all the world shares it. But upon the new plan we should obviously injure ourselves, while the injury to be inflicted upon Russia is less clear. We recently repealed the restrictions on the import of slave sugar, alleging that it was absurd to maintain here a distinction which was effaced by the operation of the neutral markets. The whole tallow of the world, the whole hemp of the world, would be open to American and German purchasers; that limited part which has hitherto been least desired would alone be available to British purchasers. What a bonus to neutral ports as against London and Liverpool! What an inducement to establish manufactories in neutral countries of all the articles of which Russian produce is the raw material!

Do we not come back to the point from which we started; viz., either we must pursue the trade of the enemy in the hands of the neutral, which we do not propose, or else we must not disturb it in the hands of our own subjects? To do so would simply be to vex ourselves.

I have observed a sort of movement in favour of restriction in quarters where I did not expect it, viz., among those who are engaged in trading in these very commodities. This circumstance naturally led to the inquiry – Are the stocks in the hands of the dealers very large, and is it their object to keep up a monopoly price? From a circular which I have obtained, the London stocks appear:–

	1853.	1854.
Hemp – –	9,083 – –	15,235
Flax – –	718 – –	2,198
Tallow – –	20,160 – –	31,725

Very satisfactory, no doubt, it would be to those in whose favour we suspended the blockade of the White Sea, that so soon as their property is safely in dock the gate should be shut.

Even if the Government see the question in this light, and adhere to their former policy, the effect will to a certain extent have been produced by the mere alarm. I append a letter now lying for answer at the Board of Trade, illustrating this position.

I have seen observations on the state of the Russian exchanges, from which it is inferred that advances continue to be made to Russia; and it is argued that they ought therefore to be stopped in the mode above referred to. My answer is that they will not be stopped, and that if your measures be, which I believe they will not be, efficacious in diverting these advances from their former channels, you will not (for the reasons above given) have injured Russia, but will simply have transferred her trade from yourselves to neutrals. It is possible that in doing so you might affect the appearance of the London exchange, but I doubt even that, since London is now the money market of the world, and its exchanges vibrate with the transactions of trade, even when British capital is not directly engaged in them.

Let us, however, consider this subject of the exchanges.[1] What does a movement of the exchanges indicate? If Russia want gold, in whatever way she be seeking to obtain it, the exchanges will be affected. If the Emperor were to sell stock in London and order the proceeds to be remitted to St. Petersburgh, the exchange would be affected. It cannot be doubted that every effort will be made to obtain gold for Russia. It does not follow from a state of the exchanges indicating a tendency of gold towards Russia, that advances for commercial purposes have occasioned it; nor if such a state of the exchanges were due to commercial reasons, would it follow that Russia was deriving a benefit from it. The following state of trade (for example) might not be such as we should be desirous to disturb, and yet its existence would be attended by an exchange favourable to Russia. Suppose the pressure of war in Russia to have diminished the consuming power of her population, and that less sugar and coffee were imported; suppose, therefore (what is, I believe, the case), that capital had been withdrawn from the indirect Russian trade; suppose that (as we have seen) the cotton manufactories were closed in Russia, and that meanwhile hemp (useful for our navy) continued to be exported; and that in other respects what is natural had occurred, viz., that the producers of flax and tallow had continued to export those articles, though at a much reduced profit, *viâ* Prussia; suppose also that inasmuch as English-

1 [Ed.: A table 'Course of the Russian Exchanges' has been deleted.]

men are considerable holders of Russian stock, they are receiving their dividends in the shape of consignments of Russian produce: this state of things would be attended with an exchange favourable to Russia, and yet I know not that it would be very desirable for us to disturb it.

But before arguing upon the state of the exchanges, would it not be well to examine the fact? Has the course of exchange any indications tending to excite alarm? In time of peace 38d. is the value of the rouble, at which gold begins to leave St. Petersburgh; and 39d. the value at which it begins to leave London. In face of the present difficulties, the exchange may, I am told, be considered inert between 37¼d. and 39¾d. At this time last year the exchange was at 39d., indicating a tendency of gold from London to St. Petersburgh. It is now at 36¼d., indicating a tendency of gold from St. Petersburgh to London.

It is true that when war first was declared, and the export of bullion prohibited by Russia, the exchange fell to 33½d., from which it has since recovered, though (as we have seen) by no means to the state of equilibrium, still less to the state at which it stood before the war.

It was natural it should recover; for the purchaser who obtained a rouble for 33½d. could make a profit of 10 per cent. by smuggling bullion out of the country.

Still, therefore, the fact remains that the exchanges actually indicate (if they indicate anything) a state of things favourable to England, and adverse to Russia. I am always reluctant to draw rapid conclusions from the state of the exchanges; because so many complicated questions are involved in them. But I see, without surprise, that, in the present instance, they confirm the conclusions which have been above derived from other, and, as I think, less deceiving proofs.

Once more, therefore, I conclude as follows, viz,:

If you operate upon the whole trade of Russia, whether with neutrals or with British subjects – and this is the effect of the blockade – you seriously injure Russia, and you suffer only little yourself; that little being only what all other customers of Russia suffer equally.

If you operate upon your own trade with Russia – and this would be the effect of the proposed regulations – you seriously and permanently injure yourself, while the probability is that you will injure Russia very little, if at all; simply diverting her trade from yourself to neutrals. Indeed, in a political point of view, I doubt whether you do not upon the whole confer a benefit upon Russia, inasmuch as you give to America and other neutrals a positive reason for espousing the side of Russia.

October 29, 1854.

THE ANGLO-FRENCH COMMERCIAL TREATY OF 1860 AND THE TREATY SYSTEM

Britain's reaffirmation of unilateral free trade in 1852 was an important exemplar to foreign nations of the benefits of unrestricted commercial relations. Yet, as the previous section demonstrated, Richard Cobden discovered on his European tour of 1846–7 that protectionism remained entrenched and suspicion of British motives unabated. Whilst the policy of 1846 sealed Britain's position as one unguided by considerations of the commercial policies of foreign countries, Continental developments were keenly observed amidst broad expectations of tariff reductions. Some idea of the magnitude of the task can be seen in Richard Cobden's astonishment at the protectionist nature of the French tariff, and his comment in 1846 to the French free trader François Arlès-Dufour that 'Your tariff is far more illiberal *now* than ours in England was a quarter of a century ago'.[1] Yet with most foreign nations reducing their tariffs on British goods in the 1850s there was some cause for optimism, and the liberalizing tendency of American tariff revision in 1846 was particularly significant on account of Britain's role as facilitator.[2] Nevertheless, no European state followed Britain in renouncing protection as state policy, and in this sense Corn Law repeal gave only a partial stimulus to European commercial liberalization in the 1850s.[3]

The Whig governments of 1846–51 paid little attention to commercial diplomacy but the minority Conservative government of 1852, attempting to exploit Louis Napoleon's wish for a better relationship with Britain, began negotiations which ultimately proved futile.[4] In the same year, Michel Chevalier proposed a wide-ranging liberal reform of the French tariff in his *Examen du Systéme Protecteur*. Whilst little came of this plan in the short-term, Chevalier, regarded as the leader of the French free traders after the death of Frédéric Bastiat in 1850, proved instrumental in the making of the 1860 treaty.[5] In Britain, the pressure for reforming foreign tariffs came largely from the Board of Trade, indignant that despite British commercial concessions French legislation 'retains in full force its hostile and restrictive character'.[6] The Board attempted to demonstrate the beneficial effects of free trade, but French policy remained stubbornly protectionist.[7] The Crimean War intervened but if any hopes were entertained of extending Anglo-French military and diplomatic cooperation to commerce, they were dashed by Lord Palmerston and William Gladstone's insistence on unilateral 'non-diplomatic' free trade.[8] In Britain, there were increases on sugar, tea and coffee duties in April 1855, but as these products were not competing with native products, they were non-protective, and levied purely for revenue purposes.[9] The view that reciprocal negotiations and bargaining were a violation of unilateralism, although long held by committed free traders, was increasingly accepted.[10]

The tense international environment of the late 1850s provided the basis for a new Anglo-French commercial relationship. The Orsini incident and French involvement in Italy, as well as the huge naval base at Cherbourg, and the construction of the first French ironclad battleship, heightened suspicion of Louis Napoleon's expansionist ambitions, and led to a serious war-scare in 1859, prompting escalating military expenditure under Palmerston's consciously patriotic defence policy.[11] In this context, making a commercial treaty served other purposes apart from reducing tariffs, and the improvement of Anglo-French relations and maintaining peace were viewed by many as its main justification.[12] Conscious that the treaty contained more commercial benefits for France than Britain, Cobden argued: 'It is not present customers we want so much as the moral & political advantages which a complete revolution in the commercial system of France will confer on Europe & the world *in proving that the Emperor has renounced the policy of war & conquest*'.[13]

The resort to commercial negotiations and bargaining, in effect a return to reciprocal commercial relationships, was strenuously opposed by doctrinaire free traders, who viewed the process as a violation of British unilateralism.[14] Even *The Times* proclaimed the treaty 'a solemn declaration against those doctrines of political economy which have regulated the practice of this country since 1846, and the theory of this country since 1852'.[15] Similarly, John Bright informed Cobden that Charles Pelham Villiers, the prominent anti-Corn Law advocate, spoke 'as if to make a Treaty were contrary to Free Trade'.[16] There was also protectionist opposition, for any agreement with France would mean further commercial concessions. Yet, protectionist pressure was far more serious in France. The Chamber of Deputies was solidly protectionist and unlikely to endorse measures of commercial liberalism. It was therefore necessary to appeal to the 'enlightened despotism' of the Emperor. Chevalier convinced Cobden that, given the vested interests of the Chamber, an agreement with Napoleon III possessed more popular legitimacy. Chevalier took the initiative, and appears to have been the author of a plan for reforming the French tariff and making a commercial agreement with Britain.[17] Cobden was initially sensitive to traditional French prejudices, and reluctant to be viewed as 'pursuing a selfish British policy'.[18] However, Cobden's meeting with the Emperor proved successful, in convincing the latter that it was in France's interest to make such a treaty. Cobden hoped this would give an impulse to commercial reform and mercantile enterprise, and as such would render a service to France and Europe.[19]

The terms of the treaty lowered British duties on French silks, wines and spirits, and renounced any restrictions on coal exports. France abolished prohibitory duties and admitted British goods at a maximum of 25 per cent within five years, with immediate reductions on coal, iron and machine tools.[20] The treaty was an integral part of Gladstone's famous budget of 1860, notable for its abolition of Britain's remaining protective duties. The British tariff now levied duties only for revenue purposes, on products that were not import-competing, such as coffee, tea, sugar and wine.[21] Only forty-eight duties remained. Loss of revenue was compensated through the sale of terminable annuities, and by raising income tax.[22] The treaty was not without critics in Britain, with many viewing the concessions made to France as excessive. British industries competing with French industries, such as silk and ribbon manufacturers, wine merchants, victuallers and distillers, were at the forefront of opposition. The silk industry at Coventry, Macclesfield and Tower Hamlets was badly affected, with more than 20,000 weavers out of work by July 1860 owing to a 74 per cent increase in silk and ribbon imports from France in the three months since the treaty. The shipping industry was an important opponent of the treaty, for France retained shipping taxes, thus placing British shipping at a disadvantage.[23]

In moving from outright prohibition to protective duties, Cobden convincingly argued that France had taken an important step.[24] Yet many felt this insufficient justification for the concessions made by Britain. In criticizing the treaty in these terms, Robert Andrew Macfie also argued that the British customs system was dangerously reliant on a small number of duties, and that entangling alliances restricted British commercial freedom. Yet even Macfie recognized the political and pacific elements of the treaty, though he held the cost of peace to be too high. In his view, the 'Napoleon of peace' had taken an effectual step towards realizing the aim of his uncle, with ships, colonies and commerce.[25] The treaty was also criticized by the more fanatically anti-French sections of the press for aiding Louis Napoleon in his 'all-encroaching, all-corrupting French Caesarism'.[26] Yet, opposition was fragmented, and there was much support for the idea of extending free trade by treaty. John Bright reported that all the Chambers of Commerce favoured the treaty.[27] Indeed, one of the more notable aspects of the treaty was the extent to which the commercial community of Britain played a part in negotiating and deliberating over tariff rates, with delegations from Chambers of Commerce visiting Cobden in Paris, for consultation on technical issues and the consequences of changes in tariff rates.[28]

Although economic costs and benefits largely dictated opinion towards the treaty, economic considerations were not foremost in the minds of Cobden or Gladstone.[29] Rejecting the view that treaties represented an abrogation of free-trade principles or a return to reciprocity, Cobden viewed them as 'peace bonds between nations' rather than pacts between rulers, and potentially the basis of 'a great international compact'.[30] Towards this end, it was important that the treaty represented only the first stage in a series of international commercial agreements, and this was to be achieved through the most-favoured-nation clause within the treaty, which automatically extended tariff reductions in further treaties made by either party. After 1860, a number of other treaties were made which resulted in a European treaty system. France became the fulcrum of the system, and treaties with Belgium, the Zollverein, Italy, Switzerland and Austria made throughout the 1860s constituted the 'nearest approach to a liberal trading regime until after the Second World War'.[31] Moreover, an Anglo-Zollverein treaty was reached in 1865 and Austrian tariff reconstruction commenced in the 1860s, although there was little progress in Spain and Russia.[32] Nevertheless, for many European nations support for free trade was determined by pragmatism rather than ideological commitment. Liberalizing commerce was an appropriate policy for industrializing nations, in terms of securing cheaper raw materials, but no European nation followed Britain in dispensing with protective tariffs. Political pragmatism was also important, with Otto von Bismarck, the grand expositor of political pragmatism, supporting low tariffs in the 1860s as a means of excluding Austria from the Zollverein, and thus consolidating Prussian political hegemony in Germany.[33] Conversely, by the 1870s, protective duties served many fiscal and political purposes for Bismarck, for in resolving the German fiscal crisis it consolidated the power of the Reich against the Federal states and Reichstag.[34]

By the 1870s the treaty system had fallen victim to escalating military expenditure, fiscal crises and economic depression throughout Europe.[35] Even in Britain, the citadel of free trade, dissenting voices were heard by the late 1860s. Central to the dissatisfaction was the feeling that the treaty system had failed to advance free trade in Europe, and had involved a futile sacrifice of national industries. MPs for areas of manufacturing industries adversely affected by the French treaty were prominent, thus anticipating the later fair trade movement.[36] The contribution of individuals, the Emperor and Chevalier for France, and Cobden and Gladstone for Britain, in making the treaty appears remarkable, and a far cry from the view of the state acting at the behest of economic interest groups. Yet this modus operandi lent legitimacy to later claims that important manufacturing interests had not been fully consulted. As a policy instrument, treaties could extend commercial liberalization, but their resemblance to the reciprocity system, through negotiation and bargaining in making agreements, was perhaps closer than many free traders cared to admit.[37] National interests clearly informed the making of such agreements, and calls for a return to commercial freedom were a foretaste of the economic nationalism that enveloped the Continent, and to some extent Britain, in the 1870s. Yet it must be remembered that by the end of the 1860s the treaty system had advanced commercial liberalism in Europe to an unprecedented extent, and there was nothing inevitable about its demise.

Notes

1. Cobden to Arlès-Dufour, 9 September 1846, Cobden Papers, BL, Add. MS 43666, fols 207–9; J. A. Hobson, *Richard Cobden: The International Man* (1919; London: Ernest Benn Limited, 1968), p. 43.
2. S. C. James and D. A. Lake, 'The Second Face of Hegemony: Britain's Repeal of the Corn Laws and the American Walker Tariff of 1846', *International Organization*, 43:1 (1989), pp. 1–29.
3. C. P. Kindleberger, 'The Rise of Free Trade in Western Europe, 1820–1875', *Journal of Economic History*, 35:1 (1975), pp. 20–55, on p. 40.
4. A. Howe, *Free Trade and Liberal England, 1846–1946* (Oxford: Clarendon Press, 1997), p. 87.
5. See Richard Cobden to Michel Chevalier, 22 March 1851, above, p. 82.
6. Board of Trade Memorandum, 23 June 1853, in D. Stevenson and J. Kieger (eds), *British Documents on Foreign Affairs: Reports and Papers from the Foreign Office Confidential Print*, part 1, series F (Europe), vol. 9: France, 1847–78 ([Frederick, MD]: University Publications of America, 1983), p. 61.
7. E. A. Bowring's memorandum on the 'Effects of the Free Trade Policy Recently Inaugurated in England, as Indicated by its Practical Results' was published in the *Moniteur*, 23 July 1855, and continued to 18 February 1860, specifically aimed at Louis Napoleon. See PRO, FO 881/902; Howe, *Free Trade and Liberal England*, pp. 87–8.
8. Ibid., p. 88.
9. O. Anderson, *A Liberal State at War: English Politics and Economics during the Crimean War* (London: Macmillan, 1967), p. 204.
10. In the 1830s, the first report on Anglo-French commercial relations argued treaties were 'generally agreements for mutual preferences, and, in so far, are encroachments upon sound commercial principles', *Parliamentary Papers* (1834), xix.[64], p. 5.
11. J. P. Parry, 'The Impact of Napoleon III on British Politics, 1851–1880', *Transactions of the Royal Historical Society*, 6th series, 11 (2001), pp. 147–75, on pp. 157–60.
12. See Gladstone's comments to Cobden, in H. C. G. Matthew, *Gladstone, 1809–1898* (Oxford: Clarendon Press 1997), pp. 113.
13. Cobden to Henry Ashworth, 2 January 1860, Cobden Papers, West Sussex Record Office, CP 103, fols 69–71.
14. A. L. Dunham, *The Anglo-French Treaty of Commerce and the Progress of the Industrial Revolution in France* (Ann Arbor, MI: University of Michigan Press, 1930), p. 106.
15. *The Times*, 23 January 1860, p. 6e.
16. John Bright to Cobden, 5 February 1860, Bright Papers, BL, Add. MS 43384, fols 179–82; Howe, *Free Trade and Liberal England*, p. 98.
17. Ibid., p. 95; A. L. Dunham, 'Chevalier's Plan of 1859: The Basis of a New Commercial Policy of Napoleon III', *American Historical Review*, 30:1 (1924), pp. 72–6, on p. 74.
18. Cobden to Chevalier, 14 September 1859, in Hobson, *Richard Cobden*, p. 244.
19. Cobden to Palmerston, 22 December 1859, Palmerston Papers, University of Southampton Library Archives and Manuscripts, GC/CO/3; Hobson, *Richard Cobden*, pp. 245–52.
20. Howe, *Free Trade and Liberal England*, p. 92.

21. See George Frederick Young, *The French Treaty, A Mockery, A Delusion, and a Snare* (1860), below, pp. 169–73.
22. Howe, *Free Trade and Liberal England*, p. 95.
23. *Manchester Examiner and Times*, 24 July 1860; A. Marrison, *British Business and Protection, 1903–1932* (Oxford: Clarendon Press, 1996), p. 112; R. L. Schuyler, *The Fall of the Old Colonial System: A Study in British Free Trade* (London: Oxford University Press, 1945), pp. 199–200.
24. See Michel Chevalier, *The History of Political Economy*, trans. W. Bellingham (1869), below, pp. 143–7.
25. See 'Commercial Treaties and Free Trade', *Economist* (1860); and Robert Andrew Macfie, 'Notes on the French Treaty', *Liverpool Daily Post*, 16 February 1860, both below, pp. 161–3, 164–8.
26. *Morning Advertiser*, 31 May, 6, 13 and 15 June 1860.
27. See H. Reader Lack (ed.), *The French Treaty and Tariff of 1860* (1861), below, pp. 154–60; Bright to Cobden, 18 November 1860, Bright Papers, BL, Add. MS 43384, fols 236–7.
28. See Cobden to Bright, 16 January 1860, below, pp. 148–52.
29. Howe, *Free Trade and Liberal England*, p. 98.
30. Ibid., pp. 92–3; for an alternative view, of the constraining effect of treaties, see 'Commercial Treaties and Free Trade', below, pp. 161–3.
31. See Cobden to E. A. Billeroche, 12 September 1861, below, p. 174; Howe, *Free Trade and Liberal England*, p. 94.
32. See [R. Morier], *Commercial Treaties: Free Trade and Internationalism* (1870), below, pp. 187–95.
33. Kindleberger, 'The Rise of Free Trade in Western Europe', p. 45.
34. O. Pflanze, *Bismarck and the Development of Germany* (Princeton, NJ: Princeton University Press, 1990), pp. 452–6; J. M. Hobson, *The Wealth of States: A Comparative Sociology of International Economic and Political Change* (Cambridge: Cambridge University Press, 1997).
35. E. Eyck, *Bismarck and the German Empire* (London: George Allen & Unwin, 1950), pp. 252–3.
36. See debate on appointing a Select Committee into the operation of the French treaty, supported by MPs representing areas of the silk, woollen and worsted industries, 'The French Treaty', *The Times*, 19 June 1869, p. 8f.
37. See 'Commercial Treaty with Austria' (1866); and Louis Mallet, Memorandum on Modifications of Anglo French Treaty, 19 August 1871, both below, pp. 196–206, 207–11.

ANGLO-FRENCH COMMERCIAL TREATY OF 1860 AND THE TREATY SYSTEM

Anglo-French Commercial Treaty

Michel Chevalier, *The History of Political Economy Taught by the History of the Freedom of Labour to which is added an Account of the Negociation of the Commercial Treaty between France and England*, trans. William Bellingham (London: Effingham Wilson, 1869), pp. 44–8.

ACCOUNT
OF
THE NEGOCIATION
OF THE
COMMERCIAL TREATY
BETWEEN
FRANCE AND ENGLAND.

Letter of M. Michel Chevalier *to* Mr. Bonamy Price.

You ask me, my dear colleague, for a succinct account of the manner in which the Commercial Treaty between the two great countries of Western Europe was made: I hasten to comply with your request.

The origin of the Commercial Treaty between France and England goes back to the Exhibition of 1855. That solemnity demonstrated that French industry was very skilful, and that there was no pretext for protecting it by absolute prohibition or by exorbitant duties. The Government, consequently, presented to the Corps Legislatif in the session of 1856, a Bill to take off prohibitory duties. It will be remembered that since the law of the 10th Brumaire, Year V., prohibition was applied to nearly every manufactured article. The Corps Legislatif, commonly so supple, rudely attacked the Bill. The Government, all-powerful as it was, thought proper to give way and withdraw; it even felt itself obliged to engage, by a note inserted in the *Moniteur*, not to remove prohibitions until the lapse of five years. I had cognisance as a Councillor of State of the hostility which the Bill encountered, for the Council of State was the mediator between the Government and the Corps Legislatif, and the pretensions of the latter had been discussed in the Council of State. One of these pretensions was that the Imperial Government, though it desired to repeal prohibitions, was deprived of the faculty which it had under the constitution of the Empire to negociate commercial treaties involving changes in the tariff, unless those changes had the sanction of the legislative power. From this I was convinced we could never attain to a customs' reform and make way towards freedom of commerce, but by making use of this power acknowledged to be in the Emperor by the constitution, to make a commercial treaty without having recourse to the Corps Legislatif to sanction its clauses. In this state of mind I only waited for a favourable opportunity to present itself.

During the same Exhibition of 1855, for which I was a member of the Imperial Commission and of the jury, I drew up a declaration which was signed by a great number of jurors and commissioners from all parts of the world, in favour of the metrical system. Upon this basis, an international society was immediately constituted for the propagation of this system of weights and measures, and I was one of its presidents. It will soon be seen that this society gave an opportunity for steps which led to the Commercial Treaty with England.

At the beginning of 1859, Lord Palmerston, who had become head of the Government, offered Richard Cobden, then in America, a seat in the Cabinet, which the illustrious orator of the League peremptorily refused on his arrival in England. Though not willing to be a Minister, Richard Cobden nevertheless supported, with his friends, the Cabinet of Lord Palmerston against the Tory party. The Ministerial majority being weak in Parliament, the Ministry had the greatest respect for the group of independent members, called the Manchester School, of which Richard Cobden and Mr. Bright were the chiefs.

At this moment, negociation between France and England for a change in the French Customs Tariff, seemed to have chances of success, owing to the political interest which both Governments would make by it. The Cabinet directed by Lord Palmerston, would, if it made such a treaty, attach to itself the representatives of the great manufacturing towns, and to that extent add strength to its majority, which it much needed. The Emperor Napoleon III., on his side, feared the overthrow of Lord Palmerston, whom he found at that time amicably disposed, while the Tory party showed hostile sentiments. He would thus very gladly give strength to Lord Palmerston, independently of which it could not but be agreeable to him to enlarge the outlet for French industry in England, and to relieve France of the fetters of prohibitions, and duties virtually prohibitive, for he sympathized with freedom of commerce. During his exile in England he had attentively followed the conferences of the League.

Having gone to England in the summer of 1859, to pass some time with one of my friends, I had met Richard Cobden in London, with whom I was acquainted since the journey he had made in France in 1846, and I had put him in possession of the provision existing in the constitution of the empire, relating to commercial treaties. I had demonstrated to him the convenience and the legitimateness in principle of a commercial treaty between France and England, with the view of strengthening the bonds between the two countries by means of a treaty which would accomplish the reform of the French Customs. I had made him understand, that such a reform, however advantageous it might be, was absolutely impracticable, if it were to be brought about by means of a law which would be debated in the Corps Legislatif, owing to the prejudices, even the violently inflamed prejudices, existing in that assembly.

Richard Cobden had at first resisted the idea of a commercial treaty, alleging that it was contrary to the principle of commercial freedom, since, he said, it would oblige England to enter into particular engagements with France, whilst the ground which she had taken up in accomplishing the Customs reform of 1846 compelled her henceforth to treat all nations in the same manner. But he soon saw that the treaty could be drawn up in such a manner that England would modify her tariff in matters that interested France in favour of all nations without exception, whilst France would confine herself to making reductions in her tariff in favour of England alone. Once agreed on this point, we separated, and Richard Cobden prepared the ground by his interviews with the members of the Government.

In the month of October of the same year, I returned to England, profiting by the opportunity afforded me by the meeting of the International Congress of Weights and Measures which took place at Bradford, and of which I had been invited to be president. In reality, the principal object of my journey was the Commercial Treaty. I arrived in London on the 8th, and the next day I advised with Richard Cobden, who expected me, and then I left for Bradford in company with Mr. Benjamin Smith, M.P., an intimate friend of Cobden's, and one of the oldest champions of commercial freedom. Thence I went to Rochdale to see Mr. Bright, to whom my coming had been announced. He declared to me plainly that he would adhere unreservedly to the contrivance of the treaty of commerce, and encouraged me to work for the cause which, in the heartiness of his conviction, he called *the faith:* this was the term which he employed when we separated. I returned to Bradford for the meeting on Weights and Measures,

I did what I had to do, and on the 14th left for London, where Mr. Cobden had admirably employed his time.

M. de Persigny, ambassador of France at London, had been put by me confidentially in possession of what I had prepared with Mr. Cobden, and he had used his personal influence to the same end. He had already declared his opinion in France, when he was Minister, in favour of a great reform of the Customs tariff, and had taken part in the changes accomplished by decree, in a provisional document, *in the first years of the Empire.*

I had a conversation with Mr. Gladstone, Chancellor of the Exchequer, in the evening of the 15th after the meeting of the Cabinet. This was Saturday. I informed him of the provision of the Constitution of the Empire and the latitude which the Emperor thus had to negociate commercial treaties. I did not dissimulate from him, however, that I had no title to treat, but I added that, in certain circumstances, I had every right to think that the Emperor would receive favourably the idea of a treaty conceived in a large spirit, especially if that treaty abolished the duties still levied, which weighed on an important French manufacture, that of silk, also articles made of fur, and a great number of articles comprised under the general denomination of *Paris goods*, and, in fine, if there resulted a considerable reduction in the enormous duty levied on wines. It is well known that this duty was nearly six shillings a gallon, or 1f. 60c. the litre. Mr. Gladstone replied that England would abolish the duties upon all articles manufactured at Paris or Lyons, and especially upon silks, gloves, shoes, millinery, and articles called *Paris goods*, and would reduce the duty on wines from the existing rate of about six shillings a gallon to two shillings.

In three quarters of an hour all was settled between the Chancellor of the Exchequer and me. The arrangements about which we agreed were nearly those carried out by the Commercial Treaty definitively signed on the 23rd of January, 1860.

On leaving Mr. Gladstone, I went to join Richard Cobden, who awaited me at the Athenæum Club. We congratulated ourselves on the favourable turn which the project had taken, and we agreed to meet in Paris, where we were to arrive separately, so as not to give warning to the prohibitionists, who, if they had suspected what we were about, would have risen in arms and made it impossible for the Government to accomplish so necessary a reform.

Richard Cobden, whose family were at Brighton, spent some days there. I took the direct road by Folkestone and Boulogne. We met on the 22nd. The Emperor was warned by M. Rouher, whom I had seen in Paris immediately on my arrival, of what I had done, and that I had put myself in communication with Richard Cobden. He received us at St. Cloud on Monday, 27th, but separately. He told us that he adhered to the project of the Commercial Treaty, and recommended us to be secret for some weeks. The negociations would commence when the Emperor would return from Compiègne, in the middle of November. The negociators were, on the side of France, M. Rouher, Minister of Commerce, and M. Baroche, Minister of Foreign Affairs *ad interim*, in the place of M. Thouvenel, then away from Paris; on the side of England, Richard Cobden and Lord Cowley. I was present, and took part in the conferences. M. Achille Fould, Minister of State, who was in favour of the Treaty, entered with all his might into the favourable arrangements of the Emperor, who, besides, had taken his part. The Minister of Finance, M. Magne, was not let into the secret, nor was the Director General of Customs, M. Gréterin, who was, like M. Magne, for the restrictive system.

The secrecy recommended by the Emperor was well kept by everybody. I may on this subject mention the following detail: M. Rouher mistrusted his officials, the direction of foreign commerce being in the hands of a man, certainly very honourable, but a declared partizan of prohibition, and connected with the prohibitionist chiefs. The officials of the Ministry were therefore completely ignorant of the work with which the Ministers were occupied. The notes of M. Rouher were copied by Madame Rouher; as those of Richard Cobden were fair copied by Madame Michel Chevalier. When the terms of the Treaty were very nearly determined, the Emperor disclosed the business at the Council of Ministers, where many objections were raised. The prohibitionist notabilities, being warned, hastened to Paris. The Emperor and the Ministers, M. Rouher especially, were besieged. But nothing shook the resolution of the Government, and the Treaty was signed.

The name of freedom of commerce is not mentioned in it, nor in the reports and documents relating to the business. But the part which Richard Cobden and I had taken in it proved to every one, and especially to the prohibitionists, that freedom of commerce was the end which was sought. The Ministers, in conversation, did not dispute this. It must be acknowledged, from recent acts, that the zeal of the Imperial Government for commercial freedom seems lukewarm enough. Is this a simple political accident? Is it a sudden change? The future will tell.

MICHEL CHEVALIER.

Richard Cobden to John Bright, 16 January 1860, Cobden Papers, BL, Add. MS 43651, fols 60–7.

4 rue de Berri Paris 16 Jany 1860

Most Private & Confidential

My dear Bright

Although up to this moment nothing is signed & ~~signed~~ sealed, & although I therefore consider that nothing is really done, yet as only a week now ~~elapses~~ <is wanting> until the meeting of Parliament when the result must be declared, I cannot any longer abstain from telling you, in strict confidence, how the matter stands.–

When I came here in Octr & had my first interview ("audience" is the proper word) with the Emperor, I told him that if he were disposed to resort to his constitutional power of altering the tariff by a "decree", consequent on a Treaty of Commerce, our government would be able to make great reductions in articles coming from France which might give him some éclat in his wine districts, Lyons, Paris, &c – He asked me to give him, through M. Rouher the Minister of Commerce, a precise statement of what I thought could be done.– I did so; you can of course guess what they were.– He then sent Fould & Rouher to me to know what I should expect him to do in return.– I handed in a written plan in which among other suggestions I said their tariff ought gradually to be brought (say at the end of 3 years) to the following scale 6 to 8 per Ct on such articles of production as partook of the character of raw materials, such as twist, manufactured chemicals, &c: 15 per ct on common articles of manufactures: & in no case exceeding 20 per ct for articles of elaborate workmanship.– Of course I made other suggestions, such as the complete removal of all duties on raw materials.– After the delay of more than a month, during which M. Rouher was constantly employed in drawing up a plan for the Emperor, (it is a most fortunate thing that Rouher the Minister of Commerce has not only sound views, but a great sense <of> irritation towards the Protectionists who have for years bullied & plagued him) which he at last presented to him, & it was agreed to offer to make the duties on imports range from 10 per Ct to 30.– I then asked for another audience with the Emperor, & having received his formal assent to the principle of a Treaty, I employed the greater part of an hour in trying to induce him to lower his maximum. The result was that he referred me back to Rouher, & we have agreed to 25 per Ct maximum, *where we stick at present*.– The plan is to begin at 30 <maximum> &, after a year or two, drop to 25.– I don't know whether I told you that the Emperor is under a pledge, made years ago, to the prohibitionist party, not to invade their system till July 1861.– When the Italian war broke out these protectionists, ever on the alert, put in the plea for a "longer day".– This was in the spring of last year, & the Emperor then made them a vague promise of further delay.– I have got ~~them~~ <the government> to agree to Oct 1st 1861 as the starting time for the new tariff.– The first Treaty to be signed (& which, if ~~it~~ <at> all, must be executed this week) will merely fix the maximum, & it will be followed by another (the provisions of which are to be completed before 1st July 1860) for fixing the rates of duty on each article ranging from 10 to 30 per Ct, (to be afterwards reduced ⅙th) & which will really be the important work of the Treaty.– First the *advalorem* rates will have to be fixed, & then "Experts" named on both sides to convert them into "specific" rates, generally by weight.– I of course expect that for yarns &c, the duty will be at the lowest rate; & that <the> extreme maximum will only be exceptional for manufactures.– In fact, I am full of hope that, before another six months have passed, the French tariff <(to come into operation the 1st Oct 1861)> will be the most liberal of any *large* State out of England, including Russia, Austria, the Zollverein, & even the United States.– Such a total change, from absolute prohibition to comparative Free Trade, ranging over all the articles of the tariff, is I believe without precedent.– – Even if the Emperor were not pledged by his word to a little delay, such a complete reversal of a system under which the country has been existing for centuries, could not have been effected without the interval of a year or two to facilitate so great a change.– There are such measures as the abolition of duties on raw materials to be ~~off~~ carried out, in justice to the protected interests, before the latter can be dealt with.– The Emperors letter in yesterdays Moniteur points to these preliminary arrangements. – Yet strange to say (& I now write~~ly~~ absolutely for your own eye only) I am receiving the most urgent <indeed most annoying> letters from Gladstone, begging me to get *something* into the ~~tariff~~ Treaty binding the French government to some measures of *immediate* reduction of duties, & telling me that less importance is attached to a low maximum <for every thing> in Oct 1861 than to *something* being done *now*!– And this I can attribute only to the ignorant fear which the government have of these rifle club heroes who will pooh-pooh any thing & every thing coming from this side;– *And for whose existence the Cabinet are more than any other dozen men to blame.–* I tell Gladstone that the manufacturers & merchants, whose judgements (& not the Cockney rifle corps) will decide as to the value of this treaty, are just *now* little in want of more customers, that they have as much to do as they can accomplish; but what they want is some assurance that their profitable industry will not be troubled in future by the warlike policy of Louis Napoleon.– A commercial Treaty, such as is now in hand, will do more than any thing else to give them this assurance; & if *it be intrinsically a sound & substantial measure of reform calculated to allow of a permanent commerce between the two Countries*, they will not object to wait so reasonable a time as 18 months or so for its realization.–

Since writing thus far, your letter has reached me.–[1] I wish I could talk an hour with you.– The way in which I am worried to do impossibilities, & even threatened that parties in the Cabinet ~~will~~ <may> refuse, from our side, to let the business go forward, seems almost to justify your *illiberal* suspicions, that to a large part of the government the good work of pacification would not, especially at my hands, be acceptable.– I do not complain of G – himself, through whom all my correspondence has been carried on.– – Mean time, whilst people at home are so exacting, it is not easy to realize to oneself how the <French> government is to have courage enough to carry out even the terms they have agreed to.– Public opinion is absolutely unprepared for any thing of the kind.– You could not assemble together 500 persons in France, by any process of fair selection, of which 450 – at least would not be in favor of the present restrictive system.– Men of all parties admit that the Emperor alone is strong enough to destroy the prohibitive system in this Country.– I have no hesitation in saying that if Louis Napoleon were carried off by a fit of apoplexy tonight, this Country would be deprived for 20 years, if not indefinitely, of such a measure of commercial <Reform> as may now be secured & in operation within two years from this time.– Nor must it be supposed that he has not had his difficulties.– For two months he, & Fould, & Rouher, & more lately Baroche, have been laboring incessantly to reconcile the great majority of the members of the Cabinet Council to the Treaty – The most rabid "cannon-ball" of them all is Magne, the Finance Minister, who is disputing every step, & has sometimes kept his colleagues at bay for hours in the presence of the Emperor.– Count Persigny was sent for to come over & attend a Cabinet Council, to bring his *political* reasons in favor of the Treaty to bear on Magne, but without effect.– I have given him two private lessons, but might as well have been lecturing old Spooner.– To show you how pertinaceously he & his protectionist colleagues in the Council are trying to thwart the Emperor, I may mention the latest incident.– On saturday I had an appointment to meet, at 4 oclk, M. Baroche (who is acting as Foreign Minister till Thouvenel arrives, & who will sign the Treaty) & Mr Rouher at the Foreign Office –, when I thought I should have finished matters at last.– But a notice reached me at 3 that I could not see them – It turned out that at a meeting of the Council of Ministers that morning, Magne, aided by Troplong, had so worked on the Emperor, by telling him that his honor was pledged to an *enquête* before he reversed the prohibitive system, that he consented to an "inquiry", which was intended to delay the business indefinitely, of course, *like ours at home*, but which the Emperor has resolved shall only last for two days.– In the mean time, to satisfy me that he did not intend to draw back, he sent his letter to

1 [Ed.: 12 January 1860, BL, Add. MS 43384, fols 172–5.]

the Moniteur that night, & which ~~will~~ appears this morning. You will have read ~~this letter~~ <it> with interest, & I must still <tell> you another secret (absolutely again only for your own eye) apropòs of this letter.– A week ago, he sent me, by the hand of Rouher, a copy in M.S. of the letter with a request that I would read it carefully, & make my remarks on it.– I did so, & made suggestions for a couple of additions which he has adopted,– one is where he talked of lending money to manufacturers, I recommended the word *exceptionally* to be inserted; & the other was to add an allusion to the working class to the effect that they were not so well off as the same class in a neighboring Country, & that their lot would be benefited by the application of sound principles of Political Economy.– This letter I consider commits him to the policy of the Treaty, & although it is in some parts unsound enough, in our view, in bringing the "*State*" to the aid of individuals, yet it contains much that is proper to be done, & useful in itself.– But does not all this show how much forbearance we ought to feel towards him, & how *we* <I mean the English government> ought to try to facilitate his operations, as to time & manner, in the great <& difficult> work he has undertaken to accomplish?– I may here add that nothing which I said to him seems to have had so much effect as when I ~~said~~ <told him> that ~~comparatives~~ <comparing> the operatives of England & France, I found that their wages in this country were 20 per Ct less, whilst their hours of labor were 20 per Ct greater, & they paid upwards of 10 per Ct more for their clothing,– than with us.– He has sent to me for proofs, & it turns out even worse for the French operative than I said.– The protectionists here will not hear the last of this very soon.–

I am sorry to say there is no chance of my being able to reach home at the meeting of Parliament.– Yesterday we had a fog in Paris, & I nearly lost my voice from going out of doors.– There is nothing the matter with me but this susceptibility to the effects of the atmosphere on my bronchial organs.– My physician tells me if I go to London to sit late in the House, & then expose myself to the night air in Feby or March, I shall lose my voice altogether – It is very sad, but I can't help it – I must go South for a month or two.

Believe me Yours vr ty
R. Cobden

Now you know all,– I wish you would write me a few lines by return of post saying whether I have rightly interpreted the opinion which the parties interested in the North would form of this Treaty.–[1] Of course it would be better if it could come into immediate operation, & I am trying hard to get them here to agree to reduce the duties <at once & put them in the Treaty> on *our* linens & <linen> yarns (which are not prohibited) to a level with those coming from Belgium.– They were raised by Louis Philippe.–

1 [Ed.: See Bright to Cobden, 18 January 1860, BL, Add. MS 43384, fols 176–8. Bright was cautiously optimistic.]

When I ask you to write by post by return I of course merely wish you to refer *vaguely* to what I have been writing above – & I shall understand you.

The delay in the coming into operation of the stipulations in the Treaty will not endanger their fulfilment.– Our side of the engagement will be carried out to a large extent this spring.– Whatever faults the French may have, a want of honor or even disinterestedness in their foreign relations, as a nation, is not one of them.–

Richard Cobden to Arlés Dufour, 10 August 1860, Cobden Papers, British Library, Add MS. 43666, fols 224–5.

Paris, 69 Champs Elysées

10 Aug. 1860

My dear Friend

How are you? Let me have a line to tell me that you are better.

To-day the bearers of the enclosed from Sir Joseph Paxton have called on me. They are on their way to Lyons, S^{t.}Etienne, Bale, &c to inquire on behalf of the Coventry weavers into matters connected with the ribbon trade. I shall give them a letter to your house at Lyons with a request that any introductions which can be given to St. Etienne or elsewhere or any other facilities in your power may be afforded to them. I only regret that you will not be at home. But I shall be obliged if you will write by the first post to your son to ask him to do his best for these men.

It was a good idea & worthy of all imitation to send working men abroad to see with their own eyes how their fellow-creatures are fighting the battle of life. If all England could pay a visit of a few weeks to France, & all France could return the compliment, how many hatreds and prejudices, the foul offspring of ignorance, would be for ever destroyed, & how impossible it would be for Newspapers and diplomatists & statesmen to delude Frenchmen & Englishmen into the belief that they were only made to fear & mistrust each other. We are still at our treaty work. I hope we begin to see the end of it. I hope I shall see you again.

The Memorial from the Lyons' Chamber of Commerce is highly honorable to you all.

You need not return me the enclosed
Believe me yours truly
(Sig^d.) R. Cobden

H. Reader Lack, *The French Treaty and Tariff of 1860; with an Historical Sketch of the Past Commercial Legislation of France* (Philadelphia, PA: Collins, 1861), pp. 9–19, 22.

HISTORICAL INTRODUCTION.

In order to form an adequate estimate of the New French Tariff upon British Produce and Manufactures, it is necessary to consider the system for which it has been substituted, as well as the history of commercial legislation in France which has preceded it.

It is a fact worthy of serious reflection, that so far back as 1786 a Commercial Treaty was concluded between England and France, the provisions of which were, speaking generally, quite as favourable, as regards the terms upon which British merchandise was admitted into France, as those of the Treaty of 1860.

The brief existence of this liberal Tariff was one of the results of the war which commenced in 1793, and, with occasional intervals, raged during twenty years between the two countries; and the system of prohibition and prohibitory duties which compressed, within unnaturally narrow limits, the interchange of commodities between them, and which has shackled French commerce ever since, is one of the legacies which that war has entailed upon the industry of England.

The principal features of the Treaty of 1786 were as follow: – French wines were to be admitted into England at the same rate as Portuguese wines; vinegars to pay £33 per ton; brandy, 7s. per gallon; olive oil, the same as from other nations.

It was agreed that the under-mentioned articles should reciprocally pay: –

BEER, 30 percent. *ad valorem*

Hardware, Cutlery, Cabinetware, and Turnery, and all manufactures of iron, steel, copper, or brass, a duty not to exceed 10 per cent. *ad valorem*.

Cottons, Woollens, and Hosiery (except when mixed with silk), and Millinery of all kinds, 12 per cent. *ad valorem*.

Cambrics and Lawns, 5s. per piece of seven yards.

Linens, not to pay higher duties than linens imported into Great Britain from Holland.

Saddlery, 15 per cent. *ad valorem*.

Gauzes, 10 per cent. *ad valorem*.

Porcelain, Earthenware, Pottery, Plate-glass, and Glassware, 12 per cent. *ad valorem*.

The excise duties on certain articles, in addition to the import duties, were to be charged in each country.

The Declaration of Independence by the United States of America, which act engendered a feeling of universal brotherhood in the higher circles of French society, then all-powerful, is said to have led indirectly to the conclusion of this Treaty. However this may have been, it does not appear that the French manufacturers generally received it with any favour; they were, in truth, opposed to it from the very commencement, and petitions against the new treaty were being daily received in Paris from various parts of France, when the Revolution suddenly burst forth and put a stop to all commercial undertakings.

A second general Tariff was proposed in 1791, but things remained in a very unsettled state until the decree of March, 1793, appeared, which annulled all treaties of alliance and commerce with the powers with whom France was at war.

Events thus led to the establishment on a larger scale of the system of prohibition, which has continued down to the present time, owing to the weakness and instability of successive French Governments, which prevented them from carrying into operation any reforms in the commercial policy of the country opposed to the views of the leading manufacturing interests; in short, the monopolists have always been stronger than the governments.

By decree of September, 1793, foreign vessels were excluded from the coasting trade of France; and another decree of the same month and year prohibited the exportation of all articles of primary necessity.

In October, 1793, the National Convention proscribed all manufactures of British make or origin, and the productions of any of her colonies. Offenders against this law were liable to twenty years' imprisonment in irons. The professed object of France was to force England into peace; and as she could not hope to do so by arms, she endeavoured, by attacking the industries of the country, to bring her into subjection.

Negotiations for a treaty between the two nations were entered into after the peace of Amiens, but nothing was definitively settled before war again broke out, and Napoleon conceived the idea of isolating England from the rest of the commercial world. The celebrated Berlin decree of 21st November, 1806, prohibited all dealings with England. On the 23rd November, 1807, another decree, dated at Milan, declared that all vessels were seizable which had touched at an English port; and on the 17th of September following, another decree from Milan placed the British Islands in a state of blockade, and ordered the confiscation of all vessels, French or foreign, which had been visited by a British ship.

The Tariff was altered to keep pace with these decrees, and by the 5th of August, 1810, the duties on colonial products were fixed at the exorbitant rates of 400fr. per 100 kilogrammes for coffee and clayed sugar, 600fr. for pepper, 1,000fr. for cocoa, and 2,000fr. for cinnamon and nutmegs. All seized goods were publicly burnt, and the announcements were published in the 'Moniteur.'

In defiance of the difficulties thrown in the way of commercial transactions with England, the vessels of foreign nations braved all hazards, and as the scarcity of exotic products in the English markets had so greatly raised their prices, they made for an English port, at the risk of the utter ruin of the adventure, in the hope of realising great profits.

A multitude of means were resorted to in evasion of the Continental system. Smuggling, by corrupting official *employés*, and otherwise; supplying Russia by the White Sea, and the means of supplying the Continent generally with British manufactures and Colonial produce, were found out by multitudes of English, Americans, Dutch, Hamburgers, Danes, Swedes, and even by the French themselves.

The system of a Continental blockade was impracticable, and therefore absurd: impracticable, because France, instead of having a navy at sea to enforce the blockade of the British Islands, had her own squadrons blockaded in her own ports; impracticable, from the fact that France was unable to close the ports of Europe against English commerce; impracticable, if she could have done so, because she was not in a position to supply the Continental States with the products which they required.

Foiled in the attempt to destroy the commerce of England, and wishing to relieve the commerce of the maritime cities of France, Napoleon granted a certain number of trading licenses, which permitted transactions with England under special regulations. Thus the English trade was in a great measure restored. The blockade had not proved so injurious to the trade of England as might have been supposed, for, although shut out from the ordinary channels, new markets were formed in those allied countries in which England either subsidised troops, or whom she aided with supplies of money.

We pass to the Tariff of the Restoration of 1816.

This Tariff was based upon the model of the Tariff proposed in 1791. It maintained all the prohibitions established by the laws of the 1st March, 1793, and the 10th Brumaire, year 5, independently of others which it established.

It also established a *surtax* varying according to the place of lading of the ship or flag, and adopted a new classification of articles in classes.

No changes of great importance to this country have taken place in the French tariff between 1816 and 1853, if we except the case of linens, the duties on which were reduced in 1836, but raised again in 1845, in compliance with an outcry from the spinners of Northern France.

The prohibitions on bar, angle, and old iron, on cotton-yarn of No. 170 English and upwards, and cotton lace, on undyed woollen twist, on prepared skins, on chain-cables for the navy, copper wire, and some others, were removed in July, 1836, and high duties substituted in their place.

Whether tempted by the experience of England, or pushed forward by the increasing wants of the country, the French Government has introduced since the year 1853 many large reductions in the tariff, and more especially since the Exhibition of 1855.

In 1855, considerable reductions were made in the duties on pig, bar, and sheet-iron (by from 25 to 50 per cent.); on steel, cast and wrought (by from 50 to 75 per cent.), and on coals and coke (by from 18 to 50 per cent.).

In 1856, the duties on machinery were lowered by from 11 to 40 per cent., and numerous alterations have been effected from time to time, since the Tariff of 1816, in the duties on colonials, skins, dyestuffs, timber, chemicals, and raw products, still leaving them, however, very high, for we must not forget that, though the reductions in many cases have been large, the starting-point was prohibition.

By decree of 5th December, 1857, the greater portion of the export duties were abolished.

In all the changes hitherto made in the French tariff, it is easy to perceive that each successive alteration was effected either to give increased facilities of fabrication to a native manufacturer, or to prevent foreign articles from coming into near competition with his goods in the French markets.

The *consumer* was never for one instant thought of. It was proved some years back that by excluding foreign iron France was losing one million sterling per annum; and it is a well-known fact that for years past the French consumer has paid 50 to 100 per cent. above the market price in England for many articles of ordinary use. The duties upon iron and its derivatives are still far too high, but it is hoped that the manufacturing interests in France, which are now exposed to competition with England, will gradually call for some further reductions upon this important raw material of industry.

With this exception, the New Tariff is one of a liberal and moderate character; and when it is considered that it has been substituted, in the course of a few months, for a system of custom-house legislation more restrictive than that of almost any other commercial nation, the magnitude of the change will be seen in its real light.

The following Table of *Prohibitions* on articles of British manufacture will sufficiently illustrate the amount of protection which existed in the French Tariff on the 1st of January, 1860: –

YARNS:
Cotton, plain and twisted (except unbleached of and above No. 170.)
Woollen (except long combed, unbleached, twisted, cleansed, or baked).
Hair (except of goats, cows, or other cattle, and of dogs).
TEXTILE MANUFACTURES:
Cotton (except lace hand-made and spun and twill lace).

Silk and floss silk, stuffs mixed with false gold or silver, silk twills and imitations of cashmeres.

Woollen (except carpets, sieve cloth, ferrandine, and trimmings lace and ribbons).

Of Mixed Materials.

Hosiery, cotton and woollen.

Hair (except shawls, cashmere, from countries out of Europe, blankets, and hosiery).

Horsehair (except sieve cloth, trimmings. and hats).

LEATHER MANUFACTURES (except coarse pack saddles and empty wine skins).

SKINS PREPARED (except lamb or kid, calf and swan and geese skins, parchment, vellum, and large tanned hides for soles).

STONEWARE, fine or of pipe clay.

GLASS of all kinds (except mirrors, spectacle or watch glasses, full bottles, and broken glass).

CARRIAGES on springs, lined or painted.

CABINET WARE (except billiard balls and combs of ivory or tortoiseshell).

SUGAR refined.

SOAP (except perfumed soap).

GARANCINE.

TURMERIC (except in roots).

EXTRACTS OF DYEWOODS.

CHEMICAL PRODUCTIONS not enumerated in the Tariff.

PLATED ARTICLES.

IRON:
> Forged, in lumps or prisms.
> Cast, in pigs weighing less than 15 kilogrammes.
> Purified puddled, weighing less than 15 kilogrammes.

CUTLERY.

METAL WARES:
> Copper (except plainly turned).
> Cast-iron.
> Sheet or tinned iron.
> Steel.
> Zinc.

BRASS WIRE (except for strings of musical instruments and for embroidery).

SHIPS for sea navigation.

ROCK CRYSTAL, worked.

Thus all the yarns of Manchester and Leeds – the textile fabrics of Manchester, Glasgow, Leeds, Huddersfield, Bradford, Leicester, and Coventry – the stoneware of Staffordshire, London, and Newcastle – the glassware of Birmingham, Newcastle, and London – the hardware of Birmingham and Wolverhampton – the cutlery of Sheffield, and many other of our most important industries, were entirely excluded from the French markets.

The Treaty of January, 1860, abolished these prohibitions and substituted a duty not to exceed 30 per cent. *ad valorem* in 1861, and 25 per cent. in 1864. With the exception of the duties on iron before alluded to, and a few other articles, the average rate which has been actually fixed does not exceed 15 per cent.

The immense opening thus effected at one sweep for English manufactures, must have a very beneficial result for English manufacturers in general, whilst the stimulus given to French producers by the competition of English goods thus admitted into the French markets will be the means of developing the vast resources of that country.

The importance of the French Treaty must not, however, be estimated by the benefits which it will confer upon English commerce alone. It has a much wider scope, inasmuch as the reductions granted to England by that Treaty will be offered to the other European states, on condition that they, in return, moderate their customs tariff; and, as a matter of course, what those countries concede to France, they cannot long refuse to England. A Treaty between France and Belgium is now being negotiated at Paris, and the preliminaries for another are being considered at Berlin.

If these intentions are carried out, the Treaty of 1860 will have been the starting-point for a general system of reduction in the import tariffs of the Continent.

It is needless to speculate on the probable advantages to commerce that are likely to accrue from the removal of the restrictions which now fetter trade in many countries in Europe. England has long afforded an illustration of the benefits which result from a liberal system of commercial legislation, and no arguments are now needed in this country to persuade people that a large commerce can only flourish in those states where such impediments as protective customs duties are unknown.

The ordinary reader who may glance at this volume, and the public in general, are not, perhaps, aware that each rate of duty placed in the tariff has not only been considered separately, but that it has formed the subject of many discussions, and been anxiously debated by the representatives of that particular branch of trade, and to whom, no matter what became of the rest of the tariff, it was the one thing to have satisfactorily settled.

The labour of adjusting a tariff, which shall be fair towards each of the innumerable interests to be affected by it, is therefore no slight one; and the difficulty is still further increased when the rival interests of two great nations are concerned.

It may not, therefore, be uninteresting to state how the present tariff was arranged.

By Article XIII. of the Treaty of January, 1860, it was agreed that the *ad valorem* duties established by that treaty should be converted into specific duties before the 1st of July, 1860.

In order to carry out this agreement, a Commission was appointed by the English Government, consisting of Mr. Cobden as Chief Commissioner, and Mr. Mallet, of the Board of Trade, and Mr. Ogilvie, of the Board of Customs, as Assistant Commissioners. The English Commissioners opened their office in Paris at the commencement of May, 1860. The French Government also nominated a Commission, which was presided over by M. Rouher, the Minister of Commerce; the other members being M. de Fourcade de la Roquette, at that time Director-General of Indirect Taxes; M. le Comte de Lesseps, of the Department of Foreign Affairs; and M. Herbet, Chief Commissioner to the Conseil Superieur du Commerce.

A sitting of the 'Conseil Superieur du Commerce' was held for several weeks, previous to the meeting of the two commissions, for the purpose of obtaining evidence as to the relative cost of production and manufacture of articles in the various branches of industry both in France and England.

The witnesses, who were examined before the Conseil, consisted of representatives of the leading French industries, and of English delegates deputed by several Chambers of Commerce and other persons in England; and it will not be out of place to mention here that this country is greatly indebted both to those Chambers of Commerce and gentlemen who, at a great sacrifice of time and labour, not only procured the most valuable information, but gratuitously rendered their services to the English Commissioners in Paris in working out the details of the Tariff. [1] [...]

It was not till the end of June following that the 'Conseil Superieur du Commerce' finished its labours, and the two Governments were prepared with the necessary information relative to prices, freights, &c. The discussions of the duties between the two Commissions then took place, and lasted until the beginning of November.

February, 1861

---

1 [Ed.: There follows a lengthy list of merchants and manufactures who attended in Paris to give evidence before the Conseil Superieur du Commerce, as representative of their particular industries.]

'Commercial Treaties and Free Trade', *Economist*, 18:857 (28 January 1860), pp. 85–6.

Within ten days at latest the Commercial Treaty which our Ministers have concluded with France will be most likely in the hands of our readers, and we shall then be able to discuss its details more satisfactorily than we can now. In general, there can be no doubt that, if confirmed by Parliament, it will bind us to reduce or abolish the duties on French manufactures, silks, wines, and brandies; and that France will, in return, engage to reduce considerably the duties which she now levies on English manufactures, coal, and iron. These bare outlines are not sufficient to enable us to form a complete judgment of the merits or demerits of this very important treaty, nor do we propose to discuss them; but we think that we may, with some hope of being useful, state the principles by which it will have to be estimated, and the mode in which, as Free-traders, we are bound to view all conventions of the kind.

In the first place, as Free-traders we must not bargain for commercial advantages. This is one of the truths that mercantile nations have found it most difficult to learn. In England, however, it is now generally understood that we are benefited by our trade with a country in proportion to the quantity and utility of the articles we import from it. We know that we obtain in that way many commodities which we could obtain in no other way, and that we economise our own labour by producing commodities in which we have the greatest facility, and in exporting them to change for others in which we have comparatively a disadvantage and difficulty. We are now aware that the value of a trade is derived from the comforts and enjoyments which we find by experience that it gives to us, and not in any balance of the precious metals or supposed pecuniary profit to be obtained by overreaching the foreigner. From this simple view of commerce, it follows that, so far from making it a matter of favour to France to reduce our duties on the importation of French manufactures, we ought for our own sakes to be desirous to reduce them. Every such duty diminishes the quantity of French commodities which we can consume, and therefore diminishes the daily benefits which France confers on us.

Secondly, we cannot be parties to a fraud on the French, or on any other foreign people. We cannot condescend even to use the language of bargaining. We cannot truthfully say to them, 'If you will take our productions free of duty, we will injure ourselves by taking yours free of duty.' Because we believe that, by so taking those commodities, we shall not be injuring, but by benefiting ourselves. We cannot allow that the profitableness of any treaty with us shall be measured by France, or by any other country, on any other principle than this. We cannot permit it to be measured by any profit and loss account computed in accordance with maxims that we disown. Of course we cannot help the economical doctrines which may chance to prevail on the Continent. But at the conclusion of every commercial treaty, and during its negotiation, our statesmen are bound to mark their disbelief of influential tenets which they know to be unsound. If they do not do this, they run a great risk of endangering the best part of every sound treaty, because they submit it to the test of unsound principles, with which very likely it may be found discordant.

These are negative principles, and show what sort of commercial treaties we should not make. The following principles show what treaties we may make under fitting circumstances.

First, if we *happen* to have protective duties which are impediments to a foreign nation and undue advantages to our own manufacturers, there is no valid objection to our engaging to relinquish them. It was an error to have them, and we shall gain by their abolition. If foreigners will relinquish also their protective duties on our commodities, we shall be doubly gainers. We must not, indeed, wait for foreign nations; we must not delay for a day the abolition of protective duties which press on the consumer because continental nations do not do the same. We are bound to carry out the principles of free trade, and it is our interest so to do. But if, during the period that the process is incomplete, and while we are in the act of carrying free-trade principles into effect, another nation would come to us and offer to reduce her protective duties, we may with propriety engage with it to abolish ours. To some extent this is our position with France. We have still a considerable number of protective duties on commodities imported from that country[1] ... Most, though not all of these duties are protective duties. The brandy duty, so far as it is higher than the English spirit duty, which it is by nearly as much again (the English spirit duty being 8s, and that on French brandy 15s), will partly rank as a protective duty. And in so far as the commercial treaty recently concluded deals with these duties, it is not inconsistent with the principle of free trade. The departure from free-trade principles was in having such duties.

Secondly and lastly, it is not inconsistent with the principles of Free trade, though it may be objectionable on other grounds, to engage with foreign countries to reduce duties which we have imposed for the sake of revenue only. If, for example, it should be desirable to cement our alliance with any particular country, we may, without any departure from abstract principles, give up some Customs duties which we have imposed on the importation of its productions. Whether we will do so or not is a question of *policy*. We have to measure the advantages of the duties which we relinquish, with the advantage of the amity which we hope to obtain. Such transactions are in the last degree delicate. They are apt to hamper us in the future. They often do not benefit us in the present.

1 [Ed.: There follows a table listing the amount of duty levied on articles imported from France in 1858.]

They connect us with the commercial matters of foreign countries so intimately, as frequently to endanger the alliances which they were designed to render closer. They complicate the fiscal system, which, especially in a country like this, is in other ways but too complicated already. Still, such a treaty is not prohibited by free-trade principles. It is, in fact, not commercial, but political. It relinquishes certain fiscal advantages for certain other advantages. In the case of the forthcoming convention with France, it will almost certainly be our duty to enter on a comparative estimate of this kind. We shall have to say whether we think the augmented intercourse we may obtain with France by a reduction of the wine duties, is or is not a sufficient equivalent for the recourse to other modes of taxation which it will render necessary. We must compare the wine duties with such modes of taxation, and form the best judgment we can. All we wish to say at present is, that it is not contrary to any abstract principle of political economy to sacrifice revenue duties for political reasons, though it may be, and for the most part is, delicate, dangerous, and inexpedient to do so.

Robert Andrew Macfie, 'Notes on the French Treaty', *Liverpool Daily Post*, 16 February 1860, in R. A. Macfie, *Cries in a Crisis for Statesmanship Popular and Patriotic to Test and Contest Free-Trade in our Manufactures*, 2nd edn (London: Edward Stanford, 1881), pp. 66–70.

NOTES ON THE FRENCH TREATY, 1860.

The following remarks by Mr. Macfie were published in the *Liverpool Daily Post* of 16th February 1860. Of course they were but imperfect at the time, and could not be expected to forecast exactly the actual working and consequences of the Treaty: –

'The Treaty with France.
'*To the Members of the Chamber of Commerce.*

'The following are among the objections a supporter of the Government has to the treaty: –

'It concedes much in return for little. This is impolitic, because irritating to the British people, and not calculated to win us the respect of foreign nations.

'It *perpetuates* the inequality between our treatment of France and her treatment of us, by confirming it and withdrawing the main inducement to lessen it by lowering duties on importations into France.

'It deprives the United Kingdom of the power of rectifying that inequality from her own side by a change of duties.

'It deprives this kingdom of the power of reverting for revenue to the Customs duties which she abolishes, whatever the future state of the national finances. Surely no treaty ought to promise more than that France shall be treated as the most favoured foreign nation. On wine we reduce the duties without the power of reverting to higher ones.

'It deprives this kingdom of the power to legislate independently in regard to affairs that are exclusively her own concern, – how she shall raise her revenue, and on what; whether she shall have export duties or not; what she shall allow to be exported, and what not. Why should we become dependent on any foreign power to say what our Customs system is to be?

'It binds us to allow the export trade in coal without restraints, or duties, or limits, even though we may be engaged in war with the nation to whom it finds its way, or anticipate war with France itself; and this in spite of the danger of our own supplies approaching exhaustion.

'It is thoroughly one-sided. Witness: –

'I. The duties on the side of France are to be 30, and, by and by, 25 per cent. *ad valorem* (including charges of freight, insurance, and commission, in the valuation); whereas those on the side of the United Kingdom are, or are to be, almost universally abolished.

'II. It allows France duties of importation on coal, though it precludes Britain from levying duties of exportation thereon, between which kinds of duties, as legitimate revenue, in effect there is no substantial difference.

'III. It expressly reserves the present differential duties in favour of French shipping, while it precludes any in favour of British, thus surrendering a precautionary power contained in our laws at present.

'IV. We make a heavy surrender of duties on wine and spirits to please France; whereas France makes a great reduction only on such articles as, according to Lord John Russell, the nation cares little about her taking (see correspondence), and which, at least, are important aids to her as a manufacturing and agricultural people.

'V. We charge the costly brandies of France no more than our own common spirits.

'VI. Provision is made for the interests of the French colonies and North African possessions, but not a shadow of advantage to the colonies of Britain! Their produce and manufactures do not seem included in the reduction of duty in France; certainly not unless imported from the United Kingdom.

'VII. Importation from France, whatever the place of growth or manufacture, insures the advantages which we concede, whereas importation from the United Kingdom is not enough, unless it also be the country of production and manufacture.

'VIII. France is left at liberty to continue her present exclusive navigation system, or adopt any other, just as may suit her will and her interests. No option is left us. We cannot help ourselves. We must adhere to our bond, whatever the consequences.

'IX. The advantages given to France are immediate; those which they give us come into operation after a considerable lapse of time.

'What are to be our advantages from the treaty?

'It will secure a large market for coal and iron. So far as iron is concerned, we may look forward to a large increase of trade; beneficial to us, and much more beneficial to France – chiefly as a means of attaining greater manufacturing capabilities and agricultural advancement. So far as coal goes, the large increase of trade will be viewed with more indifference, because it is really a transference of capital stock which our own nation may want, as well as a transference of munitions of war, and of means of manufacturing rivalry. It will open up a large market for British manufactures, but under protecting duties which will operate seriously against trade. These duties may not prevent the trade becoming considerable; but they are so high that we should not receive them under treaty as a boon to be met by an equivalent, far less by such liberal concessions as we are asked to make.

'Granting these advantages to be real and valuable, the question arises – What do we concede to obtain them?

'We compromise our independence, and we endanger our commerce and manufactures. On these points a few observations hereafter.

'What, then, will be the general effects of the treaty?

'It will deprive the British Parliament of the right and the power to impose revenue duties on articles perfectly calculated to bear it. It will prevent such legislation, consistent with free-trade principles, as may be called for to meet special emergencies and unforeseeable contingencies, such as war with some other maritime power. It will give the Emperor of France a right to interfere in our internal affairs, as it already gives him the prestige of exacting and obtaining high-handed terms. It will expose British manufacturers and merchants to competition, for ten years, with rivals whom it effectually favours; for, as a matter of fact (witness the establishment of the beet-sugar trade), protection does, in a multitude of cases, answer its end: whether that end be legitimate, and the means to attain it expedient and fair, is another question. By means of differential duties to foster French shipping – and foster that branch of industry it will most powerfully – it must throw very much of our trade into the hands of the French. By the operation of French bounties (such as in the sugar trade, at any rate, are well known), and by exemptions from the monopoly in the use of new processes and the heavy royalties for that use where permitted, to which British patent laws subject our own people, manufactures will be stimulated on the other side of the Channel. The new Customs charges would augment this tendency.

'It will besides, and in all cases, confer a double advantage on the French manufacturer. He works without liability to the income-tax of 4 per cent. which the British is to pay; and he gains the benefit of protective prices on whatever part of his manufactured goods he sells at home. If he sells a half at home, and he can secure even only four-fifths of the protective rate, he pockets a 10 per cent. boon, which is denied to our countrymen. That the French will regard this protection as a valuable privilege, there can be no doubt to any one who knows what are the feelings that prevail within protected trades. That its value may and will be overrated does not materially affect the argument, which is, that belief in the value of protection, and its nearly-guaranteed continuance for ten years, will stimulate manufacturing industry among our clever neighbours, who, if outdone at the first by the cheaper and better productions of Britain, will ere long find out the way to improve. Perhaps we may by-and-by see the effect of the revocation of the Edict of Nantes reversed. That unhappy interference with the rights of man led to the settling in England and Scotland of many skilled artisans, and the introduction among us of new arts. This chivalrous interference with the natural course of events may cause the expatriation to France of thousands of our noble working population at the instigation of French manufacturers. Some of our own *masters* may themselves calculate that, as on what they send to France they have to pay 25 to 30 per cent., it may be more for their interest to remove their establishments to that kingdom, and supply their own country from thence. A similar transference of ownership of ships may perhaps arise sooner than most expect. There is apparently no benefit whatever in being a shipowner of the United Kingdom, but much in being a shipowner of France.

Merchants and shipowners, by a law of their nature, like eagles to the rocks where their eyrie is to be formed, tend, though with less rapid flight, to their best place for settling and fixing their home. It will make France the great depôt and their ships the great carriers of Europe. By having a bulky article like sugar, which she will have abundantly, as heavy freight, and coals as a return freight from Newcastle on the east coast, Liverpool on the west, Cardiff on the south, and the ports of Leith and Glasgow on the north, she will be able to lay down produce, attracted from all parts of the earth to Marseilles, Bordeaux, and Havre, at these various parts of this island at a mere nominal rate of freight, and on more favourable terms, than the British merchant can from London. It will be natural, and become usual, for goods to be warehoused in the French ports in preference to the English, because thereby a choice of markets will be obtained, which is a pecuniary advantage of no mean amount. But this choice is more than a pecuniary advantage to manufacturers – it is in their case deeply connected with the secret of success. The true means of the growth of manufactures is the extent of open markets, the certainty of large and ready sales. This will be secured to the French. And just so with regard to shipowning. Success there depends on the amplitude of employment and return freight. The tone of British legislation has no doubt been in this direction, independently of the treaty, but so far it has been unconstrained, and liable to review as new circumstances develop themselves. Under the treaty the advocacy of free-trade by Britons will go for little, because foreigners will hold we are not free to act on contrary opinions.

'Undoubtedly, the Emperor shows himself in this treaty the Napoleon of peace. He takes the most effectual step possible to realise the cherished desire of his uncle, – ships, colonies, and commerce. We may wish him success; but why concede our national independence as the condition? Why put our neck under the intolerable yoke of a treaty which, unlike former ones, is unequal, and must be galling, because it gives much for little, and not only secures for Frenchmen more favour than for our own people, but prevents our doing otherwise for ten years, whatsoever be the call or the necessity? Would it not be better to throw all our advantage from the treaty to the winds, and make a *present during pleasure* of every advantage it is intended to bestow on the French, rather than come under such a fetter? The great hero-patriot of our island learned from his uncle those memorable lines, which stirred him up to manly vigour, and secured the freedom of his country: –

> 'A maxim true I tell to thee:
> Nothing so good as liberty.'

'Let us, then, preserve our freedom of legislation, – our right to do what we will with our own; and this we can afford to do, for labour at present finds ample and remunerative employment, and we do not *need* new markets. Whether the French Treaty would, in the end, increase the demand for labour, is a question not easily solved.

'In the foregoing there is an intentional omission of reference to the supposed advantage of the treaty as a means of cementing our amicable relations with France, because it is not at all obvious that will be the permanent effect of a treaty so framed. Yet this paper will not close without ready acknowledgment of the excellent intententions [*sic*] of Mr. Cobden, its framer, and of her Majesty's Government, who, no doubt, in a most generous spirit have acted with a confidence more deserving of our esteem than our concurrence, that such an aim as theirs might justify unusual liberality.

AN EX-DIRECTOR OF THE CHAMBER OF COMMERCE.

George Frederick Young, *The French Treaty, a Mockery, a Delusion, and a Snare* (London: Richardson Brothers, 1860).

DEDICATION.

To Duncan Dunbar, Esq., Chairman, and the Members of the Committee of the General Shipowners' Society.

Gentlemen,

The duties and the responsibilities incident at all times to your position, are immeasurably increased at this moment, by the critical condition of British Navigation, and the universal and unreserved confidence reposed in you by the Shipping Interest of the United Kingdom. It has been throughout an extended life, my pride and my pleasure, to co-operate to the best of my ability with your Society, in defence of the interests connected with British Maritime Commerce, less from their identification with my own, than from my undoubting conviction that on the success of that commerce greatly depends, not only the prosperity, but even the safety of the State. If in the present struggle, the little effort I venture here to present should in any degree aid your efforts, it will afford gratification to

Gentlemen,
Your friend and fellow-labourer in a good cause,
GEO. FREDK. YOUNG.

Oakfield Lodge, Reigate,
28th February, 1860.

THE FRENCH TREATY,

A MOCKERY, A DELUSION, AND A SNARE.

'Free trade,' says the *Times*, in a recent article, 'is a thing easy to talk of, but difficult as a fact.' The columns of that journal, afford daily evidence of the facility; – the French Treaty aptly illustrates the difficulty. It is not to be surmounted by the piratical assumption of a name; – the Treaty is neither equitable, nor politic; – and it violates every principle of free trade. It is as our title designates it, a mockery – a delusion – and a snare.

It is a mockery. For after declaring its purpose to be 'to improve and extend the relations of commerce' between the dominions of Her Majesty and those of the Emperor of the French, it not only seeks that end by a surrender of British interests totally uncompensated by any adequate concessions of French restrictions, which is inconsistent and unjust, but by the third Article it absolutely sanctions the most obnoxious and injurious of French commercial regulations, by expressly stipulating that '*it shall not interfere with the differential duties in favour of French shipping.*'

The Emperor of the French, as the ruler of an independent state, has a perfect right, if he see fit, to pursue a policy calculated to extend the maritime commerce of France by a jealous exclusion of English shipping from her trade. But British negotiators have *no right*, spontaneously and formally, to recognize and virtually to approve that policy; and to admit such an approval into such a Treaty, renders the Treaty itself as a Free Trade measure, an insult to common sense, and a *mockery* to the nation.

It is a delusion. For assuming to be based on on [*sic*] the principle of a mutual abrogation of the impediments interposed by existing commercial regulations, to the friendly intercourse between the two nations; it seeks the relaxation of those regulations, not by providing for reciprocal and equivalent concessions; but by stipulations involving immediate and enormous sacrifices of public revenue, and of private interests, on the part of Great Britain; in return for the removal it is true, of absolute prohibitions from the French tariff, but by the substitution for them of a scale of duties which will still be in many instances little short of prohibitory, and in all be highly protective; and even these changes are to be postponed to a period comparatively distant. It is thus a *delusion*.

It is a snare. For holding out to many separate British interests the prospect of separate advantage, to secure the support of *each*, it conceals under cover of its multifarious details, the insidious and hazardous nature of its tendencies, as affecting the interests of *all*. It engages also the public sympathies, by falsely assuming a connexion with the popular principle of freedom of trade; thus rendering the public mind comparatively regardless of its dangerous bearing on objects of the highest public importance, as connected with the national safety. Thus it is a *snare*.

With these views, we denounce the Treaty, as a dangerous imposture. We proceed briefly to illustrate them.

In this illustration, to enter into minute detail is needless; the blots in the Treaty are 'gross as a mountain, open, palpable.' It sins practically against every acknowledged general principle.

It is an avowed dogma of political economy, that all liberations of commerce from restraint should be adopted on the spontaneous volition of the liberating State, founded on the principle, that freedom of commerce must in itself, and with certainty, promote the prosperity of every Country. Hence, even treaties of reciprocity are condemned by free traders, as inconsistent with the very principle of free trade. The French Treaty *is* presented as a treaty of reciprocity, and ought therefore on that account by free traders to be opposed. Lord John Russell's distinction is worthless and absurd. He would support treaties favourable to the emancipation of commerce, but oppose those that would fetter it. Can the Foreign Minister cite any reciprocity treaty not founded on the basis of a relaxation of restriction? The plea is simply ridiculous.

It is opposed to all *equity* and fairness in its arrangements. As between the two countries, it opens instantly the markets of Great Britain to all the products of France, while it keeps the French markets all but closed to British productions, by the continuance for a time even of prohibitions; and by the permanent retention of duties which may, under its provisions, amount to 30 per cent. As between the several interests of the State, it provides for the benefit of the Manufacturer, the Miner, and the Merchant, while it not only omits all provision for the Shipowner and the various interests connected with maritime commerce, but, by Article III, actually rivets on that commerce the fetters of exclusion.

It is at variance with every principle of *prudence*, as respects both commercial competition and public security. It provides only for a freer importation into France, of all those articles which constitute important requisites for the maintenance of successful rivalry in manufactures; for internal communication, and for other branches of commercial enterprize. The introduction of our iron and our coal is to be facilitated, that her railroads and her steam-engines may be improved: of our yarns of Cotton, Woollen, and Flax, that the more profitable subsequent development of her textile fabrics may be secured: of our Machinery, that she may advance and economize her manufacturing capabilities, by aid of mechanical power; and all these advantages are assured to her by the elastic stipulation, that the duties on the various articles enumerated are *not to exceed* 30 per cent.; by which she may at all times by high charges restrain the importation of articles in which she may find herself unable to compete with British productions, and by low duties encourage the introduction of those which are essential to enable her to oppose an effectual rivalry to us. Our coal, which is indispensable to a Naval Power, that can only be needed by France for purposes of menace or aggression against us, is to be secured to her, free of export duty, for ten years; while as, if in very derision, she engages not to levy any duty on the export of coal, *which she does not possess.*

It is inconsistent with all *precedent*. The French Treaty of 1787 [*sic*], negotiated by Mr. Pitt, was a Treaty of Commerce '*and Navigation*.' The existing Treaty with France, made by Mr. Canning in 1826, was similar. In the present Treaty alone, is the ominous and discreditable omission of Navigation. The Treaty of 1826 expressly declares the desire of the Sovereigns of Great Britain and France 'to simplify and equalize the regulations relative to the Navigation of both Kingdoms, by the reciprocal abrogation of all discriminating duties;' – and further, it reserves to the Contracting Parties the power of making such further relaxations 'as they may think useful to the respective interests of the two countries, upon the principle of mutual concessions, *affording each to the other reciprocal advantages*.' The Treaty of 1860 *confirms the differential duties in favour of French navigation, and gives no reciprocal advantage to that of Britain.* The Treaty of 1826 bears the signature of *George Canning* – that of 1860 is signed *Richard Cobden!*

In this last fact lies the solution of a problem otherwise inexplicable. How is it that a compact so humiliating in its spirit; so inequitable in its provisions; so opposed to principle, to fairness, to prudence, to precedent, as we have shown it to be; so adverse to the interests, and so lowering to the independence of England, can have been concluded? How could the British public be induced to tolerate its degrading impolicy, and British legislators to sanction its anti-national stipulations? By one expedient, and one alone. By affixing to it the prostituted title of Free Trade, and by consigning its construction to the hands of Richard Cobden! We have no desire to enter on the examination of disputed theories, and neither motive nor inclination to speak with personal disrespect of Mr. Cobden; but the truth ought to be plainly told. The whole transaction of the French Treaty is disreputable to every individual concerned in it; and in spite of all the fulsome eulogies bestowed on its negotiator, by those who were its concoctors and abettors, impartial history will so regard it. But we need not the future revelations that history will record, to enable us to unmask its hypocritical character, and to expose the motives that have led to it. Its origin is political; its end and aim, conciliation of the present ruler of France, and consolidation of the present British administration; the means for its accomplishment are as unscrupulous as its objects are humiliating. Hitherto, Statesmen and Scholars, have been entrusted with the negotiation of treaties. But instead of George Canning, we have now Richard Cobden. Let Cotton Spinners and Carpet Weavers rejoice, and Statesmen hide their diminished heads! Rochdale and Birmingham may henceforward take the place of Oxford and Cambridge; – the Irwell supplant the Cam and the Isis; – Cocker supersede Euclid; – and Porter displace Tacitus. Louis Napoleon and Richard Cobden are not unfitly associated. 'The eldest son of the Church,' makes war and the Apostle of Free Trade turns diplomatist, each for 'an idea.' Perhaps each may be equally successful. When Italy is free from the Alps to the Adriatic, and the visions of 'the Pope and the Congress' are realized, then may free trade be triumphant in France. We wait both issues; and we believe we shall wait long for them.

But meantime reflecting men, free from the trammels of party and the prejudices of theories, look anxiously and with sadness, at the strange complications presented in the Ministry and the House of Commons. The Budget is dextrously entangled in untraceable and inextricable confusion with the Treaty. The flippant Premier, and the constitutional Foreign Secretary – lately so pitted against each other in political rivalry – bow down together before the majesty of France. The *Times*, which on the 16th January supported in these terms the very reasoning we have urged, –

'France has at last some prospect of beginning fairly at the beginning, of obtaining for herself cheap coal and cheap iron – the constituent elements of manufacturing success; of basing commerce on increased production, a large mercantile navy upon commerce, *and a thoroughly effective fleet upan* [sic] *her mercantile navy*,'

on the 25th February, eulogizes the Treaty it had thus, a month before, criticized. The accomplished Chancellor of the Exchequer, oblivious of his hostility to the Income Tax, on his own declared ground of its being 'the most demoralizing of all taxes,' proposes that very tax to supply a deficiency in the revenue which he himself gratuitously creates. The talented and amiable conservative member for Northumberland, dazzled by the splendid vision of coals glittering in expected export under the Treaty, supports the budget of the ministers, whose policy he opposes. The aldermanic conservative representative for the potteries, characteristically anxious to give to the luxurious Parisians porcelain in which their dinners may be served-up safely at the epicurean temperature, follows the disinterested example; while the independent conservative member for Liverpool abandons his party, entangled in the meshes of the cotton web, so artfully woven by the authors of the convention. The justly dissatisfied, because neglected Ship Owner remonstrates loudly; but his parliamentary influence is slight, and his complaints, therefore, elicit scanty sympathy, and no effectual help; albeit, the neglect of his interests may involve the efficiency of our naval defences, and consequently the safety of the Nation. The whole spectacle is to the lover of his country, sorrowful and disheartening – but we must find our consolation in the conviction that to the best of our ability, we have done battle manfully in the cause of justice and of truth; and it is in that cause we *have* denounced, we *do* denounce, and we *shall continue* to denounce the Treaty concluded between Louis Napoleon and Richard Cobden, as –

A MOCKERY, – A DELUSION, – AND A SNARE.

Treaty System and Promotion of Free Trade

Richard Cobden to E. A. Billeroche, 12 September 1861, Cobden Papers, West Sussex Record Office, CP 6, fol. 91

Midhurst 12 Sepr 1861

Sir

In reply to your letter I beg to say that I feel great pleasure in replying to M Jaffroys inquiries – for I sympathise greatly with his views. They are the heroic free traders who seek to abolish the Custom house system altogether.

I am not aware that there is any protective duty in favor of the merchandise or flag of Great Britain, either in the United Kingdom or the Colonies. There is no particular document affirming this principle of Free trade to which I can refer. The present state of things has been the gradual growth of 15 years of continuous legislation in the direction of Commercial liberty. When in 1846 the great monopoly of the dominant class in this Country was destroyed by the abolition of the Corn laws, it was known that the whole system of 'protection' as it was called was overthrown. The corn laws were the keystone of the arch of Monopoly, & when withdrawn the whole structure fell of its own weight to the ground.

The navigation laws followed; then the restrictions on the Colonial trade which favored the mother country were removed; and year after year each succesive budget purged our tariff from some of its remaining protective <duties,> until last year Mr Gladstone completed the great work begun by Sir Robert Peel in 1842. I am not aware that there is now one duty remaining in our tariff which is protective in its object. We have many duties, such as that for example on tea, which are too heavy, but they are not maintained in the interest of any British producers.

The greatest boon perhaps that could be conferred on humanity would be the abolition of the Custom House System, & the removal of every obstacle which impedes the free intercourse between the nations of the Earth. I shall not live to see this great reform realised; but I have no more doubt of its realization than I have of the triumph of truth over error in any other question in which the moral & material interests of mankind are involved.

I shall be glad if you will allow Mr Jaffroy to see this letter
With my best Compliments
I remain truly yours
R Cobden

'Memorandum on the Commercial Policy of European States and British Trade' (1879), PRO, FO 881/3834.

Printed for the use of the Cabinet. February 1, 1879.
CONFIDENTIAL.
(3834.)
Memorandum on the Commercial Policy of European States and British Trade.

VARIOUS statements having been made of late with respect to the operation of European Tariffs, hostile to British trade, on the commerce of this country, it may be useful to show briefly how the case really stands.

Apart from changes in minor details of Tariff, there have been six important alterations in European Tariffs since the existing commercial depression began.

I. *Change especially detrimental to British Trade.*
Spain, 1st August, 1877:
The Spanish Tariff was revised at this date, and British commerce was excluded from the benefit of reductions of duty then made.

II. *Change especially favourable to British Trade.*
Portugal, 15th April, 1876:
When the Tariff of the Commercial Treaty of 1866 between France and Portugal, which had hitherto been withheld from England, was extended to British trade.

III. *Changes detrimental to Trade generally as well as to British Trade.*
Austria, 1st January, 1877, and 1st January, 1879.

Russia, 1st January, 1877.
France, 1st January, 1879.

The changes in the Austrian Tariff resulted –

1. From the abrogation on 1st January, 1877, of the scale of duties for cotton and woollen wares established by the English Supplementary Convention of the 30th December, 1869.
2. From the abrogation on the 1st January, 1879, of the Austrian Conventional Tariff and the establishment of the new General Tariff in its stead.

These changes affect the trade of all nations alike. But, as the Treaty Tariff of the 30th December, 1869, was devised in the interest of English trade, there is reason to think that the abrogation of this Tariff chiefly affected some branches of our mixed woollen manufactures.

The change in the Russian Tariff was the result of a Decree by which customs duties are ordered to be paid in gold. This measure in effect raised the rate of Import duties, to what extent our statements on the subject do not agree, probably about 15 per cent., but it cannot be said to have affected British trade more than other foreign trade with Russian.

The change in the French Tariff was the result of the lapse of the Treaty of the 11th December, 1866, between France and Austria. By that Treaty duties on certain steel goods, ships, and some other articles were reduced. These duties have now reverted to the amounts fixed in French Treaties of earlier date than the Austrian Treaty. This measure, again, cannot be said to have affected British trade more than other foreign trade with France; but the latest reports from Lord Lyons indicate that it will be revoked either wholly or in favour of some articles affected by it.

It is, however, to be remembered that besides the changes of Tariff abovementioned, alterations of duties are either intended to be made, or have been in discussion lately, in most European countries, more particularly in France, Germany, Italy, Russia, and Switzerland, and that trade has undoubtedly been much disturbed in consequence of uncertainty occasioned by these proposals to alter existing customs arrangements. This has more especially been the case in Italy and in Austria.

In Italy the intended change will probably take effect on the 1st of next month. The new General Tariff will then come into force. It has already been somewhat modified by the Treaty recently concluded with Austria, and it will be further modified by the Treaties about to be negotiated with France and Switzerland.

As this General Tariff stands it is represented by our trade to be, both in augmentation of duties and in new classification of goods, extremely adverse to British commerce. Representations on the subject have been addressed to the Italian Government at various times. According to the latest intelligence from the Embassy at Rome the Italian Government seem disposed to take these representations into consideration in connection with their negotiations with France.

In France, Germany, and Switzerland changes of Tariff are proposed to be made in the course of the present year. Experience shows, however, that the discussion of Tariffs in the Legislature takes considerable time. Nothing can, therefore, be said positively as to the date when any such changes will really take effect.

In France it is proposed that a new General Tariff shall be adopted, which it seems evident will be made the basis of negotiation with foreign countries. Its duties are in excess of those of the present Conventional Tariff founded on the English Treaty of 1860, on the average about 10 per cent., and they will, in fact, be further increased by a new classification of goods; and by the scale of values adopted for the conversion of *ad valorem* into specific duties.

In Germany it is proposed to increase existing duties, and to impose new duties on goods now free. The rates and classification are not yet settled. As regards English trade, iron wares are the goods likely to be chiefly affected.

In Switzerland a new General Tariff is before the Federal Assembly. In some respects it is of a Protectionist character, but in this instance it seems possible that the character is assumed with a view to negotiation.

In Russia some increase in the rate of customs duties appears to be contemplated, but no positive information has yet been received on the subject.

On the other hand, the new Austrian General Tariff has been modified in a few details, which scarcely interest British trade, by the Treaty of the 27th December, 1878, with Italy. It may possibly be further modified by the Commercial Treaties to be negotiated, probably in the course of this year, with France, Germany, and Switzerland.

In Roumania, in 1876, as an assertion of independence, and as a means of compelling foreign countries to enter into direct negotiations, a new General Customs Tariff was established. Previously an import duty of 7½ per cent., in conformity with the Turkish Tariff, had been levied; the new General Tariff augmented these duties very considerably – in some instances upwards of 100 per cent. Side by side with this new General Tariff, a Treaty Tariff, negotiated with Austria, was brought into operation, the benefit of which, under provision for most-favoured-nation treatment, was extended to the trade of other countries. This Roumanian Treaty Tariff in its rates is alleged to be nearly identic with the previously existing duties of 7½ per cent. But its rates are almost entirely specific, not *ad valorem*; and the classification of goods adopted is represented to be framed to suit the trade and manufactures of Austria-Hungary. Her Majesty's Government have been for some time past in negotiation with Roumania for the conclusion of a regular Commercial Treaty between the two countries. No actual progress has, however, yet been made in these negotiations. In the meanwhile British trade enjoys in Roumania most-favoured-nation treatment, under a law which places on this footing the trade of nations whose Government is negotiating a Commercial Treaty with that country.

In Turkey a revision of customs duties has at different periods been suggested, but nothing has been formally done in the matter. The present duties vary between 7 and 8 per cent. Sir H. Layard was instructed last August to report on the subject. He has called upon our Consuls to send in their observations; and his Report may soon be expected. Notwithstanding some representations which have been made, it seems evident that as regards amount of duty our trade with Turkey has no just ground of complaint. There is reason to think that frauds exist in the collection of the Turkish customs revenue, and that the Treasury only receives about 5 per cent. instead of 7 or 8.

It is to be observed, generally, on the changes of Tariff in the more important countries of Europe, that although in some respects their aim, and in others their tendency, is Protectionist, yet, for the most part, they are in truth the result of financial exigencies, and of the necessity for raising revenue by means of indirect taxation. The most Protectionist measures are, as regards new Tariffs already adopted, the Austrian and Italian; as regards changes contemplated, the German. In the two former cases manufacturers have, by means of Parliamentary influence, exerted pressure on the Government; in the latter the Government has strengthened the action of the manufactures.

There does not appear to be any intention of altering existing Commercial Treaties except as to customs arrangements. At least, no material alteration of their terms in other respects seems probable. Nor does it appear probable that a policy, in precise terms, of differential treatment will be adopted. The French, however, have evinced a disposition to curtail the wide language used in recent most-favoured-nation Articles; and possibly to extend the encouragement which the system of surtaxes d'entrepôt gives to direct navigation, and to adopt further measures to benefit the national mercantile marine.

It is, however, possible, and even probable, that the system of customs arrangements likely to be adopted in Europe will, in its future effect, be adverse to British commercial interests. It is to be remembered that the Conventional or Treaty Tariffs hitherto in force on the Continent have to a considerable extent been founded on the Tariff annexed to the Conventions supplementary to the Treaty of the 23rd January, 1860, between Great Britain and France. The new Tariffs adopted or proposed, apart from financial or protective considerations, have in some cases been framed, or negotiated, with the view to meet the requirements of trade between different foreign countries. The tendency to abolish *ad valorem* duties is much deprecated by certain trades; and the manner in which these duties are transformed into specific rates requires careful attention.

Thus, while except as regards Spain, up to the present time, British commerce can scarcely be said to have suffered from the operation of hostile Tariffs, it is not unlikely that before long our commercial interests may suffer from the influences and policy on the Continent to which attention is directed in this Memorandum. It is very possible that if a commercial policy of this nature is once settled it will be adhered to for some years.

C.M.K.
Foreign Office,
January 29, 1879.

Henry Charles Carey, *The French and American Tariffs Compared in a Series of Letters to Chevalier* (Philadelphia, PA: Collins, 1861), pp. 21–9.

LETTER FOURTH.

Dear Sir: –

The following is the passage of your Address referred to in my last, as furnishing proof conclusive that the policy of protection initiated by Colbert, steadily pursued by France, recently so ably advocated by yourself, and now so firmly established by the treaty you have made, is the true and only road towards domestic and foreign peace, towards the full development of human powers, and towards an ultimate entire freedom of international intercourse: –

'The treaty of commerce between the United Kingdom and France has already given occasion to a treaty of commerce between Belgium and France. In a few weeks probably it will have determined the signature of a treaty of commerce between France and the Zollverein, or at least between France and Prussia; for that treaty has already been for several months under negotiation. In a short time, I think I can assure you of it, we shall see concluded a treaty between France and that young kingdom, called to so glorious a future, which the noble and intelligent sword of the Emperor Napoleon the Third and the patriotic perseverance of Cavour have raised from the tomb in Italy. Each one of the States which has thus signed a treaty of commerce with France in consequence of the English treaty, or which will sign one, becomes a focus of propagation for free trade; and in treating itself with other States it determines them to propagate it around themselves. It is thus that the number of laborers in the vineyard of the Lord is continually increasing.'

Your countrymen, my dear sir, have a saying from which we learn, that 'whoso shall make of himself a sheep, will be sure to find wolves ready to devour him,' and all experience proves that such is certainly the case with regard not only to men, but also to communities of men. In the world of international commerce, England has always played the part of wolf, while seeking to induce the other nations to take that of sheep – permitting her to make of her little island the one and only 'workshop of the world,' to which all other communities were to be compelled to send their products in their rudest forms, to be there changed in form, and *there taxed*. Foremost and firmest in resistance to this oppressive system has been France. Other nations that hitherto have been disposed to play the part of sheep, have recently followed her good example, and with such effect that they appear now to be grouping themselves together for the purpose of making that resistance more effectual; but that any such action on their part can be construed into an admission of the truth of the British free trade doctrine, neither you nor I can readily believe. The ends they have sought to attain have been – first, a development of the power of association and combination among their own people; second, a development of agriculture consequent upon the creation of a domestic market for the products of the farm; and third, an assertion of their right to determine for themselves the form in which their products should be exported; and it has been for the purpose of carrying those views into full effect that they have had recourse to protective measures. British free trade, on the contrary, desires to *prevent* the growth of association everywhere, while dictating to all the world the forms in which their exports shall be made; and in the pursuit of that policy England has exhibited a steadiness and determination that is wholly without a parallel in history. That she has recently abandoned certain portions of her programme is very certain; but as I propose, my dear sir, to show you, not a single step in that direction has ever yet been taken that has not been forced upon her by the protective measures of other nations.

Prohibiting her colonists from bringing to her markets, except in their rudest form, any of their products, she thereby prohibited them from combination among themselves, while subjecting them to a taxation for transportation, for changes of form, for exchanges, and for the support of government, so oppressive as to take from the poor producer, as then estimated by British merchants, more than two-thirds of the total product of his land and labor. Prohibiting them from converting their rude products into commodities required for even their own especial use, she thus increased the quantity requiring to be transported to her markets, to be there converted, exchanged, and taxed. Prohibiting them from the use of any ships except her own, she thus compelled them to pay to her, and to her alone, the enormous amount required for the transport of so much bulky freight. Prohibiting the export of machinery, and the emigration of artisans, she thus denied to them, and to the world at large, the power to profit of the great discoveries in regard to steam, and to other of the great natural forces, that had then been made. Prohibiting, to the utmost extent of her ability, combination everywhere, she compelled Germany to send her wool – Russia to send her hemp and flax – India and Carolina to send rice and cotton – Jamaica and Brazil to send their sugar in its rudest state – each and every of these commodities being subjected to the payment of heavy duties on their entry into her ports, preparatory to their re-exportation in a finished form to the countries in which they had been produced. Occasionally, and only occasionally, her tributaries were permitted to feed some slight portion of the artisans she thus employed. Taxes on the food they sent were added to those on raw materials of manufacture, and the enormous amount thus raised was then appropriated to the maintenance of fleets and armies employed in coercing the producers of food and raw materials into submission to a system more tyrannical, more destructive of morals, more antagonistic to civilization, and more in opposition to all the teachings of Adam Smith, than any other that had existed from the creation of the world.

With time, however, there came resistance – this country setting the example of a determination to compel the recognition of equality on the ocean; a movement that was followed by repeal of the obnoxious provisions of the Navigation Laws. Following in the same direction, we find our protective tariff of 1828 compelling the disappearance of the tax on cotton – that of Russia, of 1825, doing the same by the taxes on flax and hemp – that of Germany, doing it in regard to wool – and our own highly protective tariff of 1842 giving the *coup de grace* to the restriction on the import of food. Thenceforth, all foreign nations were to be permitted to bring the raw products of their various soils, and to have them so changed in form as to fit them for consumption, without the payment of any direct tax for the support of the British government – the indirect taxation to which they were subjected, enormous as it was, being held to be entirely sufficient.

Such is the history of the rise and progress of British free trade – every step in that direction having been forced upon the people of England by the adoption of measures of resistance, in the form of tariffs adopted with the view of carrying into effect your own grand idea of *acclimating among the nations of the earth each and all the various branches of manufacture*, and thus familiarizing them 'with the working of metals and of mines, with the various departments of mechanics, and with the art of navigation.' For the accomplishment of that great object, the governments of those several countries had not been forced to resort to any 'abuse of power.' On the contrary, they had, my dear sir, to use your own words, only 'performed a positive duty in seeking to take possession of all the various branches of industry whose acquisition was authorized by the nature of things,' and they were being in part rewarded by the emancipation of their people from a taxation of the most oppressive kind. Having protected their people, they had ceased to 'make of themselves sheep,' and the danger of becoming a prey to wolves had almost disappeared.

That protection is the one and only road towards freedom of international intercourse, is proved by all the occurrences of the last thirty years. Were further proof of this here required, it would be found in the fact that the idea of reciprocity is found in none of the arrangements of England with those states which are either unable or unwilling to protect themselves – those which furnish sugar and tea, coffee and tobacco.

Of the amount paid by the people of England for sugar, no less than £5,000,000 is taken by the public treasury. Were there no such claim, the quantity of money expended on sugar would not be in any manner diminished – the consumption growing with a reduction of price that would enable both producer and consumer to profit of the change. The effect of this would soon exhibit itself in a rise in the price of the whole crop, giving to the whole body of producers probably six, eight, or even ten millions of pounds per annum more than they now obtain. Such being the case, does England, in her anxiety for reciprocity, propose to accept sugar from its producers at the same low rate of duties at which she desires them to receive her cloth and iron? Not at all! On the contrary, one of the essential objects of that war which is so well described in the public document given in my last, is that of compelling the people of the tropics to devote their exclusive attention to the sugar culture – to increase the quantity thrown upon her market – to diminish the price and increase the consumption – and thus to enable her to take a constantly increasing proportion of the product for the maintenance of her government. Anxious to sell cloths, she makes a war upon China which closes with a treaty providing for the admission of cottons and woollens at very low duties, but without the slightest suggestion of remission of any part of that enormous proportion of the price paid by the British public for tea (£5,000,000) which is now required for public purposes. So, too, with tobacco, which pays another £5,000,000, nearly every shilling of which comes from the pockets of men who are surrounded by great deposits of coal and iron ore which they cannot work, because of the 'determination of British iron-masters to destroy competition, and to gain and keep foreign markets;' and who are, therefore, compelled to devote their labor to the raising of rude products for the British market. Professedly anxious for freedom of trade, she so discriminates – or quite recently has so discriminated – against refined sugar from her colonies, as to compel her own subjects to send their products to her ports in their rudest state. Anxious, too, for reciprocity, when it suits her purpose, she urges with all her force a treaty between this country and Canada, and yet refuses to permit the formation of a treaty of reciprocity between her colonists of the West Indies and those of her possessions on this continent. Such, my dear sir, is the character of British free trade practice – each and every step toward any real freedom having been forced upon the government by the adoption by other nations of policies closely resembling that which France has so long pursued, and to which you have affixed your seal in the treaty so lately made. Such being its character, and there being now – as always heretofore – a manifest determination to 'overwhelm all foreign competition,' and to accomplish this by means of a warfare of the most destructive kind, can we regard Great Britain, with all her free trade professions, as any other than the wolf she always has been, although now appearing in the clothing of the sheep? As it appears to me, it is quite impossible that we should do so.

By Englishmen generally this suggestion may be regarded as most unjust, and for the reason, that they have so long been accustomed to judge of every measure by its probable effect upon their own trade, their own profits, their own manufactures, and their own power, as to have become almost entirely incapable of occupying any other stand point whatsoever. As a consequence of this it is, that, to use the words of your most distinguished countryman, De Tocqueville: –

'In the eyes of the English, that which is most useful to England is always the cause of justice. The man or the government which serves the cause of England has all sorts of good qualities; he who hurts those interests, all sorts of defects, so that it would seem that the *criterion* of what is noble, or just, is to be found in the degree of favor or opposition to English interests. The same thing occurs to some extent in the judgments of all nations, but it is manifested in England to a degree that astonishes a foreigner. England is often accused on this account of a political machiavellism which, in my opinion, not only does not exist any more, but rather less than elsewhere.'

The real charge to be brought against her is not machiavellism, but selfishness such as is above so well described, and which wholly unfits her for taking the lead in the work of organization in which your own country, my dear sir, seems now to be so well engaged. Of all the countries of the world, England is the one that has the fewest real friends, and hence it is that she has so entirely lost her hold on Europe. How she stood, a year since, on this continent, even among those who are now soliciting her aid for the destruction of this Union, may be seen from the following extract from a speech of Mr. Jefferson Davis, now at the head of the, so-called, Confederate States, delivered in the Senate of the United States, less than eighteen months since: –

'This English teaching, this English philanthropy, is to us what the wooden horse was at the siege of Troy. It has its concealed evil. It looks, I believe, to the separation of these States; the ruin of the navigating and manufacturing States, who are their rivals; not the Southern States, who contribute to their wealth and prosperity. Yet, strange as it may seem, there only do the seeds they scatter take root. British interference finds no footing, receives no welcome among us of the South. We turn with loathing and disgust from their mock philanthropy.'

Towards France, as I believe, there exists no such feeling as that which is here exhibited, in any portion of the world; and for the reason, that her position in the world of commerce has always been that of the sheep which has desired to protect herself, and not that of the wolf desiring to prey upon the sheep. The results of this now exhibit themselves in the facts, that by means of a protective system more stringent and more steadily maintained than any other in the world, she has been enabled to obtain the admission into the British markets of many of the most important products of her vast and varied industry, while retaining for herself that thorough protection for her own manufactures which had before been promised by the Council of State; and, that she is becoming from day to day more fully enabled, by means of the reciprocity system, to bring to act in concert with her, those of the countries of continental Europe whose policy has recently been most in accordance with her own – thereby bringing the sheep to act together, and thus enabling them more thoroughly to repel the wolf's attacks. The idea is a grand one – it being the organization of Europe at large in opposition to that system which looks to having but a single workshop for the world. Fully carried out, it cannot fail to result in placing France in the lead of both the political and the commercial world.

French commercial policy tends thus to the production of union between France and the advancing communities of the earth, and brings with it, as you so properly say in your Address, 'the thought of mutual approximation and of harmony among the most civilized nations' – that is, of those nations which have most adopted your own admirable ideas as to the duty imposed on governments so to act as to secure the taking possession of all the various branches of industry for which they are fitted, and thus to promote that diversification in the pursuits of their people which is required for the production of harmony within, and strength for resistance to all attacks from without. British policy, on the contrary, tends to the prevention of any movement in that direction, and hence it is, that in all the nations subject to it, we witness nothing but growing discord at home, with steady decline in the power for self-defence, the latest proof of this being furnished in the recent history of these United States; the Germanic Union, on the contrary, furnishing the most conclusive evidence of the advantages to be derived from moving in the direction indicated by France.

Thirty years since, Northern Germany presented to view a congeries of independent states, various in their sizes and widely different in their modes of thought and action. Small as they were, each had its little custom-houses, and, as a necessary consequence, there was but little domestic commerce, and absolutely no common bond of union. Prohibited by England from obtaining machinery, their people found themselves compelled to send their food and their wool to that country in search of the spindle and the loom, and there to submit to severe taxation as a condition precedent to the conversion of the two into cloth, to be then returned to the place from whence the materials had come, and to be worn by those to whose labors their production had been due. Food and wool were, of course, very cheap, while cloth was very dear, and the farmer very badly clothed. A better day, however, was then close at hand – stern necessity having compelled the formation of new arrangements which gradually took the form of a great Customs Union – embracing 35,000,000 of people – within which commerce was to be absolutely free. Without its limits trade was to be subjected to such restrictions as were deemed to be required for carrying into effect the grand idea of 'acclimating' among the German people 'the principal branches of industry,' and 'adding to woollens and cottons all that might be required for rendering them familiar with the working of metals and mines, and with the arts of navigation' – in full accordance with the ideas that you, my dear sir, have so well expressed. Under the system thus inaugurated, the people gradually grew in strength and power – each and every stage of their growth being attended by a disappearance of some of the restrictions under which they before had suffered. First, came permission to purchase machinery in England. Next, the English duties on wool disappeared. Again, the market of England was opened to their food. With each successive stage of progress towards commercial freedom, there came a diminution in the necessity for exporting raw materials, and an increase in the power to export finished commodities, with steady increase in the prices of food and wool as compared with those of cloth and iron, and a constant increase in the productiveness and value of German labor and land. With each, there came an increased desire for the formation of a closer and more intimate union than that which then existed. With each, the government grew in strength for resistance to aggression from abroad – that strength having, within the last three years, manifested itself to an extent that could scarcely have been anticipated, even by those who had most carefully studied the Germanic movement. Here, as everywhere, my dear sir, enlightened protection has proved to be the road towards strength and independence.

Thirty years since, the American Union exhibited a scene of prosperity, the like of which had never been known – a thoroughly protective tariff having largely aided in developing the industry of the country, while so rapidly filling the public treasury as, three years later, to compel the entire extinction of the public debt. Always turbulent, South Carolina was then as anxious for a dissolution of the Union as she has recently proved herself to be, but so strong was then the attachment to the Union that she could find no second. Three years later, the British free trade system was re-inaugurated; and since then, with the exception only of the years from 1842 to 1847, our course has been dictated to us by the class of men which thrives upon the profits of transportation, and desires, therefore, that all our products shall be exported in the most bulky form. Fifteen years have now elapsed since we last abandoned that policy to the steady pursuit of which France owes her present strength. With each and every of those years, the relations of American slavery and British free trade have been becoming more close and intimate. With each, there has been an increasing alienation of the several portions of the Union, and for the simple reason, that with each there has been a diminution of the power to maintain domestic commerce, accompanied by an increase in the necessity for looking to England as the only outlet for those rude products of our soil which we have not been allowed to manufacture. Having thus made of ourselves sheep, the wolf stands now ready to devour us so soon as a fitting opportunity for so doing shall be presented. Anxious to pass from that position, and to take once more our true one, we have now established the Morrill tariff, and although, as a protective measure, it is but a very feeble imitation of your own, as well as of those to which your German and Belgian neighbors owe their present wealth and strength, it cannot fail, as I think, ultimately to bring about a state of things that shall fit us for association, on a footing of reciprocity, with all those civilized countries where the plough, the loom, and the anvil are made to work together.

The raising of raw material for distant markets is the proper work of slaves and savages, and yet it is to that work to which British policy would restrict the nations of the world. Hence it is, that slavery and British free trade have, in this country, always worked together, and hence, too, it is, that there is, at this moment, so strong a pro-southern tendency in the general British mind. The more the tendency towards converting those raw products into finished commodities – the greater the tendency towards the adoption of your own most excellent doctrines – the greater becomes the power of both communities and individuals to rise from the condition of slaves to that of freemen. French, German, and Belgian policies look in that direction, and hence it is that there is so general a pro-northern tendency in the mind of Continental Europe. That in this respect your feelings are in full accord with those of your countrymen generally, I feel very certain, and therefore it is, that I cannot but hope that further examination of our recent tariff may lead you to the conclusion that its authors are entitled to the gratitude of every friend of civilization and of freedom.

That there is a perfect harmony of all real, permanent, and well understood international interests, I feel well assured, and equally well am I satisfied that the day is not far distant when you, and all other of the enlightened men of continental Europe, must arrive at the conclusion, that the interests of their respective countries, as well as those of freedom, would, in the past, have been much promoted by our permanent adoption of the policy of which France has so long been the chief exponent, and by our absolute and determined rejection of that barbarizing system which England seeks to force upon a reluctant world – and that in the establishment of our present tariff, we have made a move in the right direction.

Begging you to excuse my several trespasses upon your kind attention, and hoping that you may live to see the time when the whole of continental Europe shall be united in the formation of such a protective union as appears to be indicated by your Address, I remain, my dear sir, with great esteem and regard,

Yours, very truly,

HENRY C. CAREY.

MONS. MICHEL CHEVALIER.
PHILADELPHIA, October 31, 1861.

[R. Morier], *Commercial Treaties: Free Trade and Internationalism: Four Letters Reprinted from the 'Manchester Examiner and Times' by a Disciple of Richard Cobden* (London: MacMillan & Co., 1870), pp. 13–30.

COMMERCIAL TREATIES.

THE reply given by the Chancellor of the Exchequer to Colonel Akroyd and the deputation from the Chambers of Commerce in regard to commercial treaties involves issues of such transcendent importance to the future commercial policy of the empire that I trust you will allow me space enough to examine the general bearings of the question, and, at a moment when an unusual amount of confusion exists in the public mind as to the *raison d'être* of commercial treaties, to inquire into the first principles which govern the subject, and to which, however we may dislike the process, appeal will sooner or later have to be made.

No man possessed of the brilliant and, as I believe, the honest intellect which characterises Mr. Lowe, could, in so short a speech as that recorded in the *Times* of the 25th ultimo, have stumbled over so many fallacies, unless his reason were cramped by the trammels of a dogma. Now the dogma to which the Chancellor of the Exchequer gave official expression on the occasion referred to may be concisely defined to be 'that commercial treaties, as such, are incompatible with a policy of free trade.'

To a person only acquainted with the modern commercial conventions of which the Anglo-French treaty of 1860 was the inauguration and has continued the type, it would, I believe, be absolutely impossible to explain by what process of reasoning this incompatibility has been established as a so-called politico-economical maxim. To enable such a person to understand the process it would be necessary to furnish him with the anterior history of commercial treaties, and to explain how an unscientific generalisation from a particular kind of treaty had influenced the imagination of political economists to a degree which caused them to mistake the accidental attribute of one treaty for a general law inherent in all treaties. It is the history of every dogma. A relative truth is enthroned by the enthusiasm of those who first recognise it into the position of an absolute truth, and, when once there, the strongest minds accept the situation unquestioningly. Moreover, the *odium theologicum* is by no means restricted to theological dogmatism, it is a vice in the blood of every dogmatic school, and in none more conspicuous than in that of the political economists. With his dying breath, M'Culloch vented his impotent anathemas on the great work of Richard Cobden, and amidst the mightiest triumphs of the French treaty the muttered protests of the school of which Mr. Lowe has now proclaimed himself the representative were audible to those who had ears to hear.

The Chancellor of the Exchequer was the most brilliant of the many brilliant luminaries who shone at Oxford at the time when Aldritch's logic was the gospel of that University; he will allow me, therefore, to use the old familiar formulas, and to demonstrate the fallacy of the school he represents according to the strict rules of the art in which he was formerly so great a proficient.

The error I am combating takes the form of the following syllogism: –

All treaties of commerce are incompatible with a policy of free trade.

The treaty concluded in 1860 with France, and the treaties proposed to be concluded with Spain and Portugal are treaties of commerce.

Therefore these treaties are incompatible with a policy of free trade.[1]

Against the formal correctness of this syllogism I have nothing to say. I join issue with my opponents on the material correctness of the major premise: 'All treaties of commerce are incompatible with free trade,' and I deny *in toto* the accuracy of the proposition.

For the mere purposes of argument it would be sufficient for me to establish this negation, and to reduce the statement to that which is a correct description of the facts, viz., 'Some treaties of commerce are hostile to a policy of free trade.'

As, with this major premise and the minor premise, 'The treaty with France and the proposed treaties with Spain and Portugal are treaties of commerce,' it would clearly be a logical fallacy to deduce the conclusion, 'Therefore these treaties are hostile to a policy of free trade,' I could throw upon my adversaries the onus of proving that the treaty with France and the proposed treaties with Spain and Portugal belonged to the particular class of treaty incompatible with free trade. I will, however, do more, and not only prove that the general proposition on which the argument is based is erroneous, but also that, *though there are treaties of commerce incompatible with free trade, there are others not only not incompatible with free trade, but of the essence of free trade and its only true and definite expression.*

It is not difficult to prove that the general terms in which treaties of commerce, as such, are denounced are wholly unscientific, and contain in themselves their own *reductio ad absurdum*. A treaty is an international agreement to do, or to abstain from doing, something. An instrument of this kind having reference to commerce

1 Nothing can be more general than Mr. Lowe's condemnation, 'He must frankly state that he is not in favour of treaties of commerce; he was not in favour of their negotiation ... the plan for negotiating foreign treaties of commerce was mother of the heresy of reciprocity as against free trade!' He refuses, it is true, 'to enter into the question of the French Treaty, the negotiation of which was under peculiar circumstances,' thus slurring over a difficulty he did not like to face – for that treaty was either right or wrong: if right, we should continue the policy, if wrong, Mr. Lowe should use his influence in the Government to denounce the treaty when the lease falls in. He will hardly venture to do that. His hostility, however, to the treaty at the time it was concluded is matter of history.

is a treaty of commerce, and there are innumerable agreements connected with commerce existing in fact, and conceivable in theory, which by no ingenuity could be described as in any way trenching upon the province of free trade. That which is meant therefore when the wholesale anathema is pronounced, is not a treaty of commerce as such, but a treaty of commerce having reference to the duties under which the contracting parties agree that the merchandise of their respective subjects shall find its way into their respective countries; in a word, it is tariff treaties that are intended, and the proposition can therefore be narrowed down to the following: 'All tariff treaties are incompatible with a policy of free trade.'

Now, if we review the tariff treaties which, from the commencement of the last century until now, have been concluded by ourselves and other European States, we shall at once perceive that, amidst every variety of detail and the greatest differences on subordinate points, they can be collected into two antagonistic groups, differing from each other as light does from darkness, the *raison d'être* and the principle of the one group being protection and monopoly, the *raison d'être* and the principle of the other being free trade and the strangulation of monopoly.

The one class has for its object to bind the contracting parties by means of international engagements *not to lower their tariffs*, the other employs the same machinery to bind the contracting parties *not to raise their tariffs*. The one compels the parties to maintain restrictions on trade, even if altered circumstances should make it advantageous to remove them, the other compels them *pro tanto* to remove restrictions from trade, and precludes them during the period for which the treaty runs from re-imposing those restrictions, even if a momentary hallucination should make the one or the other of the contracting parties long for the flesh-pots of protection.[1]

The well-known Methuen treaty concluded with Portugal in 1703 may be taken as the type of the one class, the Anglo-French treaty of 1860 may be taken as the type of the other class. By the former England engaged herself, for all time to come, not to lower her duties on French wines to the level of her duties on Portuguese wines. By the latter, both parties engaged for the period during which the treaty was to run, not to raise their duties against each other above the level fixed by the tariffs appended to the treaty, France knowing at the time she concluded the treaty that England, having given up differential duties, would at once admit all the world to the same rates of duties as those agreed to with her, England knowing that it was the intention of France to grant her conventional tariff to all states willing to negotiate treaties with her on the basis of the Anglo-

1 That this most important function of commercial treaties, in a free trade sense, should be so absolutely ignored as it is in England, with the recent experience of what has taken place in France before our eyes, is one of the many proofs to what mere lip service the Cobdenic gospel has dwindled down. Where, I should like to know, in the political hurricane which has lately swept over France, would Monsieur Chevalier and the French free traders be, if they had not had the sheet anchor of a great international compact to rely upon?

French treaty. By this great international compact, therefore, for the first time in the history of commercial treaties, the object supposed to be of the vital essence of a commercial treaty, viz., the securing of *exclusive* advantages, was solemnly discarded, an international sentence of death was pronounced against monopoly, and free trade celebrated one of its greatest triumphs. That with these facts staring them in the face a large number of intelligent Englishmen should persist in talking of that treaty as a departure from the principles of free trade is a signal proof of the iron rod with which doctrinaires rule public opinion.

How completely Mr. Lowe has failed to realise this congenial difference between the two kinds of international engagement we are discussing, to what extent his mind is still under the influence of the old form of commercial treaty, how wholly unable he is to divest himself of the idea that a treaty of commerce as such is an engagement not to lower one's tariff, is apparent from his extraordinary statement to the effect that he thought it 'extremely undesirable that a Chancellor of the Exchequer should be precluded from removing duties when they ought to be taken off.' To anybody the least conversant with the history of tariff treaties for the last ten years it must be evident that to talk at the present day of a treaty by which the contracting parties should bind themselves not to remove duties would be much the same thing as to ventilate the idea of a treaty for the extradition of runaway slaves or the surrender of heretics.

The Alpha and Omega of the modern treaty of commerce is the setting up of an international barrier against the raising of Custom duties, and, by the action of the most favoured nation clause, the securing that every tariff reduction made by one state shall be shared by the great commercial confederacy, bound together by the network of treaties which owe their origin to the Anglo-French Treaty of 1860, and to that great heresiarch Richard Cobden. By means of this network, of which few Englishmen seem to be aware, while fewer still know to whom they owe it, all the great trading and industrial communities of Europe, *i.e.*, England, France, Holland, Belgium, the Zollverein, Austria, and Italy, constitute a compact international body, from which the principle of monopoly and exclusive privilege has once for all been eliminated, and not one member of which can take off a single duty without all the other members at once partaking in the increased trading facilities thereby created. By the self-registering action of the most favoured nation clause, common to this network of treaties, the tariff level of the whole body is being continually lowered, and the road being paved towards the final embodiment of the free-trade principle in the international engagement to abolish all duties other than those levied for revenue purposes.

That such an engagement will, doubtless, be a restriction of that individual liberty of action which to the Chancellor of the Exchequer appears as the *summum bonum* of international intercourse is undoubtedly true. But that this restriction is a restriction made in favour of individual liberty, is what his school persistently shut their eyes to. We need not go back to Saint Paul to prove that law and liberty are correlative terms. To secure individual liberty we keep up a police force, whose business it is to prevent one set of citizens from interfering with the individual liberty of another set of citizens by murdering or robbing them. To argue that this is an undue interference with the individual liberty of murderers and burglars, and to protest against a police force on that ground, is to plead in favour of anarchy and *pro tanto* against liberty.

Now, what municipal law is to the individual citizen, international engagements are to the international unit. The modern commercial treaty, therefore, to the extent to which it keeps down protection, is a law preventing one set of human beings from robbing another set of human beings, and an international compact against Customs duties other than of a fiscal kind, should it ever be realised, will be a general law against international robbery.

To the policy which I have thus imperfectly attempted to describe, a policy inaugurated by us and stamped with the name of Cobden, but which our leading statesmen are now openly repudiating, we have it in our power to give an almost incalculable impulse by the negotiation of twin treaties with Spain and Portugal. By sacrificing out of our four millions of surplus some two or three hundred thousand pounds of wine duties, we could at once reduce the tariffs of those two countries to a level which would open up the markets of the Peninsula to our manufactures. But this would be but a small part of the victory gained in the cause of free trade. The conventional tariff agreed to with us would form the basis on which each of the two countries would negotiate treaties with the other states within the network; it is next to certain that from each they would in return get some remissions of duty below the present level – each such concession as shown above would not only be shared in by us, but by all those states, and thus by the time Spain and Portugal had completed their cycle of treaties, the area of what may be fairly termed the 'Anti-Monopoly International Alliance' would not only have been increased by two states of first magnitude, but the tariff level of the entire body would have been materially lowered.

The favourite argument of M'Culloch and his disciples, that because it is in the interest of a country to lower its tariff irrespectively of other countries lowering theirs, it is immoral to add supplementary inducements – in other words, that it is immoral to bribe people to do that which it is in their own interests to do, is so supremely silly as not to deserve serious refutation. We might as well say that a child who refuses to take medicine unless the taste has been first disguised, should be allowed to die rather than that the sugar should be put in, because it is for its advantage to take the medicine whether sweetened or not. I want the child free trade to live, and I maintain that it ought to be the national policy of Great Britain to use every legitimate means to save so valuable a life. Manchester, and Manchester only, can force a policy of this kind on the Government. The reorganisation of the Manchester school, on the larger and more philosophical basis of international co-operation, is an imperative necessity. The Chancellor of the Exchequer, as I began by observing, possesses, in my opinion, an honest intellect; but a man at his time of life, especially a Cabinet Minister, does not reconsider his opinions unless forced to do so. Moreover, in all he says and does there is a flavour of infallibility which points to the necessity of using considerable pressure from without. I can only hope that his utterances on the 25th of February were not made *ex cathedrâ*, and that an appeal may therefore be attempted with success, 'a Papâ male informato ad Papam melius informandum.' – I am, sir, your obedient servant,

A Disciple of Richard Cobden.

II.

'Give a good dog a bad name, and you may as well hang him,' is a saying the correctness of which is very generally admitted. I am inclined to believe that the converse of the proposition is equally true, 'Give a good name to a bad dog, and for any further use that you may hope to derive from the name you may as well erase it from your vocabulary.'

This is pre-eminently the case with the word 'reciprocity.' A more innocent word I think it would be difficult to find. Though, strictly speaking, neutral, so that it can be applied as well to the returning of evil for evil as of good for good, yet I must confess that, until lately, I had associated something of kindliness and geniality with it. Somehow it seemed to me rather the companion of such rules as 'Do unto others as you would they should do unto you,' than of maxims like 'Treat a friend as if he may some day be an enemy,' and the like. We awake one fine morning and all this is changed. 'Reciprocity' has become a by-word among the nations. It is the name of a heresy for the professors of which 'San benitos' and 'auto da fes' must be prepared. The bad dog, Protection, has re-christened himself with it, and the hue and cry of free traders and pseudo free traders are pursuing him through the streets and lanes of the town. 'Hurrah for Free Trade; down with Reciprocity' – 'Hurrah for Reciprocity; down with Free Trade,' are the delightfully logical cries which assail our ears. Now, this may be all right and proper as a question of party warfare, and is, I have no doubt, in addition very amusing to the political gallery; but to the serious political economist, who knows the imperative necessity, in every scientific inquiry, of a hypercorrect use of language, and who has been taught by experience how endless are the fallacies which crop up from the slightest phraseological carelessness, it is profoundly irritating.

The Chancellor of the Exchequer told the deputation from the Chambers of Commerce 'that the plan for negotiating commercial treaties was mother of the heresy of Reciprocity versus Free Trade.'

Let us examine the exact value and meaning of these words. The most obvious fact in connection with them is that they assert the existence of a direct opposition between the idea involved in reciprocity and the idea involved in free trade. Nothing in which the idea of reciprocity enters is compatible with free trade; nothing in which the idea of free trade enters is compatible with reciprocity. Now, what are the ideas expressed by the two terms, 'free trade' and 'reciprocity,' between which this opposition is supposed to lie?

Trade presupposes the existence of two or more parties between whom an exchange of merchandise takes place. Free trade, or rather free exchange, which is the much more correct term used by our French neighbours, implies that this exchange shall take place freely, without let or hindrance. The particular kinds of let and hindrance associated with the idea of free trade, or its reverse, are Customs duties of a prohibitive or protective kind. It is clear that until *all* these lets and hindrances are removed, it is an incorrect use of language to talk of *free* trade. If one of two countries, between which exchanges take place, lowers its Customs duties and the other does not, or if one removes them altogether and the other only lowers them, there is a diminution of the lets and hindrances, and 'pro tanto,' a step taken in the direction of free trade; but freedom of trade itself has as yet no existence. A slave has chains on both his hands and both his feet. You remove them from one hand and one foot, and he has a freer use of his limbs than he had before, but he is as much a slave as formerly; his freedom has as yet no existence.

Free trade between two countries, therefore, means the removal of prohibitive and protective duties by both countries.

Reciprocity as a statement of fact implies the existence of two parties, each of which treats the other as that other treats it. As an enunciation of principle it may either mean the putting forth of the claim that others should do unto me as I do unto them, or, the reservation of the right to do unto them as they do unto me.

We have seen that free trade cannot be predicated of the commercial intercourse between two countries until *all* restrictions in the way of Customs duties other than fiscal have been removed.

In the case therefore of two countries, A and B, one of which, A, has taken off all its Customs duties other than fiscal, and the other, B, has only lowered its Customs duties, free trade cannot be predicated. As regards these countries, free trade will only come into existence when B has done the same thing as A – *i.e.*, has removed all its Customs duties other than fiscal; *i.e.*, when B treats A as A treats B; *i.e.*, when perfect reciprocity has been established between them.

Here, therefore, instead of finding the idea of reciprocity arrayed in opposition to the idea of free trade, we find the two to be inseparable companions, and the one inconceivable without the other. Instead of a heresy, it is an article of the Catholic faith to which our analysis has conducted us.

Let us now examine the word reciprocity as descriptive of the principle authorising us to claim as a right that others shall treat us as we treat them.

The question may be thus put: Having thrown open our ports to the world, is it a heresy to free-trade principles to claim as a right that the world shall throw open its ports to us?

After what has been already said, to state the question is to answer it. For when once it is admitted that the establishment of free trade between two or more countries implies the removal of restrictions by *all* the parties concerned, it is clear that if one of these parties, having by an autonomous act removed all prohibitive and protective duties along its own line of frontier, claims reciprocity as a right, it is in reality claiming free trade as a right, and that it cannot therefore be guilty of a heresy against free trade.

Whether such a claim can be defended on other grounds, and can be brought into harmony with received rules of international intercourse, is a distinct question which I do not propose to examine, though I may incidentally express my conviction that it is implied in that great natural law which Grotius has laid down as ruling international relations, viz: that it is the indefeasible right of every nation to draw nigh to, and traffic with every other nation: – 'Licere cuivis genti quamvis alteram adire cumque eâ negotiari.'

There only remains to examine reciprocity as descriptive of the principle in virtue of which we may claim the right to treat others as they treat us.

It is clear that it is under this aspect of the question, and this only, that the cloven foot of protection can be detected. But even here there are two broad distinctions to be made. A man might combine with perfect fidelity to free trade principles the belief that, by a system of tariff reprisals, the great object of a general removal of restrictions might be effected. Supposing, for instance, that we had the absolute certainty that by hermetically closing our ports for six weeks every protectionist tariff in Europe and America would be swept away, it would clearly be the duty of every orthodox free trader to urge such a measure. It is not, therefore, from the points of view of orthodoxy or heterodoxy that the unwisdom of tariff reprisals must be condemned, but on the ground of their utter worthlessness for the object proposed.

In our search for the disguised protectionist, therefore, we are reduced to the application of the principle of reciprocity in its most purely negative form as equivalent to the axiom that no tariff reduction should be made, except in return for a corresponding tariff reduction.

That this view is held theoretically by many protectionists, and that some few fossil remains of the old school, like Mr. Newdegate, are ready to push the doctrine to its legitimate consequences, and to urge that we should re-impose our protective tariff, and wait till other nations come and offer us equivalents, is very probably true, but this is no reason for putting a strained and unnatural meaning on the Queen's English, and talking of reciprocity generally as if it could be used only in this specific and exceptional sense.

Had Mr. Lowe been addressing a deputation headed by Mr. Newdegate, I should have had no objection to his saying, 'Under the specious name of reciprocity you are really advocating a return to protective duties,' but to tell a deputation from the Chambers of Commerce, headed by Colonel Akroyd, and, therefore, a free trade body, 'In asking for a commercial treaty you are asking for reciprocity, and in asking for reciprocity you are asking for protection,' was to use transparently incorrect language, and, in doing so, to betray a misconception of the true nature of free trade.

When the cry for reciprocity was raised last autumn in England, *i.e.*, in a country in which protection is dead and buried, the natural interpretation to put upon it was that it rose from men smarting under a sense of injustice, and who claimed as a right that others should treat them as they treated others.

That the working classes should awake to the sense that foreign tariffs are an injury inflicted upon them, and that every British export prevented by a foreign tariff, represents a corresponding import withheld from the British consumer, and should be loud in their demand that these tariffs should be swept away from the face of the earth, I, as a free trader, hail as the best of omens. Could we hope that such a feeling were likely to manifest itself generally amongst the working classes in Europe and America, the triumph of free trade would not be far distant.

But for the dogmatic error in regard to commercial treaties and the laws of exchange entertained by the school of economists of whom Mr. Lowe has made himself the mouthpiece, it would, I believe, have been easy for the free traders to utilise this force and employ it as a lever to carry out their principles, instead of letting protectionists obtain a vested interest in it and use it for their purposes. I can only hope that Colonel Akroyd and the Chambers of Commerce will make up for lost time. – I am, sir, your obedient servant,

A Disciple of Richard Cobden.

'Commercial Treaty with Austria' (1866), PRO, CAB 1/1.

Memorandum.

Commercial Treaty with Austria.

THE policy of England under her free trade system with respect to Commercial Treaties has been so strangely misunderstood or misrepresented, and there appears to exist in the public mind so much confusion of thought upon the subject, that it is important upon an occasion which has already revived a controversy which ought never to have arisen, to record in a brief outline the principles upon which it has proceeded, and the results which it has achieved.

The conclusion of the Treaty with Austria is a peculiarly suitable moment for such a review, as it is the first successful application of that policy in a form which leaves no room for cavil or doubt as to its entire conformity with the so-called 'free trade principles' which have guided our commercial legislation during recent years.

First, then, let us define what is commonly meant by 'free trade principles?'

All that has ever been meant in this country by 'free trade,' in connection with any question of practical legislation, is the liberation of trade from all protective duties. The term may some day mean a great deal more; but it is not among the opponents of modern Commercial Treaties that we shall find the advocates of its wider application.

The leading principle then of the recent commercial policy of England is war against protection in every form.

I propose to consider in what way this principle has been infringed by the French or the Austrian Treaty; but it will first be necessary to recall the course of legislation which preceded this last development of the free trade movement.

Until the repeal of the corn laws in 1846, the doctrine of protection, though damaged and undermined, still retained a firm hold on the minds of the governing classes in that country.

There still prevailed an illogical idea that the conditions of production ought to be artificially equalised, and that the consumer ought to be made to support the burden of industries which were supposed to be unable to prosper without public subsidies, in other words, that the nation ought not to be allowed a free exchange of its products precisely in those cases where it would derive the greatest advantage from such exchange.

It was not surprising that under this order of ideas reductions of duty upon the produce of a foreign country came to be regarded as national sacrifices, which entitled the country making them to corresponding concessions, and hence the policy of tariff bargains, which more or less will be found to have pervaded the commercial negociations [*sic*] of the period, and which survived even so late as the Reciprocity Treaty between the United States and the British provinces of North America.

It was probably owing to a perception of this fallacy, and also in some degree to the gradual and fragmentary introduction in this country of free trade measures, that the British Government proceeded to carry through these reforms, without any reference to the legislation of foreign countries, and without any attempt to obtain their co-operation in a common effort to root out a form of human oppression, which, though resting on cunning instead of force, and applied to the produce of labour instead of to the person of the labourer, is no less opposed to justice, and no less a violation of the rights of property, than slavery itself.

Had it been possible at any one time by adopting in one great policy of commercial reform the measures which were successively introduced, and by an appeal to the conscience and interests of Europe, to obtain simultaneously the removal of corresponding restrictions in the continental countries, it is difficult to see on what grounds of principle or expediency such a course could have been impugned.

It is one thing to make internal reforms which are dictated by national interest and demanded by justice, conditional on the co-operation of foreign countries; it is another to take the occasion of those reforms to found an appeal to foreign countries resting upon international equity, and grounded in reason, to make common cause with you in a great work of freedom and progress.

More than this, the two principles are not only different, they are directly opposed to each other. The first rests upon the fallacy that to liberate trade without reciprocity is an evil, the second on the incontestable truth that free trade in all countries is better than in one alone.

But such a course was probably not possible, and it may perhaps have been on the whole better that England was left to work out her commercial salvation in her own time, and in her own way. She was enabled, moreover, the better to do this from her comparative independence of European trade: the great markets of America and of her Colonial possessions being sufficient for many years to absorb her productions. If she has thereby forfeited the power of offering tariff reductions as material bribes to other countries for commercial reforms, she has certainly acquired the right of presenting herself in the councils of Europe as the representative of a great principle.

It is this right which is questioned by the opponents of the recent commercial policy; we shall hereafter examine upon what grounds.

But admitting that this course was not only the best that was possible, but in itself the best, it must not be forgotten (and I think it has been too much forgotten) that these national reforms, however fruitful in good results, must not be regarded as constituting a complete and fulfilled policy, but as the first act in a great drama, in the playing out of which England is deeply interested, both on moral and material grounds.

It is a law of nations no less than of individuals that complete development cannot be attained alone. England, of all countries, can ill afford to disregard the policy of other countries on this vital question. Her greatness, even her existence, depends upon her foreign trade; and to place that trade upon sound foundations must be one of the most important of her interests.

To prohibit trade is to violate one of the first principles of international ethics – it is a hostile act; a restriction[1] is a prohibition to whatever extent it operates; and is, therefore, also a hostile act.

Thus England has not only the strongest motive, but the clearest right to protest against the protective laws of foreign countries, from the injury which they inflict on her trade, and the injustice which they cause to her people.

The rapid progress of our industry and commerce during recent years has led us to overlook, too much, the magnitude of the injury which we sustain from the hostile policy of foreign countries.

The full rewards of labour cannot be attained until the right has been established for all, whether white or black, to the produce of their own industry in use or in exchange.

Bastiat has well said–

'L'échange est un droit naturel comme la propriété. Tout citoyen qui a acquis ou créé un produit doit avoir l'option ou de l'appliquer immédiatement à son usage ou de le céder à quiconque, sur la surface du globe, consent à lui donner en échange l'objet de ses desires. Le priver de cette faculté uniquement pour satisfaire aux convenances d'un autre citoyen, c'est légitimer une spoliation, c'est blesser la loi de justice.'

To whatever extent British products are exchanged against the products of countries where protection is maintained, still more to whatever extent they are not so exchanged in consequence of that protection, the British consumer will bear the enhanced cost which is the result of his being debarred from buying in the cheapest market. It is true that in practice this effect may be more or less neutralized by the operation of the laws of international supply and demand; but it is nevertheless broadly and unquestionably true that whatever impairs the producing power in a country from which we draw our supplies is an injury to the British consumer, whose interests always represent the interests of the nation at large.

And it must not be forgotten that while the interests of British labour are thus injuriously affected by restrictions on the exchange of its products, no such

---

1 Of course this does not apply to duties imposed equally on native and foreign goods for fiscal purposes.

restrictions are imposed on the transfer of British capital to countries which exclude the products of British industry, and that this capital is constantly diverted from its natural channel and withdrawn from employment at home to suck profit out of these monopolies, and help to retard their doom by supplying foreign Governments with funds which they can no longer raise from the impoverished resources of their own people.

Unless, therefore, by the exchange of our products we can extend the area of our production, and thus neutralize the effects of our limited territorial resources, the day will come when our people will follow our capital, and we shall enter upon the period of our decline.

Nor is it the destiny of the working classes alone which is involved in the fulfilment of this policy. The only economical justification of the right of property in land in a country where the soil is limited as in England, is in the perfect freedom of exchange with countries where the soil is comparatively free. This is shown, I think, conclusively in Bastiat's Essay, 'Propriété et Spoliation,' and indirectly proved, I think, by the English economists–Ricardo, McCulloch, Senior, &c., in their theory of 'Rent.'

A direct connection is thus established between the full development of the free trade policy and the condition of the working classes of England, the great problem of our time, which, unless solved, will solve itself by the decay of England.

The only possible foundation of all progress, and the only hope of the future of the human race lie in the material emancipation of the people. Free trade between all nations is certainly one of the most powerful of the agencies at the command of Governments in this consummation, which is the only possible foundation of all schemes and systems of social or political improvement.

It was under the influence of these convictions that those who both in France and England had devoted their lives to the cause of free trade, set themselves to the work which ended in the conclusion of the Treaty of 1860.

It is not surprising that these measures should have roused the hostility of that party in England which has acquiesced in free trade as a political necessity, but never accepted the principles from which it springs or the consequences which must flow from it.

It is not so easy to comprehend the fierce opposition which they have met with from some professed free-traders, still less the hesitating defence of them made by some of their friends who have always assumed a semi-apologetic tone in speaking of them. It is thus that the French Treaty has been justified as an exceptional measure resting on grounds of general political expediency rather than as the first step in a great commercial policy.

That Treaty was denounced as a departure from free trade principles–as a return to an exploded theory–and as involving an unsound financial policy.

It is easy to show that it is open to none of these objections, and that it can only so be considered by those who have never taken the trouble to understand the ideas which inspired it, or the principles out of which is grew both in England and France.

Those principles may be briefly stated.

The commercial intercourse of these two countries, separated only by a few miles of sea, was so restricted and hampered by perverse laws as to be a scandal to our times, and a source of loss and danger.

The Governments of both countries resolved to remove on both sides within the limits of their power the obstacles to this intercourse.

That power was very different in the two countries, England having advanced so much farther than France in liberating her trade from protective laws; hence alone, if for no other reason, all idea of *equivalent* concessions was out of the question.

England contributed her share to the work, by sweeping from her tariff, with some trifling exceptions, all trace and remnant of protection, and by binding herself to reduce to moderate rates her fiscal duties on two of the staple products of France—wine and brandy.

France, unable to destroy at one blow the whole fabric of monopoly, nevertheless made a deadly breach in the edifice, by substituting moderate duties for prohibition on the chief English exports.

If these reforms had been made exclusively in each others' favour, they might justly have been called unsound, but they were made equally for all the countries of the world; on the side of England at once, on the side of France prospectively, and thus, instead of reverting to a system of monopoly, the differential policy of France was for ever destroyed, and the equal system of England maintained and consolidated.

If then, without the sacrifice of a single free trade principle, we were able to break up the prohibitory and differential system of France, and obtain a large increase of commercial freedom, by what law of free trade can such a course be impugned, or by what true free trader regretted?[1]

The fiscal objection remains to be considered. It has been said that it is unsound financial policy to tie your hands with regard to the amount of your fiscal duties, such as wine and spirits, as you thus deprive yourself of a resource which you may one day require.

The answer (and it is a conclusive one) is this :–

A tax which from whatever cause dries up an important source of national industry and wealth, and thus takes from the fund which is available for taxation far more than the amount gained by the revenue, is a bad tax, and ought never, if possible, to be imposed or maintained.

1 [Ed.: Original footnote omitted.]

The tax on French wines and spirits had the effect of restricting injuriously to one of the largest branches of our foreign trade, and would, if maintained, by preventing the conclusion of the treaty, have deprived us of an accession of something like 20,000,000*l.* per annum to the value of our general exchanges with France. No wise legislation could advocate the retention of such a tax in the face of such consequences. There is probably no other form of tax to which it would not have been preferable to resort rather than to maintain these obstacles to our trade with France.

Such are the principal objections: it remains to consider the advantages of the policy which as been pursued.

It is unnecessary now to allude to the direct effects of the French Treaty. These are sufficiently known and appreciated, at last, to require no further reference.

It is not so generally known what have been the indirect results upon the commercial progress of Europe.

It is a common form of British self-complacency to talk of the great effect on other countries of the successful example of England's free trade policy, but facts do not justify this boast. Twenty years have elapsed since the repeal of the corn laws, and until the French Treaty the protective Tariffs of Europe had scarcely been touched; our self governing Colonies have all more or less adopted protective tariffs, and the United States of America have lost no occasion of increasing the restrictions upon foreign trade. The French Treaty has given an impulse to free trade which it was impossible for England alone to give. Those who are acquainted with the public opinion of other countries on this question know that so long as England was the only great country which had prospered under the modern system, the example produced but little effect. It was said that England had been enabled by a long course of monopoly to bring her industries to such a degree of strength, and to increase her productive power to such a point, as to enable her to face all competition, but that a similar course could only be taken by other countries, when they had, by a similar waste of their productive forces, increased in like manner, by some unexplained and mysterious process, their productive power. As soon as France, however, the great stronghold of protection, had renounced the error of her ways, and committed herself to a course of progressive freedom, the moral effect upon the Governments and upon the public opinion of Europe was irresistible, but this was not all.

We have said that in France the differential system was only abolished prospectively. This course was advisedly taken to enable her, while reforming her own system, to ensure the adoption by other countries of similar measures; and thus, by the French Treaty, we secured the alliance and co-operation of France in breaking down the whole prohibitory laws of Europe.

Perhaps this policy of France may be censured by some 'doctrinaire' politicians as unsound.

I cannot think that any one who desires the substantial progress of Free Trade rather than the assertion of a barren theory can share this view.

If, after reasonable efforts, other countries had refused to reciprocate, it would doubtless have been wiser on the part of France to adhere broadly to her own reforms, and disregard the course taken by others; but it could not have been expected, with the example of England before her eyes, that France, whose foreign trade is far more dependent on European markets than ours, could have entered alone upon this experiment, until she had exhausted every effort to obtain the simultaneous action of other nations. And if, by postponing for a few years the full development of her policy, she has been able to secure the co-operation of every country in Europe, it surely has been wise to wait.

But with this, whether right or wrong, England has nothing to do, except to consider its effect upon her own policy; and certainly it has placed her in a position of peculiar advantage. Without sacrificing her own independent principle, she thus regained the opportunity of obtaining all that France is able to extort by the material bribe of her reformed Tariff, and wherever commercial reforms are commenced, of asserting again her right to an equal share in all their results, if, indeed, she cannot effect even more than this by moulding them by her influence, and by an appeal to the principles and example of her policy, on a sounder and freer model.

It has been questioned whether the continental countries, if left to take their own course, might not have advanced more rapidly in the direction of Free Trade. This view exhibits a profound ignorance of these countries. The Governments always profess Free Trade, but, except under the influence of external pressure, would be often unable to set aside the strong opposition[1] of the protected classes. The policy of France in withholding her Tariff affords a motive which is irresistible even to these classes, and thus strengthens the hands of the Governments effectually in overcoming their interested opposition.

Thus, in pursuance of her policy, France has already in five years made in Europe alone Treaties with Belgium, the Zollverein, Italy, Sweden and Norway, and Switzerland, by which large reductions have been made in the Tariffs of all those countries.

England has obtained an equal participation in all these reductions by claiming where she had already the right by Treaty, and by obtaining by negotiation, where such right did not exist, most favoured nation treatment.

Confining ourselves to the effect of these changes on the trade of England alone, these are the results. Taking the special trade with Belgium, France, and Italy (it is impossible to trace it with the Zollverein and Switzerland) the aggregate value exchanged backwards and forwards is as follows:–

1 [Ed.: Original footnote omitted.]

'Commercial Treaty with Austria' (1866)

		Imports £	Exports £
FRANCE	1860	17,774,000	12,701,000
	1861	17,826,000	17,427,000
	1862	21,675,000	21,765,000
	1863	24,025,000	23,294,000
	1864	25,640,000	23,825,000
BELGIUM	1860	4,079,000	3,964,000
	1861	3,817,000	4,914,000
	1862	4,876,000	4,550,000
	1863	5,174,000	5,059,000
	1864	6,410,000	5,979,000
ITALY	1862	2,618,000	6,167,000
	1863	2,358,000	7,338,000
	1864	2,181,000	6,740,000

But as the indirect effects of this liberation of trade are quite as remarkable as the direct results, it is necessary to compare our European trade generally with that which existed prior to the French Treaty.

This comparison gives the following result:–

	1860			1864	
		£			£
Imports	..	84,403,000	Imports		98,502,000
Exports	..	69,644,000	Exports		100,064,000

These results are sufficiently striking to show the advantage which England has derived, both directly from the French Treaty, and indirectly through the Treaties made by France with other countries; but great as they are, it has been felt, as said before, by all those who are practically acquainted with the nature of the continental tariffs, and the prevalent ideas on customs' legislation in most European countries, that if England could obtain no more than an equal participation in all that France secured, far less progress would be made in commercial reform by British trade, than if she were admitted to co-operate in the reconstruction of European Tariffs.

It is its assertion of this principal [*sic*] that gives a peculiar value to the recent Treaty with Austria.

That Treaty may be generally described as a most favoured nation Treaty so far as commerce is concerned, accompanied by engagements on the part of Austria to revise her Tariff upon British produce and manufactures within the limits of certain maxima rates of duty, taking English prices, to be fixed by a Mixed Commission, as the basis of assessment, and to conclude a supplemental Treaty, for the purpose of applying specific duties within those limits.

Independently of the great value of the principle thus asserted, the practical advantages of this Treaty were considerable.

1st. It provides that the Customs Legislation of Austria shall be revised in cooperation with England, *i.e.* that the external influence brought to bear on this work shall be that of a country whose policy is that of commercial freedom in the widest sense, and whose experience enables her to supply the greatest range of facts and arguments, rather than that of countries like France or Prussia, who still cling to the form and phraseology of Protection.

2nd. It annihilates the differential system in Austria, which has heretofore given the Zollverein a virtual monopoly of her markets for many articles of produce.

3rd. It affixes certain limits to the amount of possible protection, and ensures a more equal incidence of duties than now exists, by an improved classification.

The small tariff changes on both sides provided by the Protocol, only require notice, because it may be feared that from an erroneous estimate of the relative value of the stipulations of the Treaty, these mutual reductions may be taken to show that the Treaty is after all a tariff bargain. To dispose of this objection it is only necessary to refer to the primary object of the negotiation, viz., the removal, wherever possible, consistently with the principles or policy of either country, the obstacles to their mutual trade, and to say, that these duties being on both sides of a nature which enabled the two Governments to deal with them at once, and as they all of them created obstacles which it was for the interest of both to remove, this Treaty presented the most suitable occasion for doing so by common agreement. Certainly on the principle of 'equivalent concessions,' this Treaty, if a tariff bargain, must be regarded as a great achievement, for it secures a revision of the whole Customs Tariff of Austria, in return for the abolition of duty on a few Austrian staves, and the equalisation of duty on Hungarian wines in bottle and in wood!

It has hitherto been supposed by many[1] that as England had no further tariff reductions to offer to other countries, she was debarred from entering upon the negotiation of Treaties involving the reduction of foreign tariffs.

This idea proceeded unconsciously on the doctrine that a reduction of a Tariff is a concession to a foreign country, instead of being, as it is, a measure primarily and principally dictated by national interest.

But even from this point of view, the necessity which was imposed on all the countries of Europe of reforming their Tariffs, by the policy adopted by France, opened the door to the action of English diplomacy.

The language used to foreign countries has been this, – 'You are obliged to reform your system in order to entitle you to the French concessions and save you from commercial isolation. It is far better to perform this work with England, which has no special objects to promote, and works in the general interests of freedom, than by the method of Tariff bargains with France or other countries,

---

1 [Ed.: Original footnote omitted.]

to which you can, if you please, proceed from a better diplomatic vantage-ground when you have a more liberal foundation for your negotiations.' You will then have more to offer than they will have to give, and 'you may bring them down to your level.'

The policy of the recent Treaties, however, rests upon much broader foundations.

The Austrian Treaty has been negotiated on the principle that a Tariff of Customs duties is a measure of international taxation, and is therefore a proper subject for international regulation.

It is impossible to impose taxes on commodities on any rational principle without a knowledge of the commodities to be taxed; where these are, as they must be in the case supposed, of foreign origin, a correct foundation of facts can only be obtained by the co-operation of foreign countires.

England and Austria therefore agree to co-operate in framing a Tariff which while on the one hand it secures the national object of a certain measure of protection (still unwisely thought necessary by Austria) shall nevertheless attain this object in the manner least injurious to English trade, and with such a correct knowledge of the facts upon which it is founded as to insure that no greater protection shall be given than is really intended.

It is strange that in a country like England, which did not hesitate to spend millions and resort to war for the purpose of vindicating her right of trade with China and Japan, it should be thought unreasonable in the case of European countries with restrictive and prohibitory laws to hold such legislation as affording a ground for remonstrance and a claim for co-operation in reducing to a minimum the injury inflicted.

But it is said that we should not proceed by way of Treaties, that each country should be left to act by independent legislation. To this is may be answered, Why not proceed by way of Treaty? If you are in earnest in your policy and have entire faith in its wisdom, why object to bind yourself to it by an international contract? Independently, however, of the practical necessity of this mode of proceeding caused by the policy of France, my answer is this: – A Treaty is nothing more than an international statute law, and it is most important that in a matter of international concern there should exist an international guarantee that the policy adopted shall be maintained and placed beyond the reach of reactionary influences. Where would commerce be without such a security?

The argument often used, that it is inconsistent with national dignity and independence to admit a foreign country to interfere in the regulation of a Tariff of course falls to the ground when the international character of this kind of legislation is admitted; but this argument, it may be observed, is never used by those who really desire commercial reform, it is merely a device of the enemy to rouse the foolish prejudices and passions of the country, and always will be found to emanate from the Protectionist camp.

The Tariff which will be constructed in the spring in co-operation with England will henceforth be the Austrian Tariff, and will doubtless be gradually extended to all other countries by Treaties or otherwise.

Whatever, therefore, may be the direct and immediate effects of the new Tariff upon British trade, and it is not probable from the variety of causes, for some years to come, that these will be very great, it cannot be doubted that the foreign trade of Austria with the countries near her frontiers – the Zollverein, Italy, Switzerland, and her Eastern neighbours – will be rapidly increased, that her consuming power will be developed, and her resources proportionately augmented.

Thus gradually will the rich territories and large population of this great Empire be brought within the ever widening circle of commercial civilization, and contribute their share to the commonwealth of Europe.

If this be the result it matters little to England whether Austria's direct exchanges are made with her or not. She is certain sooner or later to obtain her full part in the general accession which will thus be made to the productive forces of the world.

And it must be recollected that every fresh accession to this new alliance is a pledge for its future extension.

Each new Treaty which is made has a double operation. It not only opens the market of another country to foreign industry, but it reacts on those already opened; and by the universal introduction of the most favoured nation's principles, the indispensable condition of all recent Treaties, each new point gained in any one negotiation becomes a part of the common law of Europe.

It is thus that the Austrian Treaty has obtained for France an alteration in the English wine duties, and Austria is at present engaged in obtaining for England a relaxation of the French navigation laws.

It is now certain that in a few years in every country in Europe prohibitions will have been replaced by a system of moderate duties, and a great impulse given to international trade throughout the Continent, and it may reasonably be believed that the results of these changes will lead, at no distant day, to complete and general freedom from protective Tariffs.

With such a prospect in view of the present generation, is it too sanguine a hope that the united example of the old world may lead the Great American Republic and the younger Anglo-Saxon communities still unsevered from us in which the seed of this great wrong is already sown, to turn aside from following in the track of folly and injustice which marks the slow progress of commercial freedom in Europe, that monopoly, like the still darker bondage of slavery, may be proscribed by all civilized nations, and the rights of labour universally secured by equal laws?

L.M.

Louis Mallet, Memorandum on Modifications of the Anglo French Treaty, 19 August 1871, PRO, FO 24/2/72.

CONFIDENTIAL.

Correspondence respecting Proposed Modifications in the Anglo-French Commercial Treaty of 1860.

PART II.

No. 1.

Memorandum by Sir L. Mallet.

I DESIRE to submit, for the consideration of the Government, a few remarks on the bearings of the questions now before them, in connection with the Treaty of Commerce with France, upon the general commercial interests of the country, and upon the policy of Free Trade.

It is well known that the Commercial Treaty of France was the commencement and foundation of the system of international arrangements which at present regulate the intercourse of most of the countries of Europe.

Before that Treaty the only attempts which had been made to deviate from the policy of independent action in Customs Legislation, and to place international trade under international control, were of a kind which substituted for what was bad that which was worse, by the adoption of the so-called reciprocity system, and the introduction of the principle of monopoly into the domain of international trade.

The Treaty with France of 1860 constituted that [*sic*] the Americans call a 'new departure,' and was the beginning of a new era in the history of the Free Trade policy.

Its leading principles were – the international regulation of international trade, and the simultaneous removal of international restrictions, not for the purpose of exclusive privileges and Tariff bargains, but with a view to the equalization and generalization of Tariffs – and the destruction of the differential system.

By the adoption of this new principle, a powerful leverage was obtained in the prosecution of the Free Trade policy. It was found, and the reason is obvious, that, by bringing two nations together in a common reform, the Free Trade forces were stronger than the forces of monopoly in cases where independent national efforts on the part of Free Traders were inadequate.

The practical results of the new policy have been most remarkable, obtained as they have been in the absence of any concerted or common action on the part of England and France, which entered into the views of the French Government in 1860, but was never realized.

During the fourteen years which succeeded the Repeal of the Corn Laws, nowithstanding all the Tariff reforms which preceded and followed that measure, no reduction of any importance was made in the Tariffs of Europe, and, great as was the impulse given to our foreign trade by the independence remission of duties upon our imports, the restrictions still maintained in foreign countries were beginning to be seriously felt.

In 1847, the year after the Repeal, the value of British exports to the countries with which Treaties have been since concluded was 18,394,000*l*. In 1856 it had advanced to 35,336,00*l*, but in 1859, the year before the Treaty with France, it has fallen to 32,489,000*l*. In 1868, after the conclusion of the French Treaty, and the fifty or sixty similar European Treaties to which it gave rise, the British export trade to the same countries has advanced again to 60,739,000*l*., while the total addition to our trade with them in imports and exports was no less than 84,000,000*l*.

When it is recollected that the relative increase in the trade of France and some other countries under the operation of this system, has been greater than in that of England; it is difficult to over estimate the importance of the stimulus which it has given to the international exchanges of Europe and to the Free Trade policy.

There is one point in connection with the question of the extension of our trade with Europe, which is not always sufficiently kept in view, and to which, therefore, I may here advert, viz., the greater value and importance of any developments of our commercial relations with our European neighbours, than of a similar expansion of our dealings with distant and less settled markets. I will say nothing of the moral and political side of the question, as from this point of view the case is clear: but on purely economical grounds the trade with France or Germany is infinitely more valuable than that with China or Australia. It partakes more nearly of the character of a home trade, and the return to capital being quicker, gives far greater employment to labour. It may be the same thing to the capitalist whether he gets 40 per cent. on one consignment to China or 10 per cent. on four consignments to France in the year; but to British industry it makes all the difference whether the capital is turned over rapidly or slowly. Another great element of superior value in the European trade is the greater certainty which attends it and the absence of the speculative character which attaches too often to distant ventures.

Such, then, has been the work which has been going on for the last ten years in Europe; and it is this which M. Thiers now desires to undo. The question to consider is whether any and what steps can be taken to counteract his efforts.

That the international policy of Europe during recent years will ultimately prevail I cannot for one moment doubt. It is certain that without its agency Free Trade, in the sense in which it is now accepted and practised in England, cannot be attained. The advanced school of Free Traders who object to all taxes upon trade, whether home or foreign and insist upon direct taxation, may no doubt argue logically that every nation might liberate its own trade from all restrictions, on independent grounds; and that when this had been done, universal freedom would have been secured. But to those who regard such a prospect as an unattainable ideal, still more to those who on principle do not desire it, and who think that taxes on trade, so long as they are not protective, are a legitimate source of revenue, there is absolutely no way open for the general application of their principles but that of international co-operation in the common regulation of the taxes imposed on articles which form the subject of international trade.

This is thoroughly understood both by the German and Belgian Free Traders, who aim either at the abolition of all Custom-houses and the substitution of Excise duties of equal amount in different countries, or at a careful adjustment and equalization of Customs and Excise; and to this task whatever may be the obstacles interposed, the Governments of Europe will sooner or later address themselves: but if, as I am convinced, it is only by a thorough and effectual prosecution of the Free Trade policy that England can hope to solve the social and political problems which lie before her, and which it is a danger and a disgrace to leave unsolved, it is a matter of no slight moment to this country that the ground which has been gained in Europe during the last ten years should not be lost; and that our commercial relations with the Continent should not relapse into the state of chaos which existed before that period.

This is not merely an economical question. Some of the gravest political issues which can be raised in any country will in no small degree be affected by the progress made in our Free Trade policy in the coming years.

It is impossible to deny that this policy is losing its hold on the public mind of England. It is still popular with the capitalist and commercial classes generally in the limited conventional sense in which it has been hitherto understood and applied, but even among these there is a growing dissatisfaction with the feeble response in other countries to the liberal policy of England and with the inadequate measure of success which it has consequently received.

Among the working classes, those who share their views or desire to use them, and the social reformers, I observe two sets of opinion: the first, that this policy has been tried and has failed to reach their case; and the second, that a one-sided Free Trade is worse than none, and that, in the absence of reciprocity, we had better revert to protection.

This latter notion, which it is easy for economists to despise, has nevertheless obtained a dangerous ascendancy over many minds. Hence the movement of the revivers and reciprocitarians, which is, I am told, aided by and connected with Trades' Union Associations and may one day become a formidable weapon in the hands of the party of reaction.

The present generation of economists and public writers on social questions are looking in every direction except that of Free Trade and freedom generally in their schemes of reform, and many of them are openly advocating Communism and clamouring for State aid and State interference in every department.

That this is a fair representation of the public opinion of the day, I believe to be undeniable; and it is equally undeniable that, unless the Free Trade policy can be carried through much more effectively than has to heretofore been the case, those who held the views to which I have referred will have, whenever a practical controversy arises, by far the best of the argument. There is no possible logical choice between Free Trade and Communism.

To take the case of land: the whole scientific theory upon which Mr. Mill and his disciples advocate the principles of the nationalization of the land, crumbles into dust under the Free Trade system. Without this alternative it is vain to attempt to combat their arguments on economic grounds. So long as Governments in the name of property and capital uphold monopoly, no honest man can deny to the working classes their share in the public spoil.

My object in these remarks is to lead up to the question, What can the English Government do at this conjuncture to avert the consequences of the reactionary policy of France, and give a new and decisive impulse to a policy which, if there is any truth in my view, is of such vital importance to our prosperity?

I believe that they might do much. There is ground for thinking that, by removing the protective element which is alleged by the Germans to exist in our spirit duties, the Free Trade Party in the Chamber would be enabled to carry large reductions in the Zollverein Tariff, and an addition made to our trade with Germany which would go far to compensate us for any loss which we may sustain in our trade with France. In like manner I believe that Spain and Portugal might still be ready to open their markets to our trade, at least on the terms of the most-favoured-nation treatment, if the present differential duties on their wines were removed, or even diminished. Both the domestice reforms involved in these arrangements are of a kind which, if the grounds on which they are urged can be sustained (of which there is strong *prima facie* evidence), are dictated by the recognized rules of our own legislation, and are required to remove anomalies in our Tariff which are repugnant to its principles and damaging to our reputation for consistency.

By these measures, even if they did not compel M. Thiers to modify his course, not only would any material injury which England may sustain from the curtailment of her trade with France be amply compensated, but new and more solid guarantees would be obtained for the permanence of a system which has conferred incalculable benefit upon Europe; and France, finding herself alone in her effort to throw back civilization , and to add commercial jealousy and rivalry to the other causes of discord between the countries of the world, would either renounce the attempt or hopelessly fail in it; while England would recover the ground which she has lost by the hesitations and inconsistencies of her recent policy, and add another contribution to the splendid services she has already rendered to the cause of free exchange.

L. M.

C. M. Kennedy, 'Treaties of Commerce with, and between, European Powers, with Especial Reference to the Trade of the United Kingdom' (1875), PRO, FO 881/2670.

Printed for the use of the Foreign Office. September 1875.

CONFIDENTIAL.
(2670.)
MEMORANDUM.

Treaties of Commerce with, and between, European Powers, with especial reference to the Trade of the United Kingdom.

LORD DERBY having approved the suggestion, that, in the present position of the general question of the revision of the tariffs forming part of Treaties of Commerce now in force between European Powers, a statement of the engagements which have been contracted by and towards this country in regard to foreign commerce would be useful, the following Memorandum on the subject has been prepared.

In the first place, a list is given of the Treaties of Commerce and Navigation, which, at the present time, regulate the commercial intercourse between Great Britain and the different European Powers. The latest, and what may be designated the governing, Treaties alone are inserted, that course being sufficient for the purpose of this Memorandum, which is limited to matters directly connected with the trade of the United Kingdom, without entering into all the provisions of each Treaty. To do more would encumber this paper with too many details, and would lead away from its main object. Moreover, an abstract of contents of the entire Treaty engagements between Great Britain and any particular State, so far as they bear upon their commercial relations, would more appropriately be presented, with such remarks as may then be required, when the question of the revision of those Treaty engagements arises. Conventions and Declarations which exclusively relate to the Colonies of the Contracting Powers, or special matters, such as Joint Stock Companies, trade marks, &c., are accordingly omitted from this list.

TREATIES of Commerce and Navigation between Great Britain and European Powers.

Treaties with other European Powers.

Country.	When Concluded.	For what Period.	Commerce or Navigation.	Provisions as to General Treatment.	When Terminable.
Austria	December 16, 1865	10 years from January 1, 1867	Commerce	Most-favoured-nation, with certain local exceptions	December 31, 1876.
"	April 30, 1868	From June 26, 1868, till December 31, 1877	Navigation	Cargoes and shipping dues, &c., national and most-favoured-nation	December 31, 1877.
"	December 30, 1869	Same duration as Treaty of December 16, 1865	Commerce	Supplementary to Treaty of December 16, 1865	December 31, 1876.
Belgium	July 23, 1862	10 years from September 9, 1862	Commerce and Navigation	Commerce, most-favoured-nation. Cargoes and shipping dues, &c., national and most-favoured-nation	A year's notice.
Denmark	June 16, 1824	10 years from July 1, 1824	Commerce and Navigation	National	12 months' notice.
France	January 26, 1826		Navigation in direct trade and in ballast	Most-favoured-nation and national	12 months' notice.
"	January 23, 1860 (2 Additional Articles and 2 Supplementary Conventions)	10 years from February 4, 1860	Commerce	Commerce, most-favoured-nation. Shipping dues, &c., national	June 30, 1877.*
"	July 23, 1873	From August 4, 1873, till June 30, 1877	Commerce and Navigation	Commerce, most-favoured-nation. Cargoes and shipping dues, national and most-favoured-nation	June 30, 1877.
Germany (Prussia and the Zollverein)†	May 30, 1865	From July 1, 1865, till June 30, 1877	Commerce	Most-favoured-nation	June 30, 1877.

* By Articles I and V of the Treaty of July 23, 1873.
† Lauenberg, Lubeek, and the two Mecklenburgs acceded to this Treaty January 9, 1869.

Country.	When Concluded.	For what Period.	Commerce or Navigation.	Provisions as to General Treatment.	When Terminable.
Hans Towns; Bremen, Hamburg and Lubeck	August 3, 1841	No period specified	Commerce and Navigation	Cargoes and shipping dues, national	12 months' notice.
Prussia*	August 16, 1865	Same duration as Treaty of May 30, 1865	Navigation	Cargoes and shipping dues, &c., national	June 30, 1877.
Mecklenburg Strelitz	May 1, 1844	January 1, 1854	Commerce and Navigation	National and most-favoured-nation	12 months' notice.
Greece	October 4, 1837	10 years	Commerce and Navigation	National	12 months' notice.
Italy	August 6, 1863	10 years from October 29, 1863	Commerce and Navigation	Commerce, most-favoured-nation. Cargoes and shipping dues, &c., national	Notice of termination given June 26, 1875, will expire June 25, 1876.
Netherlands	October 27, 1837	10 years from October 27, 1837	Commerce and Navigation	Commerce, most-favoured-nation: conditional. Cargoes and shipping dues, &c., in direct trade and in ballast, national	12 months' notice.
"	March 27, 1851	Supplementary to Treaty of October 27, 1837	Navigation	Cargoes and shipping dues, &c., national	If British or Dutch old navigation laws are again put in force 6 weeks' notice, otherwise 12 months.
Portugal	July 3, 1842	10 years from July 3, 1842	Commerce and Navigation	Commerce, most-favoured-nation: conditional. Shipping dues in direct and Colonial trade and in ballast, national	12 months' notice.

* Mecklenburg-Schwerin acceded to this Treaty January 9, 1869.

Country.	When Concluded.	For what Period.	Commerce or Navigation.	Provisions as to General Treatment.	When Terminable.
Russia	January 12, 1859	10 years from February 1, 1859	Commerce and Navigation	Commerce, most favoured-nation: with exceptions in regard to the trade of Sweden and Norway, and Finland. Cargoes and shipping dues, &c., national	12 months' notice.
Spain	August 28, 1814*				
Sweden and Norway	March 18, 1826	10 years from March 18, 1826	Commerce and Navigation	Cargoes and shipping dues in direct and Colonial trade, national	12 months' notice.
Switzerland	September 6, 1855	10 years from March 6, 1856	Commerce	Most-favoured-nation	12 months' notice.
Turkey	April 29, 1861	For 28 years from October 1, 1861, terminable on a year's notice to be given at the end of 14 or 21 years, but the Tariff settled under the Treaty to be liable to revision at periods of 7 years	Commerce and Navigation	Commerce, most favoured-nation. Cargoes and shipping dues, &c., national	Treaty, October 1, 1876; Tariff, April 1, 1876.

* By an additional Article of this date to the Treaty of July 5, 1814, Great Britain was admitted to trade with Spain pending the negotiation of a new Treaty of Commerce upon the same conditions as existed before 1796. This additional Article also ratified and confirmed all Treaties of Commerce which at that period subsisted between the two nations. No new Treaty of Commerce has yet been concluded with Spain.

Of the above-mentioned Treaties, the stipulations of those concluded with Austria, Belgium, the several German States, Italy, Portugal, Russia, Sweden and Norway, Switzerland, and Turkey, extend to the British Colonies. The Treaty with Greece contains provisions relative to the British Possessions in the East Indies only. The existing Treaty engagements in regard to Colonies between this country and Denmark, France, the Netherlands, and Spain, severally, are contained in special Conventions. The Treaties of Navigation with Austria and with Prussia, and those of Commerce and Navigation with Belgium and with Italy, open the coasting trade of those countries to British vessels and the vessels of British Colonies which grant reciprocity. The coasting trade of certain other countries – Sweden and Norway and Turkey, for example – is open, but not under Treaty with Great Britain.

The following Treaties contain special stipulations in regard to matters of trade and Tariff on the part of Great Britain towards European Powers, and of European Powers towards Great Britain, namely, those with France, the Zollverein, and Austria. The Treaties with Belgium, Italy, and Turkey contain some special stipulations of this nature on the part of those Powers towards this country.[1]

GERMANY – THE ZOLLVEREIN.

The Treaty of May 30, 1865, between Great Britain and Prussia and the Zollverein, is on the part of each of the Contracting Parties a Treaty in the most general terms for ensuring most-favoured-nation treatment. No Tariff is annexed to it or included therein; the only specific engagement of this nature is a stipulation that neither party shall prohibit the exportation of coal, and that no duty shall be levied on such exportation.

AUSTRIA.

By the Treaty of December 16, 1865, between Great Britain and Austria, an engagement was made on the part of this country to extend during the continuance of that Treaty to the subjects and commerce of Austria the advantages conceded to France by the Treaty of January 23, 1860, and to States of the Zollverein by the Treaty of May 20, 1865.

By the final Protocol of December 16, 1865, annexed to the Treaty, Her Majesty's Government agreed to abolish the duties payable on the importation of wood and timber into the United Kingdom, and to reduce the duties payable on wine in bottle to the amount of those payable on wine in wood upon importation into the United Kingdom.

The Tariff engagements on the part of Austria, contained in the Treaty of December 16, 1865, were not carried into effect. The arrangements in substitution for them, which are now in force, were made by the Convention of

---

1 [Ed.: There follows a detailed list of imports from France on which Britain agreed to abolish import duties (Article V of the 1860 Treaty), notable amongst which were manufactures of silk, or silk mixed with any other materials. This is followed by a detailed description of the new rate of wine duties, graded according to the strength of the wine; and further details on the tariff changes agreed by both countries.]

December 30, 1869, and provide that during the continuance of that Convention British produce and manufactures generally shall be imported into Austria at the rates of duty enumerated in the Tariff between Austria and the Zollverein; a special table of duties being, however, established for British cotton and woolen wares.

By the Final Protocol of December 16, 1865, the Austrian Government agreed to reduce the export duty upon rags to 2 ft. the zollcentner, and to reduce the import duty upon salted herrings to 50 kr. the zollcentner.

The recent Treaties of Commerce between Great Britain and other European Powers do not contain any specific engagements on the part of the former with respect to Tariff. These Treaties contain stipulations in terms more or less general to secure most-favoured-nation treatment in matters relating to commerce; and in regard to navigation also when they are Treaties of navigation as well as of commerce.

In the following instances the other Contracting Powers have made specific engagements with this country on points connected with Tariff or trade.

BELGIUM.

By the Treaty of July 23, 1862, Article XIII, the regulations established by the Treaty of May 1, 1861, between France and Belgium with respect to proofs of origin of goods, the calculation of duties *ad valorem* and expertise are made applicable to goods imported in Belgium from Great Britain and its Possessions.

ITALY.

By the Treaty of August 6, 1863, Article II, in addition to the usual stipulations for most-favoured-nation treatment, the Italian Government engages not to prohibit the importation into the Italian dominions and possessions of any article the produce and manufacture of the dominions and possessions of Her Britannic Majesty, from whatever place arriving. By Article XI it is stipulated that import duties in Italy shall be calculated on the value at the place of production or fabrication of the object imported, with the addition of the cost of transport, insurance, and commission necessary, for the importation into Italy as far as the port of discharge. It is further provided that, if the Custom-house authorities are of opinion that the value declared in respect of any goods is insufficient, they shall have the power of pre-emption, on payment, within fifteen days following the declaration of the price declared, with an addition of 5 per cent., any duty levied being returned. No provision is made for expertise proceedings.

Notice has been given by the Italian Government to terminate this Treaty, which, unless other arrangements are come to in the meanwhile, will accordingly come to an end on the 25th of June, 1876.

On the 6th of June last, the Italian Chargé d'Affaires in London communicated a draft Protocol for the renewal of the Treaty of Commerce between Great Britain and Italy. This document appears to have been drawn up for communication to the different Powers with whom Italy has concluded Treaties of Commerce[1] ... In the reply returned to this communication (Lord Derby to the Chevalier de Martino, August 2, 1875), Her Majesty's Government made use of it as an overture for negotiation; stress was laid on the intention announced on the part of the Italian Government that the object in denouncing Commercial Treaties was re-adjustment of Tariff, not to impose protectionist or differential duties; a request was made that the Italian Tariff Project may be communicated to Her Majesty's Government, as well as to the Governments of Austria, France, and Switzerland, in order that British manufacturers should have the same facilities as the manufacturers of these other countries for offering observations on the details of this Tariff; and it was pointed out that otherwise differential duties might be imposed upon British goods contrary to the interests and even intentions of the Italian Government and people. Remarks were also made on the subject of the mode of assessing duties.

Up to the date of preparing this Memorandum, no answer has been received to Lord Derby's Note.

TURKEY.

A Tariff of duties on British produce and goods imported in Turkey, and of Turkish produce and goods exported by British subjects, was drawn up in pursuance of the Treaty of April 29, 1861, and was annexed to the Treaty. Its general principle was the adoption of a rate of duty of 8 per cent. *ad valorem*, calculated in regard to most articles on bases agreed upon. The import duty was fixed to remain at that rate, while the Tariff continued in force; but the export duty was to be reduced 1 per cent. annually until it was lowered to 1 per cent., at which rate it was to be maintained in order to defray the expense of the Customs establishment. Provisions are made in the Tariff for the manner of making currency calculations in effecting payments of duties; and it is stipulated that, in the event of dispute between merchants and the Customs, the duty in such cases is to be levied in kind, according to the ancient practice.

On the 30th of December, 1873, Musurus Pasha addressed a note to Earl Granville, expressing the desire of the Porte to enter into negotiations for the purpose of revising the existing Treaty of Commerce between Great Britain and Turkey; it being understood that, although the negotiations were commenced in advance, the new arrangements should not take effect until the existing Treaty expired, on the 1st of October, 1875.

1 [Ed.: There follows an extract in Italian proposing renewal of the Treaty.]

It was pointed out to Musurus Pasha in reply (Earl Granville to Musurus Pasha, January 20, 1874), that the Porte had made a mistake of a year as to the time when the Treaty of 1861 would expire, and for giving notice to terminate it.

The Porte recurred to the subject again, in further notes from Musurus Pasha (July 1, 1874), and from Aarifi Pasha to Sir H. Elliot (June 18, 1874); and Her Majesty's Government then decided that it would be more expedient to postpone entering into any negotiation for the conclusion of a new Treaty of Commerce until notice has been formally given for the termination of the existing Treaty, which cannot be done until the 1st of October, 1875 (Lord Derby to Musurus Pasha, July 8, 1874).

The Egyptian Government, referring to the power granted to the Khedive by the Imperial Firman of June 8, 1873, of concluding Commercial Conventions with foreign States, expressed a desire, in 1874, to open negotiations with Her Majesty's Government for a Convention to regulate the commercial relations of the two countries, upon the approaching termination of the Treaty now existing between Great Britain and the Porte (General Stanton, No. 33, Commercial, April 11; No. 65, Commercial, June 13).

In reply, General Stanton was supplied with copies of the correspondence with Musurus Pasha; and was instructed not to enter into any discussion at present; but to give attention to the various questions likely to be involved in commercial negotiations between this country and Egypt (to General Stanton, No. 32, Commercial, September 25, 1874).

Mr. Acton, formerly attached to the Board of Trade, and now Director of the Department of Foreign Commerce in the Egyptian Ministry of Commerce, has lately been sent to this country to obtain information on various matters connected with trade between England and Egypt: he has been supplied with letters of introduction to Public Departments and Chambers of Commerce. It would appear that he is not, and probably will not be, authorized to make any formal communication with respect to the wishes of the Egyptian Government beyond assurances in general terms of friendly intentions on the part of that Government.

The actual stipulations into which this country has entered with foreign Powers, relative to matters of Tariff are thus comprised in the Treaties contracted with France and with Austria, and also, as to coal, in the Treaty with the Zollverein. Other Powers with whom Commercial Treaties have been concluded obtain the benefit of their several stipulations under the most-favoured-nation Article, but those Powers possess no direct Treaty security in regard to them. On the other hand, this country, under the most-favoured-nation Article in these Commercial Treaties, does possess a far more ample security in the matter. When France adopted in 1860 a liberal policy in regard to foreign trade, Treaties of Commerce, on the basis of that with England, with tariffs annexed to them, were concluded between France and the principal States of the continent. These Powers further entered into similar international engagements between themselves, and thus Tariff Treaties became established in Europe. The Reports on this point called for from Her Majesty's Missions in 1872 were not answered in a complete manner, but, with the exception, it would seem, of Denmark, Greece, and Russia, all European Powers have concluded such Treaties.

The advantages which the commerce of this country derived under these circumstances have been very great. The movement began with the Treaty and Conventions of 1860 with France, and the policy to which it gave expression was confirmed by the Treaty of 1865 and the Convention of 1869 with Austria. Accordingly the Treaty Tariff of Europe was, in effect, settled, both as to classification of goods and rates of duty, with especial reference to the requirements of the trade of the United Kingdom. While the principles of the policy of 1860 are to be attributed to Mr. Cobden, it must be remembered that the details of the arrangements with France, which are, in their bearing upon British interests, of equal, if not of greater, importance, were settled by Sir Louis Mallet, who further conducted entirely the subsequent negotiations with Austria. These arrangements were made after full consideration, in some cases, of matters of a widely different nature; in others, of subjects involving conflicting claims. The development of British trade which has taken place since 1860 affords the only adequate measure of the value of these labours.

The following Tables, taken from the Board of Trade Returns, show the total imports and exports in the trade between the United Kingdom and France, Belgium, and Italy respectively, in the three years preceding the conclusion of the existing Treaties of Commerce, the three years subsequent, and the last three years for which such Returns are published:–

Country	Year	Imports £	Exports. £
France	1858	13,271,000	9,242,000
	1859	16,870,000	9,561,000
	1860	17,774,000	12,701,000
	1861	17,826,000	17,427,000
	1862	21,675,000	21,765,000
	1863	24,025,000	23,294,000
	1871	*29,848,000	33,388,000
	1872	41,803,000	28,292,000
	1873	43,339,000	30,196,000
Belgium	1860	4,079,000	3,964,000
	1861	3,817,000	4,914,000
	1862	4,876,000	4,550,000
	1863	5,174,000	5,059,000
	1864	6,410,000	5,979,000
	1865	7,354,000	6,896,000
	1871	13,573,000	12,815,000
	1872	13,211,000	13,099,000
	1873	13,075,000	14,230,000

Country	Year	Imports	Exports
Italy, Kingdom of	1861	2,480,000	6,792,000
	1862	2,618,000	6,167,000
	1863	2,358,000	7,338,000
	1864	2,181,000	6,740,000
	1865	2,970,000	6,332,000
	1866	3,819,000	6,905,000
	1871	4,624,000	7,666,000
	1872	4,159,000	7,715,000
	1873	3,831,000	8,571,000

* These figures are to some extent abnormal: the average imports for the three years 1867–69 were 83,720,000*l.*; for 1870 37,607,000*l.*

The returns of trade with Belgium include, to some extent, that with the Zollverein. No Returns can be made out for the Zollverein or for Switzerland, or complete for Austria.

In the following Tables the Returns of trade between the United Kingdom and Germany are given for the three years 1865, 1866, and 1867; and for the three years 1871, 1872, and 1873; and Returns of the trade with the Austrian ports in the Adriatic, are also given for the same periods. The German trade itself, as also the Belgian and Dutch, is a transit as well as a direct trade.

Country.	Year.	Imports. £	Exports. £
Germany	1865	16,611,000	28,153,000
	1866	19,088,000	25,105,000
	1867	18,906,000	29,868,000
	1871	19,263,000	38,493,000
	1872	19,231,000	*43,150,000
	1873	19,926,000	36,709,000
Austria (Adriatic Ports.)	1865	677,000	861,000
	1866	1,369,000	1,056,000
	1867	1,203,000	1,123,000
	1871	1,238,000	2,085,000
	1872	911,000	1,946,000
	1873	869,000	1,815,000

* There was a large increase in the export of coal, textiles, and metals in this year; and there was a large decrease in the export of woollens in 1873.

The preceding Tables relate to countries with which Treaties of Commerce have been concluded since the Treaty with France of 1860. Similar Returns are also given for the periods 1865, 1866, 1867, and 1871, 1872, 1873 for the principal countries with which Treaties of Commerce, in terms adapted to the requirements of the present time, have not yet been concluded.

Country.	Year.	Imports. £	Exports. £
Holland	1865	12,413,000	14,960,000
	1866	11,768,000	14,877,000
	1867	10,822,000	14,948,000

Country.	Year.	Imports.	Exports.
	1871	13,970,000	22,099,000
	1872	13,108,000	24,336,000
	1873	13,272,000	24,578,000
Russia	1865	17,333,000	6,180,000
	1866	19,624,000	6,915,000
	1867	22,286,000	7,250,000
	1871	23,721,000	9,932,000
	1872	24,320,000	9,468,000
	1873	21,189,000	11,545,000
Sweden	1865	4,199,000	1,630,000
	1866	4,001,000	1,540,000
	1867	4,756,000	1,400,000
	1871	5,438,000	2,072,000
	1872	6,724,000	3,046,000
	1873	7,739,000	4,604,000
Spain	1865	4,769,000	3,015,000
	1866	5,553,000	3,143,000
	1867	6,088,000	2,985,000
	1871	7,759,000	3,983,000
	1872	9,316,000	4,309,000
	1873	10,973,000	4,527,000
Portugal	1865	2,471,000	2,550,000
	1866	2,517,000	2,369,000
	1867	2,324,000	2,119,000
	1871	3,840,000	2,199,000
	1872	4,119,000	2,677,000
	1873	4,329,000	3,338,000

With regard to the increase of trade with Holland, Sweden, and Spain, it should be observed that this country has obtained all the advantages of Tariff Treaties which those Powers have entered into, and that the fiscal legislation of Holland and Sweden has been of a very liberal character of late years. But by the letter of the existing Treaty with Holland, which contains conditional stipulations in regard to most-favoured-nation treatment, the Netherlands Government, if so disposed, might raise difficulties, as Portugal has done.

The Russian Tariff has also been considerably modified within this period.

It may be useful to show the total imports and exports in the trade between the United Kingdom and foreign countries, and also the declared real value of the total exports of the produce of the United Kingdom to European countries and their Colonies in each year from 1858 to 1873: –

Year.	Trade of the United Kingdom with Foreign Countries, exclusive of British Possessions.		Value of Produce of United Kingdom exported to European Countries and their Colonies.
	Imports. £	Exports. £	£
1858	125,969,000	96,569,000	47,103,000
1859	139,707,000	106,042,000	45,480,000
1860	167,571,000	117,988,000	50,836,000
1861	164,809,000	114,493,000	54,561,000

Year.	Trade of the United Kingdom with Foreign Countries, exclusive of British Possessions.		Value of Produce of United Kingdom exported to European Countries and their Colonies.
1862	160,433,000	120,744,000	55,481,000
1863	164,235,000	141,032,000	62,578,000
1864	181,207,000	156,891,000	62,894,000
1865	198,231,000	167,284,000	68,374,000
1866	223,084,000	181,738,000	70,031,000
1867	214,448,000	172,440,000	73,987,000
1868	227,700,000	174,060,000	77,128,000
1869	225,043,000	185,123,000	80,547,000
1870	238,425,000	188,689,000	82,610,000
1871	258,071,000	228,013,000	100,661,000
1872	275,320,000	248,979,000	113,383,000
1873	290,277,000	239,857,000	113,585,000

The results afforded by the foregoing Returns can be most conveniently given in the accompanying form:–

The total trade with the United Kingdom increased –

In the case of France, from 26,431,000*l.* in 1859, to 73,535,000*l.* in 1873.

In the case of Belgium, from 8,731,000*l.* in 1861, to 27,305,000*l.* in 1873.

In the case of Italy, from 8,785,000*l.* in 1862, to 12,402,000*l.* in 1873.

In regard to the other countries mentioned in the Tables, 1865 is taken as the year preceding either the conclusion of a Treaty or the general establishment of the new Treaty-of-Commerce system; and the Returns for that year, as compared with those for 1873, show an increase in the trade –

With Germany,	from	44,764,000	to	56,635,000
With Austria,	"	1,538,000	to	2,684,000
With Holland,	"	27,373,000	to	37,850,000
With Russia,	"	23,563,000	to	32,734,000
With Sweden,	"	5,829,000	to	12,343,000
With Spain,	"	7,784,000	to	15,500,000
With Portugal,	"	5,021,000	to	7,667,000

The total amount of the imports and exports of the United Kingdom from and to foreign countries, exclusive of British Possessions, increased from 245,750,000*l.* in 1859, to 365,515,000*l.* in 1865, and to 530,134,000*l.* in 1873. The declared value of the produce of the United Kingdom, exported to European countries and their Possessions, increased from 45,480,000*l.* in 1859, to 68,374,000*l.* in 1865, and to 113,585,000*l.* in 1873.[1]

1 [Ed.: There follows a table detailing the value of produce of the United Kingdom to European countries at five-year intervals.]

It seems unnecessary to make further remarks on this part of the subject of the present Memorandum; but it may be well to quote an observation of Sir Louis Mallet on a point often lost sight of, namely, the greater value and importance of any development of commercial dealings with European countries than of a similar expansion of those dealings with distant and less settled markets. Sir L. Mallet observes,[1] that, apart from moral and political considerations, 'on purely economical grounds, the trade with France or Germany is infinitely more valuable than that with China or Australia. It partakes more nearly of the character of a home trade, and the return to capital being quicker, gives far greater employment to labour. It may be the same thing to the capitalist, whether he gets 40 per cent, on one consignment to China, or 10 per cent, on four consignments to France in the year; but to British industry it makes all the difference whether the capital is turned over rapidly or slowly. Another great element of superior value in the European trade is the greater certainty which attends it, and the absence of the speculative character which attaches too often to distant ventures.'

Such, then, is the statement of facts in regard to the operation, with especial reference to the trade of the United Kingdom, of the Treaty of Commerce system initiated in 1860, which I was desirous in the present crisis of bringing under Lord Derby's notice. I now proceed, availing myself of his Lordship's permission to do so, to offer certain remarks on this crisis. These remarks, like the foregoing statement, will be general in their terms, it being thought that the case of the relations with each particular country can only be adequately dealt with as it arises.

First of all, it should be stated that the leading principles of the commercial policy adopted in 1860 were to liberate trade from all protective charges, and to impose duties equally on native and foreign goods alike for fiscal purposes only. In the condition of things which then existed, the commercial intercourse between the different countries of Europe was hampered with restrictions which prevented the progress of those countries, and occasioned loss to their revenue. A system of differential treatment, both mischievous and irritating, likewise prevailed. The Governments of England and France, in taking the lead to remedy those evils, resolved to remove, within the limits of their power, obstacles to commercial intercourse between the two countries. England, on her part, struck off the remaining protective duties in the tariff of the United Kingdom, and reduced to moderate rates the fiscal duties maintained on two of the staple products of France, wine and brandy.

France substituted moderate duties for prohibition on the chief English exports, and carried into further effect, by subsequent Treaties with other European Powers, the general principles on which these changes were brought about. The revision of the French tariff thus accomplished, it is most important to observe, took place in co-operation with England. By means of the Mixed

---

1   Memorandum, August 19, 1871, respecting the French Treaty.

Commission of 1860, an external influence of commercial freedom, in the widest sense and of the widest experience as to facts and arguments, was brought to bear upon the revision of the French tariff, which was a type of continental tariffs generally; and, in consequence, the influence of that co-operation extended far beyond its immediate sphere of action, and gave character to the new continental tariff system. The results thus attained have introduced new conditions of trade. Commerce is more complex in its nature now than it was in 1860; competition is much more keen. Now less than ever can England afford to disregard the commercial policy of other countries. Her greatness, if not her existence, depends upon foreign trade. It is equally as important to place that trade upon sound foundations as it is to ward off the injury that would be sustained from hostile commercial policy of foreign countries.

At the present time, however, intelligence from all parts of Europe shows that a very serious crisis has arisen with regard to the new Treaty of Commerce system. The opposition which it encountered from local interests and prejudices has now been much strengthened by financial and political considerations.

No positive information has yet been received as to what changes each particular Government proposes to make in the contemplated revision of Tariffs; but, although in some few instances duties may be lowered, there is little doubt that the tendency is to raise them. In certain cases, if cost of production is taken as the basis in fixing rates of duty, reasons may be alleged in support of an augmentation. There are grounds for thinking that statements have been made by persons interested in Birmingham and Newcastle trades which might show that in regard to those trades an argument of this nature would not be entirely unfounded. Persons interested in the trade of other places, of the Yorkshire towns more especially, have kept their own counsel; but it is very possible that here also, in certain cases, the foreign argument has some foundation.

The English negotiators with France and Austria overmatched their opponents when differences of opinion arose.

On the other hand, no positive information is possessed as to the conditions which European Powers will seek to obtain from Her Majesty's Government on the renewal of Treaties of Commerce. Italy, as it has been mentioned (pp. 13, 14), in proposing the renewal of the Treaty of August 6, 1863, has asked Her Majesty's Government to consent to differential treatment for ten months: namely, that in the event of the Treaty of July 22, 1868, between Italy and Switzerland not being replaced by new arrangements before it expires, this country is not to claim, under the most-favoured-nation Article in the English Treaty, during the period from July 1, 1876, to April 30, 1877, the benefit of the Tariff for Swiss products imported into Italy. France in 1872, sought to obtain the renewal of the stipulations of 1860 for the abolition of duty on silks, and the maintenance of the existing wine and spirit duties. It would appear that Austria may wish to obtain an alteration of the wine duties, which Spain and Portugal also desire; and, perhaps, if the Italian government are pressed to make alterations in their proposed Tariff, they may, in return, likewise ask for alteration of those duties. In these circumstances it seems quite possible, without endangering the revenue, to renew and extend the Treaties of Commerce now subsisting between this country and European Powers.

Communications have been made to Chambers of Commerce in the United Kingdom with reference to the Italian and Austrian Treaties. Their opinion has been requested on the present Tariff of those countries; and documents bearing upon the commercial policy of Italy and Austria, and the Tariff charges in contemplation, have been sent to the Chambers for their information and remarks. In this manner a mass of valuable *data* for dealing with the various points of detail which will require consideration, will be brought together. But it may be here observed generally that representations of persons in the United Kingdom interested in commercial matters should not be adopted and acted upon without due examination, in order to understand as well as to check these statements, and to reconcile differences of opinion. I believe that Mr. Cobden and Sir L. Mallet considered every point fully and carefully themselves, apart from the statements of the parties concerned. In 1872, when Lord Granville did me the honour to entrust me with the French Tariff negotiation, I sought to bring together persons from different places interested in the like business, that the conclusions finally arrived at might be settled at an official meeting. In this manner only can statements be sifted, and, if necessary, modified. Had statements been put forward on the part of Her Majesty's Government in 1872, without previous examination, they could have been so far contested as to leave the two Governments in endless controversy, and have been so far disproved as to prevent the overthrow of the Tariff of Compensatory Duties.

The present condition of things is the more serious on this account: in the negotiations which are now taking place between foreign Powers, it is not the future Tariff of one State only, but the future Tariff of each of these Powers that is under revision. The whole advantages obtained by British commerce under the existing Treaty of Commerce system are in danger; the negotiations being conducted apart from the participation of this country. There is reason to think that extensive changes of classification of goods, a point even more important than rates of duty, are contemplated, and that the new Tariffs will be adverse rather than favourable to British commercial interests, inasmuch as, in these negotiations, foreign interests are held in view, and arrangements which, for example, may be very suitable to trade between Italy and France, or Italy and Austria, may be most injurious to British trade. When these Tariffs are once settled, it will not be easy to obtain alterations in them; their effects, however, will not be generally felt until two years have elapsed.

It follows, then, that many of the Treaties of Commerce now in force between this country and foreign States are of old date, and that their stipulations are adapted to the conditions of trade previous to 1860, rather than to the requirements of the present system of international communication and trade. Practically no great harm ensues; but in the well-known case of Portugal the limited provisions of old Treaties give rise to difficulties which it would be advisable to obviate generally by measures in advance. Secondly, the nature of the crisis that has arisen in regard to the Treaty of Commerce system of 1860 has been explained; and the expediency of action before the new Tariffs are finally settled has been shown.

The question as to the course of action to be adopted by this country, with regard to foreign commercial relations, is one of policy, affecting, indeed, most vital interests.

The most pressing matter, as well as the most important, is the decision as to the renewal of the Treaties about to expire; and, further, as to the steps to be taken with regard to the several points to be dealt with in connection with the approaching negotiations and the new Treaties to be concluded. It seems to be very advisable that, beyond deciding upon the general policy to be adopted, full preparation should be made in advance for dealing with these various subjects as they arise, instead of taking them up merely at the time and in the form in which they arise. But, when that period arrives, unless foreign Governments really desire to come to a satisfactory settlement of points in discussion, and to place commercial relations with this country on a satisfactory footing, the negotiations can scarcely attain good results. If any Government tries to revert to its old commercial policy, it would seem best to decline to follow in that course, and to await events. It will not be possible to refuse assent, either formal or tacit, to some increase of foreign customs duties, but the main object in view should be to uphold the principle that these duties are to be moderate in amount and to be levied for fiscal purposes; to reduce to a minimum any increase of a possible protective character; and, unless in most exceptional circumstances, not to admit any differential treatment. On the other hand, the results to be obtained under conditions favourable to negotiation depend, it is to be observed, in great measure, upon Her Majesty's Government. Under certain conditions satisfactory results would not be possible; but, when they can be attained, the extent to which favourable opportunities will be turned to account depends on the manner in which they are met. The whole question will thus require to be considered and determined by Her Majesty's Government, both as regards general policy and the treatment of each particular case. The aim in preparing this statement has been to set forth the actual position of the question, which, as it has been observed, is a matter ready for, and in its nature demanding, early attention and decision.

Perhaps some of the observations here made may be beyond the proper limits of an Office Memorandum. But they appeared necessary for the sake of clearness; and, to state fully the several matters to which it was necessary to advert, in calling attention to the present position of the commercial relations between this country and European Powers.

C.M.K.

Foreign Office,

September 17, 1875.

FREE TRADE UNDER THREAT, 1870-9

As the previous section has shown, after 1860 Europe had been united by a network of commercial treaties which brought the continent closer to a common market than at any time before the 1950s, or even the single market of the 1990s. The strength of the 'treaty-system' lay in its interlocking nature, with gains negotiated by one power passed on to others through the most-favoured-nation clause.[1] The potential weakness of the system lay in the loss of momentum once the main treaties had been completed, and in the time period for which they were in force. The fulcrum of the system, the Anglo-French commercial treaty, was itself due for renegotiation in 1870, only a short interval of time after the completion of the bulk of the 'system' in the late 1860s.

Yet by 1870, the future of that treaty had been called into serious doubt, following the Franco-Prussian War of 1870. At the end of that War, France had been compelled to offer Germany permanent most-favoured-nation status, turning the instrument of voluntary association between nations into a spoil of war.[2] At the same time, the domestic basis of support for a liberal commercial policy in France crumbled with the Empire itself, for now free trade became open to attack as a Napoleonic eccentricity, hateful to Republicans and monarchists, and 'harmful' to the interests of the French nation. This made the renegotiation of the 1860s difficult but not impossible, and this was more widely true of the system itself. Europe in the 1870s stood poised between two economic futures: would the commercial treaty 'system' be renewed and genuinely systematized as some civil servants called for a European-wide tariff conference of the sort not in fact summoned until the 1950s; or would this vision of a 'Commonwealth of Europe' fall prey to growing suspicions that 'free trade' was a badge of subservience to Britain, that it benefited capitalists rather than landowners, trade rather than warfare, 'mere commercialism' above public virtues. In retrospect the former possibility seems utopian, but at the start of the decade it was by no means a foregone conclusion that the 'free trade interlude' was over.

Even so, the 1870s were to see the start of what became a widespread 'backlash against free trade', whose dimensions would grow into the comprehensive challenge of economic nationalism documented in Volume 3. Already by the early 1870s, there had been signs of a growing intellectual breach with free trade, especially in Germany where the 'Socialists of the Chair' had launched a vigorous assault on the damage wrought by 'Manchesterism', although interestingly Richard Cobden himself was in part exempted from its criticisms.[3] More widely, classical political economy, although reaffirmed on the centenary of the publication of *The Wealth of Nations*, was increasingly under fire for its emphasis on the self-interest of the individual within the market and its inability to promote goals wider than the opulence of states. For some the military power of the state was to be a strategic goal greater than the interests of the consumer, while for others the welfare of the working class now seemed to call for the interventionism of the state. Such interventionism, some argued, was just as applicable to tariffs themselves, which might be used to broaden the base of the economy, to build up strategic industries and to protect the peasant basis of agrarian society. Significantly, by the mid-1870s in Italy 'economic Germanism' threatened to replace the British free trade model. In France too the priority of the interest of the state was at the heart of the teaching of the economist Paul Cauwès, whose influence among civil servants was to grow markedly in the 1880s. Only perhaps in Britain was there no significant intellectual challenge to the primacy of free trade; the 'marginal' revolution reaffirmed the centrality of consumption, and only in the 1890s would the historical school, on the German model, acquire a modicum of influence.

More threatening than the power of abstract ideas was the backlash against free trade induced by the onset of what came to be seen as a 'Great Depression'. This was initially signified by the Austrian crash of 1873 but, by the end of the decade, contemporaries were increasingly aware of falling prices, declining exports, general market stickiness, overproduction and unemployment, affecting the European economy as a whole. For many, the most obvious explanation of their plight was the preceding period of free trade, for this had led to the removal of the tariff barriers so that cheap American grain or British iron and textiles, or, in the British case, bounty-fed sugar and French silk goods, could now deprive domestic producers of markets, jobs and incomes; growing dependence on foreign food might even threaten the survival of the nation itself in case of war. The 'losers from free trade' were therefore now able to organize far more successfully than in the past and to articulate a range of grievances which began to build up wider constituencies of support. In Britain, significantly, it was to be sugar refiners and silk, woollen and worsted manufacturers who were in the forefront of early demands for the restoration of fair trade in the belief that Britain had made tariff concessions to others which had not been reciprocated.[4] However, in Britain such movements found it very difficult to make headway beyond the interests immediately concerned; and no political party was ready yet to be tarred with the brush of protection. Elsewhere it became far easier to construct a political coalition around a combination of economic discontents; rather as in France it was free trade itself which lacked its own party. In Italy too the major shift towards the left in 1876 virtually determined that a new economic policy would follow to differentiate the new political regime, albeit one led by Marco Minghetti, one of the European politicians most influenced by Cobden and Frédéric Bastiat.

It was then against this background of the articulation of growing discontent with free trade that European statesmen tackled the renegotiation of commercial treaties in the 1870s. First, as Louis Mallet in his memorandum of 1871 feared, the French Republic under Louis Adolphe Thiers, a long-term critic of British free trade, would abandon free trade; Mallet was therefore concerned to limit the damage done by keeping the bicycle of free trade moving through negotiations with Germany, Spain, and Portugal.[5] Interestingly too in 1870 Mallet's close friend, the diplomat Sir Robert Morier, had publicized the 'forward case' in trade reform, urging the centrality of free trade within Britain's international policy, and its importance in limiting the potential danger of autarkic and aggressive policies to the peace of Europe. Nevertheless, their initial fears also embraced what they saw as a growing reaction against treaty-making in Britain, articulated by the 'revivers' and reciprocitarians in the later 1860s and the fear that the Liberal government would prefer, as Chancellor Robert Lowe wished, to return to a unilateral free-trade policy rather than engage in 'higgling', leaving, as William Gladstone put it, 'each nation to consider the subject in the light of its interests alone'. Even so, Gladstone resisted this temptation to withdraw from negotiations with France, and in November 1872 agreed a new treaty which only slightly modified that of 1860. As it turned out, this proved stillborn, for Thiers's government fell in May 1873 and the new French government agreed a treaty in July 1873 which in effect restored the status quo ante with the additional benefit of exempting British goods from the French shipping duties. Even so, the hopes of the forward school were far from being met; the treaty was only renewed until 1877, the date at which France's other treaties were due to expire; in addition, the opportunity to negotiate a commercial treaty with Germany was not taken up, for this would have involved recalculating the British spirits duties, upsetting a hornet's nest of vested interests.[6] Finally, in 1872, the Board of Trade lost the responsibility for negotiating treaties, which the Foreign Office reluctantly took over; when first proposed in 1864 this reform was seen as a positive one which would raise the profile and expertise behind commercial policy, but by 1872 the Foreign Office only reluctantly took over this role, while the civil servant best qualified to take charge of the new department, Sir Louis Mallet, was exiled to the India Office.[7]

In many ways between 1868 and 1874, under the Liberal government of Gladstone, the main architect of the 1860 treaty, the treaty system had been kept alive but had hardly progressed from the situation of 1869 when the Anglo-Austrian treaty had come into effect, a supplement in miniature to that of 1860.

By 1874, therefore, attention was already focused on the new round of bargaining which would follow in 1877 when France's commercial treaties were due to expire; but in Britain in 1874, for the first time since 1846, a majority Conservative government was in power, freed from the protectionist legacy but anxious to make its mark in Europe. The situation facing it however was one which, as the Cobden Club survey of 1875 showed, was far from optimistic; the Club, which since 1866 had emerged as the main international lobbying body for free trade,[8] reported many signs of the backlash against free trade,[9] but in other respects the opportunity existed for renewing the commercial arrangement put in place in the 1870s. In fact, as Gaston has powerfully argued, this inspired a remarkably visionary attempt by Benjamin Disraeli's government to promote in effect a European common market.[10] The chief official at the Foreign Office, Charles M. Kennedy, embarked on an extensive round of tariff negotiations designed to secure new commercial treaties, although the expectation was now that governments, whose revenues had been hit by depression, would increase tariffs. The British goal was to limit such increases but it was also attracted by the idea of collective bargaining along the lines of the future General Agreement on Tarrifs and Trade (GATT), with a conference to design a European tariff. France proposed such a conference as the Cobden–Chevalier treaty negotiations were renewed, and the Conservative Chancellor Sir Stafford Northcote spoke in the Commons of a 'large and comprehensive understanding come to by the Powers of Europe as to some common basis for tariffs'.[11] Even so, this prospect, with its intimations of the 1957 treaties of Rome, soon receded in favour of bilateral Anglo-French negotiations. But France was now in the driving-seat as her treaties came up for renegotiation, so that had the French government inclined to free trade, the treaty system as a whole stood a fair chance of surviving. During 1877, the auguries were good, with a French government inclined to free trade and Leon Say, a sound free trader, as ambassador in London.[12] But within an unstable republic, especially after the Seize Mai crisis of 1877, the design of a European tariff, if ever realistic, became subordinate to the exigencies of a government which needed to draw interest groups to its support in order to survive. France now looked firmly to country-by-country negotiations, with Italy, not Britain, first on the list.[13]

Nor was Britain able to press successfully for reform elsewhere. Here in large part she was limited by her inability further to reduce her wine duties; these remained essential to revenue collection yet they also remained the only bargaining counter Britain had to tempt other countries into reciprocal concessions. Again the far-sighted argued for low wine duties and increased working-class consumption but this seemed too visionary for the fiscally conservative. Free trade was successfully retained for example in Turkey, even if more visionary schemes, such as that of Robert Morier for a Balkan customs union, 'with a tariff of pure customs duties and absolute free trade', failed.[14] Elsewhere too free trade was under fire. Colonial protectionism was growing apace in both the Australian colonies (save New South Wales) and in Canada. It had come as a shock to Gladstone in 1871 to realize how autonomous and how protectionist the Australian colonies were, while the Australian Customs Duties Act of 1873 allowed the imposition of differential duties, a complete departure from orthodoxy. In Canada, the incidental protection of 1858–9 was on the verge of transformation into the National Policy of 1879.[15] Only in the Crown colonies of Malta and Ceylon did freer trade make some progress, as the Cobdenites waged war against the last vestiges of food taxes. Free traders still looked with some expectation to the United States, buoyed up by the campaigns of David Wells and Edward Atkinson, but the political weight of protectionism remained as solid in the United States as did that of free trade in Britain.[16]

Notes

1. St. K. Hornbeck, 'The Most-Favoured Nation Clause', *American Journal of International Law*, 3 (1909), pp. 395–422.
2. R. I. Giesberg, *The Treaty of Frankfort: A Study in Diplomatic History, September 1870–September 1873* (Philadelphia, PA: University of Pennsylvania Press, 1966), pp. 143–4, 161, 164, 199.
3. See D. Mares, '"Not Entirely a Manchester Man": Richard Cobden and the Construction of Manchesterism in Nineteenth-Century German Economic Thinking', in A. Howe and S. Morgan (eds), *Rethinking Nineteenth-Century Liberalism: Richard Cobden Bicentenary Essays* (Aldershot: Ashgate, 2006), pp. 141–60.
4. See Volume 3 of this edition.
5. Louis Mallet, Memorandum on Modifications of Anglo French Treaty, 19 August 1871, above, pp. 207–11.
6. J. Faucher, 'A New Commercial Treaty between Great Britain and Germany', *Cobden Club Essays*, 2nd series (London: Cassell, Petter and Galpin, 1871–2), pp. 261–339; Chancellor Lowe also blocked progress with Spain.
7. For British commercial diplomacy in this period, see A. Howe, *Free Trade and Liberal England, 1846–1946*, (Oxford: Clarendon Press, 1997), pp. 156–65; P. Marsh, *Bargaining on Europe: Britain and the First Common Market, 1860–1892* (New Haven, CT, and London: Yale University Press, 1999); J. W. T. Gaston, 'Trade and the Late Victorian Foreign Office', *International History Review*, 4 (1982), pp. 317–38.
8. A. C. Howe, 'Cobden Club, 1866–c.1982', *Oxford Dictionary of National Biography* [online version only]; Howe, *Free Trade and Liberal England*, pp. 116–41.
9. See *Free Trade and the European Treaties of Commerce* (1875); and Letters of Henry Parkes and Gower Evans, in ibid, both below, pp. 283–311, 348–51.
10. J. W. T. Gaston, 'The Free Trade Diplomacy Debate and the Victorian Common Market Initiative', *Canadian Journal of History*, 22 (1987), 59–82; see also Marsh, *Bargaining on Europe*.
11. 7 March 1876, cited in Howe, *Free Trade and Liberal England*, p. 167.
12. For Say, the grandson of the great liberal political economist J-B Say, see especially J. Garrigues, 'Léon Say: un libéral sous la Troisième République (1871–1896)', *Revue Historique*, 286 (1991), p. 119–41.

13. See especially M. S. Smith, *Tariff Reform in France, 1860–1900* (Ithaca, NY, and London: Cornell University Press, 1980).
14. A. Ramm, *Sir Robert Morier: Envoy and Ambassador in the Age of Imperialism, 1876–1893* (Oxford: Clarendon Press, 1973), p. 143.
15. For the shaping of policy, see B. Forster, *A Conjunction of Interests: Business, Politics, and Tariffs, 1825–1879* (Toronto and London: Toronto University Press: 1986); for its intellectual context, see C. Goodwin, *Canadian Economic Thought: The Political Economy of a Developing Nation, 1814–1914* (Durham, NC: Duke University Press, 1961), pp. 109–44.
16. A. Howe, 'Free Trade and the International Order: The Anglo-American Tradition, 1846–1946', in F. M. Leventhal and R. Quinault (eds), *Anglo-American Attitudes: From Revolution to Partnership* (Aldershot: Ashgate, 2000), pp. 142–67.

FREE TRADE UNDER THREAT: TO 1879

Britain, Europe, and the United States

Manifesto of the Association of 'Revivers' of British Industry **(London: Lewis & Co. Steam Printing Works, [1869]).**

Manifesto of the Association of 'REVIVERS.'

The 'REVIVERS' do not require to exact any promise from their adherents binding them to support the association, as all will see it their interest to do so; and as no payment is required the humblest and poorest can join if he or she agree with the principles.

It will be the duty of every one who sympathises with us to send or enter his or her name, trade, and the district to which he or she belongs, with as many other names as can possibly be procured, who will be true to us in heart, for we want no lukewarm consent, and shall be better without any who may differ with the opinions, as given in our Resolution passed unanimously at all our Meetings, and which is as follows: –

'That want of Employment and consequent Distress is not only local, but general throughout England; that the Importation of Foreign Manufactures, Duty Free, into this Country, supplants the labour of the British Workman; and that without other Countries meeting us with Reciprocity, and treating us as we treat them, this portion of Free-Trade Policy is a 'Gigantic Mistake, and utter ruin to Manufacturing Industry in nearly every branch."

Our objects are definite and unmistakeable, we want to encourage British Industry and the advancement of our Colonies whatever may be the effect on Foreign Countries. Let as many names as possible be gathered together by every one of us including Women and Young People written on any kinds of paper to be given in to the Association at the Meetings or as opportunity offers so that we may be able to know and declare our Numbers. The 'REVIVERS' have formed themselves into a body to look after their own material interests. The 'REVIVERS' will not encourage the introduction of General Politics or Religion at their Meetings, nor will they as a body, interfere with them. The duty they allot to themselves is to endeavour 'To restore and specially guard the Industrial Interests of THIS COUNTRY, and every Beneficial Institution in it.' It will be the interest of every one, however remotely engaged in Industrial pursuits, to join the 'REVIVERS' if they have any desire to see happiness and prosperity return to themselves and to the people of this Country. Rich drones may be shortsighted enough to hate us; Foreigners may gnash their teeth – we cannot help that – it is their own fault, for they do not reciprocate our liberality while they have the opportunity.

The 'REVIVERS' exclude no one; all are equally the same in their eyes. It will be their duty and it is their intention when their numbers reach 100,000 first to petition Her Majesty, the nature of which petition will be disclosed at a Monster Meeting at the Agricultural Hall, when it is hoped that every Reviver will attend, and afterwards to lay before Members of Parliament individually, and ultimately to the Government, a re-modelling of the Customs' Tariff concerning Foreign Vessels and Foreign Manufactured Goods that CAN be made in this country, also proposals concerning the British Colonies carefully avoiding interference with Food or Raw Material.

This being drawn up with due care, Government will be asked to save the British People from Starvation, as well as Taxation, by taking the proposals that will be made to them into their consideration, and if possible, according to the wishes of the People, if the numbers applying warrant them in so doing. People must not starve because Statesmen are too proud to own their mistake, or to please the fancies of some Political Economists.

We must do everything calmly, peacefully, moderately cautiously, and we hope to act wisely, at the same time as a great people we must proceed boldly, vigorously, and determinedly. Money is not wanted from the Poor; what is wanted is the name and district of every adherent, male and female (if the home is the Workhouse no matter, for he and she need us) – our object is to know our numbers every week. If some cannot write, put their names and marks. Should, however, any who can afford it think our object deserves his or her help, we shall be glad of it; we endeavour to make the association support itself by the sale of Publications that are necessary, but we find the movement becoming so vast and widely approved that we hope for help, so that we may be enabled to hold more Meetings, extend our advertisements, and more rapidly and extensively enrol our followers; but our Movement is no Flash in the Pan – for dear life, wives, homes, and children are at stake – and it will proceed but slowly without assistance. Let us all put our shoulders to the wheel.

THE EFFECTS OF OUR INTENDED PROPOSALS WILL BE THESE: –

Foreigners have, during the last twenty-one years, been increasing the number of their factories, and making other great and extensive preparations year after year, to deal with us FOR EVER on our own terms, that is – giving us nothing for the privilege we have given them of supplying Us, our Colonies, and Customers, with Shipping and goods of all kinds; and although we generously admit their Goods, Duty Free, and without charge, they are so greedy that they will not treat us in a similarly liberal spirit, so the 'REVIVERS' propose to stop their little game. Foreigners have now large factories – who would keep them at work if England refused to give them orders? They have large stocks of Goods ready to pour into this Country faster than we can consume them, and of which we are as yet their largest buyers for shipment and home use. Suppose we were to put a reasonable Duty on all those kinds of Manufactures we CAN make here, and which our people WANT to make – and are starving because they cannot get them to make – what would Foreigners do with their Goods? At first they would stop sending them; they would then stop their factories working, THEIR PEOPLE would be out of Employment, but this would set our Manufacturers, our Workpeople and every other class to work hard; we could then probably compete successfully with the Foreigners. If we could not do so, still our Revenue would benefit to the extent of the Duty paid, while our men could be no worse off at all events. But the fact is – if we adopted a course of inflicting heavy Duties on MANUFACTURED Goods received from all Countries which do not admit our Manufactures Duty Free, we should so paralyze Foreign Manufacturers, that we should exact Free Trade in six months, and then we must take our chance, unless our rulers of those days see fit to continue the 'REVIVER' policy.

J. ROBERTS, CHAIRMAN; W. C. WILKINS, ARTISAN SEC.

To the People of England of all classes, Male and Female.

As you cannot obtain work here, proposals for your expatriation from the land of your fathers, destroying all the sacred ties of humanity, are now being encouraged. It is said that by some of you thus sacrificing yourselves, those who remain will obtain higher wages, – vain hope! It is also said that your being out of employment is the result of the high wages you demand, – what a contradiction!! If England cannot compete with foreign nations when labourers are numerous, what reason is there for supposing she will be able to do so when they are scarce?

The Population of Great Britain in 1846 was, including foreigners: 28,002,604
And in 1867 it was ditto: 30,157,239
So that we had only increased (in 21 years): 2,154,635

This is not an important increase contrasted with the march of intellect, machinery, gold discoveries, railways, and the consequent increase in the wealth and trade of the Country. Yet men, women, and children starve in our midst; Tens of thousands are out of work; Thousands are working half-time, or at lowered wages; Hundreds are on the verge of ruin: others are in the workhouse, or undergoing penal or stone-yard punishment; while none are prosperous. Should all this be, in the greatest and wealthiest country? No! There is room enough for us all in Great Britain, if we would look upon ourselves as one family; let us forget prejudices; let us be just before we are generous; let us be patriotic first, Cosmopolitan when we are able. We now place before you a few plain questions: –

Are your wages to be gradually reduced because half-starved foreigners will work from 7½d. per day?

Are you to be out of work? Are your wives and families to starve?

Because of the introduction of labour into your Country (which you can supply) in the shape of foreign manufactures of every kind, which are here admitted duty free, while no country admits your manufactures without heavy duties.

Believe us, friends, this is the true cause of your difficulties and distress, and we warn you that you have not yet seen the bitter end, unless you defend your own material interests, for we shall fall in one common ruin, if it is not altered.

Ask manufacturers, workmen and workwomen in all the manufacturing towns in England, whether foreign competition is not ruining them? Commence with Millwall, and every ship-building port. Ask Macclesfield, Coventry, and Spitalfields; ask Leek, Preston, Manchester, and Derby; ask Nottingham, Congleton, Sandbach, Leighton-Buzzard, Luton, Newport-Pagnell, and Tring; ask Exeter and Crediton, what workpeople there are doing, and with a few exceptions the answer will be 'none are getting a proper living.' And we tell you your prospects are gloomy, nay, fearful, unless you all boldly stand up for the protection of British labour, by demanding to be allowed to do the work required to be done here, instead of letting foreigners take the bread out of your mouths.

Remember that the ruin of ship-building involves about thirty, that of watchmaking about sixty other trades, and that all are gradually passing away from us. There are few sailing vessels now building here, for foreign vessels have greater advantages, which limit the necessity for British vessels being built. British sailors, your occupation is fast passing into other hands.

The trade in Cotton manufactures at last begins to give way. The Iron trade is losing ground. Tools, Chairs, Pans, Spades, Hoes, Axes, Nails, Lamps, Tin Ware, Locks, Curry Combs, Traps, Hinges, Brass-foundry, Needles, Hooks, Guns, Swords, Jewellery, Buttons, Steel Pens, Trinkets, Pins, Wire, Tubing, Scales, Cutlery, Bronze, Japanned Articles, &c. now come in from America, France, and Germany; we have foreign Doors, Floors, and Window Sashes, Laths, and every other kind of manufactured articles in Wood, so the trade of our Carpenters,

Lath Renders, &c. who number five hundred, is gradually passing away to other Countries. The Silk and Ribbon trades are almost gone. We receive (duty free) foreign built-ships, foreign made Paper, Agricultural Implements, Umbrellas, Furniture, Dolls, Toys, and Artificial Flowers, Baby Linen, Dresses, and Baskets, Beads and Beds, Berlin Work, Blankets, Cloaks, Bonnets, Boots, and Braid, Brushes, Candle, and Canes, Cannon, Cardboard, Carpets, Caps, China, Glass, Clocks, Cloth, Damask, Delaine, Electrotype, Paper, Pencils, Fringe, Lace, Gilded Goods, Gold and Silver Articles, Hosiery, Leather, Linen, Looking Glasses, and Lucifers, Iron Bedsteads, Staves, Shoes, Silks, Ribbons, Soaps, Stays, Stationery, Machinery, Steam Engines, Coffins, Mop Handles, in fact, everything small or greater down to a penny bundle of firewood, is now supplied by foreigners, not only to the markets of England, duty free, but to our forty Colonies, and to the markets of the world. What have British workmen left to make? Could we not make all these articles here? And if we did, would there be a single man or woman out of employment? No! But even if you can find a trade not yet competed with, in a short time some foreigner will attack it. Then look at the local taxes that want of employment inflicts on those better off.

Let workmen ask themselves whether we are stating truth, when we say that unlimited and unregulated foreign competition, by the wholesale introduction of foreign labour, is displacing yours, not only in the markets of England, but in our Colonies and the markets of the world; and this is the cause why you cannot get employment. And who gains? We do not know; but some mythical persons whom no one can succeed in discovering, may rise at our meetings and let us know. Let us no longer be misled by theory, as we have facts before us.

And could any one get the necessaries of life cheaper, if they had the money to buy? Are Meat, Poultry, Eggs, Butter, Milk, Candles, Oil, Soap, Bacon, Vegetables, Beer, or Bread Cheaper? Every one of these should be duty free, because we cannot produce enough for the people.

Let us have Monster Meetings in every Town. Bring your Wives and Children, for they are equally interested. Differences in religious faith do not affect this question. Let us forget politics. Let us unite to achieve our material interests. Be we English, Scotch, or Irish, let us forget any difference of race, and form into one compact mass to secure the means of gaining our bread – Our life, our own country, our own people are at stake! For 'the payments for wages increase the power of the BULK OF THE NATION to consume and pay.'

We ask every one who reads this address, and believes in the truth of it, to attend our Meetings and to send to us, in any way he pleases, to our temporary postal address, his name and district, and with it as many others as he can gather together from his own circle, who believe and feel the truth of our facts. Our numbers are augmenting daily. Our object is to have the names of 100,000 Persons, and as many more as we can get together, with Women and young people, to enrol themselves as belonging to our Association, and who will upon occasion, if possible, muster to the call for a demonstration, simply as believing in our principles. When we have obtained a sufficient number, we shall make a bold front, and a grand demonstration of the 'REVIVERS ASSOCIATION,' at the Agricultural Hall.

Public Meetings are held every Monday. The district and place will be advertised. Our objects, intentions, and method of procedure are all clearly and plainly laid out in the MANIFESTO of the 'Revivers Association,' which will be read at our Meetings, but will be sent to any one on application.

Although we do not ask for subscriptions, from any who cannot afford it, yet there are those who can, that we trust will help us in our mighty task, the success of which will some day certainly benefit themselves, their wives and children; and they may live to be proud that they enrolled themselves under the banner of an Association whose sole object is 'TO RESTORE AND SPECIALLY GUARD THE INDUSTRIAL INTERESTS OF THIS COUNTRY, AND EVERY BENEFICIAL INSTITUTION IN IT.'

It is right that so great a movement should emanate from the Capital of England, and we hope that our Country friends will pour in their names to swell our numbers, and will everywhere form Auxiliaries to accomplish this one great end, and constitute one mighty band – the 'REVIVERS ASSOCIATION!'

J. ROBERTS. Chairman,
W. C. WILKINS, Artisan Sec.[1]

---

1 [Ed.: The text is followed by an extensive range of figures of exports and imports illustrating the points contained within the text.]

Kuklos [pseud., John Harris], *The Commercial Policy of England in 1877: A Letter to the Public* (London: John Harris, 1877).

To the Public, –

In order to present the important subject, which we are desirous to bring under your attentive consideration, with as much conciseness and directness as possible, we purpose to do so in the form of the critical notice of a leading article published in the *Daily Telegraph* newspaper of October 17th, and which article we will commence by quoting *in extenso*.

'Intelligence of the greatest commercial importance comes from Berlin. The Emperor and Prince Bismarck, it is stated, concur in the opinion of a numerous party in the Empire who believe that 'Free Trade principles have obtained greater prevalence than the country can well afford,' and that 'the comprehensive inquiry into the state of German industry and commerce demanded by the Protectionists and recently recommended by the Committee of the Handelstag will be ordered by Government.' Within the last few weeks it has transpired that the party of commercial reaction in Germany have adopted special measures to rally the public to their restrictive standard. A cheap edition of 'A National System of Political Economy,' by the eminent Protectionist writer Frederic List, has been published under the auspices of leading manufacturers, endorsing the same policy, and the sale of that work, owing to the exertions of energetic *colporteurs*, is said to be extraordinary. Herr List, who was a disciple of Henry Clay, and an opponent of Adam Smith, deals with the subject in an ideal fashion adapted to the German cast of thought, taking the lofty ground that protection is a fundamental element of political philosophy, a patriotic duty, and an indispensable condition of national regeneration. On the other hand, the 'Catheder-Sociolists,' largely composed of University professors, have combined for the advocacy of Free Trade on the score of industrial expediency; but their theories are so inextricably interwoven with Chauvinism as to have exerted little practical force upon the public mind hitherto. Nevertheless this learned body has substantially avowed the great economic principle to which England at present bears solitary witness. The 'Catheder-Sociolists' will soon hold their annual Congress at Berlin, and as they have manifestly grasped, however imperfectly, the conception of that fiscal policy which has so mightily contributed to the commercial supremacy of England, we may venture to hope that, by extended knowledge and a fuller discussion of the subject, these *savants* may yet succeed in educating public opinion and liberalising the commercial policy of the German Empire. At the same time a dispassionate view of the situation forces upon us the conviction that in Europe the commercial horizon wears a somewhat gloomy aspect. Trade with France is still hampered by high tariffs, and the revision of the treaty between that country and England which, anterior to the existing political crisis, was under the consideration of a joint commission, has been indefinitely postponed. Austria, Italy, Switzerland, and Spain have thought fit to disregard the reiterated appeals made to them by the Cobden Club to bring their Custom-house system into accord with the axioms of modern economic science, but hitherto our efforts for that object have been without result. Protection in Russia virtually amounts, as far as England is concerned, to total prohibition.

'In recently alluding to the formidable difficulties by which English trade continues to be embarrassed, Sir Stafford Northcote, after referring to the Eastern Question, said: 'I cannot forget that there is another kind of war, much less terrible of course, but still of a very unsatisfactory and even disastrous character, which is partly being waged and partly being threatened against us – I mean the war of tariffs.' In this antagonism offered to Free Trade by the nations of America and Europe, Great Britain cannot afford to be neutral. Our interests are inseparably bound up with the development of commerce, and protective barriers erected in various directions against the introduction of our trade must inevitably inflict serious injury upon our mercantile interests. The most marvellous aspect of the economic problem is that Free Trade principles, the soundness of which has been indubitably demonstrated by practical experience in this country for thirty years, should still be obstinately resisted by nearly all other civilised communities, to their own palpable detriment. With a degree of perverseness utterly incomprehensible in a nation transcendently distinguished for industrial and commercial enterprise, the people of the United States still appear to cherish, for the most part, the suicidal illusion that they are enriched in proportion as they place fiscal obstructions in the way of foreign manufactures entering their ports, provided it is in their power to match them by the products of native labour, even at a higher cost. They seem to ignore the elementary fact that if imports are artificially restricted a check, to a corresponding extent, is given to exports; for it is needless to remark that the most extensive and profitable part of commerce between different nations consists in exchange of products. Mr. D. A. Wells, the veteran apostle of Free Trade in America, has aptly compared the procedure of the United States on this question to that of a merchant whose store is well situated for business, and replete with an ample variety of marketable goods. The roads conducting to the place are well paved, and every precaution is taken that all who wish to purchase shall not miss their way. But when customers arrive they are dismayed to find that the proprietor has removed the steps leading to the building, bolted the door, and rendered access so troublesome that they prefer to travel by some circuitous route to another depôt, where such preposterous obstacles do not intervene. It is estimated that every 4,400,000 inhabitants of different States of the Union exchange annually commodities, by the agency of railways alone, to the value of 1,000,000,000 dols. Yet, in consequence of the arbitrary restrictions imposed by the American tariff laws on commercial intercourse between the 4,000,000 inhabitants of the Canadian Dominion and the 44,000,000 Americans in the United States, the aggregate value of the international business done in 1875, between the residents on either side of the boundary, only amounted to 86,000,000 dols. Let the barriers to trade between the States and Canada be razed, and it requires no superhuman perception to see how vast an accession of prosperity would result to both countries. The application of the principle we have illustrated has but to be extended to enlightened communities everywhere in order to diffuse wealth throughout the world upon a scale of unprecedented magnitude. We welcome the inception of the earnest Free Trade agitation commenced by a zealous minority in the States, and cannot doubt that eventually it will be crowned with success.

'Unhappily, the Board of Trade returns for the last two months still leave us, as regards the revival of our industry and commerce, in an attitude of vague expectancy. There was a marked decrease in the import values for September, notwithstanding that these included an unusually large proportion of food supplies at augmented prices. We have now reached the anomalous position of buying from foreigners exactly twice as much as we sell them; and when the large excess of imports, as compared with exports, is considered, it will be obvious that the lessened foreign demand for our staple manufactures, with which we have been accustomed, in a great measure, to pay for the commodities we import, cannot fail to narrow the resources of the community. American calicoes are reported to meet with increasing acceptance in Manchester. The saws and cutlery of Philadelphia and Pittsburgh are sometimes preferred to similar manufactures produced in Sheffield. The machine-made watches of Waltham threaten to supplant the solid horologic workmanship of Coventry. Leather from the United States evokes from the tanners of Bermondsey the confession that they are no longer able to sell the same material of a certain quality against the Transatlantic product. Agricultural implements bearing the trade mark of a New York Company are to be found exposed for sale in English hardware shops; and indents from the Colonies entrusted to firms in London and Birmingham for execution actually include American edge tools. The town last named was until recently regarded as the chief source for the supply of small arms to the world; and it was confidently anticipated that the present struggle in the East would have imparted a potent stimulus to gun manufacture in that locality. But for the first time in the history of modern warfare that branch of industry in the Midland metropolis has failed to reap any advantage. The Winchester rifle in use by the Turks is produced in Rhode Island; a considerable share of the heavy ordnance of Turkey is supplied by Herr Krupp; and Russia manufactures a good portion of her own war material, while she derives most of the remainder from Germany. Nevertheless we have unbounded confidence in the future of British industry. Besides, it is indisputable that every period of dull trade, without exception, has been followed by a rebound of industrial expansion, in each case more striking than the previous one. And as the average interval of stagnation after a commercial panic is known to last about four years, there are reasonable grounds for believing that in less than two years from the present time an opportunity will occur to manufacturers and merchants to recruit their resources depleted through protracted depression.'

We will commence with the remark that the *Daily Telegraph* cannot be reasonably held responsible for the commercial national policy advocated in the foregoing, and scarcely so even for its advocacy thereof. That journal is presenting to its readers, in this manner, information of especial importance to all who are interested in the commercial prosperity of the country, and in doing so, takes for granted that a theory of commercial policy, adopted by so large a majority of the leading politicians in this country, as to have become for many years the established national policy of England, must be sound, and argues in favour of it. We are about to examine how far and in what respects the information furnished by the *Daily Telegraph* logically supports the arguments by which it is accompanied, and how far and in what respects the arguments are not supported by, and do not harmonize with, that information.

There are not a few persons who may draw an inference of this kind. They find day by day articles in the *Daily Telegraph* on various subjects with which they are conversant, written with great ability and in accordance with the acknowledged rules of reasoning. When, therefore, this advocacy of the Free Trade policy by the same journal comes before them and challenges their attention, they are naturally inclined to suppose, and are likely to infer, that the same just and close reasoning which brought conviction to their minds on those other more familiar subjects, has been applied in this case also, and thus they accept the conclusions proffered to them without much, and possibly without any, particular scrutiny. Now if, on attentive examination, it appear that, in this instance, a remarkable want of rational accord between the facts stated and the conclusions deduced from them, has taken the place of sound reasoning, the inference is likely to become unfavorable to the system of policy advocated; for the mind of the reader finding the arguments logically and manifestly untenable, by which an able advocate endeavours to support the policy, will not be easily dissuaded from condemning the policy itself as irrational.

In the first place: What are *the facts* which the *Daily Telegraph* puts before us?

1. The Government of Germany has just declared its judgment to have become even more strongly opposed to the dogma of Free Trade than it has hitherto been.

2. A treatise, entitled 'A National System of Political Economy,' by an eminent writer whose opinions are strongly opposed to the Free Trade policy, has met with a sale, in Germany, so large as to be termed extraordinary.
3. France, Austria, Germany, Italy, Switzerland, Spain, and Russia, continue to turn a deaf ear to the charming appeals of the Cobden Club, and still decline to adopt commercially that mode of putting an end to a difficulty practised by the Japanese, and called 'the happy dispatch.'
4. That Free Trade principles are obstinately resisted by all civilized communities with the exception only of our own country.
5. That, with a degree of perverseness utterly incomprehensible, the United States, commercially benighted the same as the other civilized communities, insist upon impoverishing themselves by encouraging, cherishing, and protecting their own manufactures.
6. We, the subjects of Great Britain, have now reached the anomalous position of buying from foreigners exactly twice as much as we sell them.
7. American calicoes meet with increasing acceptance in Manchester.
8. Circumstantial evidence that the manufactures of the United States are displacing and superseding those of England; not only in other countries but, in some cases, even in England itself.
9. In the competition for the supply of the Turks with heavy ordnance England has been unable to successfully contend with Germany; and in the competition for supplying them with small arms Birmingham has been driven entirely out of the field by Rhode Island.

What effect does the enumeration of these portentous facts, which he has very lucidly set forth in detail, have upon the writer of the article? Does he appear to be affrighted at the imminent danger impending over his country? No. Is he inspired with the most gloomy apprehensions of coming disaster, of which the present depression is merely the precursor and commencement? Not so. What then? These facts inspire him with confidence. 'Nevertheless we have unbounded confidence in the future of British industry.' We can only picture to ourselves, the careful reader opening his eyes very wide and exclaiming with unbounded astonishment, Good gracious! The writer of the article, however, feeling that some explanation of this remarkable conclusion is called for, proceeds to explain that 'it is indisputable that every period of dull trade, without exception, has been followed by a rebound of industrial expansion, in each case more striking than the previous one. And as the average interval of stagnation after a commercial panic is known to last about four years, there are reasonable grounds for believing that in less than two years from the present time an opportunity will occur to manufactures and merchants to recruit their resources depleted through protracted depression.' So that herein is the ground upon which expectation stations itself with so much confidence in the future result ... Because British industry has, on former occasions, been in jeopardy and has escaped, and has sometimes been depressed and has hitherto always recovered, therefore we may rely upon the same sequence of depression and recovery until the end of all time. In astronomy, in regard to the periodical apparition of comets for example, this kind of confidence is found to be in a great measure justified by the event.[1] A certain comet, having appeared and remained in the neighbourhood of the earth sufficiently long for the terrestrial astronomer to make its acquaintance, returns after an interval of (let us say) seven years, and is recognized. After an interval of another seven years it again appears, and then again after a third intervening period of the same duration; after which the astronomer proceeds to predict, with a good deal of confidence, the periodical reappearance of the comet every seven years. With respect to the recovery of the industrial well-being of a great nation from commercial paralysis, depression, or decay, the case is, we submit, essentially different. The difficulty of finding a good parallel is perhaps somewhat great. We might cite the case of a great empire such as Rome or Assyria. Each of these met with occasional reverses in its onward progress, reverses which in each case were followed by recovery and the attainment of a prosperity exceeding that which preceded the period of ill-health. But at length came one of those periods when, instead of recovery, the national sickness, neglected in its earlier symptoms, assumed a more inveterate and dangerous character, and when the patient, alarmed too late, vainly endeavoured to escape the fatal termination. It may be thought that neither of these afford a very good parallel in regard to the commercial and industrial greatness of Great Britain. A closer similarity might be found perhaps in the commercial biography of some one of those great business firms now belonging to the past, which having at first being established on a comparatively small scale, became prosperous, and, in the course of a long career, successively overcoming occasional reverses, at length grew to be wealthy and powerful. A change, unnoticed perhaps, or at least unattended to, has gradually taken place, other business firms have quietly entered the same field, have been allowed to establish themselves advantageously, and a formidable competition suddenly manifests itself. The old farsighted, energetic, but cautious policy of the firm has been changed perhaps for that of reckless or ill-advised speculation, hasty counsels and feverish anxiety to do a large business now guide the helm. A fresh period of depression sets in and before long causes for apprehension and anxiety are not wanting; but these are thought but little of, and recovery, as on former occasions, is confidently expected. The unfavourable circumstances, however, on this occasion do not disappear, but increase and grow more adverse, difficulty becomes danger, danger becomes disaster, and,

---

1   Sometimes, however, even comets do not reappear at the time their re-appearance has been confidently predicted and is expected.

instead of the confidently expected recovery, fatal collapse terminates the vitality of the once prosperous firm.

We are told something of what there is to be said in favour of that great economic dogma which all other civilized communities decline to adopt, and which has now brought our country into that anomalous and extremely alarming commercial condition, set forth and defined by the *Daily Telegraph* in the sixth item of the facts of the case as they now present themselves. The commendations of the ungainly idol are supported by argument. Speaking of the Americans and their want of intelligence in failing to appreciate the benefits of Free Trade, we are told – 'They seem to ignore the elementary fact that if imports are artificially restricted, a check, to a corresponding extent, is given to exports; for it is needless to remark that the most extensive and profitable part of commerce between different nations consists in exchange of products.' Let us consider this alleged elementary fact a little closely, in order to see whether it be actually a fact, and whether, if it be in some sense a fact, it can be correctly applied in the manner the advocates of 'Free Trade' are wont to apply it: – England requires to import annually, taking one year with another, a certain large quantity of grain, which is needed for her own wants over and above the quantity of grain produced in the country itself. Now England having to buy this grain from foreign countries: what is, or would be, the effect of levying an import duty on that grain? A large sum of money would come into the hands of the Government. 'O yes,' exclaims the Free Trade advocate, 'but don't run away with the idea that the country is any richer on that account, the country which buys the grain pays the duty and practically buys the grain so much dearer.' If the Free-trader makes the whole of this statement he is wrong in regard to the last part of it, which is untrue, but if he limits the remark to the first part of the statement he is quite right: quite right as to the country being no direct gainer by the money which, as import duty, comes into the hands of the Government. But would he be right in an inference that those opposed to the Free Trade dogma base their opposition on a supposition that the country which adopts Free Trade loses thereby the amount which under the protective policy would have been received as import duty? The writer whose argument we are about to consider, might, for instance, infer that the political economists of the United States suppose their country to be enriched by the amount of the import duty on goods of foreign manufacture and produce of other countries subjected thereto.[1] It does not seem to require a very astute mind or any extraordinary degree of intelligence, to understand that an import duty is virtually a tax, a part of the internal revenue, paid by the inhabitants, and that in respect to directly enriching or directly impoverishing the country, it does neither the one nor the other. The Government must obtain the money to

---

1 We do not understand the writer in the *Daily Telegraph* to infer this, but ill-informed advocates of Free Trade not infrequently attribute to their opponents the transparent fallacy here alluded to.

defray the national expenditure from some source, and if no part of it is got by the method of import duties it must be made up in some other manner. But is this the whole question between Free Trade and Protection? Nay; does it, let us ask, correctly constitute any essential part, even, of that distinctive difference which divides Free Trade and Protection into two opposite economic policies. Take the extreme case of a country able to supply itself with all the grain it needs, and to manufacture everything it requires, and suppose that country to adopt a policy of total prohibition in respect to the import of foreign grain and foreign manufactures, for the purpose of protecting, against foreign competition, its own manufacturers and agriculturists. Would not that be a Protection policy? And yet the Government in that case would receive no duties, and the advocate of such a policy could not deceive himself (as Protectionists are sometimes supposed to do) in respect to the country directly enriching itself by fiscal duties levied on imports.

What is the meaning we are to attach to the foregoing quotation with regard to the international commercial policy which it attributes to the United States? Let us suppose the intended meaning to be this: The people of the United States being able to carry on certain kinds of manufacture in their own country, levy duties on foreign manufactures of the same description for the purpose of protecting and benefiting their own manufacturers. Yes; but if this be the meaning, where is the incomprehensible perverseness, and what becomes of the suicidal illusion? Suppose that, thirty or forty years ago, the United States had agreed with England to adopt a strictly Free-Trade international commercial policy, and had then commenced and since that time continued to admit the manufactures of England duty free, leaving their manufacturers to fight their own battle as they could, What would have been the result? The result would have been that a large proportion of the manufactured goods required by the inhabitants of the United States would have been manufactured in England. Would that have been a good thing for the United States? It is true that in the factories of Lowel, and in some other places, the American manufacturer has an advantage, in the employment of water power, over his English competitor; but, in fact, – although in the aggregate, taking all the factories in Lowel (which is a city of factories) together, the saving, compared with the use of steam power, might appear considerable – the advantage thereby derived, as a percentage in the cost of the manufactured article, can be but very small, probably not nearly sufficient to compensate for the advantage on the side of the English manufacturer from the greater abundance of accumulated wealth and the consequent cheapness of capital in England. It is this abundance and cheapness of capital in England which would have enabled the English manufacturers, had the Americans not adopted the protective policy, to shut down the factories of their transatlantic competitors.

The benefit conferred on the home manufacturers by an import duty on the goods with which they have to compete, is even greater than at first sight it may appear to be; for the effect is not only, by partially excluding the foreigner, to give him (the home producer) a larger home market, but, also, by withdrawing the pressure of foreign competition, to enable the home manufacturer to sell his productions at a higher price in the home market. Ah; now, says the Free Trade advocate, this is just what we are trying to make you understand. Cannot you see that the country has, in that case, to pay for the benefit of the manufacturer? Has not everyone else in the country to lose in order that he may gain? No: we cannot see that; but we can see very clearly that such is not the case. The manufacturer (or agriculturist) is a part of the country just as much as his customer. The producers who sell, and those who buy their productions, together constitute the whole community, and if some members of the community become more wealthy and others less wealthy, the wealth of the country is not increased or diminished thereby. The country pays nothing and loses nothing. But, does it gain nothing? Most certainly it gains very much, by the manufacture being carried on within it. The manufacture employs and supports a number of persons, and as each one of these persons is most probably a producer of wealth over and above what he consumes, the surplus is a direct gain to the country. But moreover, and herein we note a most important fact, each one of these *as a consumer* (using the word in that sense in which, we believe, writers on the subject usually employ it) is *largely a contributor* to the common *gain* of the community.[1] Let one of the men employed belong to the better class of labourers, and let his wages be ten dollars a week. Out of the ten dollars a week let him spend eight dollars. That expenditure represents his so-called consumption. In spending the eight dollars he buys with it ... bread, meat, butter, cheese, etc.; a part of it goes towards the purchase of boots and clothing, and with a part he pays rent and taxes. On each and all of these things is a profit – generally a double profit, a wholesale and a retail profit – and all of this profit is just so much gain to the country. It is gain, too, of the most valuable kind, because it is active capital very effectively employed. Speaking roundly, we may say that for every hundred men receiving eight hundred dollars a week, fully the one-half, or four hundred dollars a week, is paid over to the commonwealth and is gained by the nation or community. In the next place: we have to take into account the proprietor's gains. The manufacture yields profits; and these profits, if they remain in the country, are clear gain to the commonwealth. They may be invested in the same or some other business, may be employed in assisting to develop the natural resources of the country, or may be mainly expended in the wages of domestic servants, and in the rent of a large and costly residence; whichever way they are employed the gain to the commonwealth is substantially the same. In addition to these there are other less direct ways in which the country is a gainer by the manufacture being

1   Using the word consumer in the more strict sense, a consumer cannot as such be a contributor. But, in fact, the wages of those employed in the manufacture may be justly considered as a part of the profits derived by the country from that manufacture being carried on in it.

carried on within it, for it may be said, generally, that each one of those employed thereby is a contributor towards those advantages which a more populous has over a less populous country. Now if we admit that those who buy the goods, lose the difference between the higher price under protection and the price at which they might have bought imported goods on which no duty was levied, of what consequence even to the purchasers is or would be that difference – the small additional percentage – compared with the manifold benefits conferred by the industrial operations of the manufacturer and agriculturist being carried on in their own country? Let us not, however, be in haste to admit that the purchasers actually lose anything, for they are a part of the country (*i.e.*, the community) which gains, and the gain of the country is their gain. And this is not all, for if the manufacture was driven out of the country by the keenness of competition with foreigners, the persons and the capital employed in carrying it on would also have to leave the country. In that case, since the expenses of the country would be almost as great as before, those who remained would have to pay that part of the taxes which was previously paid by the others. And, also, capital being rendered less plentiful by a part of it leaving the country, it would become more difficult to procure and therefore dearer. When these considerations are put against the small difference in the cost to the purchaser, it becomes evident that the purchaser of the goods, as well as the manufacturer, is a great gainer by that arrangement which enables the manufacture to be established and carried on profitably in their own country.

Is not the position our country has assumed relatively to others on this question, one which we may do well to regard carefully and with some degree of distrust and suspicion? Are there good and sufficient grounds for supposing that Englishmen are so supremely and peculiarly gifted with wisdom on commercial and industrial subjects, that they can afford to contemn the opinions and reasoning of those belonging to other countries? Is it quite certain that our country is not making herself ridiculous, on this question, in the eyes of all others? ... that, whilst proposing herself to them as a great and disinterested commercial teacher, they are not contemplating her conduct as a huge example of national vanity and folly? This much *is certain*, that when England looks abroad with a condescending smile upon the surrounding nations, and says to them: 'Out upon your barbarous ignorance; listen to me and I will teach you what to do in this matter,' those other nations shake their heads and courteously decline the proffered instruction.

Unless we are much mistaken, however, the issues involved are of a much more serious character than the passing ridicule of other nations, although that is in itself undesirable. Let the reader read again the Sixth item of the information furnished by the *Daily Telegraph*: 'We have now reached the anomalous position of buying from foreigners exactly twice as much as we sell them.' Then let him reflect that England is emphatically a manufacturing and producing country, dependent upon her manufacturing and industrial capacity in a very great degree. And, having considered this, let him say whether the circumstance, thus brought under his attention, is not a very significant and menacing circumstance. As he apprehends more clearly what it does signify, anxious thoughts and queries will be apt to suggest themselves. It is plainly a stage reached in a downward career, be it observed. Now, putting aside mere confidence that all matters pertaining to England must naturally come right after a time, because they have always done so hitherto, will he not ask himself: What if this downward career should continue, even a little further? Has anything been done, or is anything being done, likely to be effective in preventing a further descent and in averting the disastrous consequences of supinely allowing our manufacturing pre-eminence to be taken from us?

It does not follow, because Free Trade as a national economic policy is unsound in theory and injurious in practice, that the old method of protecting the home productions of a country by the imposition of duties on goods imported into that country, is the best or scientific method of affording the requisite protection. In writing on this subject some time since, we proposed to substitute a more direct system, to be called 'Promotion of Home Industry.'[1] By which system, whatever degree of protection and encouragement might be considered beneficial, could be afforded by the government of the country to the manufacturers and agriculturists thereof, and, at the same time, imported goods of all kinds be allowed to come into the country free from duty. By such a system, the objection to the old method of its occasioning a sort of war of rival tariffs, between countries whose interest it might be to exchange certain of their products, would be obviated, and, at the same time, the purchaser in the home markets would buy produce and manufactured goods at the minimum price at which foreign produce and goods, admitted duty free, could be profitably sold.

It was doubtless the clumsiness in the application of the principle of Protection, and the impolicy, under circumstances such as those of England at that time, of levying a heavy import duty on grain, which enabled the sophistries of Free Trade advocates to inveigle the country into the adoption of that system. The idea is quite a common one that the soundness of Free Trade principles was established and demonstrated by the augmented development and great increase in volume of British commerce, which, for the most part, was subsequent to and followed the adoption of those principles. *Quia post hoc, propter hoc.*

By many of those reasoners who draw or adopt this inference, it is seemingly quite forgotten that the expansion of commerce and the period of industrial prosperity which followed the adoption of the Free Trade system by England, also followed the introduction of railways and steamships. To those potent agencies, to their influence and to their consequents, and not to the Free Trade principles, the commercial prosperity of that transitionary period is correctly attributable.

1 'Essays and Reviews, in Political Economy (Promotion of Home Industry, as a National Policy).' William Ridgway, Piccadilly.

Those who attribute the expansion of England's commerce, which occurred subsequently to the adoption of the Free Trade policy, to the effect of that policy, might be asked to account for the like expansion in other countries, such as France and the United States, by which that policy was not adopted. On the other hand, let it be borne in mind that it is not alone in the direct advantages, in the increased rapidity of transport and facilities afforded by railroads and steamships for the conveyance of the products of one country to another, that the cause of the commercial expansion is to be sought; to the indirect effects of those agencies very much of that expansion is correctly attributable; chiefly so, to the enormously increased area over which British commerce was enabled by means of them to extend its operations, and the opportunity to bring the pent up wealth, the accumulated latent capital, of Great Britain, to a much larger extent than heretofore, into play. And, secondary only to this, the immense addition to industrial occupation afforded by the adoption and subsequent development of the then new systems of steam locomotion and transport, together with their belongings and consequents...including the building of many large cities, of very many smaller towns, and of almost innumerable dwellings in various parts of the world. When these things are taken into careful consideration, it will be only the blindness of perversity which will be unable to see that the commercial and industrial expansion, about which the Free Trade advocate is wont to expatiate so glibly, took place in spite of and not in consequence of the adoption of the Free Trade policy by Great Britain.

Now, however, we have got through with the expansion of trade and other beneficial consequents which it has been the good fortune of our immediate predecessors to have forced upon them. Now we have to confront the Nemesis which, though sometimes apparently slow, is sure to overtake the wrongdoer. Now, as a nation, we have to pay the penalty, and deal with the consequences of choosing the wrong for the right, of straying into the bye-ways of sophistry and folly instead of keeping to the high road of reason and science. Symptoms of improvement in the mental condition of the public have latterly shown themselves, and of such a kind as to afford room for hopefulness that restoration to a state of health is yet quite possible. It is not very long since that the nation was in danger of adopting a national policy, considered, we believe, the complement and outcome of Free Trade principles, by which we were invited and counselled to divest ourselves of those things which sane nations usually consider most worthy of retention – prestige, power, honour and empire; by which it was proposed that England should denude herself of every thing which a great nation ought to possess, and then stand forth *sans* colonies, *sans* commerce, *sans* everything, as England *pure and simple*, a great example of national disinterestedness, expecting other nations to respect her for her weakness and reverence her for her impotency.

We have now become so far rational as to agree that our colonies are not only valuable appendages but constitute an essential part of the British Empire as a great power and as a leader amongst the great powers of the civilized world. Before long, perhaps, we shall come to apprehend that commerce and industrial capacity are also valuable possessions, not only essential to the greatness of the empire but also essential to our well-being as a country, and even to our prolonged existence as a nation. Let us express hopefulness that recovery will not be too late; that we may not find ourselves vainly longing to have back things which we have perversely put from us, desirable possessions which, having been given to us and committed to our care, we did not value: that we may not awake too late to do aught but cry and lament over the loss of good things which lamentations will not bring back; for of this we may be assured, that when our manufactures are driven away our commerce will soon follow, and that when these are gone, they will be *gone* ... gone for ever.

Strictly speaking, however, that confusion of ideas, which contrived to express itself in a sort of concrete form as the great Free Trade dogma, and which has since continued to exercise an influence so detrimental to the industrial interests of our country, originated in the loose notions about political economy which were at that time and still are prevalent amongst us. Chief amongst these notions is one which, believing it to be of extreme public importance, we will make the special subject of a second letter: and trusting they may prove serviceable, we will, for the present, conclude by commending the foregoing remarks to your attentive consideration.

          Respectfully,

                                    KUKLOS.

J. Slagg 'The Commercial Treaty with France', *Fortnightly Review*, 27 (1877), pp. 389–91.

I have traced at some length the difficulties which beset economic progress in France, where neither the information nor the motives of commercial action are of a very advanced type. Let me conclude by pointing out what I believe to be the principal difficulties which exist in this country, where both public opinion and self-interest are supposed to be convinced of the advantages of unlimited free exchange. The main obstacles to our progress I take to be these: – the want of a more thorough application to commercial questions on the part of our so-called commercial Members of Parliament; the absence of commercial knowledge and interest in commercial matters which generally characterizes the chiefs of our great departments of State, and our representatives in foreign countries; the complete absence of any properly organized machinery for the negotiation and transaction of matters of commercial interest between ourselves and other nations.

The time of Members of Parliament is too much taken up with party struggles, and with questions involving the expenditure of income, to admit of due attention being given to matters that affect the sources of revenue and the commercial prosperity of the country. It would surely best suit the interests of commercial constituencies, at least, if they applied some standard of commercial utility to their representatives in the House of Commons, rather than the conventional one which related mainly to mere party athletics, or the dabbling in all sorts of legislation for which they often possess neither the training nor the aptitude. Nor are we better off in the House of Lords. Few commercial men ever attain to its precincts. Commerce is there undoubtedly considered an uninteresting, if not somewhat ignoble subject; and it was far from an edifying spectacle to find a bench full of our hereditary legislators, in the matter of the India import duties, calmly throwing over both economic principle and commercial justice, in order to support a mistaken and restive colleague. But if both Houses had all the wisdom and willingness in the world, they would be unable to produce any results without a proper and efficient department for the administration of commercial matters, and no such department, nor even the semblance of it, now exists. When deputations on commercial matters are reported to have 'thanked his lordship and retired,' they are thankful for very small mercies; for with them generally retires their question and all further action in it. However convinced a minister may be as to the merits of the case, it is impossible for him to take in hand the detail-work of it, and there is practically no one else with the authority or appliances to do it.

Sir Louis Mallet, who possesses great knowledge of business and large official experience, had brought the commercial department of the Board of Trade to a fair condition of efficiency, and he had strong views as to the desirableness of extending our commercial relations with foreign countries; but the late government evidently held equally strong opinions. Sir Louis Mallet was relegated to the India Office, and lost to those commercial interests which he was so well fitted to administer. The Board of Trade has almost abolished its commercial department; for it possesses now little more than the machinery for the publication of tariff notices, statistics, &c. The late ministry decided that the commercial department of the Foreign Office, which had hitherto been merely machinery for carrying out the Board of Trade arrangements, should take up the duties formerly performed by the commercial department of the Board of Trade; but no properly authorised head was ever appointed to this new department.

Sir Louis Mallet held a position as Assistant Secretary, and was able, whenever business required, to see the head of his office, the President of the Board of Trade, and to discuss and settle matters with him. He was further placed in communication with persons holding similar rank in other countries, and could effect much quietly by that means. He was also able to communicate freely with persons in this country with whom it would be useful that he should maintain relations: moreover, he had under him a full and sufficient departmental staff. But, as things are now, those whose duty and interest call them to the commercial department of the Foreign Office know too well how utterly inadequate it is to cope with its functions. The staff seems to undergo a steady reduction, and if the members of it were ever so zealous and assiduous, they are denied the necessary power to carry out their work. It is impossible to obtain a particle of information there as to the movements of foreign countries in commercial matters; in fact, the necessary communication does not seem to exist, nor even the power to deal with persons in this country.

Meanwhile great interests are suffering from neglect of commercial questions and the means of treating them. Foreign countries are making their future arrangements, not on a basis which in many respects will suit our trade, but without us and against us. Austria has prolonged her treaty with France, but has put an end to ours. Our embassies, without help from home – and, in the absence of proper arrangements here, that help cannot be given – are incapable of dealing adequately with commercial matters. Everything is drifting and when attention is awakened, it will probably be too late. As commercial arrangements are made without our participation, it is the more necessary that our commercial department, as well as our embassies and consulates, should be in an efficient state for dealing with these matters, and should possess full knowledge of what is going on, and capacity for action in regard to them.

Our commercial department should be on a footing superior, rather than inferior, to that which existed in 1872 at the Board of Trade, and if some increase in the estimates occurs until reorganization can be effected, the money would be well invested, and there is no interest better entitled to demand a more adequate care.

Last session, a legal assistant under-secretary and some new private secretaries were appointed, without a word of inquiry or comment in the House of Commons. As to the appointment of a minister of commerce, if he were created at present he would probably be a junior cabinet minister, who would be so glad to get the post, that he might hesitate to speak up against the more influential members of the Government. It would be better at present to develop the departments in existing public offices, which might have hereafter to be thrown off into a ministry of commerce, when they had acquired sufficient weight and experience to go alone.

As to the forthcoming arrangement of a new commercial treaty with France, it rests, in the absence of a proper organization for administering the question, mainly with the commercial community and their representatives in Parliament to deal with. Let us hope that on our side a determined stand will now be made for free trade, pure and simple, and that the free traders of France will second us by repeating the famous old answer which the French merchants gave to Colbert, when he asked them how he could best promote commerce – *Laissez nous faire.*

John Slagg.

William Bateman Hanbury, *Lord Bateman's Plea for Limited Protection, or, for Reciprocity in Free Trade* (London: William Ridgway, 1877).

PREFACE.

THE following letter is not the result of any sudden impulse, induced by the pressure of the present growing Commercial Crisis, but is based on an earnest and long considered conviction of the truth of the reasoning here attempted to be enunciated.

The absence of statistics may be remarked. Seldom read, more often confusing, never infallible, these are usually the outcome of a contracted vision, and the stale stock-in-trade and never-failing resource of anonymous scribblers, and of heaven-born political economists. They will suggest themselves without difficulty to each manufacturing and exporting interest.

Let this one fact suffice. A simple inspection of the Board of Trade returns will show the alarming deficit in our Exports as compared with our Imports from foreign countries paying no duty whatever, and which latter unfortunately exceed the former at the rate of upwards of a hundred millions in value per annum!

If the great ship-building interest, all but lost to the Thames and now transferred to the Clyde; if the great Midland iron and coal trades and of the once prosperous and busy North and West; if the great railway companies, which depend for their prosperity in a large measure on the carrying trade of these industries; if the paper makers of Devonshire, the miners of Cornwall, the glass manufacturers, the sugar refiners, the silk and stocking weavers, the great agricultural interest, and last, but not least, the cotton and woollen manufacturers of Lancashire and Yorkshire, are satisfied with the operation of the present and past free trade policy, without reciprocity, and are prepared still to face the free and unrestricted imports of the world at their present enormous disadvantage, this letter will have been written in vain!

But, in the full belief that the exact contrary is the case, and in their interest, and in the interest of those operatives, and of the whole body of the English working classes, more or less dependent upon them for subsistence, the writer has ventured upon the publication of this letter, which is now offered to the calm consideration of the commercial public, with the conviction that he is expressing herein the sentiments of a vast proportion of the community, who, having hitherto accepted the free trade policy as irrevocable, are now awaking to the conviction that one sided free trade without reciprocity is entirely abortive, and therefore ruinous and disastrous to the best interests of Great Britain.

The question rests in the hands of the constituencies, with whom lies the power, if they have the will, to supply the answer.

BATEMAN.

Shobdon Court, Leominster,
Herefordshire,
November 24, 1877.

TO THE EDITOR OF 'THE TIMES.'

Sir,

At this moment of widespread commercial depression the question of the expediency of a return to a system of limited protection as opposed to that of free trade is undoubtedly once again forcing itself upon the consideration of many thoughtful minds.

Notwithstanding the appeals, from the Chancellor of the Exchequer downwards, which continue to be made on its behalf by the advocates and apologists of the free trade policy it is evident from their recently-expressed opinions that a certain uncomfortable feeling of doubt exists as to its success, and the excuses put forward for the general non-acceptance of the free trade doctrine raise an unmistakable distrust in the soundness of their views, and lead us to inquire whether a policy which requires so much excuse to be made for it, is after all the one best fitted to our peculiar interests, or one in which this country should still continue to persist.

I have used the words 'limited protection' advisedly in order at the outset to guard against any supposition that either myself or those who think with me consider it would be either politic or possible in the impending war of tariffs, or in any revision of our Custom duties, to attempt to impose any restrictions on what I will call vital necessaries, or on the recognized food of the population. In any scheme of commercial policy due consideration should always be given to the capabilities of production of the country on the one hand, and to its absolute necessities on the other.

In the case of Great Britain, owing to our area being so much restricted and to the continual increase in our population, an increase out of all proportion to the size and acreage of the kingdom as compared with the relative proportion of population to the area and extent of foreign countries, it has become virtually imperative upon us to obtain from all nations of the earth the requisite food supply.

Thus far it is willingly conceded that the exercise of free trade, though still incomplete, has conferred on the masses an exceptional and a lasting benefit. I turn aside for a brief instant to pay this tribute to the memory of the late Mr. Cobden and Sir George Cornewall Lewis, and to the foresight of Mr. Bright and Mr. Charles Villiers.

But unfortunately we have to deal with many more interests than those exclusively connected with the food supply of the people. We have to deal with our own natural and sufficient products, with our various home manufactures, and with our own skilled (and daily more expensive) general labour question. These latter, quite as important to the well-being of the community, require to be as jealously guarded and protected, exercising as they undoubtedly do, an equally preponderating influence on the prosperity or otherwise of all classes in the kingdom. It behoves us, therefore, while securing for them the best available market, to be at the same time cautious how we allow them to deteriorate, or permit rival countries unduly to compete with our native industries to our own loss and detriment.

Sir, we cannot shut our eyes to the universal collapse of trade and its accompanying distress, be it the mineral, the shipping, the carrying, the agricultural, or the general manufacturing trade. Throughout the country the cry of depression and distress and ruin is the same. We have to compete on unequal terms with other foreign countries, who are robbing us of our profits, paying nothing to our exchequer, and underselling us at the same time. When the capitalist finds that his trade is leaving him, and that his profits are reduced to a minimum, it follows that the workmen depending upon him must suffer in like proportion, and, as a consequence, the rate of wages must come down, or employment must cease – strikes, lock-outs, and painful and undeserved distress are the inevitable results. Granted that the theory of free and unrestricted commerce with all quarters of the universe is as bold as it is magnificent, granted that the idea, by whomsoever originated (and advocated by no one more consistently than by our good and wise Prince Consort) is both grand and glorious in its conception, granted that to give effect to it has been the aim as it has been the long-accepted policy of successive Governments, it cannot be denied that the sting of 'want of reciprocity' has, from the first, checkmated our philanthropic efforts, and obliged us now to confess, after 30 years of trial, that in practice our free trade is at best but one-sided; and that while we are opening our ports to the commerce and manufactures of the world, free and unrestricted, other countries, without conferring upon us any reciprocal benefit, are taking advantage, without scruple, of our magnanimous, but disastrous (because one-sided), liberality.

It is of no use to blink the question. Facts will speak for themselves. In defiance of all arguments and all persuasion, not to say entreaty, on the subject, these awkward facts still remain. Our overtures to other countries are disregarded; our commercial treaties are not renewed; our own trade is in a sinking and unprofitable condition; our exports show a lamentable, alarming, and increasing deficit; our Exchequer is affected; and, worse than all, not a single country in Europe, beginning with France and Germany and ending with Spain and Switzerland (to say nothing of the United States of America or our own Australian colonies) can be cajoled by the most specious temptation into following our example of free importations, or of opening their ports to the commerce of Great Britain and of the world, unrestricted by safeguards in the shape of duties framed to protect their own native industries.

Now, sir, in view of these undeniable facts, and of the *quasi*-admitted failure of the policy which has been so long a time in operation, and which was in fact initiated and I may say necessitated by the exigencies of an exceptional period of famine and distress, which even the most ardent Protectionists of the time were quite unable to gainsay or withstand, but which happily now no longer exist, I ask whether that grave moment of reflection and self-examination has not now arrived when it behoves all classes who feel themselves sensibly affected, to pause and seriously review the present position; and if a false step has been made, as many think, to have the courage and the energy to retrace it without delay. This is neither more nor less than what a prudent man in private, or a prudent trader in commercial life would find it his imperative interest to do. How much more imperative, therefore, is it when Imperial and patriotic interests are so heavily involved!

We have tried free trade, and it has been found wanting. We have done our best to impress other countries with the reasonableness of our policy, and in return they scoff at our blindness, and turn a deaf ear to our remonstrances. In the meantime partial ruin and wholesale depression and distress are staring us in the face. Our local burdens are increasing, our exports diminishing. Our working classes, unsettled, are waging open war in the cause of labour against capital; discontented, because unable to find the real cause of their discontent; clamouring for their participation in profits, which can hardly be said to exist, and yet unable to account for the hesitation and inability of their employers to accede to what they consider are only their just demands.

Why should we persist in such an Utopian crusade? Why have we cut adrift from our old anchorage to launch our good ship upon a treacherous torrent, which is hurling us helplessly to imminent shipwreck? In Heaven's name, if we are on the wrong tack, let us arrest our downward course. Don't let us, for the sake of a Quixotic theory, blind our eyes to the fact that our trade is ruinously slipping from us, and that we are sacrificing our best and dearest interests to an unacceptable idea.

There are indications that the tide of public opinion is undergoing a gradual and, therefore, a more convincing change. I hail it with satisfaction. After all, the argument that comes home to every one's pocket is the most cogent, and is worth all the theories and all the lectures of all the political economists in the world.

I appeal to the common sense and to the patriotism of my countrymen, and if they are convinced how great has been the fallacy of our free trade policy without reciprocity, it is for them to say, as I believe sincerely they will say, whether a return to a policy of limited protection, so far from being impossible or undesirable, is not the true and simple solution of our present difficulties, and will tend, in a more simple and natural way than any other, to retrieve our losses, increase our revenue, lighten our burdens, bring peace, contentment, and employment to our working classes, and teach them and us to bless the day which restored the old policy and the old watchword of 'Protection to native British industry.' With the object of bringing these views before the public, and of inviting their discussion and consideration, I have ventured to address you.

I have the honour to be,
Sir,
Your obedient humble Servant,
BATEMAN.

Shobdon Court, Leominster,
Herefordshire.

W. Farrer Ecroyd, *The Policy of Self Help: Suggestions towards the Consolidation of the Empire and the Defence of its Industries and Commerce. Two Letters* (London: Hamilton, Adams, 1879), pp. i–v, 1–6.

PREFACE.

The efforts recently made to direct public attention to the subject of the following letters have provoked a good deal of criticism, sometimes angry, and often contemptuous.

This movement of opinion may, of course, be a mistaken one; or, if well founded, may be lulled by some temporary return of prosperity; but it cannot be scolded into silence, or repressed by scorn. Nor, on the other hand, can its object be advanced by the impatient zeal which would drag it into the arena of party politics, for it is not a party question. No Government ought to attempt to deal with it, except upon the distinct demand of the great body of the people. To invite the attention of working men, and to put our facts and arguments temperately before them, on all suitable occasions, is therefore the present duty of those who believe a change of policy to be required.

And there must be no putting forward of class interests; no selfish and partial efforts to obtain relief for the manufacturing population at the expense of the agricultural, or *vice versa*. A well-considered and comprehensive policy can alone command sufficient support; or, if carried into effect, produce lasting benefits.

It has been said that a Government based on a widely-extended franchise can never successfully rule or hold together an Empire embracing distant Colonies, because the multitude, whether at home or in those Colonies, will never grasp a far-reaching policy, however wise and beneficent, nor make the present sacrifices it may demand, nor allow it to be pursued with the needful steadfastness.

And thus I am continually told, as the one conclusive argument against my proposals, that the working class will never tolerate an import duty on food, however moderate, even if adopted simply as an instrument to defend their own employment and wages. But they have proved, and are daily proving, by immense sacrifices made through the agency of Trade Unions, their readiness to incur present loss in order, as they believe, to secure future advantage, and to escape the consequences of over-competition. I am confident, therefore, that when better informed on this question, they will not only tolerate but demand the adoption, at whatever temporary cost, of a policy which would deliver them from the unfair competition, in the home market, of foreigners who refuse to admit their productions in return; and, from the still greater loss and danger of depending for food upon nations who will only receive their manufactures in exchange subject to import duties which operate as a heavy fine, and so depress their employment and rate of wages to the lowest level.

For it is their interests and those of their children which are most of all imperilled. The present crisis will sooner or later pass; many employers and many distributors will disappear, trodden down in the pitiless struggle for a diminished trade; and those who survive – the strongest in capital and ability – will probably enjoy a period of prosperity, because they will have fewer competitors, both in the sale of productions and in the purchase of labour; whilst many workpeople will be left without employment, and the rest will receive greatly reduced wages. Meantime, it is melancholy to see employers and workmen wasting their diminished resources in mutual injury, instead of standing shoulder to shoulder to resist and defeat that selfish policy of foreign nations which is rapidly impoverishing them both.

It is said that Emigration must be looked to as a means of relief. Yes; the forced emigration of a starving people – that exodus of English labour and capital to which Americans have all along boastfully pointed as the certain and triumphant issue of their Protectionist policy, – this is the alternative that our critics are willing to encounter, rather than abate one jot or tittle of their pedantic theory. Indeed, the whole issue of the conflict between American and English commercial policy is whether the industrial population of Britain, now dependent on foreign food, shall be permitted to remain and to labour in their native country, freely exchanging the work of their hands for such food; or shall be forcibly expatriated, and compelled to become citizens of the United States, as the only condition of effecting that needful exchange.

For, as matters stand, it is to America that they must go; it is there, and not in her own Colonies, that England has spent the countless millions of her savings, in opening out by railways the land that is to grow her corn and other chief supplies of food. And, as if the more completely at all points to play the game of American policy, she has, with a cold and pitiless impartiality, treated her Colonists themselves exactly like foreigners, steadfastly refusing to grant to their productions, on entering British ports, the least advantage over those of nations who exclude her manufactures by enormous duties. The inevitable result is that the Colonies are treating the mother country more and more as foreign nations treat her; and, unless she shall change her policy, they will go on in that course until they too shall have shut out her manufactures. She will then naturally decline any further liability to taxation for their advantage or defence, and thus the Empire will be broken up, and England reduced to the position of a second or third rate power.

And what class of society, whether in England or the Colonies, from the richest to the poorest, but will share the humiliation and the loss?

Compared with consequences like these, what matters a difference of 10 – or even 20 – per cent, in the cost of food? Have we not, during the past ten years, encountered far larger fluctuations in the price of food, of which the nation, well employed in all its industries, and enriched by foreign trade, was scarcely conscious, and which were certainly never taken into account by any manufacturer in estimating the cost of his goods, simply because they never affected the rate of wages?

Is it not plain that work and wages are as essential as cheap food; and that to let slip a large portion of our employment, in order to gain an extra turn of cheapness in our food, is a folly like that of Esau, who for a morsel of bread sold his birthright? For it is only the *last turn* of cheapness that we do gain by our present shortsighted policy; cheapness and plenty we should still have, after taxing foreign supplies 10 per cent.; since America, compelled to sell her vast production at some price, must certainly bear the loss of a portion of that impost; whilst the stimulus given to Colonial agriculture would operate to increase the total supply of food.

I have enough real respect for working men to dare to tell them, with perfect frankness, what I honestly believe. If, therefore, I have proposed to them, in the following letters, two great sacrifices of present interest, it is because I am convinced that by no other means can steady employment, fair wages, and reasonable hours be secured to them in future.

I have recommended a return to 60 hours' work per week in factories as the best course under present circumstances, though I firmly believe that, had we earlier taken steps to combat the hostile tariffs directed against us, we should have found the existing term of 56½ hours sufficient. The vast increase of labour-saving machinery, and of facilities of transit, ought naturally to bring an increase of leisure to all who labour; and if this result be not realized, it is because hostile tariffs interfere to prevent the free interchange of our productions, and compel our ironworkers and spinners and weavers to give more hours of labour than they ought, in exchange for their supply of food from foreign countries. To secure a reasonable limitation of the hours of labour we must, therefore, either break down those hostile tariffs, or make ourselves independent of the nations which impose them; and I think the following letters will show that a small tax on foreign food products is the only instrument by which we can effect this.

All attempts to persuade working men that it is designed to tax their food or lengthen their hours of labour, in the smallest degree, *against their will*, are too absurd to receive serious notice. The power to do any such thing rests entirely with themselves; but, on the other hand, should they determine to use that power, it is equally certain that no doctrinaires, of whatever school or party, will be able to forbid them.

I am accused, in many quarters, of disloyalty to the principle of Free-trade; of a lingering desire for Protection. It would be precisely as just to accuse a man of being litigious, who, after always exhibiting a singularly peaceable and forbearing disposition, should at last be driven to legal proceedings to maintain some indispensable right. In reply, I can only submit the letters now reprinted, to the judgment of impartial readers; I have nothing to retract. Protectionism resides in the motive, – in the desire for protection; its very essence is wanting in duties imposed for the sole purpose of bringing about an extension of the area of Free-trade, after all other means have failed.

In perfect sincerity, I have admitted and extolled the soundness of the principle of Free-trade; I have acknowledged that no import duties of any kind could be other than a burden and a loss to the nation during their continuance. But I have urged, with the earnestness of profound conviction, that present circumstances render it wise – nay, absolutely needful for us to take upon ourselves that burden and that loss, in a small measure and for a limited time, in order to work out our deliverance from a far heavier burden and a far more enduring loss.

W. F. E.
20th May, 1879

LETTER I.

To the Editor of the Bradford Observer

Sir, – Neither Mr. Forster's address to the Bradford Chamber of Commerce, nor Lord Derby's recent speech at Rochdale, nor the frequent articles in the *Times*, *Economist*, and other leading journals, deal at all directly or satisfactorily with the opinions held by myself and many others, which are confounded with views of a totally different character, and loosely described as the policy of reciprocity. Is it not worth while to meet our opinions fairly and answer them specifically?

We are all agreed as to the soundness and desirability of free-trade, and we must all admit that, in spite of the hopes and the constant sanguine predictions of the past 30 years, free-trade is steadily losing ground. Is it then more reasonable to drift along, resting on expectations which experience has completely falsified, or to set ourselves steadily to consider what will be our position if, as may be deemed certain, the system of protection should still grow, and gradually, during the next 30 years, overspread such nations as Turkey, China, Japan, the South American States, and our own colonies and dominions? Here is a distinct controversy, in which it appears to us that we are always met by a repetition of those vague, vain hopes which can never soothe us more, instead of a fair examination of the consequences which must fall upon our trading and labouring population if, as we see no reason to doubt, our productions be shut out increasingly from foreign markets in the future as in the past.

The dangers which must ensue for us, should foreign nations refuse to follow our free-trade policy, were, I think, always set aside by Mr. Cobden by the positive repetition of the assurance that they would never arise, for that other nations would soon be compelled by self-interest, and by the spectacle of our prosperity, to follow in our wake.

To those who doubted this, it was all along clear that we might have to pass through three stages of experience, *viz*:

1. A period of almost unbounded prosperity, during which the nations from whom we purchased our supplies of food and raw materials, *not having the means as yet of manufacturing for themselves*, must of necessity take our productions in exchange. During this period, any protective duties they might levy would not affect us, and would only enhance the cost to themselves.
2. A transition period, during which these nations, gradually increasing their own manufactures under the shelter of protective duties, should become more and more independent of ours; yet during which the increased prosperity of our home trade and the growth of markets in semi-civilised lands should suffice to maintain our prosperity.
3. A period of contraction and difficulty, when – being obliged to import half the food of a dense and delicately organised population – we should find the nations excluding, by hostile tariffs, those products of our industry which are all we have to offer in exchange in the long run.

To escape this difficulty, we should at first force our goods on such markets as remained open, sustaining an illegitimate trade by unsound financial and banking operations; and thus, as long as possible, obtaining, even at a serious loss, the means of paying for our food imports.

Meantime, whilst excluded from the ordinary healthy current of demand for manufactures in America and on the Continent, we should be subject to a most trying and dangerous set of spasmodic influences.

For whenever, at a moment of prosperity, the demands of those countries should happen to exceed their existing means of production, we should receive large orders for iron and textiles, which would (as in 1871–72) disturb our equilibrium, raise prices and wages, induce great and sudden extensions, and excite and demoralise our people, and then as suddenly cease, leaving us to regain our balance as we could. Thus we should occupy the insecure position of 'Deferred Stock Holders,' receiving no demand till A, B, C, D, and E were satisfied, and then taking temporarily the *whole surplus demand*.

The moral and pecuniary results of such a series of excitements and depressions must be equally disastrous, and must culminate in a fourth and final period, such as I will not attempt to pourtray [*sic*]; let every English patriot pray that no vision of it may ever haunt his dreams.

Such then are the dangers which we see and fear – such the fate in whose grasp we already feel ourselves; whilst we believe that it is not too late for England, by the adoption of a large and far-sighted policy, to avert them completely, and to lay strong and deep the foundations of a steadier and more lasting prosperity.

But before describing this policy, let me say once for all what we do *not* want, and therefore what we trust our critics will cease to attribute to us, or to expend their energy in denouncing.

We do *not* want *protection* against our foreign competitors, (I write as a manufacturer); we will cheerfully compete with all comers; and if the French or others can beat us in some specialities, all honour to them. No nation can be vain enough to expect to excel the world at every point, surely.

We do *not* want *retaliation*, as commonly understood; a complex system of import duties, graduated to meet the varying follies of foreign protectionists, would be a remedy too silly for discussion.

We do *not* want an import duty levied on the raw materials of our industries; that would be a simple act of suicide.

We do *not* want the *coercion* of our colonies and dependencies into a free-trade policy; that would be to provoke resentment where we ought to attract and conciliate.

What we do want is that certain great objects should be clearly, resolutely, and persistently pursued; I place them in the order of their importance.

1. That the United Kingdom and its colonies and dependencies be gradually welded into one great Free-trade Empire, capable, if the protective system be finally adopted by other nations, of supplying all its own essential wants.
2. That our fiscal arrangements be directed to discourage the growth of our food, and the further investment of our capital in those countries which impose duties on our productions, and to divert the current of investment and emigration to our own dependencies.
3. That we abandon the system of commercial treaties until, by the temporary imposition of special duties, we shall have regained, in every instance, the power of bargaining for equal treatment.

To attain the first two objects, our course of action is clear; to impose and maintain, for at least 30 years to come, a moderate import duty on articles of food and mere consumption received from foreign nations; admitting the like commodities from all parts of our own empire *free*. We need not wish our colonies to impose similar duties, as their enjoyment of a profitable transit trade would greatly aid their development, which, and not revenue, is our primary object. Thus American food products would come, to a large extent, by way of Canada, enriching her railways, merchants, and shippers, instead of those of the United States.

I have already said that no duties would be levied on the raw materials of our industries, from whatever quarter they might come.

A steadfast adherence to this policy would necessarily, though no doubt gradually, transfer the trade of growing food and luxuries for the English market from foreign protectionist nations to the various portions of our own grand empire, which, were its resources fairly developed, is undoubtedly capable of supplying five times our requirements, well and cheaply.

A large field for emigration, and for the legitimate and safe investment of English savings, would thus be opened out, to the discomfiture of the floaters of foreign loans, American railway bonds, and unsound limited companies.

Our dependencies, thenceforth bound to the mother country by the strong ties of material advantage, as well as those of sentiment and affection, would be more ready to meet our wishes, and to establish free-trade with us and with one another, in return for the great privilege accorded to them. No coercion would be needed or thought of; but an inspiring sense of renewed youth, an assured hope of a secure and glorious future, independent of the caprices of foreign legislation, would be felt by the citizens of the British empire throughout the world. A Free-trade Empire of 300 millions of people, embracing every variety of soil and climate, and strong to maintain the freedom of the seas, would be no mean World in itself.

And what is the sacrifice requisite to attain this end?

An enhancement of the cost of some articles of food and luxury perhaps equal to one-seventh the amount now spent in intoxicating liquors; perhaps less then the annual interest of the capital lost during the past ten years in foolish loans to foreign governments, and foreign railway and other companies; a loss likely enough to be repeated during the next ten years, if our present aimless national policy be continued.

But is it said that our manufacturing population would not endure the imposition of any import duties on articles of food.

That depends upon the amount, and still more upon the purpose of such duties.

I have conversed much with working men on this subject; many of them are keenly alive to the danger of our increasing dependence for food upon nations who will not admit our manufactures in return; and I am convinced that no class in the country is more ready to appreciate such a policy as the foregoing, or to make whatever present sacrifices may be needed to realise it.

They fully understand that even the increase of cost would not be lost, but that the produce of the import duties would go either to lessen other taxes or to reduce the public debt. They also recognise the tremendous pressure at present felt by our agriculturists, which is seriously damaging the home trade, and thus lessening their own employment; and they do not think that any class can long profit by the ruin of another. On the principle of 'Live and let live,' they would, therefore, not regret any advantage which might accrue to the agricultural population.

They trouble themselves little, so far as I can judge, about foreign competition here; but a great deal about the increased exclusion of their own handy work from foreign countries by protective tariffs, especially when this is done by nations whose best customers they know themselves to be. They would, therefore, regard with a rather contemptuous indifference any duties levied by England upon foreign manufactures *for their own protection*; but would highly approve them as means of exercising pressure abroad to obtain fairer treatment for British manufactures.

But there is growing in their minds a strong feeling of distrust, almost of resentment, against those who on the one hand declare that our Government cannot and ought not to do anything to meet and foil the selfish policy of foreign protectionists, and on the other hand that we must encounter their hostile tariffs by lowering wages till we can force a demand in spite of them. For they see clearly that, to do this, their wages must always be lower than those of the foreign workman by the amount needed to overcome the tariff which protects him.

Whatever may be the judgment of working class constituencies upon a policy such as I have tried to sketch, I dare venture to assert that its advocates will, at least, receive more favour at their hands than those who have no policy to propose but that of passively drifting into the straits prepared for us by the protectionist nations. – I am, sir, yours faithfully.

W. FARRER ECROYD

Lomeshaye Mills, near Burnley

January 23rd, 1879.

Sir Louis Mallet, *Reciprocity: A Letter Addressed to Mr. Thomas Bayley Potter MP* (London, Paris and New York: Cassell Petter & Galpin, 1879).

March 17th, 1879

DEAR MR. POTTER,

I was asked last year by the Committee of the Cobden Club to write a paper for them on the subject of the recent cry for what has been known by the name of 'Reciprocity.'

The constant pressure of other work has hitherto prevented me from complying with this request – but I am bound to add that I have been deterred by another cause.

Whenever I attempted to address myself to the task, I was confronted with an insuperable difficulty.

In spite of much reading and a very sincere desire to understand the objects and arguments of the advocates of this new commercial policy, I have entirely failed in finding any statement of their case, or any programme of practical measures which will stand the test of serious discussion.

So that whenever I approached my adversary, I found him to be a man of straw.

I wish, therefore, frankly to lay my difficulties before the Committee; and, unless they can help me to a more distinct comprehension of the position which I am asked to assail, to submit to them a proposal which may, I hope, have the effect of eliciting the desired information.

For the present I can only deal with the crude opinions and proposals which have been put forward from time to time in the public press and at public meetings.

I take the following statement of the case on the part of the 'Modern Reciprocitarian' from a pamphlet by Lord Bateman, entitled, 'A Plea for Limited Protection or for Reciprocity.'

'Granted that the theory of free and unrestricted commerce with all quarters of the universe is as bold as it is magnificent; granted that the idea, by whomsoever originated (and advocated by no one more consistently than by our good and wise Prince Consort), is both grand and glorious in its conception; granted that to give effect to it has been the aim, as it has been the long-accepted policy, of successive Governments; it cannot be denied that the sting of 'want of reciprocity' has from the first checkmated our philanthropic efforts, and obliged us now to confess, after thirty years of trial, that in practice our free trade is at best but one-sided; and that, while we are opening our ports to the commerce and manufactures of the world free and unrestricted, other countries, without conferring upon us any reciprocal benefit, are taking advantage, without scruple, of our magnanimous but disastrous (because one-sided) liberality.'

It is necessary here to point out that there is no apparent connection of ideas between the statement of facts (even if they were correct) in this paragraph and the conclusions at which it seems to point, viz., that we are suffering not only from restrictions abroad, but from freedom at home.

No one would, I presume, deny that the system under which British trade is now carried on is not one of free trade, nor that a complete system of free trade is better than a one-sided free trade; but if, as is alleged, protection is only sought for the sake of reciprocity, it is impossible to understand why a one-sided free trade should not be better than no free trade at all.

The mutual relaxation of restrictions is a mutual advantage; the mutual creation of restrictions is a mutual injury. If one tariff is bad, two must be worse. It matters nothing whether the barrier be raised in one country or in another, the effect is precisely the same. It would be as rational, if the French railway from Boulogne to Paris doubled its charges, for the South-Eastern to do the same by way of reciprocity, as for the British Custom-house to raise the duties on French produce because France raises them on ours.

It will be said, perhaps, that the railway tariff affects the French exports as well as the British imports, and that, therefore, the case is not parallel; but this is a fallacy. A moment's reflection will show that the French tariff affects French exports as well as British imports. If a French wine-grower is made to pay a higher price for his Lancashire cloth, or, what is the same thing, gets less of it for a 'barique' of his wine, he will raise the price of his wine or give less of it in exchange; and his trade, as well as that of the British manufacturer, will be burdened and restricted by the tax.

To repeat this process at the English port would simply double the burden on both the French and the English trade. As Sir Robert Peel said long ago, the only way of fighting hostile tariffs is by free imports.

For what is reciprocity? The essence of all trade is and must be 'reciprocity.' Every transaction of commerce by which one man voluntarily sells his produce or property to another is an act of reciprocity, and is complete in itself. The imposition of a duty by one country on the produce or manufactures of another only affects the transaction by rendering it less profitable both to the seller and to the buyer; the variations of supply and demand will cause the incidence of the tax to fall upon the seller and the buyer, the producer and the consumer, in varying degree; but, in the long run, it will be equally shared between them.

This may be put in a way which leaves no door open for dispute or discussion. It must be admitted that, in principle, the effect must be precisely the same whatever the amount of the tax or the extent of the restriction – whether a duty of 10, 50, or 100 per cent. be imposed, there must be a point at which a duty becomes a prohibition. What is true in this extreme is equally true at every point and at every stage of the protective process. To whatever degree a country protects its own productions, it protects in precisely the same degree the productions of the countries with which it trades; for to whatever extent it closes its ports on foreign commodities, it prevents foreign countries from importing its own.

If this be true, and it cannot be otherwise, it follows that the more nearly the tariffs of foreign countries approach to the limits of prohibition, the more will the British producer be protected in his own market.

Those, therefore, who desire this kind of reciprocity – viz., the reciprocity of monopoly – must rejoice at every new restriction placed upon British trade abroad, as necessarily involving increased protection to British trade at home.

I am sometimes almost led to think, in reading the speculations of those who are always raising the cry of alarm at the importation of foreign goods, that they are still under the influence of the exploded mercantile theory of the Balance of Trade, according to which the advantage of commerce to a country resides in what it parts with and not in what it obtains – in its exports and not in its imports, the balance being paid in money, which was supposed to be the only wealth.

I am unwilling to believe in the survival of this delusion; but if it still prevails in any quarter, it is so important to dispel it, that I am tempted to quote at some length the clearest exposition which I know of the phenomena of international trade.

'All interchange is in substance and effect barter: he who sells his productions for money, and with that money buys other goods, really buys those goods with his own produce. And so of nations: their trade is a mere exchange of exports for imports; and whether money is employed or not, things are only in their permanent state when the exports and imports exactly pay for each other.

'When this is the case, equal sums of money are due from each country to the other; the debts are settled by bills, and there is no balance to be paid in the precious metals. The trade is in a state like that which is called in mechanics a condition of stable equilibrium.'[1]

Mr. Mill goes on to show that a country which wants more imports than its exports will pay for has to pay the difference in money; that by this transmission of the precious metals the quantity of the currency is diminished in such a country and increased in the countries with which it trades; that prices fall in the former and rise in the latter; and that the imports are checked and the export trade stimulated until the equilibrium of prices is restored, and the imports and exports again balance each other. He adds: –

'The equation of international demand under a money system, as under a barter system, is the law of international trade. Every country exports and imports the

---

1   Mill's 'Principles of Pol. Econ.,' cap. 21

very same things in the very same quantity under the one system as under the other. In a barter system the trade gravitates to the point at which the sum of imports exactly exchanges for the sum of exports; in a money system it gravitates to the point at which the sum of the imports and the sum of the exports exchange for the same quantity of money. And since things which are equal to the same are equal to one another, the imports and exports which are equal in money price would, if money were not used, precisely exchange for one another. ... In international as in ordinary domestic interchanges, money is to commerce what oil is to machinery, or railways to locomotion, a contrivance to diminish friction.'

Some apology appears to be necessary for thus reproducing a statement of doctrine which I always have thought had been thoroughly understood and accepted by all economists, but there would appear to be a wide-spread belief among certain classes of our countrymen that importing and exporting are two totally distinct processes, with no necessary connection between them; and that to place our foreign trade in a thoroughly satisfactory condition we should direct all our efforts to exporting as much as possible, and importing nothing in exchange. It cannot, therefore, be too broadly stated, or too often insisted on, that the two processes are as inseparably connected as the ebb and flow of the tide – that without imports there can be no exports, and without exports there can be no imports.

These two factors do not, of course, show the whole extent of our commercial intercourse with foreign countries; but they are most important elements in it, and their relative value is more easily calculated. We have heard of late a great deal too much about the enormous excess of our imports over our exports, as if this were necessarily a symptom of unsound trade. There can be no greater fallacy. Even if the values of our imports and exports were strictly accurate, which they are very far from being, they would convey no correct idea of the real conditions of our foreign trade, unless we could be presented with a balance-sheet giving a Dr. and Cr. account of all the items in our dealings with all the countries with which we trade, including capital lent or borrowed, and the interest thereon, both in the form of public loans and private investments, and every particular of international indebtedness.

Without this knowledge it is of little use to talk about our trade accounts; but upon two points we may feel an absolute certainty – first, that we cannot import without giving a *quid pro quo;* and, second, that whatever may be the balance, it is only in certain cases, and within very moderate limits, that it is cancelled by a bullion payment.

As has been shown above, a country which does not produce the precious metals can never effect its purchases in gold or silver, except in liquidation of some comparatively trifling balance. And, as a matter of fact, the imports of gold and silver bullion into the United Kingdom have in recent years exceeded the exports. In 1878 the excess amounted to nearly six millions sterling, and the average annual excess in the last five years has been nearly five millions.

So far, then, from seeing anything disquieting in what is called an 'adverse balance of trade,' it appears to me to be a feature on which we have every reason to congratulate ourselves, showing, as it does, that we are liquidating our debts in the least inconvenient way to ourselves, *i.e.*, by means of commodities which we can produce at less cost than other people.

If foreign countries are content to accept £50 worth of British goods in exchange for £90 worth of their own, are we to complain of their generosity? The preachers of the new gospel of reciprocity would apparently answer in the affirmative. 'Our policy,' they say, 'is to induce foreign countries to take more of our goods and give us less of theirs in return.' If this is what is meant by reciprocity, I fear it is not a doctrine which is likely to be very popular either with the producing or with the consuming classes in the country; but it would certainly be a better practical illustration of what Lord Bateman calls 'our magnanimous but disastrous liberality' than a system of Free Trade.

It may then be stated broadly that every Englishman who sells or buys in a foreign country, whatever be the tariff of that country or the tariff of his own, is already in the possession of complete reciprocity; and it must be apparent that the term 'reciprocity,' if applicable to the object of which we have lately heard so much, must be used in a different and much less accurate sense.

This sense would not be far to seek were it not for my second difficulty.

I might have supposed that a policy of reciprocity meant, in a rough-and-ready way, the policy of Mr. Huskisson and his successors in negotiating what were called 'reciprocity treaties,' by which two countries mutually engaged to relax or remove restrictions on each other's trade or navigation, and to extend to each other 'most favoured nation' treatment in a conditional or unconditional form.

In a still more general sense – viz., in that of a simultaneous reduction of tariffs – I might have supposed that the commercial policy of Mr. Cobden's Treaty with France in 1860 was in the minds of the modern advocates of 'reciprocity;' but it was at once apparent that their aims were very different from those of Mr. Huskisson and Mr. Cobden.

The kind of reciprocity which Mr. Huskisson and Mr. Cobden had in view, although their methods were different in some essential respects, had this in common, that they both recognised the vital importance, in the cause of Free Trade, of international action.

Sir Robert Peel, probably very wisely, at the time of his great reforms in our commercial system, resolved to proceed independently of the co-operation of foreign countries, and trusted not unnaturally to the effect of sound principles, and to the example of success in provoking the reciprocity which he was at the time unable or unwilling to invite.

I am very far from disputing the wisdom of the course which was then pursued; on the contrary, I am quite disposed to think that it was the only course which it would at that time have been wise to take; but it became clear, after twenty years of trial, that great as was its success, the policy of 'masterly inactivity' towards other countries had entirely failed in securing their adhesion to the Free Trade cause, and so far defeated the expectations of its authors.

It was under these circumstances that Mr. Cobden was led to consider whether any means could be found of giving a new impulse to tariff reform and international progress.

It was impossible to revert to the discriminating system and the conditional engagements of Mr. Huskisson; this would have been reaction, and not progress: but there could be no deviation from the strictest rules of sound economic policy, on the occasion of a sweeping reform of our own Customs system, in securing the co-operation of France with a view to simultaneous reductions which were not intended to be in favour of England and France alone, but to be general in their application.

Unfortunately, the sound maxim of Sir Robert Peel at the time of his reforms, that the best way of fighting hostile tariffs was by free imports, developed, by some strange process of reasoning in the minds of certain English economists (to say nothing of politicians, from whom anything may be expected and forgiven), into a notion which found ultimate expression in the maxim, 'Take care of your imports, and your exports will take care of themselves.'

This school of English Chauvinism has always strenuously denounced and resisted all attempts to secure the co-operation of foreign countries in establishing reciprocity of freedom, as if it were only less objectionable than reciprocity in monopoly, and has succeeded in doing two very mischievous things.

1. It has prevented the execution of a commercial policy which had been eminently successful in promoting freer trade on the Continent of Europe, and which, if completed as it might have been, would have effectually barred the course of the present reaction.
2. It is to a great degree responsible, if, indeed, it has not directly caused, the present blind cry for reciprocity. By discouraging and discrediting all attempts to obtain reciprocity of free trade, and by ignoring the incontestable truth that you cannot have free trade without reciprocity, the still grosser error has been generated in a section of the public mind that it is better to have reciprocity without free trade. The doctrine that half a trade,

is as good as a whole trade has led, logically, to the opinion that no trade is as good as half a trade.

But in their haste to find rest in a comfortable abstract doctrine which should at once flatter the national vanity by asserting our independence of other countries, and save all further trouble, the advocates of this rule of policy entirely overlooked their facts. They forgot that, until the French Treaty, our tariff was bristling with import duties, many of them protective, and that even now we draw a larger revenue from customs than any country in the world, except the United States. They forgot that their own condition was absent – that, in the sense of admitting them free, we do not take care of our imports.

I am very far from wishing in the slightest degree to palliate the attempts which are now being made by some foreign Governments – and, I regret to add, by Governments of our own possessions with even less excuse – to pursue still further a protective policy, and to plunder their people at large for the benefit of a privileged class.

On the contrary, I regard these attempts in the present state of Europe as little less than criminal; and I foresee a day of heavy reckoning, when Socialism, which is the direct offspring of Protection, claims its inheritance, and demands a share for the many in the dishonest gains of the few.

But if we were unable to raise even half our present Customs' revenue without having recourse to duties which were (as the phrase goes) incidentally protective, and our choice lay between such duties and direct taxation, I fear that there are some among us whose virtue would hardly be equal to the strain.

In thanking God, then, that he is not as other men, or even as this foreigner, the British Pharisee must not be allowed to deceive himself by a phrase. So long as we continue to raise half our revenue from customs and excise, our fiscal system may be very convenient, but our trade is not free. We may, if we like, rejoice that our wretched climate enables us to levy millions on wine, tea, and tobacco without recourse to excise duties – and the risk of subsidised domestic industries; but no trade can be called free till all fiscal impediments to its freedom are removed.

It is no consolation to the grower of wine in France or of tobacco in America to be told, when he is trying to promote a wider trade in these commodities, that our duties are imposed 'for revenue purposes only,' and are, therefore, above criticism. He very naturally replies, 'It is true you do not grow wine or tobacco, but I do; and, on the other hand, there are many things which you do produce, and which I wish to buy of you, but, to enable me to do so, you must accept payment in the only coin which I have to offer – namely, my wine or my tobacco. The more you take of these, the more shall I be able to take from you in exchange.'

The maxim of 'free imports' has never yet been tested, and never can be till our own tariff is purged.

This kind of reciprocity is, however, clearly not the object of the present agitation, which aims at the contraction and not at the expansion of our foreign trade, and invites us, in spite of the teaching of our wisest statesmen and of the conclusive evidence of our own experience, to enter upon a course of retaliation and a war of tariffs.

I must, therefore, ask those who are disposed to listen to this appeal how they would set to work.

Reciprocity in their sense means, I suppose, that we should treat other countries as they treat us, whatever the effect upon ourselves – *i.e.*, that we should apply to each foreign country a tariff of duties which would correspond, as nearly as might be, with that which it enforces against us.

Let us see where this would lead us.

Our imports may be divided broadly into three classes.

    1. Raw products or raw materials.
    2. Manufactured and half-manufactured goods.
    3. Articles of consumption, as food, drink, or tobacco, subdivided into (so-called) a. Necessaries. b. Luxuries.[1]

I presume that it can only be in respect of the second of these three classes that any new scheme of taxation could be proposed; for it is improbable that our manufacturing industries would desire to curtail their supply of raw material, or that the people of England will ever again submit to Corn Laws or Sugar Duties, and return to their small loaf and dear grocery, while our so-called luxuries, such as spirits, tobacco, wine, beer, tea, and coffee, are already so heavily taxed that the less we say about them the better.

It is, therefore, only with an eighth part of our import trade that we are, at the most, free to deal, and from this no inconsiderable deduction must, I presume, be made, for I can hardly believe that our manufacturing interest, as a whole, would desire duties on half-manufactured goods, intended for further processes which employ British capital and labour.

If, then, for the purpose of a policy of reciprocal restriction, it were proposed to re-impose duties on this small class of our imports, how could that purpose be attained?

Let us examine the sources of our supplies, and see how far they correspond with the foreign countries upon which we desire or are able to retaliate by restrictions on their trade. And first on the list of offenders stand the United States of America.

1 [Ed.: There follows a valuation of imports in 1877 for each of these classes.]

What manufactures do we import from them? In value less than £2,000,000 sterling, of which more than half consists of tanned and curried hides! There is little room for reciprocity here, for no one would dream of taxing their raw cotton and bread stuffs, and we had better leave them to tan and curry their own hides than attempt to do it for them.

Next in the illiberality of their tariffs come Russia and the Peninsula. But here the case is even worse, for we import no manufactured goods worthy of enumeration from any of them, while in the case of Spain and Portugal we already tax their wines not only heavily, but in a way which, in practice, affects them differentially, and derive from them a revenue infinitely greater than that which they raise from our exports to them.

Reciprocity here, therefore, would lead us in a contrary direction altogether from that which is desired.

But France, it will be said, which sends us every year a value of £16,000,000 in silks and woollens, shoes, and gloves, and 'articles de Paris' and other finished manufactures – surely here at least we can do to others as we do not wish them to do to us. No doubt we could; but to retaliate on a country which as a rule taxes our imports about 20 per cent. or less, while we leave untouched a country like the United States, which taxes them double, may be good or bad policy, but it is not reciprocity.

Nor could we give effect to such a policy without a further gross departure from the principle of reciprocity, by placing similar taxes on the manufactures of Belgium, Holland, and Switzerland, the tariffs of which are more liberal than those of France; for in these days of railroads and transit trades the antiquated machinery of differential duties and certificates or origin could never be made effectual again.

And what applies to France applies still more to Germany, whose trade must always largely pass through Dutch and Belgian ports, as well as to Russia, whose produce would always find its way through Germany to the sea.

It may also be as well to ask whether we might not get the worst of it in a game at which two can play, and whether we should not injure ourselves more than we should injure France by a war of tariffs?

The following table gives the total value of the trade between France and England in 1859, the year which preceded Mr. Cobden's treaty, and in 1877, the last year for which the account is complete[1] ... This table shows that in that part of our export trade which consists of British produce and manufactures, the proportionate advance since 1859 has more than kept pace with the progress of the total importations from France, and we have seen that the importations of manufactured goods from France do not greatly exceed the amount of the Brit-

1 [Ed.: The table has been deleted from the present text.]

ish exports. Any check which might be imposed on the French trade in silks and woollens would be dearly bought by the corresponding check which a return to the policy of 1859 would place upon our export trade.

'*Ex uno disce omnes!*' It would be tedious to repeat a similar story with respect to other countries on the continent of Europe. I append for reference a list[1] showing the value of the manufactures which we imported in 1877 from most of the countries with which we trade, from which it will be seen that, even if possible, a policy of retaliation would be utterly futile.

Of India and China, which for commercial purposes must be considered together, it is unnecessary to speak in connection with this subject, for we levy on one of their products – tea – alone little less than the whole amount of their joint Customs Revenue!

I turn to the British Colonies, and take the Dominion of Canada and the Australian group as the largest and most important of our customers.

What is the prospect for this kind of reciprocity here? We look in vain for a single item in the list of their exports which we could afford to tax, whatever their treatment of our manufactures may be. Canadian timber and Australian wool have become the breath of our industrial life, and must be admitted free.

Any attempt, then, at a discriminating reciprocity of restrictions must be abandoned in despair; not only would it fail in giving effect to its essential principle, but it would land us in inextricable confusion. There is only one course left – viz., that of placing a general import duty of a 'moderately' protective character, say 10 per cent., upon all foreign manufactures.

But this cannot be intended, for it would be a simple return to a policy which we have already tried, and which we have abandoned step by step from a bitter experience of its disastrous results; and I would ask what reason there is for supposing that such a course would be more profitable in the future than it has been in the past.

If any one wants a proof, let him look at the history of our foreign trade, in that branch of it alone (if he likes) which consists of British exports.[2] ... Mr. Caird, in his recent valuable work on the landed interest, states that thirty years ago not more than one-third of the people of England consumed animal food more than once a week. Now nearly all of them eat it in meat or cheese or butter once a day, more than doubling the average consumption per head. He adds that within the last twenty-five years the capital value of the live-stock of the United Kingdom has risen from £146,000,000 to £260,000,000; and he puts the total gain to the agricultural interest – landowners, farmers and labourers – in rent, farm capital, and wages, at £445,000,000 in the period under review.

1 [Ed.: Not included in the present text.]
2 [Ed.: There follow a number of tables detailing the progress of British foreign trade under free trade.]

Agricultural wages have risen from 9s. 7d. to 14s. 6d. since 1850; and it is needless to add that the wages of manufacturing labour have increased in a similar manner.

Among collateral indications of the national prosperity, which has, at all events, coincided with the adoption of our recent fiscal and commercial policy, I may refer to the growth, in the assessments of income tax in Great Britain:–

In 1843 they were   £251,013,000
In 1875   "   535,708,000

To deposits in savings banks, which were –

In 1840, £23,471,000, or 17s. 9d. per head of population.
In 1876, £70,280,000, or 42s. 6d."

And to the decrease in the percentage in pauperism to the population, which was –

In 1841 ... 8.2
In 1876 ... 3.1

And to other facts given in a recent interesting paper on the strength of England in the *Fortnightly Review*, by Mr. Farrer.

Can this be all? or is there yet some undiscovered policy which I have failed to divine?

If not, and if further reciprocity of restrictions is unattainable, I have yet one consolation for its advocates. In a still more general sense, but in a sense very distinctly affecting the conditions of our foreign trade, their policy is actually in force.

It will, no doubt, be a source of unmixed satisfaction to them to find that our so-called 'revenue duties' cannot fail to produce results as injurious to the exporting industries of the countries affected by them as their protective duties cause to our own trade.

The £20,000,000 which we annually raise in duties on foreign goods may be roughly divided among our different neighbours in the following proportions.[1]

And of all these countries there is hardly one which draws as large a revenue from the taxation of British produce. To take only two examples, the United States and France. The total value of British produce exported to the former country in 1877 was £16,300,000; making allowance for the entry of a certain amount of goods duty free, the average rate levied can hardly be put higher than 30 per cent., which would give a total revenue of about £5,000,000; while in the case of France, the duties actually levied on British goods in the same year amounted to a little over £800,000.

What more could the most strenuous advocate of a retaliatory policy desire?

1   [Ed.: There follows a table detailing revenue duty receipts from foreign countries.]

There is one ground upon which protective duties have been urged which appears at first sight rather more plausible than those which have been hitherto discussed. I mean the claim set up by our manufacturers in compensation for restricted hours of labour and exceptional taxation. It is said that if the Legislature chooses to place disabilities on particular industries, the country at large should bear the cost, and not the particular industries.

Now, in the first place, any such disabilities as are here in view are not imposed intentionally by the Legislature. The assumption has always been that cheap labour is not necessarily efficient labour, and that a system which leads to the degradation of the working class, and prevents them from attaining a certain moral, intellectual, and physical standard, directly impairs their productive energy.

But if it can be shown that any restrictions on labour or any special disabilities really diminish the efficiency of the industries which they affect, it should be the object of our reformers to address themselves to the very legitimate task of obtaining relief from unwise or unjust laws, and not to extend their operation to the whole community.

For to what does the claim amount?

Because the cost of production is increased in certain industries by an undue interference with labour, we are asked to raise the cost of living all round to the whole community.

Because an injustice is done to a section of the people, it is to be extended to all. To enter upon such a course would be to move further in a vicious circle, which could only end in the general impoverishment of the nation.

If the aid of Government is sought to equalise conditions of production at home and abroad, let it at least be invoked to diminish our burdens and not to add to them!

But, after all, what a hollow cry this is about foreign competition! A country which exports her manufactures to a value of £150,000,000 per annum to rival and neutral markets, is represented to us as on the road to ruin, because she cannot succeed in preventing the importation of £50,000,000 worth of foreign goods!

I have now combated various imaginary propositions, but end as I began, without having discovered one which accounts for the action and language of so many of our countrymen on this matter of reciprocity.

Will you think me very uncharitable if I say that an unworthy suspicion has sometimes crossed my mind that the policy which we are called upon to adopt might more fitly be called by another and a less innocent name?

Can it be that while the hands are Esau's hands, the voice is the voice of Jacob, inviting us, in the name of reciprocity, to barter our Free Trade birthright for a mess of Protectionist pottage?

I prefer to believe that the fault is mine, and to seek for further light.

The proposal, therefore, which I have to make to the Committee is that they should offer a prize for the best essay explaining the objects of this much-debated policy, and the means by which it is proposed to carry it into effect.

I shall await the result without impatience, but not without curiosity, for the prize essayist must at least succeed in proving that no bread is better than half a loaf, and that because we cannot sell in the dearest, we ought not to buy in the cheapest market.

I am always,
Dear Mr. Potter,
Yours sincerely,
LOUIS MALLET.

Free Trade and the European Treaties of Commerce (London: Cobden Club, 1875), pp. 74–86, 88–106, 112–22.

CORRESPONDENCE ON THE PROSPECTS OF FREE TRADE.

ON THE PROSPECTS OF FREE TRADE IN AUSTRIA AND GERMANY.

From Herr MAX WIRTH, *Vienna, late Director of Statistics at Berne.*

So great a part of the economical progress made not only in England, but also in the other nations of Europe, has been brought about by the influence of the noble man in honour of whose memory the Cobden Club assembles, that I feel highly gratified in doing what you ask of me, and drawing, in a few touches, the present position of Free Trade in Central Europe.

All questions, either religious or political, either scientific or economical, bear more or less an international character, science being in itself of a cosmopolitan nature, for the reason that culture is nourished by the great thoughts of all nations, and that, with regard to civilisation, there is no 'God's chosen people.' This international character becomes more apparent than ever in the question of Free Trade, which in itself must be international. Switzerland was the first country which introduced, I will not say Free Trade, but so low a tariff of customs that they scarcely deserve the name of finance customs. Again, the ideas of Free Trade began to find their way into German Universities ever since the beginning of the century, by means of Adam Smith's precepts. Although they were put into practice in the Prussian States by statesmen like Schön, &c., yet Free Trade did not obtain life and action until after Richard Cobden's great work was crowned by the abolition of the Corn Laws.

The establishment of the German Zollverein was an event of European importance, yet its principal aim was a political one, as the re-establishment of the German Empire, including all but Austria, has subsequently shown. Austria found out too late that it was wrong in remaining apart from these aims, and thus isolating herself. On the question of Custom-tariffs the Zollverein was still, in its majority, inclined towards Protectionism. The duty on imports from Switzerland had been raised by the Zollverein, so that Switzerland's young industry was brought into a very dangerous position, from which it was saved by beginning commerce with countries across the ocean. For this reason the beginning of Switzerland's commerce on international markets dates from this time.

At the time when List expounded his system of national work, and thereby gave Protectionism a scientific *raison d'être*, by showing the necessity of educating domestic work-power, there were not the elements of a Free Trade party in Germany, and still less in Austria, to oppose him. In Austria manufacturing industry possessed influential leaders, because even high aristocracy by birth did not disdain to undertake industrial establishments on its own account. A Free Trade party, however, formed itself, after the abolition of the Corn Laws in England, and after the change in the universal opinion which began about the year 1848. It was at first represented by the 'Frei-handels Verein,' founded at Hamburg, which numbered amongst its members men of importance from the west of Germany. The influence of these men was confined to the press; and although politicians refused to take any notice of Free Trade for ten years longer, still the former found means of gaining a large majority of German newspapers for the good cause. When a change came over public life, by the accession of the Prince of Prussia, the present Emperor of Germany, in the year 1858, and congresses and societies were formed in whose meetings the ideas of Free Trade were freely discussed, the ground was well prepared, and a firm trust in the final result of their aims was obtained by Free Traders, when they observed the imposing activity of the English Free Trade League. All this did not fail to stimulate Government leaders, and to give them so favourable an opinion of Free Trade, that when the time for action had come they refused to listen to the protestations of Protectionists. This was at the time of the international Treaties of Commerce, the favourable realisation of which is, in a great part, owing to Richard Cobden. Although the Treaties of Commerce are based on a compromise of both economical parties, of which the most influential obtained some advantages over the other – thus, for instance, France and Austria granted greater advantages to Protectionism, whilst England, Germany, Italy, and Switzerland favoured Free Trade – yet public opinion was quite contented with this piece of progress, so that it occupied itself with other questions of more immediate importance, especially with the position of the working classes.

Through the initiative of Governments and Parliaments, in which Free Trade, which is beginning to gain ground even in Austria, had its representatives, further progress was made. In Austria an additional convention, dated 1869, was made in connection with the Treaty of Commerce with England of 1865, and in Germany the duty on pig-iron was entirely done away with on the 1st October, 1863, whilst it was determined to abolish the duty on import of cast-iron from the year 1876. The latter measures of great importance were easily passed in the German Reichstag, when compared with the difficulties encountered by Free Trade in former times on both sides of the British Channel, the time being very favourable to them. After the war between France and Germany, all the rolling stock of the railways was in so defective and neglected a state as to render the conveyance of goods difficult for many months after the peace was concluded. But when, at the end of the war, a million of strong men returned to their work and exchanged the sword for tools and machines, – when iron-works and factories had all hands full of work with the repair of the rolling stock of railways, – when both in Austria and Germany numerous new railways were undertaken, – when new factories were established and old ones provided with new machinery, – when Germany's ironclad men-of-war began to be built – then all at once the demand for iron reached dimensions never seen before. Of course the price of iron in the country itself rose in the same proportion, and as iron-works and furnaces had in consequence plenty to do, at a price they had never before obtained, they could not well oppose the abolition of duty on iron. The progress then made by industry both in Austria and Germany turned into over-speculation, which must needs end with a crisis. Over-speculation was then principally produced by the payment of the French milliards, and the hopes which men of business founded on them. It is in part owing also to the German Currency Reform, and the mistake committed by the German Government, viz., issuing new gold crowns side by side with the old silver currency, by which means the circulation of metal had been increased by 750 millions of marks within the years 1872-74, according to the confession of the President of the 'Reichs-Rauzleramt' himself. The latter measure helped to raise the expectations awakened by the war-contribution as to the capital ready for new undertakings. By the repayment of a great many of the German States' debts, a large amount of private capital was set free, and ready for new investment, by which means over-speculation spread to Austria, and reached dimensions never before attained except with the bubbles of the South Sea Company at the beginning of last century.

With the destructive outbreak of the crisis, which, although it began at the Bourse, soon reached every branch of industry in Austria as well as in Germany, Protectionism reappeared, and offered to heal the wounds received by industry in the crisis. To effect this, Protectionism proposed giving up the Treaties of Commerce, all of which cease with the year 1876, and raising the duty on imports. The wool manufacturers of Brünn were the first to utter an opinion of this kind, because they found themselves at a disadvantage, occasioned by the additional Treaty of 1869. Next came the owners of iron-works; and both branches of industry succeeded in obtaining the attention of the Government and the Reichsrath, so that their position was made the object of an official *enquête*. In the spring of 1875 Protectionism succeeded in obtaining a triumph over Free Traders in the Austrian Congress of Economists, but merely by a local majority of voices, declaring itself altogether against the renewal of the Treaties of Commerce, and for autonomy in the tariff, which is in future to be raised.

At the same time the Protectionist party gave signs of life in different parts of Germany, especially in the Prussian Landtag and in the Bavarian Reichsrath. Now instead of naming the real cause of the bad condition of industry, quite an unexpected reason was given for it. Had Protectionists mentioned the true cause of the crisis, they would have been reminded, both by the Government and the Representative Power, that not Germany and Austria alone suffer from the crisis, but all Europe, North and South America, a part of Africa and Asia – not alone some special branches of industry, but the whole of the small trade of commerce and of agriculture. They would have been reminded that every branch of industry in the nation has the same claims to the protection of the Government. It is for this reason that Protectionists both in Austria and Germany, to arrive at their purpose, use the pretext of care for the commonwealth. The balance of commerce must be upheld, and the depression of industry is exclusively ascribed to the circumstance that in Germany import has in the latter years, especially in 1872 and 1873, exceeded export by a great deal. In Austria alone, in the years 1870 to 1874, it amounted to 600 millions of gulden. In a Bill presented to the Bavarian Reichsrath in the beginning of April a demand was made according to which the Treaties of Commerce are to cease, and duty on import, especially on cotton, is to be raised, solely because in the year 1872 325 million thalers' worth more goods were imported than exported. In 1873 import exceeded export by 589 millions of thalers. On the question of duty on iron, Protectionists demanded nothing besides suspension of the projected measure of abolishing duty on cast-iron. The preamble of the above-mentioned Bill did not name a single of the reasons on which the disproportion in the commercial balance of Germany and Austria depended. On it was founded the conclusion that both industry and the country itself are approaching their financial fall, from which they could be saved by nothing except a return to a pure system of Protectionism. The leaders of the party of Free Traders did not fail to refute these suppositions by explanations, which may perhaps be of interest to you.

The first fact to which attention was called is the truth discovered in England – viz., that the amount of export is always less exactly registered than the amount of import, because, with the former, duty is but rarely levied.

Secondly. We have no official authority to confirm the correctness of the value given for import into Germany, as goods imported pay duty not by their value, but by their weight. The amount of value given is drawn from a valuation made since 1872 by the Imperial Statistical Office.

Thirdly. It has been said that in normal times the value of import must always exceed the value of export, because for import a higher sum for conveyance, insurance, and interest on capital must be brought into account. Protectionists were reminded of the normal course of British commerce, with which, for a great many years, import has outweighed export.

Fourthly. It was clearly shown that in this special case the disproportion in the balance was to be ascribed to two reasons, so clear that they cannot possibly be refuted. These reasons are of so extraordinary a nature that they can never, or at least very seldom, recur, and cannot therefore be taken as the basis of a change in the legislation and in Custom-tariffs. One of these reasons is over-speculation before the outbreak of the crisis. In the latter part of the year 1871 the import of raw materials for the use of industry, especially of iron, began to increase both in Germany and Austria in quite an abnormal manner, owing to the enormous amount of new manufactures and railways undertaken. The capital consumed in the establishment of new companies and societies amounts to about 300–400 millions pounds sterling. I cannot give further details on the subject in these pages, but I recommend all who wish for further information to read my 'History of Commercial Crises' ('Geschichte der Handelskrisen,' second edition, Sauerländer in Frankfort O/M.), and, furthermore, a book which is shortly to appear in Vienna, editor G. T. Manz, and which will be called 'Wiedergeburt Osterreichs aus den Nachwehen der Krisis.' In these works I have clearly shown how every crisis has been accompanied by an enormous increase of import, that import always grows in proportion to over-speculation, and that this was the case with the crisis of 1857, and much more so with the crisis of 1873.

Fifthly. The reason which would by itself suffice to explain the disproportion of import both into Germany and Austria, is the importation of foreign capital into Austria, as well as Germany. It would be superfluous to explain to a learned assembly like the one I am addressing, that the exchange of capital from one country to the other is mostly effectuated in goods. For the same reason the payment of the French war-contribution was almost entirely effectuated in bills, which for the greater part represent goods. The mere fact that of the bills written for the war-contribution, 2,485 millions of francs were to be paid in thalers, 235 were to be paid in gulden, and 265 in mark banco, which were, therefore, all due in Germany; this fact alone proves that the bills represented goods. The excess of import over export in the years 1872 and 1873 is therefore explained by the payment of the French milliards, which took place within those two years. Another proof of this fact is that the import of the year 1874, the valuation of which has not yet been published, has decreased by a great deal, so that the Exchequer levied 18 million marks less in duty.

In a similar manner the over-balance of goods imported into Austria, which within the last five years amounts to 600 million gulden, is explained. Within these five years railways have been built to the extent of over 5,000 English miles. Of course, inland capital alone did not build these railways. The excess may therefore be put down to the investment of German and English capital in Austrian railways.

You see by these arguments, which have never yet been refuted, how weak is the basis on which the Protectionists found their demands. We very much doubt whether these demands will in any way be regarded by the Governments and Parliaments of Austria and Germany. We may found this supposition on the manner in which the Minister of Finances, Camphausen, treated the insinuations of the Protectionists advanced in the Prussian Landtag. He admitted that the depression of industry, in consequence of the crisis, renders the further reduction of the duty-tariff impossible. He, however, declared that legislation cannot make a step backwards out of regard for a passing misfortune. The German Government will doubtless renew the old Commercial Treaties on the footing on which they stand at present, and the Reichstag will not refuse its approbation, if only for this reason – that it requires all its forces on another side.

As to the Austro-Hungarian Monarchy, the Austrian Government has presented a project for a new Custom-tariff to the Austrian Chambers of Commerce, and these have, with scarcely an exception, pronounced themselves for raising the duty on import, especially with regard to cotton, wool, and iron. Now, although a number of other branches of industry have come into existence and get on well without Protection, which would greatly suffer from an increase of duty on the import of the materials required by them, and although almost the whole of the Austrian Cabinet is in favour of Free Trade, yet the demands of the Protectionists might, on account of the general depression of industry, be taken into consideration, had not the Government of Hungary expressed a very decided opinion on the subject. It is a well-known fact that after the Treaty of 1867, which turned Austria and Hungary by treaty into one Custom territory, no new arrangement with foreign countries may be made without the approval of both halves of the Monarchy. By a mere chance, the renewal of the Treaty of Customs and Commerce between Hungary and Austria and that with foreign countries will have to be made about the same time. Consultations on the first have already begun at Vienna. Hungary is not quite firm in its principles of Free Trade; for when, last autumn, Austria demanded a continuation of the momentary abolition of duty on the import of corn, which had been made because the harvest of 1873 had brought such bad results with it, it was Hungary which would hear nothing of the kind, on account of the competition with Roumania. The commercial policy of Hungary has, however, undergone a change since that time. The working power of the Board of Trade is an economist of reputation, the Under-Secretary of State, who did not fail to recognise that Hungary, an essentially agricultural land, must ultimately profit most by favouring Free Trade. The Hungarian Government has already returned from the above-mentioned policy in regard to corn, and furnished a deputy to the consultations on the renewal of the Treaty, with instructions quite in compliance with Free Trade. The Austrian Ministry is far too well informed to comply with the special interests of single branches of industry at the expense of the common weal. It will notice the demands of such branches of industry as are in immediate danger of extinction; it will be regardful of cases where a large amount of capital might be lost or numerous work-people be ruined. As Hungary has always known how to defend its political interests better than the sister nations of the Monarchy, it is most probable that the Treaties of Commerce will be renewed on very much the same footing on which they stand at present, with perhaps a few exceptions. Free Traders should by no means be inactive; they must not allow their fire to extinguish, or even to flag, for they have found out, from this last attack of Protectionism, that Protectionists have certainly learned one thing from them, and from our immortal friend, Richard Cobden – energetic and persevering defence of their own interests. They cannot, however, rob us of our principles!

MAX WIRTH.

From Herr GEORGE VON BUNSEN, *of Berlin.*

12th July, 1875.

GENTLEMEN, – You did me the honour some days ago to ask my opinion as regards the prospects of Free Trade in Germany at the present time, and though I can have no pretension to say anything either new or important, yet I know that in cheerfully obeying your command I do that for myself which is next best to enjoying the company of so many distinguished men as are wont to assemble at your Feast of Nations.

My answer can be brief. There is little hope, perhaps, of present speedy *advance,* but, on the other hand, still less ground is there for apprehending serious or lasting *retrogression,* now or hereafter, *on the path of Free Trade.*

On the first proposition let me say nothing. We know that Free Trade is the child of hope and the mother of goodwill. Then we must be satisfied with her holding her ground in a period of history marked by languid pessimism and by a reaction, even among eminent statesmen, to practices of national isolation!

But I foresee no retreat from the position attained. It is true that, in Germany too, plaintive voices have made themselves heard in Parliament and in the press or among manufacturers. When they speak much – and certainly not too much – of the astounding advance of French manufacture, do they attribute it to its real cause, viz., a fixed, patriotic determination to work very hard, to work very well, and to work for fair wages peaceably? No! Protection, forsooth, must have done it – the new laws of 1871 and 1872 were the panacea – and nothing but M. Thiers' reaction against those very principles, which the Anglo-French Treaty of Richard Cobden has formed into a leaven of the civilised world, could have saved France! The same error of judgment induces the same people to ascribe the present discouraging appearance of trade in Germany to our return to those more advanced economic rules which Prussia, to her honour be it remembered, was the first to inaugurate so early as 1818.

Besides these querulous voices one attempt, and one only, I think, has been made to influence legislation by embodying the same crude notions in a petition to the Central Government, signed by certain manufacturers, and praying that the legal term for the abolition of the last remnants of duty upon iron (law of 7th July, 1873) might be put off from January 1st, 1877, to a later period. This petition, set in motion at Bremen, fell ignominiously to the ground. It was met by a counter-petition from Remscheid, of representative manufacturers in the same trade and of the self-same district, protesting against Protection, and pointing to *more work, better work,* and *cheaper work* as true and lasting remedies for the present stagnation of trade and commerce.

I am proud to say that, with such few exceptions, public opinion, as represented in the press of this country, in the Economic Congress, in the meetings of the Handelstag, and, more authoritatively still, in the German Parliament, and by our leading statesmen, has been unanimous in the right direction. It will be sufficient to epitomise a remarkable speech by Herr Camphausen (Prussian Finance Minister, Vice-President of the Prussian Cabinet, and a member of the German Bundesrath, or States' Council) on this very question. 'We believe,' he said, in answer to a Protectionist complaint, 'that the worst is over, and that better days are coming. We have unbounded faith in that policy, leading, as it does, circumspectly but safely to Free Trade, which my friend and colleague, Herr Delbrück, and I, as his humble companion, have been enabled to pursue. And so strong is our conviction of its excellence that, if Germany should resolve upon a change in her economic policy, this change would certainly be preceded or accompanied by a change of Cabinet.' Loud cheers from all benches followed this declaration.

As for the Chancellor of the German Empire, you are aware, Gentlemen, that with him the love of Free Trade is not an *acquired taste,* for the landed gentry of Prussia are essentially Free Traders. This hereditary predilection has, however, grown into a broad principle in his mind. It has been observed that the advisers on economic matters whom Prince Bismarck has drawn round his person have acquired that public estimation which gave them a claim to the places they occupy by years of disinterested advocacy of those principles for which the Cobden Club labours to obtain universal acceptance.

I am not sure whether Free Trade ever had seasons of more critical import to pass through. Were it not for the genius of Cavour still ruling the destinies of *Italy* – if we could not trust Hungarian interests to outweigh an ignorant cry for Protection in parts of *Austria* – and if *Germany* was vacillating, which she is not – where would be the prospects of Free Trade on the Continent of Europe?

Will you pardon me, however, if, at the close of this far too lengthy epistle, I try to explain why, at its beginning, I qualified my statement by saying that I could apprehend no *serious or lasting* retrogression? Notice should, I believe, be taken of two complaints of the landed gentry of Prussia, to whom I have just referred as being natural allies of the Cobden Club. They have a grievance of old standing against English legislation, and a new one; both are affecting their purses seriously; *a cry for reprisals* is beginning to be listened to more readily by them every year, and I am bound to confess that a temporary backsliding on the road of Free Trade in the German Parliament by a combination of this and some manufacturing interests may be the result. Of course I am speaking of the manner in which English revenue is raised on *spirits,* and of certain measures caused by the advent of *rinderpest.* It has been said, and said with truth, that the conclusions which led to the preservation of the former and to the introduction of the latter had nothing whatsoever to do with Protection; and I am unable to judge whether or not protection of the English distiller in the one case and of the English cattle-breeder in the other is indeed the *effect* of those measures. If, however, they should, on renewed examination, be found to have that effect, who would doubt the efficacy of that wise and sound principle which the late Mr. Cobden rendered dominant in the councils of Great Britain, to wipe out from her statute-book obnoxious excrescences which weaken the hands of well-wishers and Free Traders abroad? among the humblest and staunchest of whom be pleased, Gentlemen, to number

Your obedient servant,
GEORGE VON BUNSEN.

From JAMES MONTGOMERY STUART, Esq.

ON THE PROSPECTS OF FREE TRADE IN ITALY.

Rome, July 20*th.*

GENTLEMEN, – In compliance with the request which the Cobden Club has done me the honour of addressing to me, I propose in the present letter to give a sketch of the present movement amongst Italian politicians and economists with reference to Free Trade and Protectionist views, and the partial recognition of the second by some very influential Italian statesmen.

One has been so long accustomed to regard Italy as the classic land of Free Trade, that it is at first somewhat difficult to realise the fact of any strong Protectionist movement in that country. It should, however, be recollected that the only Italian state in which Free Trade doctrines were not only generally accepted in theory, but embodied in legislative action, was Tuscany; not indeed that there were wanting advocates of liberal views in the other provinces, and even royal decrees of a much earlier date than those of Peter Leopold, attesting the recognition of the principles of commercial liberty in the councils of other absolute princes. Still, during the whole course of Mr. Cobden's memorable Italian tour of 1847, his great legislative victory was everywhere hailed in the Peninsula as one in which Italian economists might feel a legitimate pride, because, in fact, a victory due to the triumph of truths which they had long and strenuously upheld. Foremost amongst the admirers of Mr. Cobden was Count Cavour, who, in a masterly essay, sketched out in grand broad outlines the beneficent results which the revolution in the commercial policy of England must sooner or later produce in all civilised lands. The great prestige of Mr. Cobden's name strengthened the hands of all liberal economists throughout Italy; tariffs were modified in a liberal sense; and such force did the movement acquire that, in the reforming period of the new pontificate, Monsignor Corboli, charged with negotiating a Customs' union between the Papal States, Sardinia, and Tuscany, had precise instructions from Pius IX. to carry out this work in the most liberal spirit. So much indeed had the present Pontiff this at heart, that the proposed participation in the negotiations of the distinguished economist, Antonio Scialoia, then residing at Turin, was, I have been assured, owing to the personal initiative of the Pontiff, who was desirous that one so well known for his Free Trade principles should be in direct relation with the diplomatic agents of the three Governments.

The political reaction of 1849 brought, everywhere except in Sardinia, an economic reaction in its train. In Sardinia, during that period, Count Cavour, first as Minister of Agriculture and Commerce, and afterwards as head of the Cabinet, succeeded in embodying in the commercial legislation of the subalpine kingdom those principles of commercial liberty no longer regarded with favour in the rest of Italy. Even in Tuscany the strongest diplomatic pressure was put on the native statesmen who sought to maintain their economic traditions; and it is almost certain that but for the moral support they received from England, these statesmen would have found themselves obliged to give way.

No wonder, then, if the successive annexations to Sardinia of the other Italian states, and the immediate extension to these states of the commercial legislation sanctioned in the North, were regarded as the definitive victory in Italy of Free Trade over Protectionism. Ancient historical traditions and recent political experience combined – at all events appeared to combine – in making a policy of commercial freedom a prominent element in the national programme. How comes it, then, one is naturally tempted to inquire, that only fourteen years after the death of Count Cavour the possibility of a Protectionist reaction with any chance of success should be so much as dreamt of? I believe that the explanation must be sought in various and quite different causes. In the first place, the prodigious personal energy and the astonishing political successes of Count

Cavour enabled him to do things in the Sardinian Parliament and Administration which none of his successors have been able to achieve. Even in the short period that elapsed between the annexation of the kingdom of the Two Sicilies and his death it was evident that in the bureaucratic spheres at Naples he would have to encounter a strong Protectionist opposition. The winter of 1860–61 was one marked by the high price of provisions in Naples, and Count Cavour was made the object of unceasing remonstrances and complaints from the great southern capital, all ascribing to his Free Trade policy the scarcity prevalent at the time. The violence of that opposition was not even known until after Count Cavour's decease, when questions unexpectedly presented themselves respecting the regularity, and indeed the legality, of certain administrative measures taken at the time. But all this was not a very favorable omen for the general acceptance of Free Trade principles in Southern Italy, and for the contingent of moral force which the deputies from those provinces were likely to bring to a Government of enlarged commercial views. Meanwhile Protectionism but too naturally and too easily found its adherents in the various manufacturers of Northern Italy, who at each stage of their progress have been appealing more loudly and more urgently to each successive Italian Cabinet for protection against foreign competition. They have been favoured by the course of political events. The excitement consequent on the transfer of the capital in 1864, from Turin to Florence, at once threw the Government into the hands of a strongly Piedmontese Cabinet, presided over by a statesman who represented in Parliament Biella, one of the chief citadels of Piedmontese Protectionism. The annexation of the Venetian provinces in 1866 had amongst other results that of swelling the Italian Parliament with a group of theoretical politicians who had already in their writings committed themselves to Protectionist doctrines, and whose controversial energy in that line most certainly did not contribute to diminish the aspirations of the Venetian producers and manufacturers for a Protective policy of the same kind as that already demanded by their Piedmonstese brethren. All these demands in a Protectionist sense will be found embodied in the reports of the Government Commission on the state of Italian trade and commerce which, in the early part of last year, visited the principal Italian cities, received in each city the evidence of the leading merchants and manufacturers, and has published its reports and evidence in two large volumes, one devoted to the oral, another to the written communications, with a most formidable appendix of other volumes containing more special details. What I have already stated may in itself suffice to throw some light on the actual conditions of Italian Protectionism. But there are two other causes, one of a general, the other of a quite personal character, which must likewise be taken into account, and without which most incorrect and incomplete views would be formed.

In the first place, there is no use disguising the fact that the true soil, the really favouring influences, in which Italian Protectionism grows up and flourishes – that this soil and these influences are to be found in the system extending over the whole country, of the municipal octroi duties. By means of that octroi system there is raised every year a sum amounting, according to the last calculations I have seen, to about a hundred and thirty millions of francs, of which sixty millions, in virtue of special agreements, are paid in to the public national treasury, and the other seventy millions to the separate municipal treasuries. With the exception of the sixty millions which the Government derives from the lottery offices – with that single and most scandalous exception – the sum obtained from these octroi duties is the one got in with the greatest loss to the national wealth and the greatest check to the national enterprise. Every close commune in Italy – by close commune I mean one entitled to fence itself round with an octroi barrier – becomes *ipso facto* a citadel of Protectionism. Its leading municipal and provincial councillors, who are generally landed proprietors in the immediate neighbourhood, have an interest that the system be worked for their individual advantage, and to the exclusion of a more distant competition. One might fill a volume with the calamitous results for the national production. In the first place, there is created an immense disproportion between the price of provisions in close and open communes, and between the town and the country. The causes creating this disproportion, whilst acting first and immediately on home, do not the less act with crushing effect on foreign trade. Take for example the product in which, from its geographical position and its territorial conformation, Italy seems, as it were, destined by Providence to be one of the world's great exporters, quite as much so as France, or Germany, or Spain – I mean, of course, wine. By the octroi system almost every motive, so far as the home market is concerned, is taken away from the landed proprietor, and much more from the common peasant cultivator, to improve his wines. The law gives to the municipal councils the power of establishing a tariff with a *minimum* and a *maximum* duty. The *minimum* duty is constantly imposed for such articles as vegetables, which, most easily supplied from the immediate neighbourhood, are furnished by the local proprietors; whilst the *maximum* is just as regularly imposed on the wines which may enter into competition with those grown by the same proprietors. The distant wine grower has, therefore, to encounter the double obstacle of the cost of carriage and the maximum duty. The clearest instance is seen in the capital itself, in Rome. There the additional population of some fifty thousand brought by the change in the seat of Government would naturally prefer to drink the much better *Chianti* or *Barolo* wines, to which they had been accustomed in Florence and Turin. The Municipal Council of Rome lost not a moment in imposing the maximum duty on those wines, so that the public functionaries have the choice of drinking a bad Roman wine which they detest, their own native wine, or a French wine at almost the same high price, or, worse still, an adulterated wine professing to be Chianti or Barolo, but in reality manufactured in Rome itself from a common Roman wine, with perhaps a slight infusion of the Tuscan and Piedmontese or many much less desirable ingredients. And the same cause produces similar effects in a sometimes incredible degree. The Minister of Agriculture and Commerce has frequently published in the *Official Gazette* the prices on a given day of some forty of the principal articles of food in about a hundred and fifty of the chief communes in the kingdom; and the disproportion in the prices, though in part explicable from deficient communications, is in a very great degree to be ascribed to the working of the octroi system. But to return to the wine, not only the actual but the possible, the apprehended effects of the system scare the peasant cultivator in many districts from attempting to increase and improve his vintages. He has enough for himself and his own family; he has a small but sure market amongst the neighbouring peasants; why should he incur the hazards of sending his wine to a town where he must face a certain and, for him, heavy outlay in the payment of the octroi duty, without feeling assured of a corresponding gain? But all the obstacles to the natural and regular and healthful development of home industry do not proceed from the octroi system. The railway management and the railway tariffs certainly do their best to make these obstacles almost insurmountable. There is not a single city in the centre of Italy – a peninsula washed on one side by the Mediterranean and on the other by the Adriatic Sea – which might not with the existing net of railways be well supplied every morning with fish. But they would be bold fishmongers who should contract for regular supplies from Venice and Ancona, or from Leghorn and Naples, with the knowledge that they must not only encounter high octroi duties and railway tariffs, but that, through the never-ending pedantic formalities imposed by the railway companies, hours and hours, nay, sometimes an entire day, may pass over before they are able to remove the consignment of fish from the railway station. An Italian sun, though favourable to the growth of wine, is not equally favourable to the conservation of dead fish: no wonder if the speculation presents very decided risks. What is true of fish is equally true of fruit. Whilst the Ligurian, Neapolitan, and Sicilian shores exhibit one long and brilliant succession of lemon and orange groves, the Italians in an inland provincial town must, from the same causes, pay a far higher price for lemons and oranges than is paid in Norwich, or Perth, or Cork. The honest German who descends the Alps into Italy with the echoes of Goethe's song ringing in his ears – 'Knowest thou the land where the lemons flourish, and where the gold oranges glow through their dark leaves?' – has considerable difficulty in recognising that land, in its commercial aspects, the first time he buys a lemon or an orange in his progress. Why, it may be asked, are not more active measures taken to remedy such a state of things? The answer, I fear must be found, not only in the fact that so many local interests are involved, and that in connection with the system a great amount of local patronage has sprung up, but in the peculiar character of the Italian Parliament.

There is a want of political men who devote themselves practically and usefully to such special questions. The deputies in general think them below their notice. The fruit and fish trade are matters of primary moment for the whole Italian people, just as are the silk, and oil, and marble, and sulphur, and borax, and other branches too numerous to mention of agricultural, mineral, and animal production. But the deputy who would make these subjects the object of questions and motions in the Chamber would run the risk of being nicknamed Lemon Bruni, or Oyster Bianchi, or Parmesan Cheese Neri, and the mere thought of being obliged to go through the world with such a *sobriquet* would arrest him at the outset.

I would now, however, advert to the last and more special, indeed personal, cause by which the character of the present Protectionist movement in Italy has been determined. I have already alluded to the fact that there had sprung up in Northern Italy a school of accomplished writers, whose views have received their chief colouring from the teaching of recent German economists. In their works, as in those of their masters, a much larger share of action is accorded to the State than was granted by the political economists of the school of Adam Smith. From the incontestable necessity of Government action in such matters as factory labour and the education of the humbler classes, these writers very clearly give us to understand that they desire to proceed to a system of Protectionism in commercial policy, and to the revival of that fostering influence, once regarded as all-powerful, by which Governments formerly sought to rear native manufactures under natural conditions most unfavourable. Every one, on a moment's reflection, knows that the true causes why manufacturers in Piedmont or Lombardy could not stand against an English or Belgian competition are the want in Piedmont and Lombardy of coal and iron, and of a population long trained to manufacturing pursuits. The present Italian Protectionists try to keep these facts as much as possible in the background, and to obscure the whole question by vague and cloudy theories on the action of the State. In the migratory commission of inquiry, held at the commencement of last year, their views were in various cities for the first time publicly avowed. At the commencement of the present year it was resolved to open, in the same sense, a theoretical campaign. With this view a congress was held at Milan. It was not very successful, but one of the resolutions come to was to found in as many Italian cities as possible branch clubs or societies, all based on the common principle of invoking in commercial and industrial matters a more direct action on the part of Government. Meanwhile the partisans of Free Trade, or, to speak more precisely and correctly, those who regarded this new movement as a mere mask to cover Protectionist tendencies, were not idle. Professor Francesco Ferrara, generally regarded as by far the most learned of living Italian economists, led the way in a very powerful article, contributed to the *Nuova Antologia* of Florence, in last August. The article was entitled 'Economic Germanism in Italy.' In this paper the German professorial or academic socialists, and their Italian disciples of the Lombardo-Venetian school

– such was the name given to them by Ferrara – were roughly handled. In fact, it was a regular throwing down of the gauntlet to the new party. That gauntlet was taken up in the next number of the same periodical by Luigi Luzzatti, formerly professor at Padua, Secretary-General some few years ago of the Ministry of Agriculture and Commerce, and at present one of the most active members of the Chamber of Deputies. Luzzatti's acceptance of the challenge was in itself a reply to one of the taunts that this new Protectionist party was acephalous; and Luzzatti, beyond all question, is the animating spirit of this new school of Italian Protectionists: the establishment of the committee of inquiry was mainly his work; the Milan congress was brought together through his efforts; the two journals of the party which have appeared in succession at Rome and Padua have owed to him their inspiration; and the leading part which he is now taking in the negotiations for the renewal of the Commercial Treaties with France, Austria, and Switzerland will certainly not be found in contradiction with these antecedents. The Free Traders, on the other hand, have established in Florence a most ably-conducted weekly organ, *L'Economista*; and one of their earliest proposals, when organising themselves for regular action, was that of an 'Adam Smith Club.' Nothing, indeed, is more remarkable in all this movement than the unceasing war waged around the name and the fame of Adam Smith. The most eloquent passages in Ferrara's article are those in which he vindicates the glory of the Scottish economist from the sneers of his German and Italian detractors. Not the least significant passage in Luzzatti's reply is one in which he describes Adam Smith as a creature like Rousseau, of the 'age of reason,' which aspired to build 'universal' truths on metaphysical premises, and dealt with man apart from his historical antecedents and social surroundings.

There is much truth in the remark of Ferrara, that in all this glorification of the State its admirers overlook the very prosaic fact that no such thing as an ideal State exists, and that the actual State is simply the men who for the time being govern it. France is a socialist State when confided to the direction of M. Louis Blanc, becomes an enlightened Free Trading State so far and so long as it reflects the economic views of a Napoleon III., and reverts to a very pristine condition of Protectionism in so far as it is controlled and governed by M. Thiers. Italy was a Free Trading State under Count Cavour. His disciple and successor, the present Premier, Signor Minghetti, loudly protests that he has not abandoned Count Cavour's commercial policy. If such be really the case, why has he entrusted the practical direction of the very important negotiations for the renewal of the Commercial Treaties between Italy and other countries to a politician professing, as openly as circumstances will allow, Protectionist principles? The plain fact is, that in commercial policy the present Italian Premier wishes at once to keep his cake and to eat his cake – to gratify the wishes and secure the parliamentary support of the Protectionist interest in Northern Italy, and yet not to forfeit the prestige of commercial freedom which the Italian Government has inherited from Count Cavour.

Facts, however, in such questions are stronger than all theories, and it must somewhat have startled the partisans of Italian Protectionism to read, ten days ago, in the columns of the semi-official *Opinione*, the announcement that Italy must abandon all participation in next year's Philadelphia Exhibition, because the high Protective tariffs of the United States completely excluded any prospect of Italian industry and commerce deriving benefit from the same. The confession was not the less instructive because made in the columns of the very journal which a few weeks before had, notoriously under Signor Luzzatti's inspiration, been breaking out into lofty Protectionist dithyrambics on the future triumphs in store for the native industry of Italy.

What the members of the Cobden Club have the right to expect at the hands of the present Italian Cabinet is, that its head, the Prime Minister Minghetti, shall not in practical statesmanship abandon the principles and forego the hopes to which the patriot writer Minghetti gave frank and fearless utterance at the very moment when Mr. Cobden achieved his victories.

Signor Minghetti's essay on the reform of the English Corn-Laws, and on the immense benefits likely to accrue to Italy from the same, written in 1846, and republished three years ago by the author, may be profitably recommended to the perusal of the new school of Italian economists. As lovers of their country, they will rejoice that the prospects of a more extended national commerce, united in Signor Minghetti's speculations with a possible Italian customs' league, may now be realised by the energies of a single undivided state. They will feel no less gratification from the fact that the return of Eastern commerce to its ancient European channels has already in part fulfilled the glowing predictions contained in Signor Minghetti's concluding sentences. But they may also, it must be hoped, feel some misgivings on the soundness of their Protectionist views, when they read Signor Minghetti's scathing exposure in a few sentences of the Protectionist fallacies. And if they dwell in the fitting spirit on the eloquent picture presented by the author, of the economic apostleship of Richard Cobden and his fellow-labourers, they will perhaps carry away the impression that a blind antipathy to Cobdenism is not the best preparation for negotiating new commercial treaties, forming as it does a painful contrast to the aspirations and hopes of the patriot statesman who, under Pope Gregory XVI.'s grim and gloomy reign, hailed in Cobdenism a most welcome guarantee of Italian prosperity and progress.

I have the honour to be, Gentlemen,
Very sincerely yours,
JAMES MONTGOMERY STUART.

The PROSPECTS of FREE TRADE in the UNITED STATES.

From the Hon. DAVID A. WELLS.

July 12, 1875.

MY DEAR SIR, – Although it has not been possible for me to accept your kind invitation to be present at the annual re-union of the Cobden Club on the 17th, I have the pleasure of being able to report to you a marked progress in the United States during the past year, in the direction of national emancipation from legislative restrictions on the freedom of extra-territorial trade and commercial intercourse. To those accustomed to judge of progress by outward manifestations only, and who are not cognisant of quiet changes taking place beneath the surface, this assertion may not seem warranted; for the friends of Free Trade have no special agency in the United States, as they had a few years ago, devoted to the work of disseminating economic truths, while 'Free Trade' and 'Protection' alike have so ceased to be discussed generally by the press, that in the opinion of some both subjects are no longer living issues before the country. But during all this time the people of the United States have been learning more rapidly than ever before in that costly school which nations, alike with individuals, seem to prefer to any other – namely, the school of experience.

For fifteen years now the experiment of '*Protection to home industry*' has been tried in the United States on the largest scale, and under the most favourable circumstances for success that the world has ever seen; and under its influence the domestic industry of the country, to use a slang expression, 'has been getting no better very fast.' Every prophecy so confidently made in the past as to the results of Protection in inducing national prosperity has been falsified; and one has only to pick out the separate industries which have been especially protected to find out the ones which are more especially unprofitable and dependent. Thus, in the manufacture of pig-iron, excessive profits have given rise to such excessive competition as to render the whole business ruinously unprofitable: a condition of affairs from which there can be no recovery, except through a continued suspension or curtailment of production, the utter abandonment of many furnaces, and the utter loss of a vast amount of recklessly invested capital. In the manufacture of silk, the manufacturers, although enjoying for many years the protection of a *sixty* per cent. duty on all manufactured imports, and a free admission of all raw material, are desirous of a still higher duty, and unanimously of the opinion that an abatement of the existing duties to even the slightest degree would be to them altogether ruinous. In the manufacture of wool – an industry in which the representatives of Protection were allowed to dictate without interference the exact measure of Protection which seemed then desirable, and caused the enactment of duties ranging from fifty to one hundred and fifty per cent. – it is sufficient to say that the existing depression and stagnation is without parallel: eight of the principal mills of the country having been sold, on compulsion, within a comparatively recent period, for much less than *fifty* per cent. of their cost of construction; the Glendam Mills in particular – one of the largest and best equipped woollen establishments in the United States, advantageously located on the Hudson, about fifty miles above New York, and representing over one million of dollars paid in – having changed hands since the first of April last, for a consideration of less than two hundred thousand dollars. Possessing also mines of copper of such unexampled richness, that their owners are able to export their products to Europe, and sell the same at a profit in competition with all the world, the copper manufacturers and copper consumers of the United States have been obliged, through the agency of the tariff, to pay a higher price in their own market for copper, than that at which the same article, the product of the same mines, has been offered to the consumers of other countries. And coming down to the administration of a tariff whose average rate of duty approximates forty per cent., it is a fact not to be denied, that if the Federal Government, during the last eight years, had carried out the intent of its representative officials, it would have arraigned the reputation and impaired the credit of nearly every important mercantile house in the city of New York engaged in foreign commercial transactions.

All these things the people of the United States have noticed and thought about; and no teachers have been needed to convey and impress the full meaning of the involved lesson, so that if to-day the further continuance of the Protective policy on the part of the nation could be submitted to a popular vote, I have no question that Protection would go under by a most decisive adverse majority.

The following are additional facts confirmatory of the above conclusion. 1st. There are now no important newspapers in the United States, outside of Pennsylvania, which especially advocate and defend Protection, except such as capitalist manufacturers have organised or bought up for such special purpose, and have caused to be edited under instructions. American journals that exist by their own merit do not walk in the paths of Protection, even if they do not advocate Free Trade. 2nd. Outside of the State of Pennsylvania, it would be difficult to name one American university, college, or school of high character in the teaching of which Protection is not condemned as an unsound economic system, antagonistic alike to civilisation and material development. Furthermore, in most American institutions of learning a belief in Protection would be regarded as disqualifying a person for teaching political economy, almost to the same extent as would a belief in the communistic views of Prudhomme, or the fiscal theories of John Law. 3rd. Of the two great political parties which divide the country, one – the Democratic, which may fairly be held to represent at least one-half of the population – is nearly unanimous in holding as an essential political principle, 'that taxation should never be imposed for any purpose other than revenue;' while no inconsiderable part of the other great party – the Republican – also makes positive affirmation of a belief in the same doctrine.

I think, therefore, I am warranted in asserting that the time draws near when the people of the United States will demonstrate by legislation that they are fully satisfied of the utter unprofitableness of the doctrine, 'that the way to get rich is for everybody to give as much as possible for everything,' and that scarcity and high prices are productive of abundance.

I am, yours very cordially,
DAVID A. WELLS.

From HORACE WHITE, Esq., *Editor of the Chicago 'Tribune,' U.S.A.*

London, June 28, 1875.

MY DEAR SIR, – Being unable to attend the annual dinner of the Cobden Club on the 17th proximo, I comply with your request that I should give some account of the progress of Free Trade opinion in the United States.

The commercial and industrial condition of the United States at the present time is one of severe depression, being part and parcel of the panic of September, 1873. This depression has perhaps been greatest in the iron trade. A large number of furnaces and mills, started under the stimulus of high Protective duties and rapid railway extension, have suspended operations and been sold out under the hammer at a fraction of their original cost. Others maintain a precarious existence on a declining market, and in the midst of angry strifes with their workmen. For the first time since the year 1861, when the Morrill tariff was enacted, we have heard no invocation of Congress on the part of the ruined ironmasters to bolster them up with higher duties, and for the obvious reason that the present deplorable condition has come upon them at a period of the highest duties that the country could by any means be brought to bear. And what is true of the iron trade is true to a less extent of all the other protected trades. With all their audacity, they have not the assurance to charge their woes to the account of Free Trade. Their calamity has come in the teeth of the most grinding and indefensible tariff that the ingenuity of man could conceive. Instead of calling for more tariff, some of their most prominent leaders are calling for an addition to the volume of depreciated paper currency – a device no less dishonest and disastrous than the Protective system in which they and their customers are floundering. But their appeal will be altogether in vain.

The state of facts to which I have alluded, viz., a great commercial crisis in the face and eyes of a high Protective tariff – so contrary to the whole philosophy of Protection – has arrested the attention of large numbers of the honest believers in the system, and thus many ears have been opened to Free Trade arguments that were formerly closed to us. The farmers of the Western States, who are the principal sufferers by the Protective system, have taken more decided steps during the past eighteen months toward the emancipation of trade than I have observed in the previous ten or twelve years. The National Board of Trade, an organisation composed of delegates from local commercial bodies, has also been moving gradually but decidedly in the same direction. The State of Massachusetts contains an active and most intelligent body of Free Trade thinkers and workers, whose influence is perceptibly increasing, although the political power of the State is still dominated by the special interests which the tariff was intended to favour.

The causes to which I have referred, although to a large extent extraneous and accidental, have been potent in preparing the public mind to receive the truths of Free Trade; and I am quite convinced that there has been no time since the Protective system got the upper hand with us when it was so weak and so liable to be overthrown as now. As it required a period of dire distress to overturn the same system in England, so it seems that a period of great stringency and depression is most favourable to Revenue reform with us. There is no special Free Trade agitation in the United States now, but the discussion is more general, more temperate, and more clearly to the advantage of the friends of Free Trade than it has been at times when special efforts were on foot.

These are, in brief, my views of the present drift of public opinion in the United States on the subject which you have asked me to write about.

I am, Sir, your most obedient Servant,

HORACE WHITE.

From WILLIAM LLOYD GARRISON, Esq., *of Boston, U.S.A.*

Boston, July 1st, 1875.

DEAR SIR, – I have received your official notice of the time of the annual dinner at Greenwich, on the 17th instant. An intervening ocean will prevent my bodily attendance; but in understanding, heart, and soul I shall certainly be with the Club on the occasion referred to, to join in paying a grateful tribute to the memory of him whose honoured name it bears; to signify my hearty approval of the principles of political economy and international amity it so ably inculcates under his leadership (for, 'though dead, he yet speaketh'); to respond to every noble sentiment in recognition of those ties of common relationships, common rights, common interests, and common needs which should bind the nations of the earth indissolubly together for the common welfare.

It is not less pitiable than strange that a Republic claiming to be the most enlightened on earth, and never failing annually to rehearse with special emphasis in the hearing of the world the grand 'self-evident truths' set forth in its boasted Declaration of Independence, should still be found adhering to a policy of 'Protection,' so called, which is as narrow in spirit and as exclusive in aim as it is irrational in theory and injurious in practice. But as, under that Declaration, it required the sad experience of almost ninety years before a vast and hideous system of chattel slavery could be abolished – and then only through Divine retribution – the marvel is not so great that the same people should be clinging to a delusion, in regard to what concerns their best interests, incomparably less demoralising in its tendency and disastrous in its operation.

For one, I do not hesitate to avow myself to be a Free Trader to an illimitable extent, without any other restraint or drawback than the ordinary risk of industrial interchange and commercial enterprise, in all those productions which serve to comfort and bless mankind. To innocent and serviceable exchange, sale or purchase, let no selfish barrier be erected. As freely as waters run or as winds blow, let all peoples present the finest efforts of their skill and industry, the richest specimens of their mineral resources, the best results of their agricultural and manufacturing pursuits, in a world's market, to be bought and distributed *ad libitum*, according to the needs, tastes, and purchasing means of the parties interested; interdicting only what in itself is so fraught with evil as to imperil the general safety and welfare. Protection by all justifiable methods against hostile invasion by a foreign enemy; protection against infectious or contagious diseases by stringently regulated intercourse for the time being; protection against wrongs and outrages perpetrated upon the citizens of one country by another; protection against whatever is destructive of the rights and liberties of a people – all this is in accordance with the instinct of self-preservation. But protection against the achievements of human skill, invention, labour and enterprise, in the matter of food, clothing, and other material wants, because of a geographical separation, and on the plea of advancing the home interests, is as preposterous as would be an attempt to regulate the law of gravitation by legislative enactment. The welfare of one portion of the globe is not above that of any other; for mankind are one in relationship and destiny, and only those principles should be acted upon in human intercourse which are universal and world-embracing, and which cannot be violated with impunity.

Yours for 'Liberty, Equality, Fraternity,'

Wm. LLOYD GARRISON.

DISCUSSION ON THE TREATIES OF COMMERCE AND PUBLIC OPINION IN EUROPE,

At a Meeting of the Political Economy Society of Paris,

August 6th, 1875.

M. MICHEL CHEVALIER PRESIDING.

THIS meeting was attended, in response to an invitation, by several foreign *savants*, who had come to Paris to take part in the labours of the Congress of Geographical Science, as well as French members of the Congress, and deputies of the National Assembly.

The President delivered an address, in which he thanked the strangers who had honoured the meeting by their presence, and expressed his pleasure at seeing them assembled with the French *savants* on the neutral ground of scientific discussion. Every international congress, he said, even if military affairs be the subject, should have the effect of establishing peace and international harmony, because it is impossible for distinguished men to assemble and exchange their ideas and their lights without conceiving sentiments of mutual esteem and sympathy. But the present congress, thank God, had nothing to do with war. M. Chevalier saw with pleasure among those present Economists and Statisticians – men, therefore, devoted to identical studies; for statistics are inseparable from Political Economy, and the organisers of the National Institute understood this when they united in the same section these twin sciences, both closely allied to geography, from which they derive precious lessons and useful co-operation. What, in fact, is Political Economy but the science of exchanges? and how could exchange, without which neither society nor civilisation could exist, be established between nations, if they knew nothing of one another? The knowledge of geography, taken in the widest sense, as it is understood and taught by a learned academician, a member of the Society of Political Economy, is therefore indispensable to the development of exchanges, on which depends the prosperity of nations. Now, geographical science owes its progress in great measure, no doubt, to brave explorers such as Cook, Lapeyrouse, Bougainville, Franklin, Livingstone; but it is indebted also to those industrious men who patiently study the manners, the institutions, the products, the intellectual and material resources of nations, and who are all more or less Economists; and all are, or are becoming, adherents of commercial freedom. This freedom, as every one knows, is one of the objects which Economists pursue with the greatest ardour, because they see in it the solution of one of the greatest social and international problems of our age. M. Chevalier said that he would be glad if the foreign Economists present at the meeting would give some information respecting the economical ideas which appear to them to prevail in the councils of their respective governments, and in the public opinion of their respective countries, and to say whether the Commercial Treaties which have nearly expired appeared to them to have some chance of being renewed on a liberal basis.

Baron VON CZŒRNIG, Corresponding Member of the Academy of Moral and Political Science, late President of the Geographical Society of Vienna, was the senior among the Statisticians present at the meeting. He has for a long time been Director of Statistics for the Austro-Hungarian Empire, and he bore witness to the happy results produced in that empire by the lowering of the customs' duties, and the other barriers which the old economy of the State opposed to international exchanges. In consequence of economic reforms, the imports had been seen doubled, tripled, quadrupled from year to year. Not, he said, that there is no Protectionist party in Austria, but there is good ground for hoping that it will not succeed. A congress of liberal Economists has assembled this year at Vienna, with the object of acting on the deputies who will have to renew or modify the Treaties of Commerce; and everything leads one to believe that these treaties will continue the true, nay, still more pronounced expression of the progressive ideas which dictated them.

Signor PERUZZI, a member of the Italian Parliament, Mayor of Florence, would not venture to repeat the assurances which he gave some years ago at a banquet of Economists assembled at Paris, on the occasion of the International Exhibition, and which was attended by one of his friends, the eminent Economist, Signor Luzzatti, who shared his convictions then more than he does now. They conversed on that occasion about the probable consequences of Commercial Treaties, so differently estimated in Italy. They discussed also the Treaty of Navigation, which, according to many Italians, must ruin the Ligurian coasting-service for the benefit of that of Marseilles. Now it is found, after practical experience, that the Ligurian coasting-service has never been so prosperous before. Still, the renewal of the treaties may meet with some obstacles in Italy. In the first place, the Italian Parliament, it is well known, established in 1870 an inconvertible paper-currency, which, like all measures of the kind, has produced unexpected results. Thus the currency in question constitutes a real system of protection, a protection very costly for the industries which are supported in the interior of the country, while the other industries – and likewise the consumers (who are no more heeded than the theorists) – are suffering seriously by it. Another obstacle to the renewal of the treaties, which we have to dread, is the poverty of the Exchequer and the necessity which the Government alleges in Italy, as elsewhere, of raising money by all means at its disposal. We hear people talk also of the law of compensation, which obliges us, they say, to impose on foreign merchandise charges equivalent to those borne by the commerce and industry of the country. Lastly, Signor Peruzzi expressed misgivings with regard to the influence of the new School of Economy which was formed a short time ago in Italy, and which is demanding the intervention of the State in questions of exchange and labour. This school has founded a society under the direction of Signor Luzzatti, and there is a rival society, the counterpart of it, on his own side, of which Signor Peruzzi has been elected President. The latter has entitled itself after Adam Smith, thus asserting its firm attachment to the liberal doctrines propounded by the great English publicist. The Economists who give the tone to the new school do not positively differ from those of the old, as far as concerns commercial freedom; but there is reason to fear, that, in virtue of the large part which they assign to the State in the direction of economic movements, they will suffer themselves to be drawn into approving the Protectionist measures which may be proposed. The two schools are represented in the Italian Parliament. Signor Peruzzi foresees that the struggle between them will be a hard one; he declares that the banner of commercial freedom shall be lifted high by his friends and himself, but he is not absolutely sure of the issue of the debate on the Treaties of Commerce.

Dr. JULIUS FAUCHER, Editor of the *Quarterly Review of Political Economy*, Berlin, trusts that the economic policy inaugurated by the Treaties of Commerce will be maintained in Germany. The Protectionists there are not numerous nor influential, especially in the Parliament, and the attempts at reaction which have been made have met with no success. Moreover, the situation of Germany counsels fidelity to the principle of Free Trade. Germany has no inconvertible paper-currency; she has received a large amount of gold from France – that is to say, the Government has received it, not the people. This influx of specie has caused a general rise of prices; her imports have largely exceeded her exports, and the gold has returned to France through a thousand channels. But these circumstances have not shaken the friends of Free Trade, who only think of securing the future, and they, too, are engaged in a struggle, often very lively, with the Economists of the new school, whom they call the 'Socialists of the Pulpit.' There will be, next year, a Congress of Economists at Munich. We shall see if the Protectionists are represented there; but Dr. Faucher strongly doubts it.

Herr ENGEL, Director of Statistics for the Kingdom of Prussia, stated confidently that the division between the new and the old school of Economists is not so deep as is represented, and that both are agreed in favour of promoting exchanges by the lowering of customs' duties. The Statistical Bureau of Berlin is a real school, a nursery of Economists, from which Dr. Faucher himself came, and which produces neither Socialists nor Protectionists. The question between the two schools, to which reference had been made, is simply, whether in economic affairs the State ought to be reduced to the part of night-watchman, or whether it has an active and useful part to fulfil in production and exchange. The new school adheres to the latter doctrine, and M. Engel appeared to hold with it. In any case he emphatically exculpated this school from the Protectionist tendencies, of which it is suspected, and he declared that it is not in that quarter that Free Trade will find opponents.

Herr MEITZEN, Assistant Director of Statistics for Germany, knows all the young professors of the German Universities, and wishes to state that there are no Protectionists among them. He desired also to correct what Dr. Faucher had said regarding the economic situation of Germany of late years. Being in charge of the statistics of internal commerce, M. Meitzen well understands the facts, and he can affirm that the French milliards count for next to nothing in the excess of imports noticed by Dr. Faucher. This excess (considerable, it is true) is limited to cereals, meat, and metals (iron and copper), and is very simply explained. On the one hand, Germany has had bad harvests; she has been desolated by cattle-plague, which has forced her to go to foreign parts for cereals and meat. On the other hand, she has been obliged to purchase iron and other metals to satisfy the requirements arising from the development of her railways and her mining industries.

Herr UNFALVY, President of the Geographical Society of Pesth, said that economic questions in the present situation of Austro-Hungary were generally associated with the rivalry of the two parties in the Empire, but that, in relation to foreign countries, opinion was generally favourable on both sides to commercial freedom.

M. CLAPIER said that, having had the honour of belonging to the Commission appointed to examine the proposed tariff, which the Italian Government had laid before the French Government, he thought he might, without departing from the reserve imposed by negotiations still pending, furnish some information to the meeting on the subject. The treaty which existed between France and Italy, having been denounced with due notice, will cease to have effect during the course of next year. Italy has submitted to the French Government the draft of a tariff which she proposes to put in force at the expiration of the treaty. She has not formally proposed the renewal of the treaty, but she desires to take the opinion of the French Government on the tariff which she proposes to establish at home, so that nothing may interfere with the good understanding which exists between the two nations.

This communication raised a preliminary question: is it well for us to be linked with Italy by a formal and obligatory treaty? or, would it not be better to limit ourselves to an understanding which, maintaining nearly the present state of things, would leave to each of the two nations its liberty of action? A formal treaty appeared preferable to the majority of the Commission, as offering more security to industry, and rendering a longer term certain. The Commission therefore felt bound to examine and discuss the draft tariff submitted by Italy, on the supposition that it might serve as the basis of a treaty.

This tariff appeared to them the result of three distinct motives: – 1st. A desire to furnish supplies to the Italian treasury; this purely financial motive raised no objection. 2nd. A desire to convert *ad valorem* duties into specific. *Ad valorem* duties, though apparently more equitable, are nevertheless a source of disputes and frauds; the Italian Government loudly complains of them, and all Economists interested in the question recognise that this conversion is indispensable; but the transition from one species of legislation to another is not free from difficulties. Specific duties, founded on average values, have the inconvenience of weighing more heavily on common goods than on rich products, which is an economic mistake. This difficulty can only be escaped by dividing each species of product into a certain number of categories, and marking with great nicety the external signs and conditions of composition which are to serve as the basis of each category. The Italian draft exhibited unfortunate gaps in this respect; the French Government, enlightened by hints furnished by our principal manufactures, and by the stipulations of the English treaty, thought that it could point out these to Italy. 3rd. A certain Protectionist motive, revealed in several provisions of the draft tariff, gave occasion for some remarks on the part of the French Government. The Italian Government repudiated this intention, affirming that the maximum duty which it is proposed to place on foreign goods is not more than 10 per cent. The French Government admitted that duties restricted to this limit did not exceed the measure of protection which a State may reasonably accord to its industry, without doing violence to the good relations which exist with neighbouring States; and, taking note of this declaration, consented to make it the general basis of negotiations, with certain partial exceptions which circumstances might render necessary.

Signor PERUZZI reverted to some of the considerations which he had put forward, and which M. Clapier had just confirmed, while presenting them in a new aspect. As to the question which divides the Economists of the new school and the orthodox Economists, Signor Peruzzi, borrowing M. Engel's simile, said that in his opinion the State ought to be a 'night-and-day watchman,' but not to interfere in economic questions, otherwise than by clearing away the obstacles and the shackles, which, by paralysing exchange, prevent wealth from multiplying and prosperity from becoming general.

M. A DE BOUNSCHEN, President of the Geographical Society of St. Petersburg, briefly informed the meeting of the progress which has been effected in Russia since 1851 in economic ideas and circumstances. At that date, legislation being completely protectionist, the customs' duties were raised and industry slumbered. In 1857 there was a first revision of the tariffs, with some concessions made to liberal ideas; the duties were lowered and industry began to spring up. In 1867 there was a new revision and new concessions. The great cotton manufacture cried out for a protection, which it did not need; but the Government did not stop to listen to these complaints. As for the public, it remained neutral. Other special revisions have taken place since, and always with a tendency towards Free Trade. At the present time Russia, although protecting her iron manufacture, imports one hundred million pounds of foreign iron for her railways. She protects other industries also, but with exceptions so numerous that they reverse the rule. If the liberal intentions of the Government meet with impediments, it is on the part of France, from whom they ask only for reciprocity. In short, economic ideas are making progress, and one may hope that the next revision of the treaties will be favourable to the extension of exchanges.

M. BAUMHAUSER, Director of Statistics for the Netherlands, spoke of the treaty relating to the regulation of the sugar-duties, which interests, besides the Netherlands, Belgium, England, and France. The upshot of his evidence was that the general tendency in Holland is favourable to Free Trade.

M. CLAPIER then said: As the question of the sugar-duties is raised, I have the good fortune to be able to furnish some accurate information to the meeting on that subject; for I belong to the Parliamentary Commission to which this question is actually submitted.

You all know the convention of 1865. At that date there was a very keen contest between England, Holland, Belgium, and France, to get hold of the exportation of refined sugar to the great consuming countries. This contest issuing in the award on the part of each country of premiums on the exportation of refined sugar more than covering the duty paid on the importation of raw sugar, the convention of 1865 had for its object to place the four contracting powers on the same footing, and to provide against imported sugars being subjected to duties other than those paid by the sugars made or refined at home. This convention raised loud complaints on the part of England, who alleged that the French refiners had in the facilities provided by the French legislation an indirect premium, which crushed their own refinery; a certain number of the manufacturers of the home-grown sugar, making common cause with the English refiners, maintained that this indirect premium caused an enormous loss to the French exchequer, and under this impression the National Assembly decided that, at the expiration of the convention, which terminated on 1st August, 1875, the French refineries should be subjected to the excise. In the interval, England abolished all duties on sugar, thus leaving her market open to all nations. On the other hand, the French Government, not wishing to inflict the annoyances of the excise on her refineries except this excise should be equally established in the two other contracting countries, negotiations were opened. Belgium formally refused to establish the excise in her refineries, but she offered by way of compensation to reduce by half her internal duty on sugars, which reduced by half the indirect premium which her refiners possess in the facilities provided by her legislation. She offered also to raise by some degrees the tax on her beet-juice, subject to the system of simple *abonnement*. Holland did not oppose an absolute refusal to the establishment of the excise in her refineries, but before committing herself, she expressed a desire to know the system which would regulate the mode of application of the excise in France. France officially communicated a proposed scheme of regulations, but reserved the liberty to modify it according to the greater or less latitude of the Dutch regulations. Moreover, she showed herself determined to see the internal duty imposed on raw sugars, on their entry into the refinery, on the basis of their real richness, determined not by mere shades, but by chemical analysis and the observations of the saccharimeter. England, although not interested in the question, insisted nevertheless on intervening in the treaty, under a promise (which, coming from Lord Derby, costs her little) that if ever she re-establishes a duty on sugar at home, she will subject her refineries to the excise; taking advantage of this simple promise, she demands very peremptorily, as the fulfilment of a formal undertaking, that the French refineries should be subjected to the excise.

Such is the state of the question, and as its solution will require some further adjournment, the contracting parties have agreed to prolong the convention of 1865 to the month of March next; a law ratifying this agreement was passed by the French National Assembly at the end of last session.

This question, very difficult in itself – inasmuch as the legislature in intervening must conciliate at once the rights of the Treasury and those of the French and colonial sugar-producers with those of the sugar-refiners, and establish between the contracting nations, in default of an identical system which they reject, a system of compensation which maintains complete equality between them – is further complicated by the fact that we have now to deal with powerful competition outside the four contracting nations, such as that of Germany, of Hungary, and that of the United States, which must unquestionably destroy the equilibrium which is sought to be established by legislative combinations. The introduction of a system of impediments and restrictions such as are demanded must undoubtedly strike a blow against one of the fairest industries which France has created for twenty years, and demonstrate once more that both at home and abroad liberty, honest competition, the incessant improvement of the product, and reduction of the cost of production, are the surest basis of the commercial prosperity of a country.

M. Zemeroff, Director of Statistics, St. Petersburg, confirmed in a few words the information furnished by his fellow-countryman, M. de Bounschen.

Senor Fr. Coello, of Madrid, assured the meeting that in Spain opinion is favourable to Free Trade; and this tendency is conformable to the manifest interests of the country, which must desire an outlet for its agricultural and mineral products. Unhappily, Spanish publicists are concerned at present much more with politics than with economic science; the country is wasted in civil war;

but the speaker hoped that internal peace will shortly be re-established, and that the commercial relations of Spain with other countries, and particularly with France, will speedily resume their normal course.

M. Joseph Garnier summed up the explanation which had been given by the different speakers, and from which this salient fact appears among others, that the new school of economy formed in Germany and Italy agrees with the 'orthodox' school in demanding commercial freedom.

(*Translated from a Report in the Economiste Francais, August* 14, 1875.)

The Colonial World

Cosmopolite, *Free Trade and No Colonies. A Letter Addressed to Lord John Russell* (Edinburgh and London: Blackwood & Sons, 1848).

June 10, 1848.

My Lord,

Our colonial policy has of late years undergone so radical a change, and the results have already been so important and instructive, that the time appears to have now arrived when the wisdom of that policy and its probable consequences may be fairly made the subject of investigation.

In considering this subject, your Lordship is well aware that no assistance can be derived from the experience of other nations, whether ancient or modern; for, as our recent policy has been altogether peculiar and unprecedented, its wisdom must be tested solely by its own results. The principle upon which our colonial, and indeed the whole of our recent commercial legislation is based, is new in the history of civilised states. The doctrine of free exchange or unrestrained competition between nations, may be said to constitute the entire basis of that legislation. It has long been maintained by a certain section of the modern school of political economy, that this principle of universal competition is the true path to the material prosperity of nations; and after much contention this principle has been adopted by the British Legislature. If, therefore, it is right, it must necessarily admit of receiving full effect; if it is wrong, the farther it is carried out the more disastrous must be the results.

Now, it is obvious that this principle of competition is one derived from the notion of self-reliance or self-dependence. The state which adopts it necessarily presupposes that it is at least on a footing of equality with all others; for we cannot imagine any nation deliberately to expose itself to the rivalry of a neighbour its superior in all the great branches of industry. No nation will, in fact, adopt it unless it expects to derive immediate advantage from the change; because the commercial spirit, which necessarily directs the legislator upon this point, is the one of all others which looks to speedy results. And this consideration ought amply to account for the rejection of our Free-Trade principle by the statesmen both of Europe and America. Our legislators considered, whether justly or not I shall not now stop to inquire, that we had nothing to lose and everything to gain by a free competition with foreign states, while they seem to think that they have much to lose and nothing to gain by a free competition with us.

The same principle of freedom has been applied to our colonial as to our foreign commercial policy, and this circumstance leads me to the point upon which I have been induced to address your Lordship. If we examine, however cursorily, the colonial systems of all modern European states, we shall find that the connection between the mother country and its foreign settlements has been founded on the observance of a totally different principle. That connection has had its foundation on a system of mutual dependence and support. The very notion, indeed, of a modern colony implies dependence, while that of the parent state implies support, as well in a political as in a commercial sense: and under the colonial system of Great Britain a trade of reciprocity between the foreign dependency and the parent state was a natural result. Let us suppose that under that system the British North American provinces exchange their raw produce for the manufactured produce of the mother country; although such a trade, from its exclusive nature, may be liable to speculative objections, it is still, upon the whole, as Adam Smith has expressed it, 'greatly advantageous' to the parent state.[1] It is true, indeed, that England might be able to obtain her corn and timber from a cheaper market, but the loss which may arise from this circumstance is more than compensated by the gain she derives from the exclusive possession of the colony trade. Abolish the colonial system, and introduce in its place the principle of free competition, and a great change necessarily takes place. England finds that she can obtain her corn and timber at less cost from the Baltic than from America; and the Canadian provinces, in their turn, may find that they can buy their manufactures cheaper in Virginia than at Manchester. In such a case, supposing the free principle to be in full operation, it is obvious that the import and export trade between the colony and the parent state would greatly diminish, if it did not entirely cease. The colony trade would, in fact, be exchanged for a foreign trade; and this would be attended with a double result; for, in the first place, the more certain would be abandoned for the less certain market; and secondly, we should retain the responsibilities of our colonial sovereignty without its commercial advantages. Without participating, to any beneficial extent, in the trade of the colony, we should still be called upon to contribute to the expense of its maintenance in time of peace, and to defend it in time of war.

If it is alleged that, from our superiority in manufactures, or from any other cause, the case adduced is not likely to occur, I reply that that is no sufficient answer, because, if the universal freedom of trade is the true principle of commerce, we are bound to follow that principle through all its legitimate consequences. In the foregoing case, however, I have assumed that the industry and

---

1 Vol. ii. p. 445.

commerce of the British colony have not suffered from foreign competition; I have only assumed that they have found a different channel. But, to take a further illustration from existing circumstances, it is now a matter of certainty that the British colonies in the West Indies are unable, in their present condition, to compete in the production of sugar with Cuba and Brazil. Carry out the free system to its full extent, and in all probability the cultivation, in a commercial sense, of these colonies, must very shortly cease. The most ardent advocates of that system are now led to this too palpable conclusion. Struck, indeed, by the impending destruction of so great an amount of capital, but unwilling to question the truth of their theory, they boldly assume that the ruin of our sugar colonies was inevitable; but, while they are eloquent upon the subject of past imprudence, they have failed to enlighten us as to the future; they have failed to inform us whether the burden of maintaining these showy, but profitless appendages, is to fall upon the mother country; and yet, if we pursue our present course, there seems to be no choice between this bitter alternative and unconditional abandonment.

While upon the subject of these unfortunate colonies I cannot refrain from noticing a popular error, which may be said to have formed the groundwork of our recent West Indian legislation. It was asserted, on the authority of certain economists, that free labour is cheaper than slave labour, and that our colonists had therefore nothing to fear from the competition of the latter. This opinion may be traced to Adam Smith, who, in one portion of his work, states his reasons generally for entertaining it. In another, however, he cites an example in proof of this opinion, by referring to a statement of Montesquieu, to the effect that the Hungarian mines were wrought at less expense by free men than the Turkish mines, on the neighbouring frontier, by slaves.[1] There seems to be no reason for questioning the truth of this statement; but general conclusions can seldom be safely drawn from isolated facts. We have now for the last ten years had a continued trial of free labour in our East Indian dominions, where it is both cheap and abundant; but that which may be true on the banks of the Danube has not been proved to be true on the banks of the Ganges; for the planter of Bengal is unable to compete in the production of sugar with the slave-owner of Brazil. Again, if we look to the West Indies, we find that the island of Barbadoes, although for a long period in a state of high cultivation, and plentifully supplied with labour, is equally unable to compete with the neighbouring island of Cuba. The opinion in question, therefore, has not been proved to be correct; and if we were to investigate the cause of the apparent inconsistency of the experience of Montesquieu with our own, we should most probably find it in the simple fact that the Turk is a more humane taskmaster than the Brazilian or the Spaniard.

1   Vol. iii. p. 39.

Nor can the partial success of free labour in Porto Rico be referred to as at all conclusive of the truth of Adam Smith's theory. By far the greater portion of that island being occupied by small proprietors of European descent, who cultivate their plantations in many instances with their own hands, the state of society in that island is so totally different from that of the neighbouring British colonies that no satisfactory comparison can be drawn between them.[1] Judging, therefore, from the experience of the present age, it is impossible to resist the melancholy conclusion, that the balance of testimony is decidedly against the truth of the proposition contended for by Adam Smith, and relied upon by a great portion of his followers.

But to return to our new commercial system, it is obvious that, supposing it to be in full operation, no trade will be carried on between England and her colonies unless the advantages to be derived from that trade are more immediate and direct than those which would be derived from an intercourse with foreign states. And as there are few articles of British colonial growth which cannot be obtained at less cost from foreign states, it follows that the commercial ties between the colonies and the mother country must become rapidly weakened, and liable to be snapped asunder at any time when cheaper markets may be discovered.

I do not think, my Lord, that I have over-stated the probable consequences of our recent legislation. It would, indeed, be an easy matter to fill pages with startling evidence of Canadian disaffection and West Indian despair – to dwell on the vast importance, at the present time, of emigration, and to point out the mighty augmentation of imperial power which colonial dominion has brought to England. But as the whole of our recent commercial policy has been based on a certain defined course of action, I prefer tracing that principle to its source, in order to ascertain, if possible, whether it is just in theory, although it may have hitherto proved unsatisfactory in practice.

On the occasion of the introduction of the budget for the present session of parliament, your Lordship took occasion to state, more than once, in order apparently to silence all objection, that our new commercial policy had been adopted in accordance with the opinions of Adam Smith. But your Lordship is well aware that that philosopher is not infallible; and there are strong reasons for believing that, in our recent commercial changes, we have generally rejected his opinions when they happen to be right, and adopted them when they happen to be wrong.

In confirmation of this assertion, I do not allude to his well-known opinion on the navigation laws, which are now under the consideration of the Legislature. I allude more particularly to his opinion upon a matter of even more fundamental importance, and which, in fact, goes directly to the root of the whole doctrine of free trade.

---

1 See Colonel Flinter's work on Porto Rico, *passim*.

Adam Smith states that the home trade is twice as advantageous, in a national point of view, as the foreign trade; and as the proposition is one, in an economic sense, of the very highest importance, I shall give it in his own words: –

'The capital which is employed in purchasing in one part of the country, in order to sell in another the produce of the industry of that country, generally replaces, by every such operation, *two* distinct capitals that had both been employed in the agriculture or manufactures of that country, and thereby enables them to continue that employment. When it sends out from the residence of the merchant a certain value of commodities, it generally brings back in return at least an equal value of other commodities. When both are the produce of domestic industry, it necessarily replaces, by every such operation, *two* distinct capitals which had both been employed in supporting productive labour, and thereby enables them to continue that support. The capital which sends Scotch manufactures to London, and brings back English corn and manufactures to Edinburgh, necessarily replaces, by every such operation, *two* British capitals which had both been employed in the agriculture or manufactures of Great Britain.

'The capital employed in purchasing foreign goods for home consumption, when this purchase is made with the produce of domestic industry, replaces also, by every such operation, *two* distinct capitals, but *one* of them only is employed in supporting domestic industry. The capital which sends British goods to Portugal, and brings back Portuguese goods to Great Britain, replaces, by every such operation, only *one* British capital: the other is a Portuguese one. Though the returns, therefore, of the foreign trade of consumption should be as quick as those of the home trade, the capital employed in it will give but *one half* of the encouragement to the industry or productive labour of the country.'[1]

It is remarkable that the researches of the most eminent of the French economists have led him to precisely the same conclusion. '*The British Government*,' observes M. Say, 'seems not to have perceived that the most profitable sales to a nation are those made by one individual to another *within* the nation, for these latter imply a national production of *two* values, the value sold and that given in exchange.'[2] How far this remark may be applicable to the recent commercial policy of the British Government I shall leave your Lordship to determine; but it is almost superfluous to observe that the opinions of these two authorities – and none higher can be produced in their respective countries – are obviously and necessarily inconsistent with the principle of free trade, or universal competition. If the home trade is more advantageous than the foreign, why allow the latter, in any instance, to displace the former? for even if foreign nations, as was predicted, were to reciprocate with us, which they do not, the free exchange of

1 Vol. ii. book ii. chap. v. p. 62.
2 Say's Works, translated by Prinsep, vol. i. p. 248.

our produce with theirs would, according to the opinions of Smith and Say, be only half as advantageous as if an exchange took place within the nation itself.

In further corroboration of his opinion, M. Say, in another place, makes the following remarks: –

'The most productive employment of capital for the country in general, after that laid out on the land, is that of manufactures and the home trade; because it puts in activity an industry of which the profits are gained in the country, while those capitals which are employed in foreign commerce make the industry and lands of all countries to be productive without distinction.'[1]

Again, these views entirely coincide with those of Adam Smith, while treating of the different employments of capital. 'After agriculture,' he says, 'the capital employed in manufactures puts into motion the greatest quantity of productive labour, and adds the greatest value to the annual produce. That which is employed in the trade of exportation has the *least* effect of any of the three.'[2]

It will be observed, therefore, that the commercial legislation of the last six years has been mainly directed to the increase of that branch of industry which Adam Smith considered the least advantageous to the state.

Adam Smith does not indeed appear to have perceived that the inferences to be drawn from his opinion, as to the comparative advantageousness of the home and foreign trade, were at variance with other portions of his work. But later writers, observing that they stood directly opposed to the universal freedom of trade which they advocated, were compelled to question the doctrine of Smith and Say upon this fundamental point. Mr. Ricardo has accordingly constructed an argument to show that that doctrine is erroneous.[3] He found it necessary to overthrow the theory of Smith and Say, before he established the truth of his own; but he has entirely failed in the attempt. Any one who will examine his argument, will find that it is based upon a palpable fallacy, which it is surprising should have escaped so acute a reasoner.[4] Mr. M'Culloch has since come to his aid, and assailed the position of the two great economists, but with no better success than his predecessor.[5]

The question, then, remains precisely where it was left by Smith and Say; and if their opinion is correct, there is an end of the so-called doctrine of 'free trade.'

1 See 'Political Economy,' by Ricardo, who cites this passage, p. 492.
2 Vol. ii. p. 58.
3 Ricardo's 'Political Economy,' p. 444.
4 See 'Principles of Political Economy,' by William Atkinson, where this fallacy has been ably exposed, p. 17.
5 See M'Culloch's 'Commerce,' p. 13, *et seq*. In a former work Mr. M'Culloch stated broadly that the question admitted of '*no satisfactory solution.*' – *Prin. of Pol. Economy*, p. 147. In the work first cited, however, he qualifies this assertion by stating that the question '*does not, perhaps, admit of any very satisfactory solution.*' We need not be surprised to find, therefore, that the arguments he has brought forward to overthrow the position of Smith and Say are 'unsatisfactory' and inconclusive.

If it is erroneous, it is incumbent upon the advocates of the latter system to show it to be so.

With all submission to your Lordship, therefore, I maintain that we have not adopted the more matured opinions of Adam Smith and the better informed economists; we have become the disciples of a newer and a bolder school, and allowed our policy to be guided by the theories of legislators who dream of never-failing markets and eternal peace. I do not, indeed, maintain that our old commercial system was incapable of improvement; but our object has been, not to amend, but to destroy. We have thrown away the substance for the shadow. We are deliberately ruining our colonial, in the mere hope of extending our foreign trade; we are encouraging the continental artisan at the expense of our own. Nor is it difficult to account for the temporary success of this national delusion. It was addressed as well to the selfish passions of the many, as to the more elevated sentiments of the few; for while the capitalist and the trader anticipated a speedy increase of their profits, the philanthropist contemplated with satisfaction the idea of a vast union of civilised nations, bound by the peaceful ties of commercial brotherhood. Of the mode in which these captivating doctrines obtained their temporary triumph – of itinerant agitation and political apostacy – I shall not speak; but of all the gross delusions to which they have given rise, none surpassed the assumption that they would ameliorate the condition of the labouring class. It is evident that, of all classes, they are the most exposed to foreign competition; and it is a significant fact, that the localities in which the greatest amount of destitution at present prevails, are those which may be supposed to suffer most from the importation of commodities from abroad. There is more distress, comparatively speaking, in London and in Nottingham, than in Manchester and Liverpool. If we refer to the actual condition of national industry, as exhibited by the last published returns of the Board of Trade, we find that during the month ending the 5th of May, there was a falling off in the gross value of our exports, of 1,483,046*l*. as compared with the same period in 1847.[1]

This enormous diminution of our export trade may, no doubt, be accounted for in a great measure from the present unsettled state of Europe. But the same cause ought to affect our imports; yet of these there has been a large and general increase. In the article of silk manufactures[2] alone, the imports, during the period referred to, nearly double those of 1847. What precise effect these increased importations may have on our domestic industry, I shall not take upon myself to determine; but it is well worthy of remark that the classes most likely to be injured by them, and who, not two years since, were ardent supporters of

---

1   See the city article of the 'Times' of June 9, 1848.

2   Silk manufactures for home consumption, in 1847, 39,668 lbs.; in 1848, 72,570 lbs. See 'Times' of the same date.

the free trade movement, are now beginning to demand protection against the foreign producer.[1]

It is to be observed, that the first victims of free trade are the weaker and more dependent interests of the state – viz., our working classes at home and our colonists abroad. But the evil cannot rest there, for, in the political, as in the physical frame, the serious injury of a part must affect the whole; and it is not difficult to foresee the war of conflicting interests which we are still destined to witness. It has, indeed, been customary of late to treat the question of free trade as settled, and to thrust aside its opponents as bigots who would vote back the Stuarts or restore the Heptarchy. But it is neither probable nor desirable that the manufacturing interest should retain its present influence in the councils of the nation; and there are symptoms of reaction and resistance now abroad which promise its speedy diminution. There is no truth of history more satisfactorily established by the unvarying experience of all countries and all ages, than that manufacturing prosperity is variable and ephemeral, when compared with that derived from the cultivation of the land. Yet it is for the supposed aggrandisement of this one interest that the whole of our recent policy has been directed. But a few months more and the British agriculturist will be exposed to the competition of the Russian serf, as our colonist now is to that of the blood-stained slave of Cuba. But a few years more, and the mill-owners of Lancashire may find themselves engaged in a struggle of life and death with the manufacturers of the United States. Before that time arrives, however, the nation may have awakened from its delusion. We may have discovered that a moderate restriction upon the importation of foreign grain may have the effect, not only of preserving our agriculture, but of increasing a falling revenue, without materially enhancing the price of corn. We may have discovered the value of our colonial empire, which the presumptuous quackeries of a pretended science have placed in jeopardy. And last, not least, the working classes of the nation may have spoken in a voice that will be heard against this all-devouring spirit of free trade, which the genius of our great dramatist seems almost to have typified in the following words: –

> 'The everything resolves itself in power,
> Power into will, will into appetite,
> And appetite an universal wolf
> Must make perforce an universal sway,
> And last eat up himself.'

But, to return to the more immediate subject of this letter, I need scarcely remind your Lordship that, independent of all recent legislation, the home administration

[1] An account of the proceedings at a meeting of the artisans of London, published in the 'Daily News' of the 27th of April last, and the resolution that was passed respecting foreign competition.

of colonial affairs has long been a matter of just complaint. I mean no flattery when I say that, during the last twenty years, no minister has conducted the business of that department with greater success than your Lordship; no one, therefore, can be better aware of the general inefficiency of the system, and the necessity that exists for some important alteration in the management of our colonial empire.

It is to be observed that our colonies have two interests which are essentially distinct; the one is local, and confided to the representative assembly, or if it does not enjoy that privilege, to the executive government of the colony; the other is imperial, and confided to the general legislature and the executive government of the empire; and it is to the latter that I now venture to draw your Lordship's attention.

I assume, therefore – for it would be a waste of time to prove the fact – that the imperial interests of the colonies do not receive that degree of attention from the home government which their great importance deserves. At the present time, in particular, when the subject of systematic colonisation is forcing itself upon the public mind, the want of some organised means of effecting that desired object is powerfully felt. With the double object, therefore, of obtaining justice to the colonies, and at the same time of rendering their resources most available to the mother country, I have to suggest one of two remedies. The first is to enlarge both the administrative power and the responsibility of the Colonial Office; the second, and more effective plan is, to allow the colonies the right of direct representation in the imperial Parliament.

Your Lordship is doubtless aware that the scheme of direct colonial representation was strongly advocated by Adam Smith, and as resolutely opposed by Burke. 'There is not the least probability,' observes the former, 'that the British constitution would be hurt by the union of Great Britain with her colonies. That constitution, on the contrary, would be completed by it, and seems to be imperfect without it. *The assembly which deliberates and decides concerning the affairs of every part of the empire, in order to be properly informed, ought certainly to have representatives from every part of it.* That this union, however, could be easily effectuated, or that difficulties, and great difficulties, might not occur in the execution, I do not pretend. I have yet heard of none, however, which appear insurmountable.'[1]

The objections of Mr. Burke to this scheme are principally founded on the distance of the colonies from England, and on the unavoidable difficulties and delays which would occur in the election and return of members to the seat of government.[2]

It is scarcely necessary to observe, however, that circumstances have very materially altered since these conflicting opinions were expressed. The principal,

---

1 Vol. ii. p. 473.
2 Burke's Works, vol. i. Observations on a late state of the nation.

and in fact the only valid objection of Burke, can hardly be said now to exist, at least with reference to our American possessions – and he has confined his argument to them. A voyage from Boston or Halifax can now be performed in as short a time as a journey from the north of Scotland or the west of Ireland in the days of Burke; and throughout the year the West Indies are probably more accessible than the Shetland Islands. In proportion, therefore, as the force of Mr. Burke's objections has been diminished by circumstances, the reasons adduced by Adam Smith in favour of colonial representation have received additional strength. And there is another circumstance to be considered, which, although for obvious reasons he has not directly referred to it, could scarcely have failed to operate on the mind of Burke, while treating of this important question. At the period when he wrote, the close boroughs afforded a ready means of representation to the colonies; a means which no longer exists. Practically speaking, therefore, the colonies were represented in the imperial legislature in his day, although not so efficiently as if they had been allowed to send their own representatives direct to Parliament.

In order to avoid the possibility of contested elections, and the great delays that would necessarily attend them, the colonial legislatures, which must still remain, might be empowered to send members to Parliament in the same manner as the separate legislatures of the United States send members to Congress.

As direct imperial representation must necessarily imply imperial taxation, those colonies only would send members to Parliament which could afford to contribute to the revenue of the mother country, in some proportion to the expense of their maintenance. The smaller colonies, therefore, and those generally which have no local assemblies, would remain governed as they now are, although they too would derive great advantage from the presence in Parliament of men who might be personally acquainted with their actual condition and resources.

If your Lordship asks for a precedent for so important an innovation, I fear, indeed, that none can be furnished, either from the history of this country or of any other. As the idea of representation was unknown to the ancients, we cannot look to them for information. Among the maritime states of the middle ages, however, we may perceive the necessities that sometimes existed for colonial representation at the seat of government. During the fourteenth century, a colony[1] of Venice claimed the right of sending deputies to the great council of the Republic, but this privilege was denied by the exclusive legislators of St. Mark.[2] During the grandeur of the Spanish monarchy in the sixteenth century, the great foreign dependencies of the crown were represented at Madrid by a separate council or board, which appears to have superintended the affairs of the dominions committed to their care, without the intervention of the Cortes. Even this would be

1   The island of Candia. Cornewall Lewis on the 'Government of Dependencies,' ch. x.
2   Id.

an improvement upon our loose and changeful system of colonial management; but no remedy would appear to be so efficient, so constitutional, and at the same time so conducive to the strength and stability of the whole empire as the one already suggested.[1]

And if no historical precedent can be adduced in favour of this proposed measure, it is also to be borne in mind that the circumstances of the case have no parallel in the annals of mankind. With an overflowing population at home, and a boundless extent of colonial territory abroad, it is the obvious destiny of this nation to employ its indomitable energies for centuries to come, in civilising and peopling those vast regions of the earth which Providence has committed to our care. Such, in spite of the temporary triumph of theory over reason and justice, is our inevitable course. Nor would anything more facilitate the accomplishment of this great work, by diffusing just notions of the wants and capabilities of our colonial dominions, than the presence of their representatives in England. If it is asked how they would affect the deliberations of the supreme legislature, it may be safely replied that they would add generally to their interest and utility; because under the plan proposed the ablest men only would be returned. From their education and their habits there is also every reason to believe that they would cherish a firm attachment to the constitution of their forefathers, and thus, in addition to the increased intelligence which they would bring to Parliament, they would form an important element of resistance to that destructive spirit now abroad, which, whether under the attractive guise of a popular league, or the bolder front of Chartism or Repeal, aims really at the destruction of our institutions and the subversion of society.

I have the honour to remain,
My Lord,
Your Lordship's most obedient servant,
COSMOPOLITE.

---

[1] The following extract from a speech delivered on the 9th of February last, by an influential member of the legislature of New Brunswick, is worthy of attention at the present time: 'Let the voice of the colonial subject be heard within the halls of her Imperial Legislature. It was love for the venerable institutions of their forefathers which prompted him to speak so plainly. If they saw a friend about to take a road which they knew to be beset with danger, would they not warn him to beware of the path which he was about to pursue? Was it not, then, his duty, and the duty of that house, if they saw danger in the policy of Great Britain, to warn her of the dangers which surrounded her colonial empire? Did they not see the whole of the noble colonies of the West Indies laid prostrate by the policy which brought the produce of foreign islands and slave labour into competition with them in the British market? and if they believed as he did, that the same policy, if persisted in, would produce similar effects in this colony, would they stand quietly by until the evil day had arrived, which would throw them helpless and ruined into the arms of foreign states?' See speech of Mr. R. D. Wilmot in 'The Colonial Advocate' of the 17th February last. This language is ominous, and reminds us of that held by the colonists of the United States before their separation.

John Dunmore Lang, *Freedom and Independence for the Golden Lands of Australia* (London: Longman, Brown, Green and Longmans, 1852), pp. 248–53.

SECTION VII. – PROPOSED CONDITIONS OF THE TREATY OF INDEPENDENCE CONTINUED – NO HOSTILE TARIFF, NO CUSTOM-HOUSE.

The second of the grand objects of colonization is the creation of a market for the surplus produce and manufactures of the mother-country; and I should consider it expedient and necessary for Great Britain, in conceding entire freedom and independence to any of her full grown colonies, to make effectual provision, in any Treaty of Independence, that no hostile tariff should be established against her in the country acquiring its freedom, for a certain fixed period at least – say FIFTY YEARS.

But although it would be expedient and necessary for Great Britain to insist upon such a provision for her own interest, I would by no means propose it on the part of the colonies as a special exemption in her favour. On the contrary, I would propose, as a measure of the best possible policy for the future good government of the Australian provinces, that all import duties, and other restrictions on the importation of goods of any description from all foreign parts, should forthwith be discontinued, and all custom-houses abolished.[1]

As a proposition of this kind may at first sight seem somewhat startling, it may not be out of place to ascertain the grounds on which it may nevertheless be urged with the utmost propriety.

1. It can be no reason, therefore, why there should be a custom-house in Australia, for the levying of duties on foreign trade, that there is one in England, another in France, and a third in the United States. The circumstances of the

---

1 Mr. Roebuck proposes, in his scheme of *Municipal Independence*, which is rather *a post too late now for Australia*, that the same privilege, as I propose should be guaranteed by treaty, should be secured by Act of Parliament. 'Neither for purposes of regulation or taxation should any power be given to tax the produce and manufactures of the mother-country or of her colonies; and the mother-country ought to resolve not to tax the produce of the colonies.' – *The Colonies of England*. By John Arthur Roebuck, Esq., M.P., p. 153. But *he would allow the colonies to tax the productions of other countries as much as they pleased*. Now this is too bad, Mr. Roebuck! To use the language of the poet:

'Free as the winds, and changeless as the sea,
Should trade and commerce unrestricted be.
Wherever land is found, or oceans roll,
Or man exists from Indus to the Pole,
Open to all, with no false ties to bind,
The world should be the market of mankind.'

countries contrasted, in each of these cases, with Australia, may be totally different from ours. There is an Established Church, for instance, in England, and *one in Ireland, too*; there is an immense standing army in France; and there is the institution of slavery – worst of all – in the United States: but what need have *we*, in Australia, for any of these *transmarine institutions?* Besides, the universality, whether of a custom, or of a custom-house, is no better argument for its propriety, than its great antiquity: and it is well observed by an able French writer, 'Ancient customs are sometimes nothing but great abuses, which are only the more dangerous the more respectable they are considered.'[1] A country over-burdened like Great Britain with debt and taxation, could scarcely give up her custom-house with safety to the State; but what has that to do with the case of Australia? We should not even desire to be exempted from customs' duties on Australian produce in England, as Mr. Roebuck proposes for the colonies, on the reciprocity system. We should only desire to be placed on the footing of the most favoured nation.[2]

2. Custom-houses are a great obstacle in the way of trade, and frequently a perfect *incubus* upon it. It is universally acknowledged that the public lose far more in the additional price they have to pay for their taxed commodities, than the State derives from the taxes in the shape of duties: and all this loss has to be sustained by the community.[3]

    1   ' Les anciennes coûtumes ne sont quelquefois que de grands abus, d'autant plus dangereux qu'on les croit plus respectables.'–*L'Abbé Millot*. To the same effect, the celebrated Christian Father, Cyprian, in his Epistle to Stephen, bishop of Rome, when testifying against Roman traditions, observes, 'Consuetudo sine veritate, vetustas erroris est.'–*Custom, without truth for its basis, is merely the antiquity of error*. The same excellent observation will apply equally to custom-houses.
    2   It is somewhat singular that in one of the most ancient treaties of peace and commerce in existence – viz. between the Carthaginians and Romans, – free-trade and no customs' duties forms one of the stipulations. Polybius (Book 3. chap. 22.) has preserved a copy of a treaty of peace and commerce between the Romans and Carthaginians, concluded so early as in the year after the expulsion of the kings of Rome, under the consulship of Junius Brutus and Marcus Horatius, that is, 28 years before the expedition of Xerxes into Greece, and 246 from the building of Rome. It is remarkable for the entire freedom of trade which it establishes between the rival republics, while it jealously guards against expeditions of war or invasion. The Free-trade proviso, translated into Latin by Isaac Casaubon, is as follows: – 'Qui ad mercaturam venerint, ii vectigal nullum pendunto, extra quam ad præconis aut scribæ mercedem.' *Let those* [Romans] *who come* [to Carthage] *for purposes of trade, pay no customs' duties, with the exception of the fees of the auctioneer and clerk of the market*.
    3   'The last remedy which I would propose is one which I feel persuaded would not only be attended with beneficial results to New Zealand, but also to all the Australian colonies: – it is the doing away with the Customs, and declaring the ports of New Zealand free. The impetus that such a measure as this would give to trade in this and the neighbouring colonies is incalculable. The loss in revenue could easily and equitably be made up by means of a property and income tax, which I doubt not the people would cheerfully pay. The present taxes on imported goods are made to press heavily on the honest trader alone, the facilities for smuggling being so great in a country possessing such fine harbours, and such an extensive coast line as New Zealand as to require a more efficient Coast Guard than that of England or Ireland for its prevention. To such an extent is smuggling carried on in the article of tobacco alone that a short time ago it could in this country be

3. The taxes levied through the custom-house are unequal in their pressure, and consequently unjust in their operation: they are paid chiefly by the humbler classes, who are least able to bear them. The industrious mechanic consumes perhaps as much sugar and tea as the squire himself, especially if his wife happens to be a tidy body, and at all fastidious in her taste; but he virtually contributes greatly more to the State.

4. The cost of an efficient custom-house establishment for such a country as Australia would be enormous, and out of all proportion to the amount of revenue to be derived from it. Already the cost of the custom-house establishment at Twofold Bay, in New South Wales, exceeds the whole amount of the duties received by it; and there are several suspicious places along the coast that must be vigilantly watched, and defended by a custom-house force, without the least prospect of duties, in the way of a Preventive Service. Such a Service, for a coast line of several thousand miles in extent, with numberless bays, creeks, and roadsteads, would be greatly too costly for any country, but especially for a young country to bear.

5. The custom-house system is already interfering materially with the productive industry of the colonies, and promoting extensive demoralization. The cultivation of the vine, for example, is now becoming both extensive and profitable in New South Wales; but it is found, in the process of wine-making, that much of an inferior quality has to be made into brandy, as for instance when the grapes happen to have been saturated with rain. But the Government derives an import duty on all French brandy imported, and to prevent the diminution of the revenue derivable from this source, which would be a serious matter for a Government with so much unnecessary and expensive machinery to keep up, the colonist is actually prohibited from making brandy for sale from his own vineyard, *lest he should interfere with the importation from France!* So preposterous a system can only have one result – illicit distillation and extensive demoralization – and accordingly a considerable seizure of colonial brandy was effected, just before I left the colony. It was coming to Sydney, from one of the northern settlements, *under the denomination of tallow!*

6. Revenue, arising from indirect taxation, always holds out a strong temptation to unnecessary and extravagant expenditure; and has uniformly been the egg from which the ill-omened bird, War, has been hatched by unjust and dishonest statesmen.

7. The amount of patronage which a custom-house system would throw into the hands of the executive would be dangerous to the character, as well as to the

---

bought at 10*d.* per pound, duty paid, or said to be paid, while the duty itself was a shilling.' – *New Zealand in 1842, or the Effects of a bad Government on a good Country.* By S. M. D. Martin, M.D., Auckland, New Zealand, 1842.

stability and permanence, of the national institutions. This is deeply felt already in the United States, and it will be much more so by and by.

8. A custom-house system for the Australian provinces would be quite unnecessary; as a revenue of sufficient amount for the support both of the provincial and national governments could be raised by other means, and from other sources, with perfect facility. It is scarcely necessary, however, to indicate these means and sources at present.

9. In the event of the revenue required for the support of Government being raised as at present, through a custom-house, it would be impossible to ensure such a distribution of the public expenditure as to prove satisfactory to all parties. For example, the district of Hunter's River, in New South Wales, contributes very largely to the public revenue, but has hitherto obtained only a very small share of the public expenditure. This, it must be evident, cannot be tolerated long; and accordingly, in the year 1850, one of the members for that district, Donald M'Intyre, Esq., a gentleman of liberal opinions, who had previously resided for many years in the United States, and had seen and experienced the benefits and blessings of the State governments of that country, told the Council very plainly that, if the district he represented were not more equitably treated in future, it would demand separation from New South Wales, like Port Phillip. But if there were no indirect taxation, the money raised in each district for public improvements would generally be expended in that district under the eye of those who raised it: they would consequently have no ground of complaint against other districts, and they would doubtless look very carefully after the expenditure of their own money.

10. The absence of such a system would render it comparatively easy to extend the National Government over any number of additional provinces, to be formed, for instance, among the islands of the Western Pacific, which might be the subject of future and progressive *annexation*; but with a custom-house system of the usual character, such an extension of the area of the National Government would be neither practicable nor desirable.

George Ward Cole, *Protection as a National System Suited for Victoria: Being Extracts from List's National System of Political Economy* (Melbourne: George Robertson, 1860), pp. 30–5.

LESSONS FROM HISTORY.

AT all times, and in all places, the intelligence, morality, and activity of the citizens have been regulated by the prosperity of the country; and wealth has increased or diminished according to these conditions; but nowhere have labour, economy, the spirit of invention, and the spirit of industrial enterprise accomplished any thing great, where civil liberty, the institutions and laws, external policy, the internal government, and especially where national unity and power have not lent their support.

History everywhere exhibits an energetic mutual reaction of social and individual powers. In the Italian and Hanseatic cities, in Holland and England, in France and America, we see the productive powers, and consequently the wealth, of individuals, increasing with the advance of political and social institutions, and the latter in their turn, finding in the increase of the material wealth and productive power of individuals the elements of their improvement. The impulse of the industry and power of England dates from the establishment of her liberty. The industry and power of the Venetians and the Hanseatics, of the Spaniards and the Portuguese, were extinguished at the same time with their liberty. It is in vain that individuals are industrious, saving, intelligent, and inventive; these free institutions are still needful for the proper application of these qualities. History teaches, in fact, that individuals draw the greatest part of their productive power from the social condition and the institutions of society.

The influence of liberty, of intelligence, and knowledge upon power and consequently, upon productive energy, upon the wealth of the country, appears nowhere so clearly as in the shipping interests. Of all the branches of industry, navigation is that which requires the most energy and courage, the most boldness and perseverance, all qualities which can only flourish in the atmosphere of liberty. In no other department of industry are ignorance, superstition, and prejudice, indolence, cowardice, and effeminacy so fatal, in none is the sentiment of personal independence so indispensable. History furnishes no instance of an enslaved people who have excelled in navigation.

The nations of India, the people of China and of Japan, have from the most ancient times confined themselves to the navigation of their canals, their rivers, or along their coasts. In ancient Egypt maritime navigation was discouraged; the priests and kings fearing, apparently, that it might furnish ailment to the spirit of liberty and independence. The freest and most civilised nations of Greece were also the most powerful at sea; with their liberty, their maritime power came to an end; and history, which relates so many victories gained on land by the kings of Macedonia, gives no account of their naval victories,

When were the Romans powerful at sea, and when do we hear no more of their fleets? At what time did Italy rule like a sovereign the whole Mediterranean, and since what time has even their coasting trade fallen into the hands of foreigners? The Inquisition pronounced sentence of death upon the Spanish fleet long before it was executed by the fleets of England and Holland. From the day when the mercantile oligarchies arose in the Hanse Towns, their power and courage deserted the League. In the Spanish Netherlands the seamen, without other aid, achieved their liberties; those who submitted to the Inquisition were doomed to witness the closing even of their rivers. The English fleet, by conquering that of Holland in the British Channel, did no more than take possession of the maritime supremacy which the spirit of liberty had long before assigned to it. Holland, however, retains to this time a great part of her marine, whilst that of the Spaniards and Portugese [sic] is nearly annihilated. Eminent statesmen have in vain attempted to make France a naval power, for fleets constructed under the rule of despotism always disappear. In our time the mercantile and military marine of France are upon the increase. The independence of North America had scarcely been achieved, when we see them struggling successfully against the gigantic fleets of the mother country. But what is the navigation of Central and South America? So long as their flags shall not float upon every sea, the solidity of their republican governments must remain questionable. Look at Texas; no sooner is she awake to separate existence, than she claims her part in the Empire of Neptune.

Navigation is but an element in the industrial power of a country, an element which can grow and flourish only under the support of all the people, and by the power of the whole nation. Navigation, internal and external commerce, agriculture itself can at no time or place become prosperous but where manufactures are permitted to become prosperous. But if liberty is the fundamental condition of the development of navigation, how much more is it the essential condition of the increase of manufacturing industry and of all the productive powers of a country? History records no instance of a rich nation addicted to commerce and the arts, which has not, at the same time, been a free nation.

Where manufactures flourish, we find also the means of communication, the improvement of river navigation, the construction of canals and roads, steam navigation, and railways; all which are an essential condition of advanced agriculture and civilisation.

History informs us that arts and trades have travelled from city to city and from country to country. Persecuted and oppressed in one country, they have fled to cities and countries where they were assured of liberty, protection, and assistance. They passed thus from Greece and Asia to Italy, thence to Germany, Flanders, and

Brabant, and from the two last to Holland and England. In these cases it was folly and despotism which drove them away, and the blessings of liberty which attracted them. But for the extravagances of the continental governments, England could never have reached her industrial supremacy. Is it not more rational, however, not to wait until other nations are insane enough to drive out their artisans and compel them to seek refuge among us, but without trusting to such contingencies to attract them, by offering to all the highest advantages our position affords? Experience teaches us, it is true, that the wind carries with it the seeds of one country to another, and that desert places have thus been changed into heavy forests. But would it be wise for the proprietor of waste land to wait for the wind to perform this office of planting and transformation during the lapse of centuries? Is it folly in him to force nature by planting his uncultivated lands, that he may attain his object in a score of years? History shews that whole nations have successfully accomplished what the wise landowner always achieves.

A few free cities or small republics, limited in their territory, their population, and military power; a few associations of such cities and such states, sustained by the energy of a new-born liberty, favoured by their geographical position, and by a fortunate concurrence of circumstances, became distinguished by their industry and commerce long before any of the great monarchies attained such distinction, through their free communication with the former, to which they furnished agricultural products in exchange for manufactures. Such cities and countries arose to a high degree of wealth and power, as, for instance, Venice and the Hanseatic cities, Flanders, and Holland.

Free trade was, at the beginning, not less beneficial to the large States than to those mentioned. Considering the abundance of their natural resources and the rudeness of their social condition, the free admission of foreign manufactured products, and the free exports of their agricultural products were the the [*sic*] most certain and effectual means, developing their productive powers of inuring to labour, people who were idle and contentious; of interesting the nobles and the proprietors of the soil in industry; and of awaking a spirit of enterprise in sluggish merchants; in short, of increasing their culture, their industry, and their power.

England, especially, has derived these benefits from her relations with the Italians and the Hanse Towns with the Flemings and the Dutch. Having arrived, by the aid of free trade, to a certain development, the great States soon began to comprehend that the highest point of culture, power, and wealth, could be reached only by uniting in the same country manufactures and commerce with agriculture: 'it became obvious to them that the infant manufactures of a country commencing that career, could not live and prosper in free competition with manufactures long established in other countries;' that fisheries and mercantile navigation, which are the basis of maritime power, could prosper only by special assistance; and that merchants and manufacturers exposed to competition with foreigners, superior in capital, experience and knowledge, must finally succumb and continue to be paralyzed. They endeavoured, consequently, by restrictions, by favours and encouragements, to transplant to their own soil the capital, skill, and enterprise of foreigners; which they did with more or less success and rapidity, according as the means employed had been used with more or less discretion, and applied with more or less energy and perseverance.

England, especially, had recourse to this policy; but, kings wanting intelligence, or abandoned to their passions, civil disturbances, or foreign wars, having frequently interrupted its application, it was only after the reign of Edward VI. and Elizabeth, and after subsequent revolutions, that England had a system fixed and appropriate to its object. For what effect could the measures of Edward III. have, when we remember that down to the time of Henry VI. it was not permitted to transport grain from one county of England to another, nor to export it abroad? When we recollect that under Henry VII. and Henry VIII., every kind of interest, even the profits of exchange were regarded as usury; and when the government endeavoured to encourage industry by low taxes upon woollen cloths and upon wages, and to promote the production of wheat by discouraging the increase of sheep. How much sooner would the woollen manufacture and the navigation of England have reached a high degree of prosperity, if Henry VIII. had not considered the high price of wheat an evil? if, instead of expelling in a mass foreign artisans, he had, after the example of his predecessors, exerted himself to draw thither a larger number? if Henry VII. had not rejected the Act of Navigation, proposed to him by his parliament?

In France we have seen manufactures, free trade at home, commerce abroad, fisheries, mercantile navigation, and naval power, – in a word, all the attributes of a great, powerful, and rich nation, – obtained by England only after centuries of effort, – rise in a few years as by enchantment, at the bidding of one great man, and disappear as suddenly under the iron hand of religious fanaticism and despotic rule.

We have seen the principle of free trade struggling without success in unfavourable circumstances against restrictions enforced by power; the Hanseatic League annihilated, and Holland succumb to the attacks of England and France.

The decline of Venice, Spain and Portugal, the retrograde movement of France after the revocation of the Edict of Nantes, and the history of England, where liberty went hand in hand with industry, commerce, and national wealth, shew that *restrictive* policy is efficient only so far as it is accompanied by the development and progress of civilisation and free institutions.

On the other hand, the history of the United States, and the experience of England, demonstrate that a very advanced culture with or without free institutions, if not supported by a wise commercial policy, is but a feeble guarantee of the economical progress of a nation.

Modern Germany, deprived of an energetic and united commercial policy, abandoned in her territory to the competition of a foreign manufacturing industry superior in every respect; excluded at the same time from foreign markets by arbitrary and often capricious restrictions, far from accomplishing an industrial progress in harmony with her degree of culture, could not even maintain her old rank, and became like a colony, a prey to the very nation of which, a few centuries before, she had taken the same advantage through her merchants, until, at last, her governments determined, by a strong and common system, to secure their home markets to their own industry.

The United States, in a better posture than any country before them, to take advantage of free trade; influenced, moreover, in the very infancy of their independence, by the lessons of the cosmopolite school, made a greater exertion than had ever been before, to apply that principle. But twice were their people obliged by wars with Great Britain to manufacture for themselves commodities which, under the system of free trade, they had imported from abroad; twice, upon the return of peace, were they carried by free competition with foreign countries to the very verge of ruin; and admonished by this lesson, that in the present state of the world, a great nation must, above all, seek by a suitable and harmonious development of its own productive powers, to make sure the guarantees of its prosperity and independence.

History teaches that restrictions are much less the creation of speculative minds than the national consequences of diversity of interests – the struggles of nations for independence or supremacy, and consequently, of national rivalries and wars; and that they are to cease, at the same time with the conflict of national interests, or under some new system of international law. The inquiry, how nations can be united in a federation, and how in the disputes between independent people judicial decrees are to be substituted for the power of arms, is equivalent to this: How can universal free trade be substituted for national systems of commerce?[1]

---

1   We think there is some error involved in this. It seems, indeed, to be the opinion of List that in certain conditions of the world free trade may be assumed as a sound doctrine in the sense in which it is supported by the school which maintains it as a fundamental principle. We deny that it ever can be sound doctrine in their sense. In our view, free trade is a policy, a means, not a doctrine, or a philosophical truth, or a principle. Free trade is now the true policy of Great Britain. We do not believe that under any probable circumstances it could be the policy of all civilised nations; for if all now possessed equal advantages with Great Britain, a severe and destructive competition would take place, making it necessary to resort again to the protection of the labourers of each nation. The object of industry, that labour by which men live, is not the greatest development of foreign trade; it is the comfort, well-being, and moral progress of the masses of each separate nationality. We say each nation, because each separate people must take care of themselves. Their power reaches no further, and their comprehension of their own interests must be more full than that of others. Under no circumstances that we can conceive, then, can it be the duty of any government to give up the care of the labour, that is, of the labourers of the country. Now, if free trade were the great object of human life, it should, of course, be the effort of governments to attain to it as quickly as possible. Or, if free trade could secure

more effectually than any other policy the welfare of the masses, then it should be pursued for that reason. But when we remember that the welfare of the masses has no place in the theory of the free trade school, we may well apprehend that the development of their system will not be directed to that object, nor be found to subserve it. The truth is, the care of men in social life is a task so complicated, so changing, requiring such faithful guardianship and finally such kindly and charitable regard, that it can never be left to a system of political economy which does not even profess to have it in view. There is no doubt that the advocates of free trade imagine that under its sway all the industrial interests of nations and their people would find their right position, and every labourer his true place as one of the cogs in the vast machinery which manufactures wealth. So, indeed, in the view of the system every man would always be in his place, that is, where the force of circumstances would place him, over which, neither he nor his country could exercise any control. The system has no provision for any inquiry whether any one man or any class of men, is happy or miserable, well or ill-fed, or clothed, or lodged, or educated; it gives men the privilege of free trade whose lot in life is nothing but labour.

But this system regards only international trade, and makes every other interest bend to what will promote the progress of foreign trade. The palpable error involved in this may be seen by recurring to the fact that no nation or people can by any possibility derive more than one-tenth of their consumption from other nations. The average of the consumption thus imported among civilised nations at the present day does not reach five per cent cent. [sic] of their home production. Nine-tenths and more of what people eat, drink, wear, and consume, is of home production. The welfare of people, so far as it depends on the necessaries and comforts of life, and the welfare of labourers or producers, so far as it depends upon the rate of their compensation or the extent to which they are permitted to enjoy the products of their own labour, should be independent of foreign trade, and especially should not the producers and consumers of the nine-tenths, or rather the nineteen-twentieths, be injured, or their products be reduced in quantity by any influence of foreign trade. Foreign trade, over the commodities of which, or the labourers who produce them, no nation can exercise any control, except when crossing Its boundary, should be so regulated, then, as in no way to diminish the efficiency of that industry upon which people are mainly dependent, not only for the articles of their consumption but for the opportunity of producing, as well as of earning and enjoying them. Foreign trade being shorn of its power to do injury, every nation might make it as free as it pleased. Many of the positions of free trade theorists would, in fact, be then sound and forcible. The error now committed in that system is that the industrial welfare of men is left to the chances, changes, and variable results and influences of foreign trade, instead of being made, as it, more than anything else deserves to be, the direct and principle object of public care and legislation. The friends of free trade say, let free trade prevail, and all will come right with the people. We say, let all be made right with the people, even if in making all right, free trade should be one of the means. We are unwilling to assume any other starting point for the development of a social system than the best interests of the people; we are unwilling to regard free trade in any other light than as one of the means which may or may not, in the exercise of an intelligent discretion, be applied to that object.

It is not difficult to divine why the economists of the Say school are such strenuous advocates of absolute free trade. In the last analysis it is the single leg upon which their system rests; take from it this prop, and it comes to the ground. They wish to establish a law of social economy or science, to take the subject out of the domain of sound discretion and common sense. Their rules are laws of science, which admit no contradiction. The law in this case is free trade; any interference with it is a violation of science, and a disturbance of the natural order of things. Looking upon all the producing agencies, man, machinery, and the powers of nature, as being merely agents under the stimulus of their law of demand, they take no account of industry, or its processes, or its labourers; they merely receive its products when brought upon the scene of distribution; they take little account of consumption except in the light of demand and supply, nor of prices, except so far as they may hinder or facilitate distribution, one of two great works over which the so-called science of political economy presides. To admit any interference with this distribution, founded upon considerations of humanity or policy, or the special interests or well-being of the people of any nation, is to violate a law of politi-

The experience of certain nations adopting the principle of free trade in the face of nations superior in industry, riches, and power, and protected by a restrictive commercial system, for instance, such as that of Portugal in 1703 of France in 1786, of the United States 1786, and 1816, of Prussia from 1815 to 1821, and of Germany for centuries, proves that the prosperity of a country may be thus sacrificed without any benefit for mankind in general, and for the sole advantage of the power which sways the sceptre of commerce and industry.

Switzerland forms an exception that proves too much and too little, at the same time, for and against either system.

Colbert is not, in our opinion, the inventor of the system to which the Italians have given his name; we have seen that the English had elaborated it long before his time. Colbert only put in practice what France was to adopt soon or late for the accomplishment of her destiny. If any censure is to be applied to Colbert, it would be that of having attempted to execute a work under an absolute government, which could not have long duration until after a great change in her political institutions.

To justify Colbert, it might be answered that his system, if pursued by wise monarchs and enlightened ministers, would, in the way of reform, have overcome the obstacles opposed to the progress of manufactures, agriculture, and commerce, as well as those in the way of public liberty, and thus spared France a revolution. It might be said that if France, stimulated in her development by the mutual action and reaction of industry and liberty, had persevered in this policy, she would have been for the last half century the fortunate rival of England in manufactures, internal communications in general, commerce and colonisation, as well as in fisheries, and in her mercantile and military marine.

History teaches us, finally, how nations, endowed by nature with all the means of reaching the highest degree of wealth and power, can, without inconsistency, and should, change their system in proportion as they advance. At first, indeed, by free trade with nations of higher culture, they emerge from barbarism, and improve their agriculture; then, by means of restrictions, they give an impulse to manufactures, fisheries, navigation, and foreign commerce; then, finally, after having reached the highest degree of skill, wealth, and power, by a gradual return to the principle of free trade, and free competition in their own and foreign markets, they keep their agriculturists from inaction, their manufacturers and their merchants from indolence, and stimulate them to wholesome activity, that they may maintain the supremacy which they have acquired. In the first of these stages we see Spain, Portugal, and Naples, in the second, Germany and North America; France appears to be on the limits of the latter; but England alone has not only reached, but maintains an industrial and commercial supremacy.

---

cal economy. To change the natural order of distribution, to make it a subject for sound discretion, or the exercise of common sense, is absolutely to shake the whole foundation on which Say's system of political economy is built.

Henry Ashworth, 'Our Colonies: Their Commerce and their Cost', a paper read at the Meeting of the Society of Arts, 26 March 1862, in Henry Ashworth, *Pamphlets and Other Papers by* (Manchester: William Irwin, 1872), pp. 10–11, 15–16, 19, 23.

We will next proceed to a consideration of the AUSTRALASIAN COLONIES, including New Zealand.

The number of British troops employed is 2,947. The Imperial military expenditure has reached about £49,000, and Western Australia, which is a convict settlement, costs us from £20,000 to £26,000 for troops.

At the 75th anniversary of the establishment of the Australian Colonies, held on the 12th February last, His Grace the Duke of Newcastle, Secretary of State for the Colonies, expressed his congratulations upon the successful foundation of so powerful, happy, and prosperous a community, having a population of 1,250,000, and a revenue of £6,500,000. He stated that their imports now amounted to £25,000,000, of which no less than £16,000,000 came from the mother country. The exports of these colonies were valued at £21,000,000, and within the last ten years they had raised and exported more than £100,000,000 in value of gold, principally to this country. The export of wool had also reached a value of £2,000,000 annually, all of which afforded material evidences of prosperity. The laws they had framed had been after the example of England, and, by way of conclusion, he added, 'if they thought their strength was sufficient to allow them to stand alone, we should not seek to restrain them by force.' Referring to the distinguished men identified with the rising prosperity of the Australian Colonies, who honoured this anniversary with their presence, and bearing in mind the significant remark of the Duke of Newcastle respecting their capability of self-government, it will be interesting to ascertain, on some future occasion, whether they wish to set up for themselves in a state of independence or desire to remain under their allegiance to the British Crown.

We may also adduce the cheering proofs we have before us of prosperity and enterprise embodied in the following account of the expenditure for public works in these colonies. In the last ten years there has been expended there on –

Railways	£8,000,000
Telegraphs	163,476
Roads and bridges	5,272,620
Other public works	3,500,000
	£16,936,026

The imports into Victoria in 1860 amounted to £15,093,730, being nearly £28 per head.

With such evidences of material prosperity before us, it may reasonably be inquired why do not these colonists, so high-minded as they showed themselves at this anniversary, pay their own expenses of military defence? The reply is one which will be found exceptional, and, as far as it goes, favourable. In the year 1851 the Australian colonists entered into an arrangement with Earl Grey, at that time Secretary of State for the Colonies, that they should be allowed by the mother country a certain number of Imperial troops, and if they required more they agreed to pay for them. This arrangement has continued in force, and has worked well throughout.

The tendency of import duties levied on manufactured articles has usually been found to generate a desire for native manufactures, and it would appear that Victoria, abounding to so remarkable an extent in natural resources, is by no means an exception to this rule, for example: – Mr. Mayes, the successful writer of a prize essay, reminds the colonists that in the year 1858 they had imported woollen goods of the value of £528,000, and in the same year had exported wool of the value of £1,678,290; showing that whilst they possess the raw material in such abundance, it was important that they should endeavour to manufacture some of these imported goods, and he proceeds at once to furnish an outline of the processes which are necessary to convert wool into woollens. The colony of Tasmania is also, on the same principle, endeavouring to establish native manufactures. [...]

The tariffs of many of our principal colonies have been remarked upon as being more unfavourable to British commerce than those of most foreign countries. During the negotiations on the French Treaty, the protectionists of France expressed their surprise, that the English should demand of them a lower scale of duties than they themselves allowed to be imposed on British manufactures imported into their own colonies. The effect in Canada of such a policy must, in the end, be suicidal to her commerce, by the restriction thus imposed on consumption; indeed, this has already been disclosed in their commercial returns, showing, that while the average of the colonial trade of Canada for the five years ending with 1857 was £4,800,000, the average of the four years ending with 1861 was only £3,700,000 – being a decline of 23 per cent., notwithstanding the increase of population and the great improvement in the condition of the country.

One of the important pecuniary advantages ever present to the mind of the emigrant is that of his being entitled to enjoy in our colonies the privilege of an inhabitant of the mother country, in his exemption from those fiscal burdens imposed for purposes of 'protection;' in this respect he finds himself disappointed.

It may be asserted that the object of these high duties is not protection – but revenue. It cannot, however, be concealed that protection formed some portion of the object of the Legislature. There are admissions to that effect, and, under the encouragement afforded by these high duties, corporations and companies are in course of formation to establish local manufactures. The following extract, from the 'Annual Review of the Trade of Toronto, for 1861,' most fully confirms this view of the subject: – 'The trade in home manufactured woollens has been large and very successful.' The writer proceeds to enumerate about a dozen of those manufacturing firms who have established 'first-rate mills in the province,' and congratulates the public on the enterprise embarked in the cotton manufacture, although regretting that it is now unhappily being held in suspense for want of cotton, owing to the American rebellion.

Having indicated the bearing of the policy which, as a mother country, we have adopted towards our colonies, and having more particularly brought under observation what has been the character of the return we have received from our Canadian fellow subjects, it now becomes the duty of our countrymen to consider the future of our proceedings, and to make selection of that course of policy which may be deemed most pregnant with successful results, both to our fellow-subjects in the colonies and to ourselves. [...]

Potent as the figures of arithmetic may be in determining a question of commerce, the delusive effect of an unsound commercial policy could not be more completely set forth than we find it in the advice of Jeremy Bentham, addressed to the National Convention of France, and headed, 'Emancipate your colonies. What should colonies be worth to you but by yielding a surplus of revenue beyond what is necessary for their own maintenance and defence? Do you, can you, get any surplus from them? If you do you plunder them and violate your own principles. 'Oh, but the produce of our colonies is worth so many millions a year; all this, if we were to give up our colonies, we should lose.' Illusion! The income of your colonies your income? Just as much as that of Britain is your income. Can you take a penny of that income more than they choose to give you? or should you if you could? We have no such pretension. 'Oh, but of this income of theirs a great part centres here; it comes to buy our goods; it constitutes a great part of our trade; all this, at least, we should lose.' Another illusion! Must you govern a people in order to sell your goods to them? Is there that people on the face of the earth who do not buy goods of you? You sell goods to Britain don't you? And do you govern Britain? When a colonist sends you sugar, does he give it you for nothing? Does not he make you give him value for it? Give value for it, then, and you will have it still. 'Oh, but we give ourselves a monopoly of their produce, and so we get it cheaper than we should otherwise, and so we make them pay us for governing them.' Not you, indeed, not a penny; the attempt is iniquitous, and the profit an illusion.' [...]

The colonies are entirely independent in the conduct of their foreign trade, and the trade they carry on with the mother country does not amount to one-half of the whole general trade. Therefore, in the name of British commerce, we may venture to disclaim the existence of any advantage as derivable from colonial dependence to Great Britain.

During the last century, it was supposed that we derived some sort of exclusive advantage, which in effect amounted to a taxation of them; but since then colonial affairs have become so far changed that the colonists are now taxing us. Whatever portion of this annual drain upon our exchequer is deemed to be necessary or expedient for Imperial purposes, is an affair which must be allowed to rest with the Legislature to determine. We have looked in vain for any evidence in support of this wet-nursing of our colonies; the system has evidently had its day, and the result has been a mortifying disclosure of ill-success.

George Reid, *Five Free Trade Essays* (Melbourne: Gordon and Gotch, 1875), foreword, pp. 67–75.

TO THE ELECTORS OF VICTORIA.

GENTLEMEN, –

I venture to inscribe to you the following humble product of my leisure and reflection. Both sides of the great question it discusses have been presented to you from the hustings, in Parliament, and in the columns of an able Press. But I do not recollect to have met with any effort to deal with the subject in a systematic and complete form, which is obviously quite beyond the scope of the longest of speeches or the most comprehensive of articles. When we consider the importance of the controversy it is much to be regretted that its literature is not more extensive.

I may state at once my profound conviction that any community, whether young or old, which leaves enterprise as free and living as cheap as possible pursues a policy the most likely to promote both individual happiness and national greatness. I believe that any system which places enterprise in leading strings, in order that it may become bold and adventurous, which represses commerce in order that it may thrive, which tears Industry in its infancy from the generous breast of Nature to suckle it on duties of Customs, and compels it in youth to lean on crutches that it may become strong in mature age, is as disastrous in its consequences as it is contradictory in its principles. Holding these opinions, I venture to lay before the great electoral mind of Victoria the grounds on which they are based. If I am wrong I do my opponents a service in enabling them to expose the fallacy of my arguments. If I am right I may render some slight service to the cause in which I believe. I am confident that in either case my motive will recommend itself to your approval.

The people of Victoria and the people of New South Wales are equally bound to remember that so long as the issue between Protection and Free Trade continues to divide them Australian unity must be deferred. All I am sure must therefore hope that the contest may soon be decided, and that the Australian populations, if they may not become one in name and government, may speedily be united by the strongest and most enduring of all ties, harmonious policy, free intercourse, and mutual prosperity.

Your most obedient servant,

G. H. REID.

Sydney, New South Wales, April, 1875. [...]

CONCLUDING ESSAY.

The industrial development of mankind has proceeded by three broad stages. In the first stage flocks and herds chiefly constituted wealth; in the second the soil and its fruits became more valuable; and in the third handicraft is most valuable of all. In other words, society advances from pastoral to agricultural, and then to manufacturing pursuits. As population grows its wants vary and enlarge. That 'necessity is the mother of invention' is exactly true of the exigencies of population. The conversion of resources keeps pace with demand, and the pressure of life will always force enterprise into new modes of production. China has been alluded to as a remarkable exception. But is the exception surprising when we recollect that the genius of the wonderful race inhabiting that vast empire has for ages been repressed by the most rigid and comprehensive system of Protection the world has ever known? However small a territory may be its resources never fail to expand with the needs of its population if its institutions and commerce are free. So long as freedom in politics and freedom in trade are preserved the spirit of a people can never decay. Their warlike prestige may decline. Their political importance may disappear. But their industrial prosperity will abide with them.

England is perhaps the most notable specimen of national growth. Six hundred years ago she was still in the first stage of development. The flocks which roamed over her pastures were her chief wealth. In the 'Ordinance of the Staple,' passed in the reign of Edward III., wool was styled 'the sovereign merchandize and jewel of our realm.' The advance of agriculture was strangely slow, but during last century it may be said to have risen into pre-eminence. Its supremacy, however, was short, for towards the close of the century the manufacturing interest began to surpass every other, and its progress from that time may be considered as the greatest fact in the annals of human industry. How completely manufactures have eclipsed the pastoral and agricultural interests of Great Britain may be gathered from the statistics of the import trade, which show that in 1872 the import of wool was 306,378,664 lbs., and the import of live stock, provisions, corn, &c., for the year was valued at £85,000,000. Of the exports for the same period only £2,300,000, in a total of £256,000,000, can be referred to the two industries which were regarded by our ancestors, the one as 'the jewel of the realm' and the other as 'the pillar of Church and State.' It is the circumstance that Great Britain has reached her third stage of development, and is so great a manufacturing country, which enables her to be the splendid customer she is for the raw material produced in her Colonial Empire; as it is, on the other hand, the progress made by the Colonies in the production of raw material which enables them to become such good customers for British manufactures. So far from the case being as a Protectionist puts it, that the interests of British industry are hostile to the interests of Australian industry, the truth is that the Mother

Country and her Colonies constitute a magnificent co-operative concern, and the closer their relations and the freer their interchange, the greater will be their mutual advantage. If a Colony choose, as Victoria has done, to adopt a Protectionist policy, and legislates so that her markets shall be free to sell to but not to buy from England, she not only disturbs the harmony and assails the unity of the Empire by so selfish and mistaken a policy, but actually injures herself far more than the parent country; for whilst she must leave the rest of the world open to the British manufacturer she must shut out the whole of the world from the local consumer. The influence of Great Britain on the development of her colonies generally applies, for as one division of the globe attains the higher forms of industry it leaves room for the advance of another in the lower forms. The march of civilization on one continent gives greater value to the unpeopled wastes of another; for the multiplication of wealth and wants in one country must lead to a similar advance in others. The force of demand ever gathering strength stimulates more and more the productive energies of mankind, and its action and reaction on all nations draw them nearer the millennium of plenty and universal peace. Surely the glorious truth will soon be made plain that the scattered peoples of the earth are one in interest, and ought to be one in sentiment and policy? That every upward step achieved by one nation leave a step free for the rest? It was the greatness of Europe in handicraft that made the greatness of America in agriculture, and of Australia in pastoral pursuits. Assuredly, when America achieves the greatness of Britain in manufactures, and Australia the greatness of America in agriculture, extensive areas now barren and neglected will be brought within the range of settlement and cultivation.

It is a dangerous thing to interfere with the free play of private enterprise. When the interference is an attempt to reverse the ordinary laws of progress it is more than ever likely to prove a mistake. It will be admitted that the Australian Colonies are not yet past the first stage of development. Their wealth and importance are still chiefly derived from live stock. Owing to modern appliances and knowledge, agriculture can now be developed in new countries with a rapidity which forms an extraordinary contrast to its previous history; and the agricultural interest in these Colonies is already very considerable. We might well be prepared for the progress of both interests, for both have many conditions in their favour. They have ample room, ready markets, and a genial climate. There is a magnificent market always open for Australian wool, tallow, and hides, and there will soon be as wide a market for our grain, wine, and meat. No one can say that private enterprise has made a mistake in following these primary industries. No one can say that capitalists could have done better than produce the raw material which is now the basis of our wonderful prosperity. They knew that the world would be an eager customer for that raw material. They are wiser in their day and generation than our Protectionist friends. They knew that the world would laugh at them if they attempted to obtain a market for

Australian manufactures. Why? Because the world can buy manufactures elsewhere much cheaper than we could make and export them. In the case of this branch of enterprise our advantages count for very little. Indeed, the great success which has attended the other industries to which we have referred is the most formidable difficulty of the manufacturing interest. If the profits in these other branches were not so large labour would not be so much in demand, and with low wages and hard times for our working classes the prospects of cheap manufacturing would speedily brighten. If we conceded that under a temporary system of Protection, our artisans and manufacturers could surpass the British operatives and manufacturers in skill and management, the two most serious obstacles in the way of Australian manufactures would remain to be disposed of. We mean *short hours and high wages*.

Do the electors of Australia think the short hours and high wages which Australian labour enjoys a calamity? If they do, Protection is about the best device for lowering wages they could adopt, for it very effectually reduces the value of wages in increasing the cost of subsistence. But why should we tax ourselves all round to keep up a struggle to compete in manufactures which are confessedly our weakest point, and in which we find all the great nations arrayed against us, when we can become supreme in the production of raw material, and when those who can beat us in manufactures are for that very reason our best customers in raw material? Is it not worse than ridiculous to throw away time and money on the one when we can do so well with the other? Would not a tradesman be thought deranged if he persisted in making an article for which there was no demand in preference to an article for which he could get a good sale? Would not a consumer be thought deranged if he insisted on making an article for his own use when it would pay him better to buy it, selling a different article at a profit? Is it less absurd for Australian electors to vote for a system which is to compel them to forego a part of their earnings because those industries which pay are followed in preference to those which do not? Is it less absurd for a whole people to insist on making articles which they can buy more cheaply ready made? Was there ever an individual or a community of individuals who did not buy as well as sell? Is it not complete folly to act as if we could reverse this universal rule?

It was once argued that State-aid was necessary to religion in these Colonies; but our experience is that the Churches are more energetic and prosperous without it. Thrown on their own resources the better part of each has asserted itself. Protection, whether in religion or in trade, is more likely to blunt than to sharpen the edge of enterprise. It appears somewhat irrational to expect that enterprise will put forth its full strength when an endowment of any kind meets it half way, and the more liberal the endowment is the less chance is there of enterprise being safe, or going as far as it ought. State-aid is the bulwark of mediocrity: freedom and self-reliance are the germs of power. It is true that some forms of State endowments can scarcely be dispensed with – for example the educational grants. But, apart from the transcendent moment of education, as the germ of every form of national growth, the best defence of such grants is that they are the only way of securing the great end in view, that is, the instruction of the poorer, for those who are in comfortable circumstances can and will educate their children whether public schools are established or not. Besides, in our grants for public instruction there are two effectual safeguards against abuse. One is the principle of 'payment by results' and the other 'efficient inspection and control.' In public instruction the quality and extent of the work done can be thoroughly tested. It was not so in the case of State-aid to religion, and especially is it not so in the case of State-aid to manufactures. We have pointed out that there is a great deal to be said in favour of the bounty system, although we are not to be understood as approving of it, which cannot be urged in favour of Protective duties; and the chief reason for a preference is that bounties are given on the principle of *payment by results*. The Protective system has no such safeguard. Indeed, a system like that adopted by Victoria offers many bribes to mis-directed enterprise, for it offers liberal inducements for the establishment of industries which any man of business can see to be terribly bad speculations. And there is no pretence of State control. There are no means of determining whether the different encouragements are too liberal or inadequate, when they ought to be reduced, and when they ought to be repealed. If in the history of the relations between manufacturers and the State, under Protective legislation, there is one thing more true than another it is this: that manufacturers were never known to admit the propriety of the reduction or repeal of the duties in which they were interested. A proposal to withdraw the protection, however long it had been enjoyed, has always elicited from them a cry of real or affected despair. We might refer, as a good illustration, to the case of 'State-aid to industry' in the United States, where, after a long period of liberal encouragement, the manufacturers insist on the maintenance of a tariff averaging 40 per cent. *ad valorem* as absolutely necessary for their protection.

There is a vast difference between industries which Protection conceives and those which are founded by private enterprise. Manufacturing industries such as those which exist in New South Wales under a Free Trade tariff, and those established in Victoria before a Protective tariff was made law, are an unqualified benefit to the community. Their development can never be a direct loss to the public, as protected industries are at first and may continue to be. If a capitalist make a mistake he finds it out and abandons a losing concern. The public are not compelled to pay 10 or 20 per cent. on the articles he offers for sale in order to convert his losses into gains, thus making everybody but himself suffer for his blunders. If the man prove a shrewd speculator, on the other hand, his venture is profitable to him and injurious to nobody. This is a set of conditions in harmony with the rules of business. But it is a state of things which Free Trade alone can preserve. Adopt the policy of Protection and the whole position is at once reversed. The Legislative Assembly takes industrial speculations in hand. The Legislative Assembly decides what industries ought to pay, and it has the power of making them pay very easily, by taxing the people so as to 'rig' the market. Thanks to these taxes on unfortunate consumers the worst speculation may become for the time a very good one indeed. Conscious perhaps of their inability to discriminate in such matters, the Legislative Assembly of Victoria adopted a tariff which appears to proceed on the extraordinary presumption that nearly every description of industry can be made profitable in that Colony. They have enacted an industrial destiny for the future generations of Victoria which must have been fashioned by the rule of thumb. A capitalist is very careful to weigh the chances of profit, and he tries to know exactly what he is about. But gentlemen who owe their seats to a 'cry' are not in a position, if they have the ability, to act in that way. They must say 'yes' to everything which resembles the cry on which they were returned. Hence a tariff which made the clumsiest if any, attempts to distinguish between industries which might and those which could not pay was passed into law with slight difficulty. A number of mushroom industries will spring up, and however absurd they may be the people are compelled to keep them going. Neither the legislator who failed in discrimination nor the capitalist who errs in judgment is made to suffer. The latter of course is in a worse position than the former, for he has something at stake. He may flatter himself that 'so long as the duty is kept up' he is safe. But we think when he depends on the protection of a Parliamentary majority he trusts to a very frail support. Does he imagine that the laws of Victoria are as those of the Medes and Persians? Does he think that the working classes will never get tired of paying 50 or 100 per cent. more on the consumption of their families than they need pay? When they find out 'where the shoe pinches' are they likely to consider the interests of the manufacturer?

We believe that the Free Trade party is as sensible of the value of the Manufacturing interest as the Protectionist party. But the Free Trader does not fall into the error of placing that interest above all others, or of striving to increase it before the time for its profitable development arrives. Good foundations are laid slowly and with great care. A foundation built in haste may turn out well, but is not that highly improbable? Are not some of the stones likely to be wrongly placed, and will not the whole edifice be shaky? But the man who lays the foundation of his house without levels is not so rash as the statesman who would build up an industrial interest on Protective encouragements. Confusion and failure must attend such a policy. Some parts might prove sound, but some would not, and the whole would be precarious. Under a policy of Free Trade the Manufacturing interest is bound to rise upon sure foundations. That which will not stand the strain of profit and loss will be rejected. Each stone of the 'palace of industry' will fit into its proper place. Those which ought to adorn the apex will not be found at the base, weakening the whole superstructure. In other words, industries will take their places in the ratio of their profitableness, and those that will prosper at once will not be confused with those whose time has not yet come. We venture to believe in the unassisted sagacity of Australian enterprise. We do not think our capitalists are so ignorant that any Parliamentary majority can teach them the true sources of profit. If we were a horde of savages the interference of Government might be intelligible. But our capitalists and our working men are far more likely to invest their capital and labour to the best advantage than Parliament for them. It ought to be a self-evident proposition, if we are worthy descendants of Englishmen, that private enterprise will work out our industrial greatness on more safe and lasting foundations, left to its own intelligence, spirit, and resources, than when tempted by reckless bribes, and taught to rely on artificial supports.

It may seem strange that the capital cities of Victoria and New South Wales have already a larger relative population than the capitals of the oldest and greatest nations. But such is the fact. Of the whole population of Victoria, which was 792,476 on the 31st March, 1874, no less than 231,008 were congregated in the metropolitan district! Of the whole population of New South Wales, which was, according to the census of 1871, 503,981, no less than 136,483 were congregated in the metropolitan district! Thus, nearly thirty per cent. of the population of the two Colonies is massed in and around their capitals! Let us compare these proportions with those of older countries: –

Belgium (1870), 5,087,105; Brussels, 314, 077, 6 per cent.
Denmark (1870), 1,784,741; Copenhagen, 180,866, 10 per cent.
England and Wales, (1871), 22,704,108; London, 3,251,804, 14 per cent.
France (1866), 37,067,094; Paris, 1,825,274, 5 per cent.
Italy (1871), 26,796,253; Rome, 836,291, 3 per cent.
Prussia (1871), 24,693,066; Berlin, 826,341, 3 per cent.
Russia in Europe (1867), 63,658,934; St. Petersburgh, 1,160,930, 2 per cent.
Turkey in Europe (1844), 12,787,000; Constantinople 1,000,000, 8 per cent.
New South Wales (1871), 503,981; Sydney, 136,483, 27 per cent.
Victoria (1874), 792,476; Melbourne, 231,008, 29 per cent.

If we take the most populous city in the world – London – which is the capital of the greatest Empire in existence, and the commercial centre of the whole globe, we discover that its population of three millions and a quarter *would have to be doubled* to bear the same proportion to that of England and Wales which the population of the young capital Melbourne bears to that of Victoria, or Sydney to that of New South Wales! That a metropolitan population of thirty per cent. of the whole can be supported in comfort and comparative luxury by a rural population so inadequate is a strong proof of the wonderful productiveness of the Colonies. But is it anything to be proud of? We think it is much to be regretted. In newly settled and extensive territories an undue tendency to gravitate towards the metropolis is surely an unhealthy sign? Would it not be infinitely better if the attraction were towards the vast and fertile interior? In the United States the movement of population was always onwards towards the West, and we behold the result in the thirty-four great states which constitute the American Union. In Australia the opposite tendency has prevailed. New arrivals are only forced into the country when they can get nothing to do in town. This is a sure sign that they are not the class of immigrants we want. A system of free or assisted immigration that would settle hardy and enterprising British agriculturists on our lands is the great need of Australian colonization.

But the plain effect of a policy of encouraging the premature development of a manufacturing interest is to aggravate the evils of centralization. Its aim is to draw our young men into the factories of the city, when they should in every possible way be induced to go to the country. Its effect, if not its object, is to convert our young women into sempstresses, working away their bright and precious life and stamina in unhealthy garrets, on starvation wages, and under conditions as unfavourable to morality as to health, when they ought to be in every way encouraged to go into the kitchen and the farm-yard, to become the honest wives and sturdy mothers of a brave and stalwart Australian peasantry.

If we examine the statistics of the countries which excel in manufactures, we find that *female* and *juvenile* labour is a chief factor in the result. This may be unavoidable in old countries, but it is not yet necessary in Australia. In our domestic life, the great trouble is, not to provide suitable employment for our young women, but to persuade them to take it. The employment of the gentler sex in factories affords nothing of which any people can be proud. It signifies either the pressure of want, the selfish heartlessness of husbands or parents, or the depravation [sic] of domestic instincts. Every one must sympathise with efforts to elevate the condition of woman, and to provide for them desirable means of subsistence. But we heartily denounce the policy which would, in the hey-day of our prosperity degrade the mothers of our future nation into factory hands! That civilization which chains our women to the car of industrial progress is more cruel than beneficent. It tends to degrade the hallowed relationship of the weaker to the stronger sex. It destroys the charm and sanctity of domestic life. Whatever the industrial future of Australia, we fervently hope it will be achieved by the strong hands of our men, and not purchased, at too dear a price, at the expense of the comfort and true happiness of our womanhood. May the day be far distant in which the bright daughters of Australia will be reduced to the condition of artisans, compelled to struggle for existence in employments which unsex them, and destroy the delicacy and sweetness of home.

Another obvious effect of Protective policy is that it increases the cost of subsistence. One would think that the great aim of all statesmen would be to reduce the cost of living to its lowest point, as the best way of increasing the comfort of the masses to its highest. In most countries the poorer classes are in so desperate a plight that any serious increase in the cost of living, if it did not expose them to absolute starvation, would scarcely fail to excite the most dangerous commotion. But where labour is degraded Protection is unnecessary. Provided capital and raw material are at hand nothing further is essential. But in Australia labour is so well off that the Protectionist can only mount his hobby by trampling on the prosperity of labour. He consequently strives to counterbalance high wages by high taxes. He is not content to wait until wages fall or labour is in better supply. But we would ask why the people should be worried by taxation because they prosper in other industries than those which are the pets of the Protectionist? What is there in the products of the factory that makes them more valuable or attractive than the fruits of Nature? On what ground of common sense or expediency should we diminish the prosperity we derive from the primary stages of development in a hurry to advance before the proper time to the more advanced stages? Is it not rash, to say the least, to push on the finishing processes of our industrial destiny before the primary are half completed? Ought not the foundations to be completed before the superstructure is begun? If this great dispute were a mere question of theory – if only the symmetry of our national development were imperilled – the extraordinary conglomeration sought to be suddenly forced into existence might be more tolerable. But when all these experiments are to be carried out at the expense and risk of poor men, and of the comfort of their families, this policy, so illogical and illiberal in its principles, becomes positively cruel and disastrous in its consequences. We can conceive of no invasion of liberty more wanton than that of the Protectionists on the means of the poorer classes of the population. Our working men have always a sufficiently hard task set them to provide for their families the necessaries and decencies of life. Surely a scheme of public policy which would debar them from supplying their wants in the cheapest way open to them is little less than an outrage on humanity?

National greatness is one thing – national happiness another. England is perhaps the greatest nation in the world, and the Australian Colonies are not yet risen to the level of a nation; but the people of Australia are as much above their English brethren in general prosperity as they are beneath them in greatness. We believe national happiness to be of more consequence than national greatness. When, therefore, the Protectionist assures us that although his policy may be burdensome for a time it will ultimately make us a great nation, we think it much better to cling to the prosperity we have, and we would prefer to advance with it, however slowly, than to hasten before it, however rapidly. That would be our policy even if we could trust to the predictions of our Protectionist friends. But whether our ambition should be to advance the Colonies in the scale of national greatness, or simply to promote the individual prosperity and happiness of their inhabitants, our profound conviction is that with either end in view the shortest and the safest road is through a development of the advantages with which Providence has endowed us, which no Act of Parliament can make or unmake, and which only need for their conversion into magnificent sources of both happiness and greatness the free application of unflagging industry and enlightened enterprise.

What shall we say of those who, enjoying the privilege of free institutions, impose slavery upon themselves? Who whilst they would resist foreign tyranny to the death, welcome a system of domestic tyranny which oppresses them at every turn, which enacts what they shall eat, what they shall wear, and what they shall pay? Is that liberty which they hold so priceless in political affairs so worthless in the affairs of ordinary life? Can it be true that whilst the Imperial fortunes of our race have risen to unequalled grandeur under the inspirations of freedom, our Colonial destinies can expand only under a miserable system of pupilage and compulsion? Is that free enterprise which enabled Englishmen to conquer and civilize an empire which reaches from the rising to the setting sun a worthless tradition to their descendants settled on these rich and boundless territories? Shall it be that free by a glorious birth-right we are slaves by choice? That, proud of our civil freedom, we at the same time forge for ourselves the chains of *commercial slavery*? This is no empty figure of speech. The reproach of commercial slavery is branded on the fair young brow of Victoria. It is solemnly enacted by her laws. It has consigned her to an antiquated dungeon when it is of the first importance she should be free! The more she clings to her fetters the more desperate her case becomes.

We fervently trust that so mischievous a barrier to the union of the Australian Colonies as Protection will soon be broken down; and that the genius of commercial liberty will speedily emerge from her temporary eclipse, and diffusing her equal blessings over our scattered populations, will bind them as closely in the relations of free trade and good-will as they already are bound by the ties of kindred blood, and the promise of a grand future.

Letters of Henry Parkes, George H. Reid and Gower Evans, in *Free Trade and the European Treaties of Commerce* (London: Cobden Club, 1875), pp. 106–11.

THE PROSPECTS OF FREE TRADE IN AUSTRALIA.

The Hon. HENRY PARKES (late Chief Secretary of State, Sydney, New South Wales) writes: –

The doctrines of Free Trade are making sure way among the Australian populations. In Victoria (which is the nursery of Protection), the policy of artificial aids to industry is breaking up, and the very public men who some years ago introduced the 'thin end of the wedge' by taxes in favour of the local manufactures, are now seeking to obtain political support as Free Traders.

I do not think the new Government here will do much to forward the cause, but they certainly will do nothing to throw it back. For the next year or two our fiscal relations will probably remain stationary. But when any change is made, it will be in favour of more complete commercial freedom.

Sydney, New South Wales, 13 *May*, 1875.

DEAR MR. POTTER, – Presuming upon the enclosed introduction from Mr. Parkes, I beg your acceptance of some *Free Trade Essays*, which I am about to publish in Australia. I propose to send a few additional copies to the Cobden Club, through Messrs. Gordon and Gotch.

If there is anything in the Essays which seems likely to be useful to the Club, I place it completely at your disposal.

During a recent visit to Melbourne, I found the symptoms of a reaction towards Free Trade doctrines amongst the more intelligent electors. Of course the mass of the working classes forms the bulwark of the Protective laws of Victoria; and it is against that, as you will observe, that I have directed the chief effort of my work.

In New South Wales our common cause is out of danger. There is no Protectionist party whatever here; and the general desire is to throw open our trade and resources as much as possible, conscious as we are that the freedom of commerce is as essential to our future greatness as it is in accordance with the genius of a free constitution and the instincts of a free people.

Allow me to add my humble testimony to the service done by the Cobden Club publications in this part of the world. You will perceive that in one of my Essays I have largely quoted from them.

Permit me, in conclusion, to express my ardent admiration of the principles on which the Club is founded, principles whose complete triumph in levelling for ever the barriers which selfish folly interposes between the blessings of God and the necessities of man will do something more than free the commerce of the world, for they will confer on all the scattered races of mankind the germs of universal peace, civilisation, and goodwill.

I am, my dear Sir,
Your faithful servant,
G. H. REID.

THOMAS B. POTTER, Esq., M.P., *Hon. Secretary of the Cobden Club, London. From* GOWER EVANS, Esq., *of Melbourne, Australia.*

Hayes, July 15, 1875.

DEAR SIR, – I have great pleasure in complying with the wish of the Committee of the Cobden Club, that inasmuch as I have recently arrived in London, after an eight years' residence in Victoria, I should acquaint them, as far as in my power, with the present position of the Free Trade movement in Australia. I must mention, by way of preface, that as far as my own colony is concerned, it is difficult at this moment to make a precise statement. The Parliament of Victoria commenced its session at the end of May; and a telegram from Melbourne, dated May 25, informs us that the Government policy includes a remission of Customs' duties. How far this remission goes, and whether it will be acceptable to Parliament, it is of course at present impossible to say.

On the whole, however, I am happy to be able to state that the prospects of the Free Trade party in the Australian colonies are more hopeful than they have been at any previous period during the last ten years. For that space of time, as the Committee are doubtless aware, the whole group, including Tasmania and New Zealand, have been, mainly through the initiative of Victoria, more or less under the influence of Protectionist ideas. The first symptoms of uneasiness under oppression of the Protective tariffs manifested themselves in the desire to establish a system of inter-colonial Free Trade. After repeated appeals, the Imperial Government acquiesced in this desire of the Australian colonies, and an Act was passed empowering the colonies to enter into Commercial Treaties and to impose differential duties. No advantage has been as yet taken of the privileges conferred by the Imperial Act, and the present able Governor of New South Wales, Sir Hercules Robinson, in an exhaustive State Paper, has pointed out the difficulties which must inevitably occur in any attempt to carry out the Act on any principle except that of general Free Trade. Partly, I consider, in consequence of the ideas suggested by this paper, and partly from a belief in the soundness of the general principle, the New South Wales Government some two years ago took an immense stride in the direction of Free Trade, by the abolition of the *ad valorem* duties. The Government that, under the leadership of Mr. Parkes, adopted this sound policy has since fallen, but their successors have avowed their adherence to the same principles, and purpose to proceed further in the same direction; and at the last general election not a single candidate presented himself in support of reactionary views. The action of New South Wales has had a sensible influence on Victoria. The oppressive duties levied in Melbourne have for some time past tended to divert the inter-colonial trade from Melbourne to Sydney, in spite of the natural advantages of the former port. In addition to this, the classes in Victoria, such as the miners and farmers, who do not in any way benefit by Protection, but who have supported the Protective policy under the mistaken idea that they were furthering the interest of their fellow-labourers in the towns, are beginning to feel the burden of the tariff without being able to convince themselves that they really have served the interests which they intended to promote. Owing to the depression in the mining districts, the revenue of Victoria has shown symptoms of decline. It is in these circumstances that the Victorian Government has been induced to reconsider its fiscal policy, and, as the telegraph informs us, to propose a remission of duties. I am not sanguine as to the extent of this remission, nor can I write with confidence in respect to the amount of change that has taken place in public opinion in reference to the main principle of Free Trade. That some change, however, has occurred in the right direction is certain, but so much class-feeling has been generated by the long struggle, and so many interests have grown up under the Protectionist règime, that a complete return to Free Trade is not to be expected for the present.

We must be contented to know that the movement is in that direction; and we may hope that at no distant period Victoria may be found ranged with New South Wales, and that the colonies will march together to the completion of the policy. South Australia, it is encouraging to learn, so recently as June 17th, under a change of Ministry, has adopted the New South Wales tariff. When the three adjacent colonies move together, the others, which have never gone so far as Victoria, must inevitably adopt the system. Thus, as I said at the commencement of my letter, the moment gives occasion for a more sanguine feeling than Australian Free Traders have for some time experienced; and although patience is still required, I am justified in expressing the opinion that the present members of the Cobden Club will have the opportunity of celebrating the return of the whole of Australia to a sound fiscal policy.

I am, yours faithfully,

GOWER EVANS.

August 19.

P.S. – Since the foregoing was written, we have been informed by telegraph that the Victorian Ministry then in office had brought forward a budget of a Free

Trade tendency; that it had been left in a majority of one; and that, having been refused a dissolution by the Acting-Governor, it had resigned, and had been replaced by a Protectionist administration, under a Mr. Berry. I would remark, in the first place, with respect to this change, that, taking the worst view of it, a Ministry coming into office with a minority, even though the minority be only inferior to the majority by one, cannot be a very strong one. But there are circumstances connected with the position of the retiring Ministry which, coupled with the character of that which has replaced it, lead me to take a still less gloomy view of the situation. The late Ministry consisted, in the main, of Free Traders who had consented to carry out a Protectionist policy. They were, consequently, not very warmly supported by the non-official Free Traders in the House. When they proposed to modify the Protectionist tariff, they also announced the intention of imposing a property-tax and a tax upon bank-notes. It may possibly be the case that their modification of the tariff may not have been considered sufficient to justify the imposition of new taxes, and the ranks of the ultra-Protectionists may have been swelled by the addition of some dissatisfied Free Traders. Then, again, the list of the new Ministry does not contain a single name of political or social eminence. I am perfectly sure that every one acquainted with Victorian affairs regarded it with unmixed astonishment. Although, therefore, as I have said in my letter, I am not prepared to indulge in sanguine prophecy with respect to the extent of change that public opinion has undergone in Victoria on the subject of Protection, I am still inclined to think, for the reasons I have given, that a change in the right direction is taking place; and I do not attach any importance to the accession to office of such an administration as that of which we have in the last few days received the list by telegraph.

GOWER EVANS.

G. C. WARR, Esq., *Secretary of the Cobden Club.*

COPYRIGHTS AND PERMISSIONS

John Charles Herries to George Frederick Young, [8?] January 1849; Minutes of a Special Meeting of the Acting Committee of the National Association for the Protection of British Industry and Capital, 15 October 1849, at the London Tavern, Chaired by G. F. Young; J. C. Herries to G. F. Young, 15 November 1849, Herries Papers, BL, Add. MS 57423, fols 104–6, 143–4, 147–8. Reproduced with permission from the British Library, London.

Lord Stanhope to G. F. Young, 29 May 1849; Lord Stanhope to G. F. Young, 8 June 1849, Young Papers, BL, Add. MS 46712, fols 97–8, 99–100. Reproduced with permission from the British Library, London.

Sir James Graham to W. E. Gladstone, 13 November 1852, Gladstone Papers, BL, Add. MS 44740, fols 167–70. Reproduced with permission from the British Library, London. Copyright © Charles Gladstone. Glynne-Gladstone Collection. Reproduced with permission.

Sir James Graham to W. E. Gladstone, 19 November 1852, Gladstone Papers, BL, Add. MS 44163, fols 64–5. Reproduced with permission from the British Library, London. Copyright © Charles Gladstone. Glynne-Gladstone Collection. Reproduced with permission.

Richard Cobden to Marco Minghetti, 21 May 1847, Minghetti Papers, Bibliotecha dell' Archiginnasio, Bologna. Reproduced with permission.

Richard Cobden to Michel Chevalier, 22 March 1851 (copy), Cobden Papers, West Sussex Record Office, CP 290, fols 271–3. By courtesy of the Governors of Dunford House and with acknowledgement to the County Archivist, West Sussex Record Office. By courtesy of the National Council of YMCAs. Copyright © Elizabeth Cobden Boyd. Reproduced with permission.

The Abortive Anglo-French Commercial Treaty of 1852, 19 February 1853, PRO, FO 881/551. Reproduced with permission from the National Archives (Kew, Surrey).

Lord Clarendon to Lord Palmerston, 20 April 1856, PRO, FO 27/1169. Reproduced with permission from the National Archives (Kew, Surrey).

Cardwell Memorandum on Commercial Policy towards Russia, 29 October 1854, PRO, 30/29/23/4, fols 181–8. Reproduced with permission from the National Archives (Kew, Surrey).

Richard Cobden to John Bright, 16 January 1860, Cobden Papers, BL, Add. MS 43651, fols 60–7. Reproduced with permission from the British Library, London. By courtesy of the National Council of YMCAs. Copyright © Elizabeth Cobden Boyd. Reproduced with permission.

Richard Cobden to François Arlés-Dufour, 10 August 1860, Cobden Papers, BL, Add. MS 43666, fols 224–5. Reproduced with permission from the British Library, London. By courtesy of the National Council of YMCAs. Copyright © Elizabeth Cobden Boyd. Reproduced with permission.

Richard Cobden to E. A. Billeroche, 12 September 1861, Cobden Papers, West Sussex Record Office, CP 6, fol. 91. By courtesy of the Governors of Dunford House and with acknowledgement to the County Archivist, West Sussex Record Office. By courtesy of the National Council of YMCAs, Trustees of the Cobden Estate. Copyright © Elizabeth Cobden Boyd. Reproduced with permission.

'Memorandum on the Commercial Policy of European States and British Trade' (1879), PRO, FO 881/3834. Reproduced with permission from the National Archives (Kew, Surrey).

'Commercial Treaty with Austria' (1866), PRO, CAB 1/1. Reproduced with permission from the National Archives (Kew, Surrey).

Louis Mallet, Memorandum on Modifications of Anglo French Treaty, 19 August 1871, PRO, FO 24/2/72. Reproduced with permission from the National Archives (Kew, Surrey).

C. M. Kennedy, 'Treaties of Commerce with, and between, European Powers, with Especial Reference to the Trade of the United Kingdom' (1875), PRO, FO 881/2670. Reproduced with permission from the National Archives (Kew, Surrey).

For Product Safety Concerns and Information please contact our EU representative GPSR@taylorandfrancis.com Taylor & Francis Verlag GmbH, Kaufingerstraße 24, 80331 München, Germany

Printed and bound by CPI Group (UK) Ltd, Croydon, CR0 4YY
08/05/2025
01864526-0003